C0-AUG-204

# INTERACTIVE GRAPHICS IN CAD

# INTERACTIVE GRAPHICS IN CAD

Yvon Gardan and Michel Lucas

*With Additional Material*
*by*
*Richard G. Budynas*

NEW YORK

Translated by Meg Tombs

First published 1983 by Hermes Publishing (France)
52 rue Rennequin, 75017 Paris, France


English language edition first published 1984
by Kogan Page Ltd, 120 Pentonville Road, London N1 9JN

This edition published in the United States by UNIPUB



ISBN 0 89059 036 2

Library of Congress Catalog Card Number 84 - 51343

Printed and bound in Great Britain

# Contents

# Introduction

In a society in which the use of information technology is becoming commonplace it is natural that pictures and images produced by electronic means should be increasing in importance as a means of communication. Computer graphics have only recently come to the attention of the general public, mainly through animated drawings, advertisements and video games. The quality of the pictures is often such that, unless informed of the fact, people are unaware that they are created with the help of computers. Some simulations, those developed in connection with the space shuttle for example, represent a great and rapid progress. In industry, computer graphic techniques are used not only for the presentation of business data, but also in design and manufacture processes.

Such computer-assisted systems are collectively represented by the acronym CAX. In CAD/CAM (computer-assisted design/manufacture), interactive graphic techniques have attained considerable importance. In CAD/CAM systems a dialogue can be established between the user and the machine using a variety of easy to operate communication devices.

Due to the recent developments in hardware and software (for modelling, visual display, etc), a designer is now able to make decisions based on the information presented (plans, perspective drawings, graphics, etc) with the help of interactive, graphic techniques. These constitute the most visible and perhaps most spectacular aspect of CAD/CAM systems. It should be noted, however, that the two are quite separate and independent of each other, and can be used both to complement each other and separately, to good effect. Some CAD/CAM systems do not involve the use of graphics and certain graphic applications (non-technical drawing, for example) exist independently of CAD/CAM. For this reason, Chapter 1 is concerned with the role of graphics in CAD/CAM. In Chapter 2 the components of a typical CAD/CAM system are described and considered from the point of view of graphics production. Hardware already commonly in use in other systems is not discussed at great length here, since information on these can readily be found elsewhere.

It is a common mistake to confuse the information displayed on the screen with the data stored inside the CAD/CAM system. It is the model that is of fundamental importance – whether it be of an object to be manufactured, a tool or a unit – and this is the logical representation of the object. The quality of this model (and particularly the geometric model) determines the quality of the CAD/CAM system. The graphical use of models can also involve simulations, based on information contained in the model. Chapter 3 considers the subject of geometric modelling, one of the most important aspects of CAD/CAM systems.

Chapter 4 is concerned with visual display techniques, and the different types of graphics (comprehension, communication) that are used. Algorithms associated with visual display are also explained (elimination of hidden parts, etc).

The dialogue techniques discussed in Chapter 5 depend, at least partly, on available hardware, but are treated here from the point of view of quality and levels of dialogue according to the operations of interest. In Chapter 6 examples are used to illustrate the points mentioned in previous chapters.

*Chapter 1*

# The role of graphics in computer-assisted design/manufacture

## 1.1 Design procedures

The life of an industrially produced object, whether a car, a piece of furniture, a building or simply a bearing, starts with its design and ends with its manufacture. In the design and manufacturing process, two different sequences can be identified, depending on whether the product is *new* or *standard* (see Figure 1.1).

### 1.1.1 DESIGNING A NEW PRODUCT

This can be divided into five stages:

1. *the pilot study*: definition of external constraints, choice of technology, basic calculations, prototype design and trials;
2. *initiating the project*: product industrialization phase and establishment of definite plans;
3. *preparation for manufacture*: vital transitional stage between design and manufacture; requires close coordination between the planning and manufacture stages (1 and 4);
4. *manufacture*: product launch and manufacture; CAD/CAM techniques are used most frequently in this stage and will be increasingly so in the future, partly because of the expected increase in the use of robotic techniques and flexible manufacturing systems, which allow direct use of the data contained in CAD/CAM systems;
5. *maintenance and support*: mentioned only in passing here, this is an important factor to be taken into account should computer breakdown occur; the importance of an efficient and expert after-sales team should be stressed, as should the provision of replacement components.

### 1.1.2 DESIGNING A STANDARDIZED PRODUCT

Standard products can be based on existing products and this type of design is characterized by a much shorter pilot study phase. Generally, the components involved in the pilot study are already familiar to the

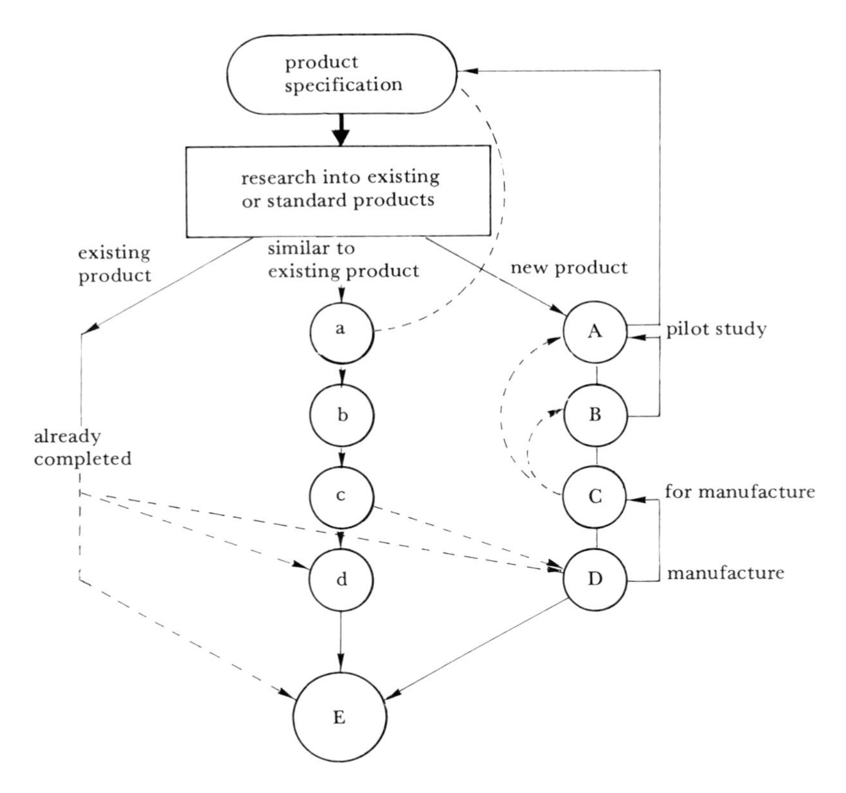


**Figure 1.1.** *The various stages in the development of manufactured products*

design team and development of a prototype, whether real or simulated, is not usually necessary. The main aim of a pilot study is to produce an estimate, based on previous research, to enable a solution to be found that comes to that set down in the product specification. It should be noted that there may be several attempts at each stage, and that the design process is not necessarily linear. Some technical choices may be thrown open to question as the study advances, causing the designer to reassess previous work. This situation can also occur when several possible solutions are being considered at the same time, with the best being retained, judged in relation to existing criteria. However, these criteria can change as the project progresses and the solutions which proved most attractive at one stage may be unsatisfactory in the light of other considerations established later.

Design procedures can also be analysed from a completely different viewpoint, without considering procedural sequences, but only the type of procedure followed. The following basic types of procedure can be distinguished (see Figure 1.2):

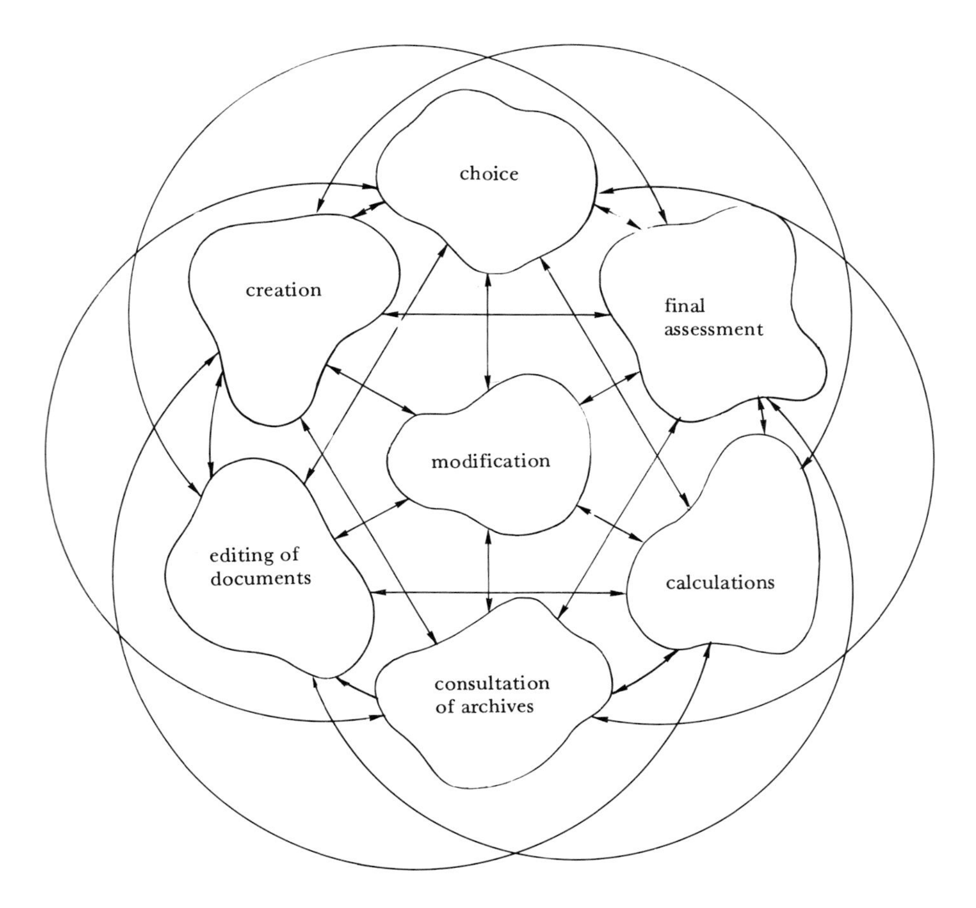


**Figure 1.2.** *The interrelationship between the various types of design procedures (the sequence of procedures is not relevant)*

1. *creation*: the invention of new objects or techniques to solve a given problem. It is necessary to be able to describe objects that have not actually been manufactured, and to store them for later use;
2. *modification*: with existing objects, changes and improvements may be necessitated by technological advances;
3. *editing of documents*: this concerns both alphanumerical documents (estimates, lists, etc) and graphical documents (plans, diagrams, etc);
4. *calculations*: the most important of these are the simulations which will be used to carry out work on potential prototypes;
5. *choice*: using the technical elements available (plans, calculations, etc) a choice must be made as to which will be retained, and in which direction the project will proceed;

6. *consultation of archives*: this involves the scanning of existing solutions as well as the use of individual items of information, and verification of a product's record of development;
7. *final assessment*: the stage during which the designer attempts to finally solve the problem, or choose between different solutions.

The following points should be noted:

1. The order in which these procedures are listed has no significance because, in practice, they take place in different sequences and combinations at different times. In Figure 1.2 the arrows are intended to signify this, showing that there is no real priority in the order in which these procedures are followed.
2. The amount of time devoted to each of the procedures can vary considerably. The concept of work pace has an important influence on this, and should not be seen simply as a function of financial return or of productivity, but should take into account that the rate of design may tend to vary. So, at certain times it may happen that the designer is working towards a certain idea and the pace of work may become rather slow. At such a time he will not, for example, be inconvenienced by a delay in response to a question concerning archive information. However, once he has fixed on an idea the pace of the work will increase, and he will require a faster turn-round from colleagues in order to achieve a maximum input of ideas.
3. It is evident that the procedures are not applied to a static object in the course of the design process, since the product is constantly modified. The fact that similar procedures are used in the various stages of development of an object suggests that CAD/CAM systems would be more attractive and acceptable if the tools they incorporate could be used in the same way for a given type of procedure, even at different stages of development. In other words, more emphasis should be placed on the type of procedure than on the type of object being handled.

### 1.1.3 CAD/CAM – TOWARDS A DEFINITION

From the concepts discussed above it is possible to attempt to define CAD/CAM. This can be said to take place when a computer system is used to facilitate the work involved in any one of the procedures described above. This definition raises a number of points that should be considered. In some ways, the idea of 'assistance' runs counter to that of automation. It concerns the provision of a number of carefully chosen tools intended to facilitate the work of the designer. In the final analysis, it is the designer who chooses which tool to use – the machine only provides the options. Sometimes, not all procedures are assisted, either because it is not necessary, because the amount of work to be done is not sufficient to make it worthwhile, or because the data processing involved would be too complex.

Of the task division between operator and machine, it is obvious that some should fall naturally to the machine (for example, everything concerning the storage of information and control of archives) whereas others are naturally reserved for the operator (for example, definition of new products to be developed). Within certain procedures there are some parts that could be assisted, and others which could not. For example, written documents may be edited automatically, but not with a CAD system.

This definition reflects the flexibility in the levels of integration of CAD/CAM systems. The introduction of CAD/CAM into a business can be carried out progressively by selecting specific areas of activity which would be particularly suitable for computerized assistance. Many businesses use CAD/CAM without realizing it, using specific computer programs to facilitate the work of designers.

## 1.2 Graphics and CAD/CAM

There is a common tendency to confuse computer graphics with CAD, a confusion often shared by industrial computer users, because even though they use calculation and simulation programs, they do not consider that they are using CAD/CAM because they do not produce graphics with the computer. This confusion arises for two reasons. In traditional design and manufacturing processes, information is communicated through text and plans. So, whether the products in question are new or standard, most of the documents used are in graphic form – plans, graphs, diagrams or other forms of graphic representation (see Figure 1.3). In research establishments, the breakdown of graphics activity is roughly as follows (see also Figure 1.4):

drawing 70%
archive work and updating 15%
design proper 15%
- copying out 70%
- variations 20%
- errors 9%
- invention 1%

The production of graphical documents is the most impressive part of CAD/CAM. A demonstration of the interactive production of documents is considerably more striking than the execution of a simulation program that provides a numerical output. It would be useful to consider here the contexts in which interactive software can be used (see Figure 1.5).

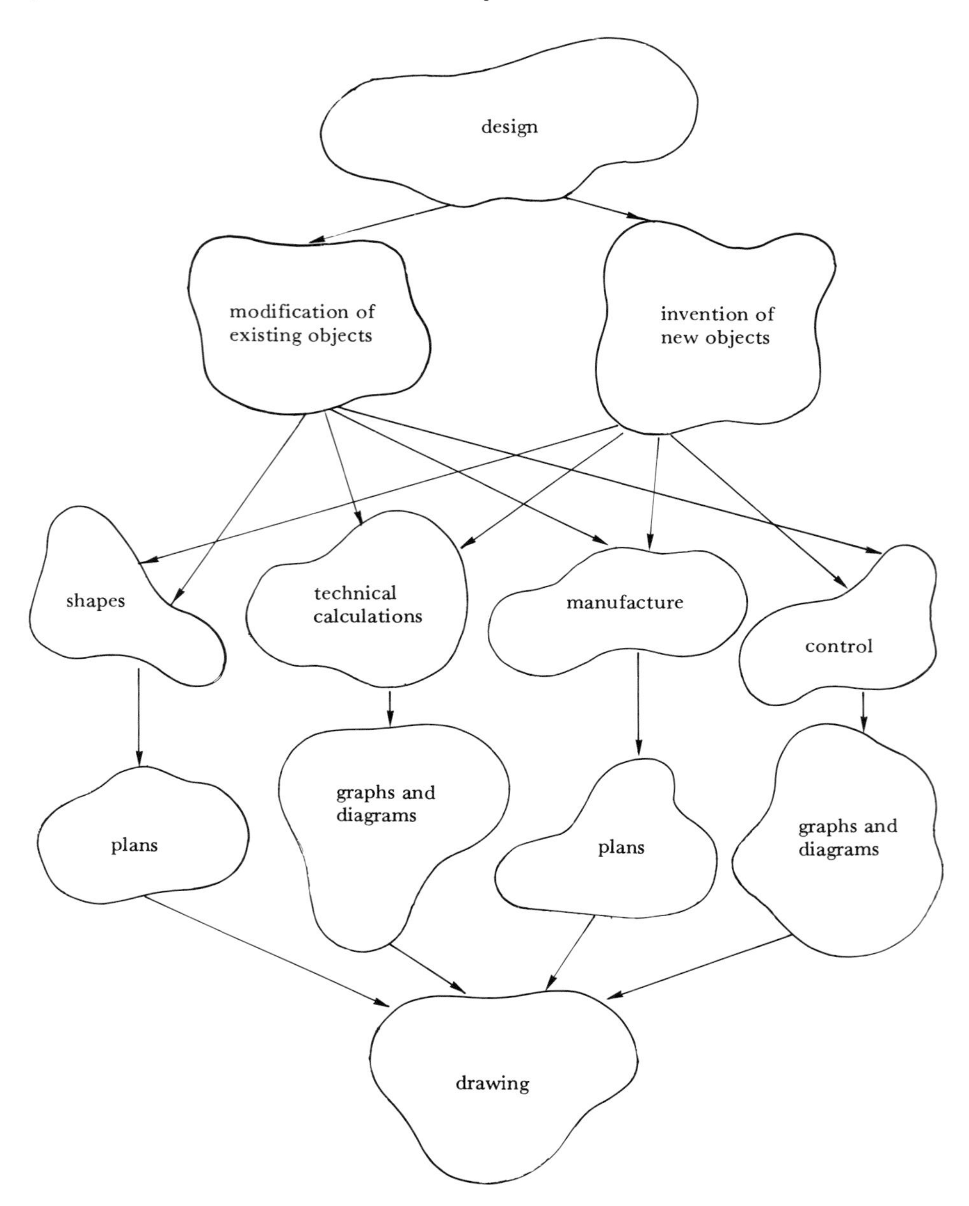


**Figure 1.3.** *The drawing, a vital input medium for CAD/CAM, is accepted in a variety of forms by the system*

The application program is central to the production of computer-assisted graphics, and carries out the calculations concerning a given area of interest. The program makes use of information stored in the computer's data bank. This data can be permanent (ie stored on file for

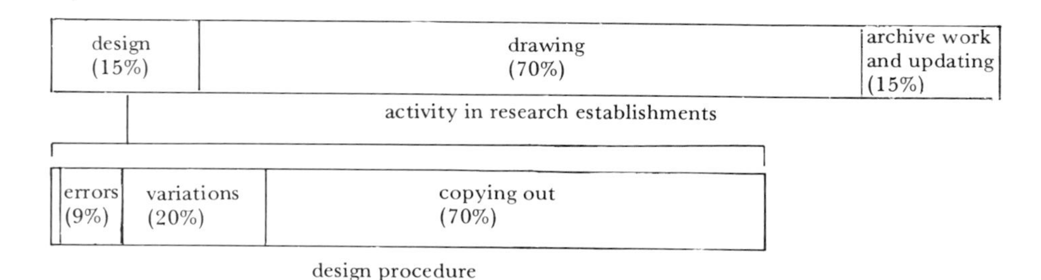


**Figure 1.4.** *The percentage breakdown of the different procedures in research establishments, showing further breakdown of design activities*

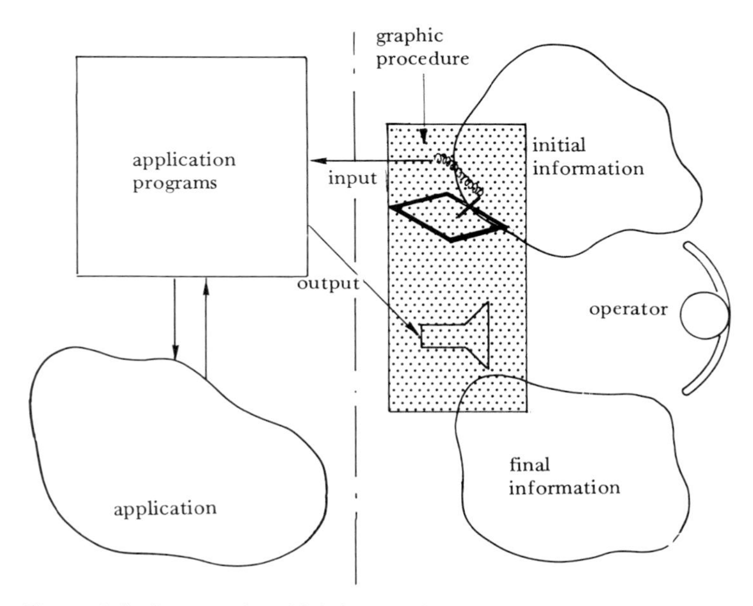


**Figure 1.5.** *Context in which interactive graphic software is used*

use in successive applications), or temporary (for intermediate calculations). The initial information is supplied through the input procedures and the results are obtained from the output. The input/output operations are instructions intended to create a link between machine and operator. Interaction or dialogue is characterized by the presence of an operator, who, having considered the output, will influence the program by inputting new initial information. This process continues until the required result is obtained.

Interactive graphic techniques are used only in a limited number of input/output operations. It is clear, therefore, that they have only a limited role, and, in general, the application programs themselves are the most important component. This is the way in which CAD/CAM can be used without any graphics being produced. On the other hand, CAD/CAM can take a more simple form, used to assist in the production of technical drawings. So, to maximize usefulness, it might be necessary to develop a number of programs which do not involve graphics.

To sum up, computer graphics are an integral part of CAD/CAM, but still represent no more than a part, and not necessarily the most important nor the most difficult to use. The following section is an attempt to analyse the various levels of assistance, and illustrates the range and complexity of systems used for assisted drawing.

## 1.3 Graphic processes in CAD/CAM

Assisted drawing systems are intended basically to ease the production of technical drawings. This means providing a description of the geometric primitives of the surface of an object so that the relevant documents can be produced more quickly. Increased speed is achieved in a number of ways:

1. the use of a more or less formal description of the drawing as a whole, leaving the computer to perform most of the line drawing;
2. the use of catalogues of symbols related to the work in progress and appropriate to the CAD/CAM system in use (the designer requests a symbol and the machine automatically draws it);
3. time is saved at the modification stage, when the designer needs only indicate what has to be changed and the computer readjusts the whole drawing accordingly; erasement and re-copying are thus totally avoided.

The first computer-assisted drawing systems involved the designer in virtual programming of the drawing to be made, through the use of parameterized geometric primitives. For example, a circle was produced by describing the coordinates of its centre and its radius. The use of collections of simple parameterized objects has come to be quite common. An example is shown in Figure 1.6; it can be seen that in order to draw a symbol, no matter how complex, it is necessary to give only the name of the symbol and a number of parameters which describe the symbol as a whole. The designer must think in geometrical terms, and organize the drawing according to the basic elements available. If a mistake is made the faulty instruction is deleted and the sequence of parameters modified accordingly. Producing a technical drawing thus becomes equivalent to writing a computer program, which means that the designer or draughtsman will require specialized training.

There are other basic operations which allow the designer to save time. For example, by introducing the concept of contour (and therefore of

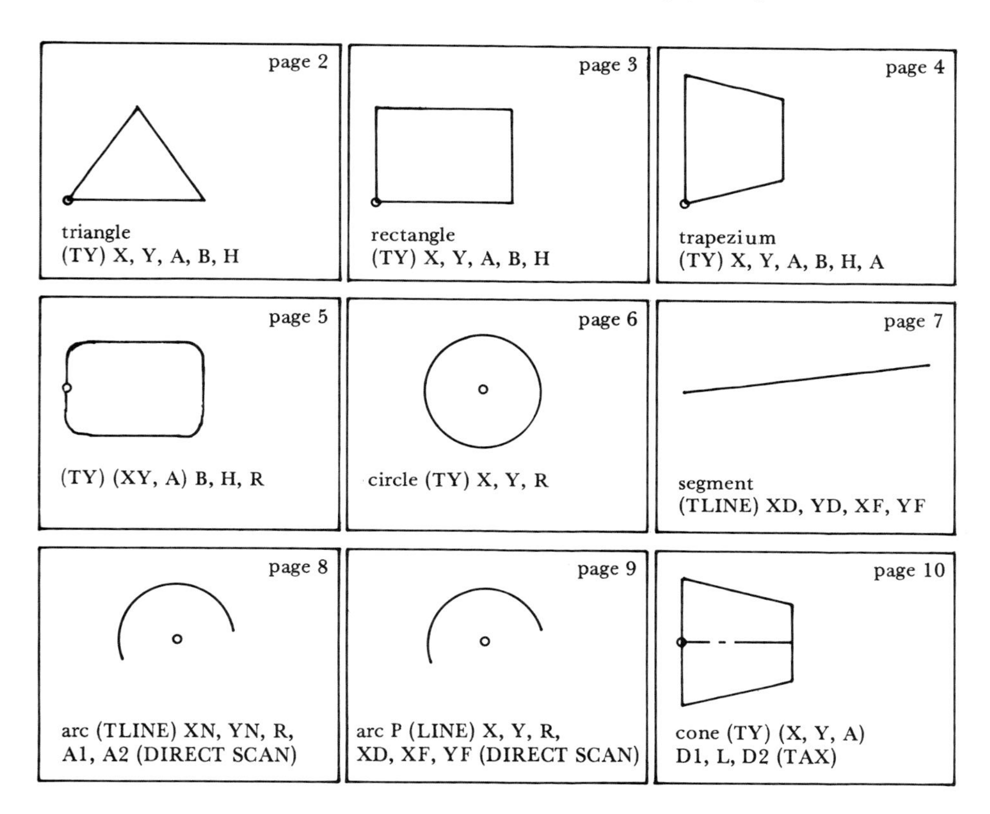


**Figure 1.6.** *Simple parametrized objects: in order to draw a shape only the name and a number of parameters need be given*

surface) it is possible to incorporate cross-hatching into the program. Figure 1.7 shows an example of this, in which the designer need only specify the contours of the parts to be shaded and the intensity and angle of the cross-hatching. This type of work is typical of the repetitive activities which, though of little interest to the designer or draughtsman are, nonetheless, very important for the efficient communication of information. The time the designer can save by using a computer for this type of work represents a real advantage over traditional methods.

Another example of the advantages intrinsic to computer-assisted drawing methods is in the production of geometric constructions, which will be discussed in detail in Chapter 5. Three examples are given in Figure 1.8:

1. Using a symmetry facility only one half of a shape needs to be defined, the other half is drawn automatically by the computer.
2. When a shape which is not altogether symmetrical is required, the shape drawn by the computer can be modified by deleting the inappropriate section of the drawing and replacing it with the

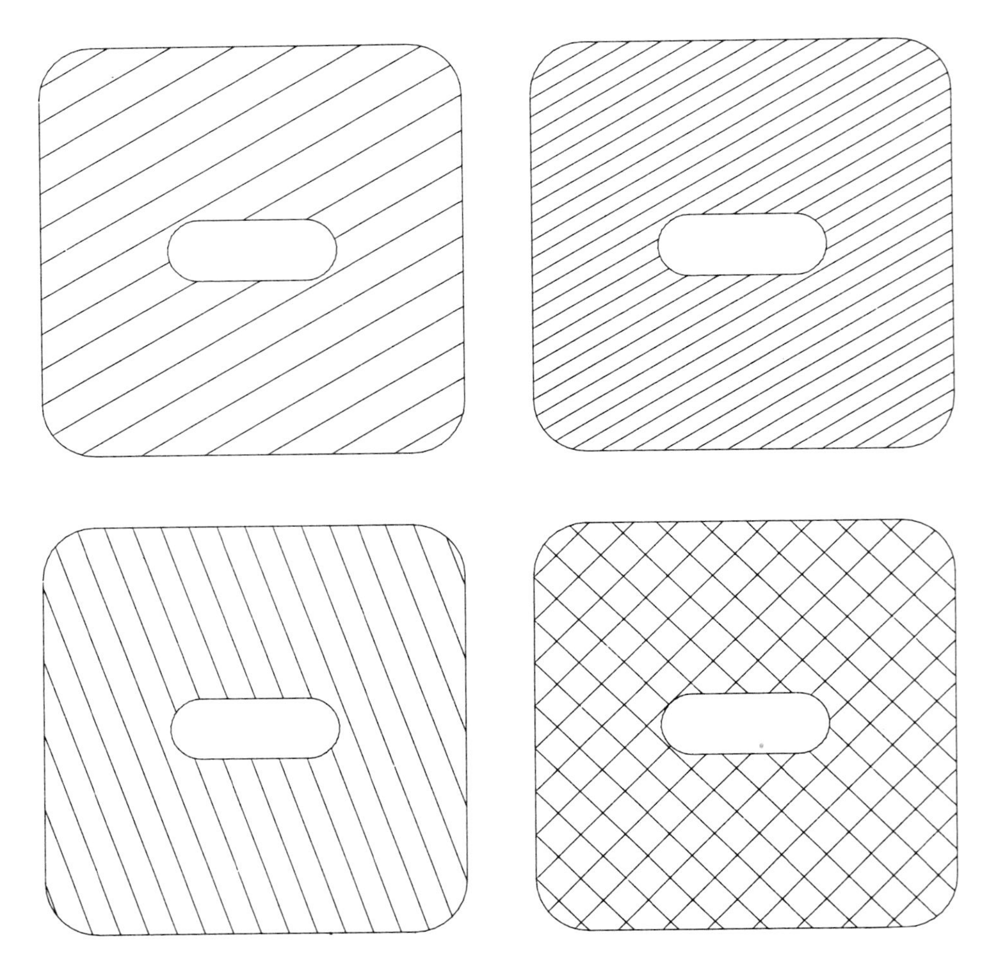

**Figure 1.7.** *Different types of shading on identical shapes – these are drawn in automatically*

asymmetrical shape. The designer can organize his work in such a way as to find elements which display a degree of symmetry, so as to simplify the description of the shape, and leave the computer to complete the drawing according to specifications input by him.

3. Details concerning the joining of components can be left to the computer. The designer is thus not required to carry out precise calculations of say, the radii and centres of the different arcs of circle necessary to draw the intersections of joined parts. Once the information concerning the parts to be connected is input to the computer, it automatically carries out the rest of the procedure.

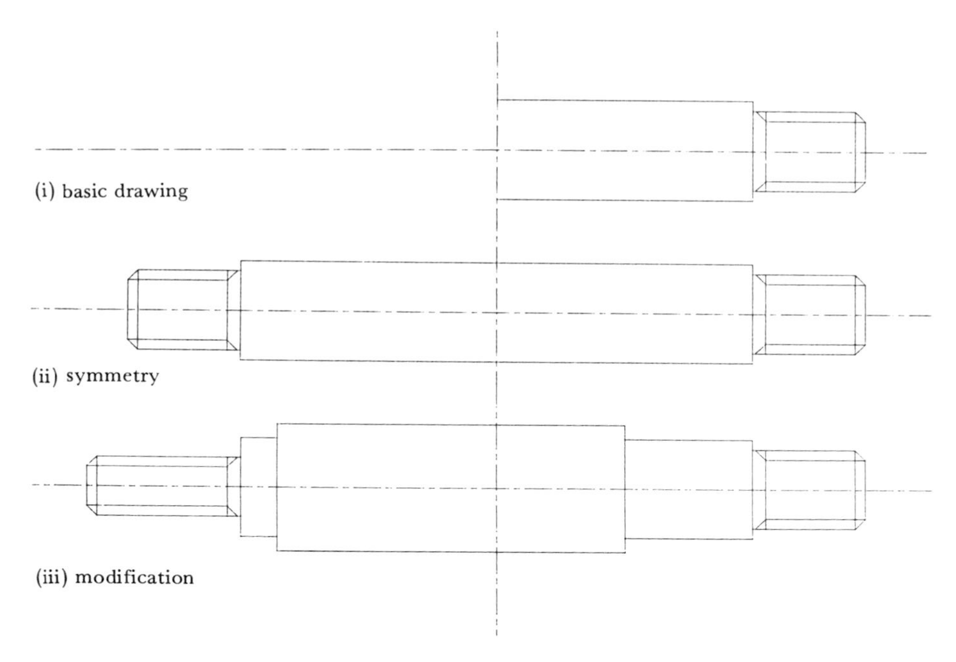


**Figure 1.8.** *Construction of a drawing using a symmetry facility (i) only one half of the drawing is provided; (ii) the system provides the other half; (iii) the system modifies drawing (ii)*

Two observations can be made at this point:

Modern software is generally interactive by nature, that is, the construction of a drawing can be carried out using a dialogue, with the instructions being carried out immediately and the result being displayed on a screen. The designer can thus judge the effect of his instructions immediately, which is extremely useful when making modifications. One of the drawbacks of the earliest systems was that it was not possible to judge the effects of any instruction until a relatively long time, sometimes hours, had elapsed. A mode of operation, characterized by processing in batches, is generally used only for the production of finished plans, whereas the preparation of plans is carried out using a dialogue.

In so far as these systems can be used to produce any type of technical drawing, it is possible to create documents representing three-dimensional objects. Under these conditions, the computer does not modify the work methods of the designer, but simply offers assistance within the framework of standard graphic techniques.

A new development has occurred over the last few years in which systems capable of graphic representation of three-dimensional objects have been developed. These systems make use of three-dimensional geometric modelling and allow various types of graphical representation

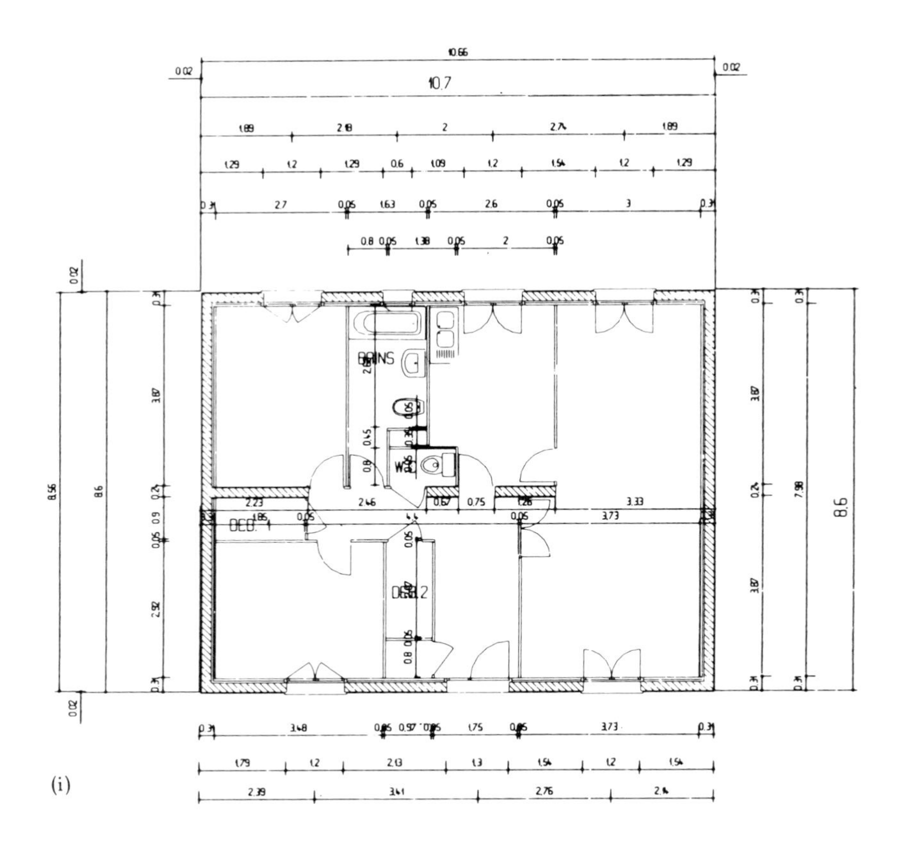


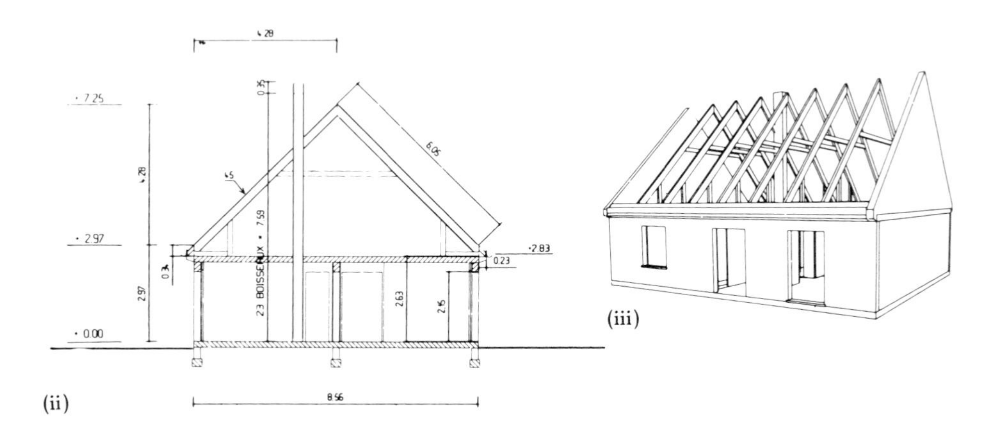


**Figure 1.9.** *Three views of the same building (i) plan; (ii) vertical elevation; (iii) perspective drawing with hidden parts eliminated*

**Figure 1.10.** *A work station*

to be derived from these models. For example, Figure 1.9 shows three different views of the same building, including a perspective view with hidden parts eliminated, a plan and a vertical elevation. These systems (see Figures 1.10 and 1.11) have introduced a new way of designing. The designer can work directly on a three-dimensional model and can then request perspective views, cross-sectional views or plan drawings, etc. The various components of this type of system will be discussed later.

Bearing in mind that all computer-assisted drawing or design systems make use of geometric models (both two and three-dimensional), the following points should be considered. The model allows the graphic elements of the design to be described effectively. There are then two types of situation that can arise:

1. In the first case, there is no connection between the elements of the geometric model and the elements contained in the scheme of the application data. This means that the only significance attached to graphic elements is geometric, and that there is no interaction between the operations carried out on the drawing and the state of the application data.
2. Or, there is a semantic, constantly maintained link between the elements of the geometric model and the structural elements of the application data. Thus, any modification of one structure

**Figure 1.11.** *Use of a work station to design an electronic circuit*

must be reproduced in the other, so as to ensure that each is consistent.

In both cases, it is possible to carry out CAD/CAM procedures in accordance with the definition given earlier. The procedures will be better integrated in the second case, as they are more closely connected at a data processing level, than in the first.

*Chapter 2*

# Components of a CAD/CAM system

## 2.1 General points

A CAD/CAM system brings together the user (designers, engineers and draughtsmen), hardware (computers, visual display and dialogue systems) and software (programs for calculation, archiving and presentation of graphics). This combination facilitates the solution of problems, the aim being *assisted* design and not *automatic* design. A division of labour may be made between the user, hardware and software, depending on the respective capabilities of each (see Figure 2.1).

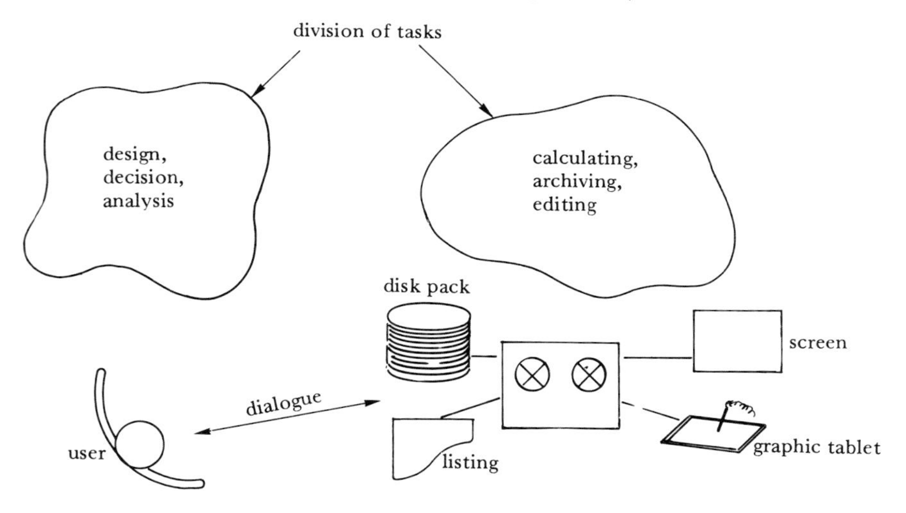


**Figure 2.1.** *Division of tasks between user and machine*

The *user* generally takes responsibility for the conceptual tasks which may include the design of the product itself (the original idea), making a choice between several solutions, analysis of the various possible directions that can be taken and of the advantages and disadvantages inherent in each. In practice, the human operator makes use, above all, of his capacity for synthesis.

The *computer* is generally responsible for repetitive actions, for example, the analytical combination of parameters and the storage and handling of large amounts of information, which involves the formation and adjustment of data bases and consultation with the data bases of other catalogues. The computer's capacity for calculation is used extensively, especially in simulation procedures. Finally, the computer is required to present results in a way which can be immediately understood, particularly in the form of graphics.

The 'user' input is important, because it is usually the engineer alone who is capable of presenting the problems to the computer. It is important that the hardware and software components of the CAD/CAM system are 'user-friendly'. Indeed, the role of those who design CAD/CAM systems is crucial, since the acceptability of their systems will depend on their ease of application.

## 2.2 Hardware

### 2.2.1 GENERAL TECHNIQUES

The hardware available to users of CAD/CAM systems can be divided into a number of categories (see Figure 2.2):

1. *The computer*: made up of one or more processors. The various types of processor available will not be discussed here, but the following trends should be noted:

(a) Currently, most CAD/CAM systems depend on microcomputers with a fairly high calculation capacity. The use of 32 bit processors is widespread, and allows a high standard of performance in terms of calculation, visualization and simulation.

(b) The development of microcomputers has lead to the use of more compact hardware, which it seems, will soon be as powerful as the minicomputers in use at present. The first 32 bit micros have become available recently, and are not significantly less powerful than the larger minicomputers. Although these micros can be used very effectively in specialized systems, their future use in CAD/CAM systems will be limited.

(c) With the introduction of computer networks, it is possible to envisage a system whereby individuals would work with a local system of comparatively small capacity, and be able to gain access to a powerful central processing unit when necessary. The concept of splitting a CAD/CAM application in this way would, however, pose problems and would particularly influence the type of software used. However, such developments are in keeping with the trend towards the use of a new generation of hardware based on multiprocessors and local networks.

2. *The storage device*: designed for the storage of large amounts of information. This subject will not be discussed at length here because it

extends beyond strictly graphic applications. The increase in the number of cheap, high-capacity storage methods available – disks, diskettes, drums and magnetic tape – has encouraged new attitudes and approaches. It is possible to process enormous quantities of data from the first design stage to the manufacture and distribution stages, at relatively low cost. The real problem is to know how to create these data units. In particular, the creation of catalogues or the simple introduction of existing plans could seriously hold back the development of a CAD/CAM application – network structure could cause new problems on the subject of data sharing (local data or data common to a group or profession).

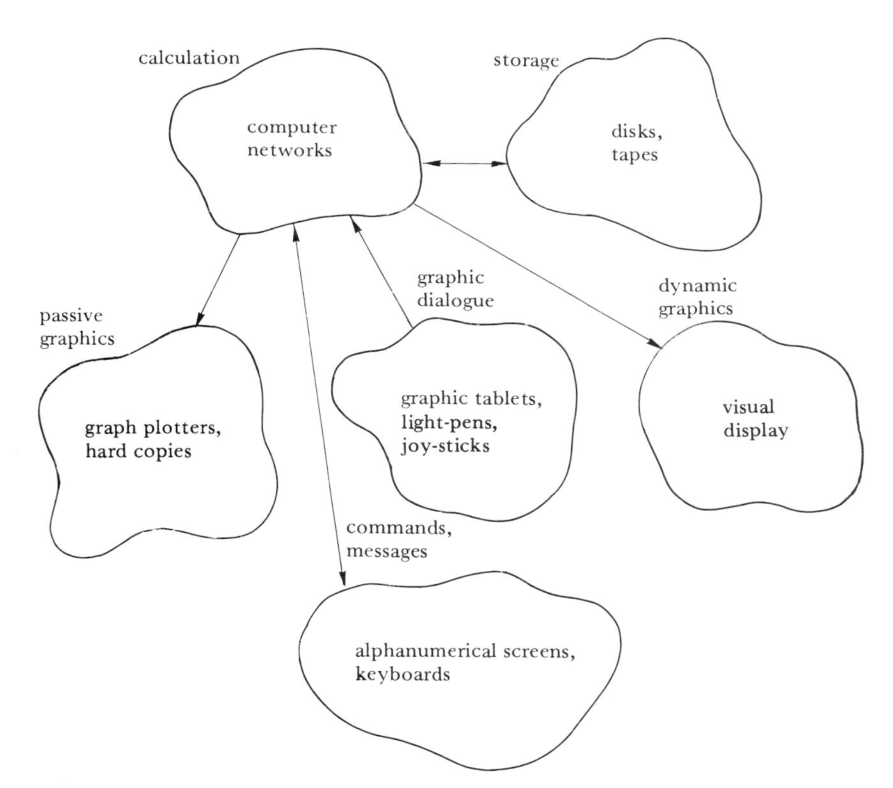


**Figure 2.2.** *CAD/CAM hardware; the system comprises processor and storage, graphic and communication devices*

3. *Graphic devices*: include *passive systems*, in which the drawing or image remains static and cannot be modified in any way, and *dynamic systems*, in which the image can be modified at any time.

4. *Communication devices*: include *graphic systems*, designed to transmit information, such as coordinates, and *non-graphic systems*, for example, alphanumerical keyboards and screens.

Graphic and communication devices will be considered in greater detail later.

In practice, the designer only considers these different types of hardware from the point of view of his own work station (see Figure 2.3) which comprises the devices that allow him to create and design objects, using both graphic and non-graphic instructions and data. The extent to which a work station is well-equipped depends on a number of factors:

1. the number and type of screens (for example alphanumeric or graphic);
2. the variety of means of communication available to the designer;
3. the various ergonomic factors taken into account in its design (work space, positioning of equipment, use of non-reflective screens, etc).

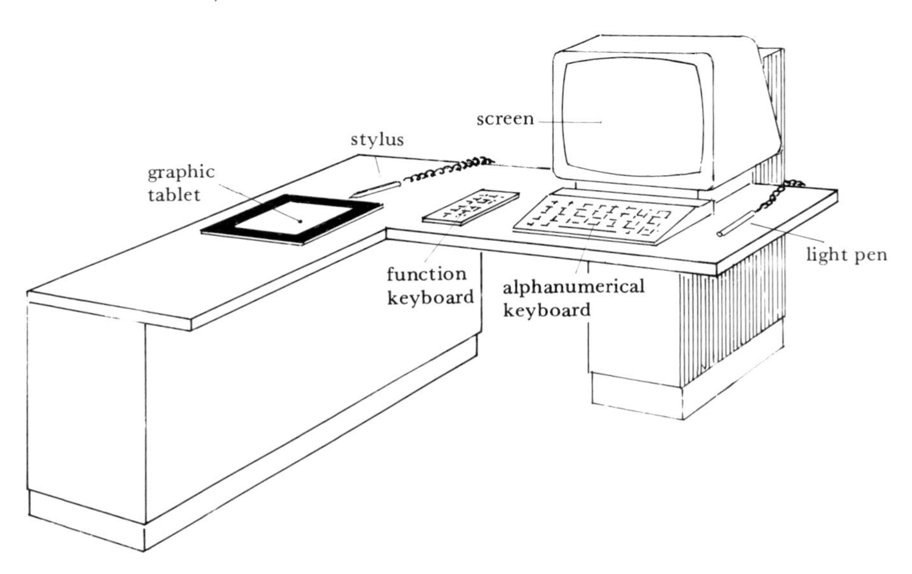


**Figure 2.3.** *A typical work station*

It should be noted that the ease of use, or the adaptability of the unit to the task to be performed, depends on the hardware, but to an even greater extent depends on the software and thus on the utilization procedures laid down by the designer of the CAD/CAM system. Thus, an effective work station represents a compromise between the need to offer high performance but expensive visualization and dialogue devices and less efficient and thus less costly systems. Certain features, however, are indispensible, and if these are not provided to a high enough standard, the entire unit will be rejected as inadequate. The importance of the various hardware and software components of CAD/CAM systems will be assessed later.

### 2.2.2 PASSIVE VISUALIZATION

Systems which provide for graphic presentation to be obtained with permanent input will be considered here. The main characteristic of this type of system is that once displayed the graphic presentation cannot be modified. Moreover, the input medium itself cannot generally be reused.

The most widely used devices are without doubt curve tracers and other such drawing machines. These are based on a variety of technologies (flat, roller or drum tracers), in which the basic parameters are the operational dimensions, precision and speed of tracing. Two basic types can be distinguished:

1. those which allow line drawings to be made, for example, *graph tracers.* The basic graphic element is the straight line segment. As it is difficult to distinguish different areas of an image differentiated only by the level of greyness, cross-hatching is generally used to obtain such effects;
2. those which allow surfaces to be presented effectively, for example *electrostatic plotters*, with which areas can be shaded – invaluable in some applications.

These devices are designed to produce perfect documents and are generally used for the production of plans, or in a wider application, for what are referred to as *communication documents.* For these applications they can be used not only in real time, for work on-screen, but also for delayed processing (overnight, for instance). Screen copying systems also fulfil another function: they can provide the designer with a copy of what appears on the screen (say, a design) at any given moment. This copying facility will obviously reproduce any faults which may be present in the design at the time, but has the advantage of being able to make permanent copies at any stage in the design of an object, and to have them available almost immediately is very useful. Documents of this type are important more as an aid to the design process than an example of communication documents as such. It should be noted, however, that such documents can be fairly elaborate. There are systems available that can produce colour copies and provide proofs of photographic quality.

The two types of system mentioned are thus complementary, in that they may be used at different times during the design process. It is possible to use a curve tracing device to copy a screen image, but the speed at which the image is produced on a real screen copier cannot be matched, and the factors of cost and convenience only emphasize the fact that these devices are not really interchangeable.

### 2.2.3 DYNAMIC VISUALIZATION

Visual display screens are devices that enable images, by nature transient, and thus modifiable, to be viewed. There are two basic types of screen:

1. *Alphanumerical screens*: the main function of these is to display texts of a fixed number of lines and characters.
2. *Graphic screens*: graphic elements, for example line segments or dots, can be displayed on these. By combining graphic primitives it is possible to form characters so that these screens can also be used for alphanumerical display.
3. *Semi-graphic screens* are alphanumerical screens in which the character generator can display simple shapes. Combinations of characters placed side by side can be used to form more complex graphic symbols. Such screens could be used in applications in which a highly schematized graphic display is sufficient, but could never effectively replace a proper graphic screen.

The fact that part of a designer's work is carried out in the form of an alphanumerical dialogue with a computer has often lead to work stations being designed with an alphanumerical screen and a graphic screen. The former is used for interchange of instructions and messages between designer and computer, and the latter reserved exclusively for the presentation of graphic documents. These may include some textual elements, but the graphics used for the text are so much more complex, with different type-faces, colours, sizes, etc, that they can be considered an integral part of the document. The text of the instructions and messages, however, are not considered as part of this type of document, and thus would not appear in the final version of the document.

We shall be concerned here mainly with graphic screens, because these are more specific to graphic assistance in CAD/CAM. There are many factors to be taken into account, each of which can dramatically affect the performance of a system. Many different types of technology are presently in use and the performance standards of systems vary considerably. Here, attention will be paid to screenload capacity, colour display and degree of interaction.

#### *2.2.3.1 Screenload capacity*

This is a measure of the number of graphic elements that can be displayed simultaneously. Normally, the image produced on the screen fades very rapidly and must be redisplayed at least 25 times per second for a persistent image to be created. There are two ways in which the image can be regenerated, using very different techniques:

1. *Calligraphic plotting*, in which the image is reproduced on the screen in such a way as to respect the logic of the design. The beam follows the lines defining the graphic representation, going from one point to the next as prescribed by the shape of the design. In this type of scanning, the more complex the design, the longer it takes to complete the display. Indeed, if the design takes longer than one twenty-fifth of a second to complete, an unpleasant flashing effect is produced which soon causes eye discomfort. The number of elements that can be displayed is thus limited, and is often not great enough for certain types of application, for example, for displaying the circuitry of a microprocessor.
2. A method in which the *regeneration of the image* is carried out, independent of the design is similar to the way in which storage tubes, television tubes and plasma panels work. The general idea is that the entire surface of the screen is scanned every twenty-fifth of a second, and the dots which were lit before remain lit.

In *storage tubes* the surface of the screen is constantly bombarded with electrons which pass through a grid that carries the design. The design is then reproduced on the screen in the form of an arrangement of positive charges. In *television tubes* the surface of the screen is scanned line by line, the information being stored in a memory containing a 'word' of between one and twelve bits for each dot on the screen. This is referred to as 'raster scanning'. In *plasma panels* all the gas dots are covered by a maintenance signal, which keeps all the dots which are already lit in the same state. Thus, if necessary, the entire screen can be lit, without any noticeable flashing effect being produced. The screenload is therefore not limited, as in the other scanning method. However, a bottleneck can occur in the production of this type of image, since the time required to display the information can be considerable, and depends on the speed of transmission between the processor and the viewing console.

### *2.2.3.2 Colour*

The use of colour is also an important variant. Certain CAD/CAM applications may require colour or may require a large or small range of colours. For example, to display an electronic circuit the use of five or six colours may be adequate, but for town planning applications it may be necessary to portray the environment in as realistic a way possible, and this may involve a larger range of colours and shades.

The technology currently in use for graphic display imposes considerable limitations. Calligraphic plotting screens can only display line drawings using a range of about five or six colours. Using raster screens, on the other hand, images may be formed on all parts of the screen, and up to 4096 colours can be displayed in the most sophisticated versions. Memory tubes can provide only monochrome images, with possible simulated variable light intensity. By using a selection of gases, plasma screens can be made to display some colours. However, the range is not wide and the resolution can deteriorate as a result. The choice of screen is made according to the intended application; some screens will be completely unsuitable, because colour simulation by cross-hatching is only acceptable in certain cases.

#### *2.2.3.3 Degree of interaction*

The degree of interaction can be measured in two steps:

1. Modification of the graphic image: that is the deletion of part of the image displayed – in calligraphic plotting screens, this operation is carried out by inputting an instruction into the maintenance memory which blanks over the section of the design to be deleted. The updated image is formed almost instantaneously. In storage tubes, however, the whole screen must be cleared and the new image reconstructed; this can take several seconds. Television tubes and plasma panels fall somewhere between the two: modification is carried out by rewriting the new information over the existing display.
2. Time of response for a request for identification to be carried out: that is, the time taken for the processor to make the association between a graphic element on the screen and the object it represents is measured. In calligraphic plotting, the buffer memory contains a structured description of the design, which allows the graphic element to be immediately associated with the graphic instruction being carried out. Identification takes something in the order of a few hundredths of a second. In memory tubes and plasma panels there is no buffer memory and in television tubes the buffer memory is analytical and it is therefore necessary to simulate a structured buffer memory for use during identification requests. The response time can be as long as a few seconds.

It is clear that the hardware involved can vary substantially. If the hardware chosen is not entirely suitable it should be adapted so that the performance of the system approaches that required. An example of a technique used to compensate for a specific weakness in a system is that of *pre-recorded update*, which is widely used in conjunction with storage tubes. The operator should be aware that the image displayed at a given moment does not correspond exactly with the actual state of the design, because successive modifications are not taken into account unless specifically requested. The screen must first be cleared and the image is then reconstructed in accordance with an evaluation of a sequence of modification commands, stored in the memory during the preceding updating request. Although, by re-assembling the deletion and reconstruction operations, this technique saves time, the quality of graphic representation is reduced.

Some types of screen can function simultaneously. For example, some memory tubes allow part of the image to be displayed *and* updated, which allows the benefits of both systems to be enjoyed. Table 2.1 summarizes the main characteristics of dynamic visualization surfaces:

| | *calligraphic* | *television tube* | *plasma panel* | *storage tube* |
|---|---|---|---|---|
| *image load* | limited | unlimited | unlimited | unlimited |
| *buffer memory* | structured | dot by dot | none (screen) | none (screen) |
| *intensity levels (one colour)* | 2–16 | 2–128 | 2 | 2–6 (simulated) |
| *colours* | 1–6 | 1–4096 | 2 or 3 | 1 or 2 |
| *selective deletion* | yes | yes | yes | no |
| *identification* | immediate | long | long | long |
| *degree of interaction* | high | medium | medium | low |

**Table 2.1.** *Characteristics of visualization surfaces*

### 2.2.4 COMMUNICATION DEVICES

These are used to communicate messages and data to the computer. There are three types of communication device:

1. *Keyboards*: allow information to be transmitted using a number of keys. These include *alphanumerical keyboards* which are identical to typewriter keyboards, and *function keyboards* which consist of a number of keys that, when depressed, cause a corresponding numerical character to be transmitted to the computer. Sometimes these keys can be lit up by the program to show at a given moment which ones are available for use.

2. *Direct designation devices*: can be used to describe an exact screen location. This category includes *light pens* (photocells with which light can be detected), *reticules* (formed on the screen by two straight lines, one vertical and one horizontal, that intersect at a given point), and various methods involving designation using a touch sensitive pad. The positional accuracy with which points can be described on the screen can vary (due mainly to errors caused by parallax). However, reticules are very accurate since the image is placed directly on to the screen.

3. *Indicate designation devices*: allow coordinates to be obtained off-screen and the equivalent position to be shown on-screen in the form of a luminous symbol. Included in this category are graphic tablets, rolling balls, joysticks and other types of 'mouse'. It should be noted that the use of graphic tablets provides a high degree of precision, whereas other systems have been designed for simplicity of application (the mouse) or for high tracking speed (joysticks).

Some of the techniques used with these devices will be discussed in Chapter 5. The basis for the operation of these systems is the emission of a signal to the computer (causing an interruption) and the transmission of an item of information, the nature of which will depend on the device: a key number for a keyboard, a position (x, y) for designation devices, an alphanumerical sequence for an alphanumerical keyboard, etc. The procedure is shown diagrammatically in Figure 2.4, and shows why work carried out in dialogue mode tends to disturb the normal operation of the system: the frequency of interruptions is such that calculations cannot be carried out in the time available. This is one reason for equipping the visual display console with a processor to manage the communication devices and to leave the computer free to carry out the necessary calculations.

### 2.2.5 GRAPHIC PROCESSORS

All visual display consoles (and all graph tracers) are equipped with a graphic processor, which varies in complexity from model to model. The basic function of this type of processor is to carry out instructions received from the computer, such as:

1. *drawing instructions*, including at least point, vector and character following;
2. *page format instructions*, including primitives for window specifications and surface geometric transformations (change of scale, rotations and translations);
3. *in calligraphic plotting screens* there is a structure for the buffer memory and instructions for the control of the memory.

An elementary graphic processor is illustrated in Figure 2.5; it is made up of a register X, a register Y and a light register L. Behind these registers, a digital-analog converter directs the beam of electrons so as to display the point of coordinates (X, Y), with luminosity L. The computer carries out instructions such as 'load register X, load register Y, load light register L'. In scanning screens, the computer is mainly engaged in loading the different registers in order to maintain the image on the screen, and so cannot be used for anything else (if it was used the image would fade). A slightly more sophisticated

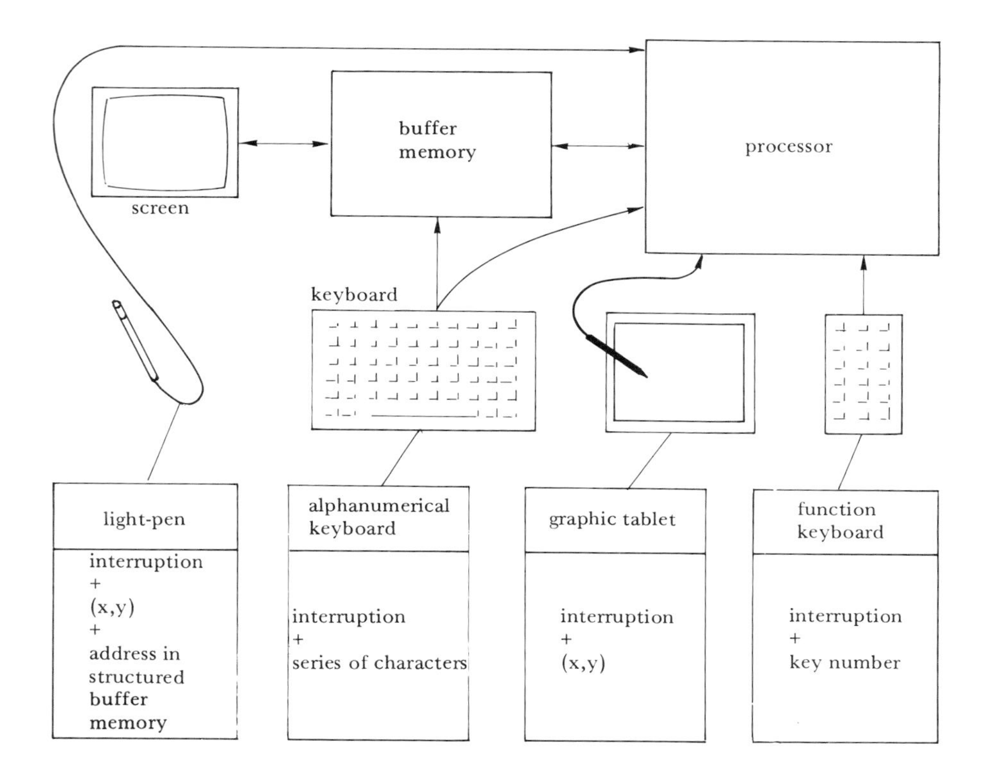


**Figure 2.4.** *Modes of operation of communication devices*

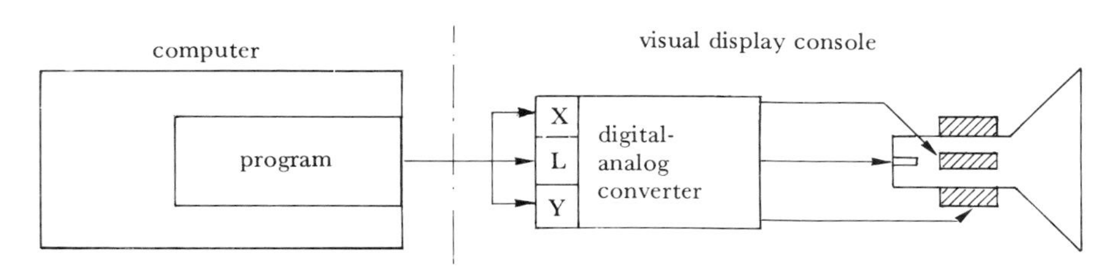


**Figure 2.5.** *Structure of a simple graphic processor*

structure is shown in Figure 2.6. Here a buffer memory has been included between the computer and the console proper. The series of instructions is then transmitted by the computer into the buffer memory, and the console maintains the image. The computer is now free to be used for other purposes. In the diagram a character generator and a vector generator have also been included; these allow the quantity of information to be transmitted from the computer to be reduced. It is this arrangement (minus the buffer memory) that is used in graphic plotters and storage tubes.

The common tendency is to integrate one or more microprocessors

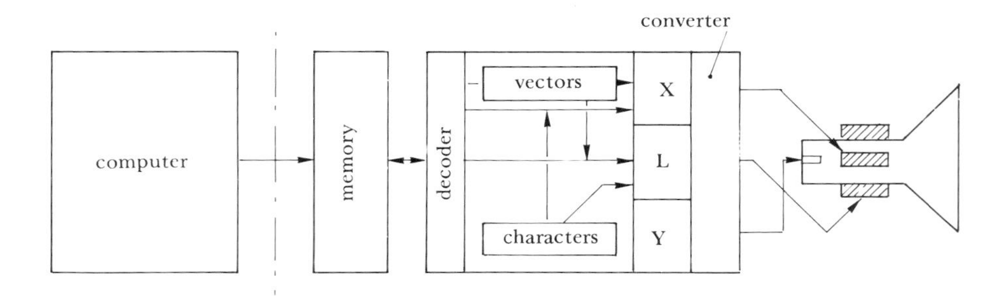


**Figure 2.6.** *Structure of a more sophisticated graphic processor with buffer memory*

into the visual display console, so as to be able to effect a maximum number of calculations. Consoles with an extremely sophisticated range of graphic instructions are now available, particularly for large visual display lists, using symbols and sub-designs which can be modified with windowing and page format operations virtually in real time. These are likely to become more widespread because the price of microprocessors is decreasing exponentially and their performance standards are improving. It is not unreasonable to suppose that systems for processing three-dimensional scenes will soon become available. On the other hand, the means of incorporating dialogue techniques are not yet particularly well developed, and it is this area in which most progress has yet to be made.

## 2.3 Software

### 2.3.1 BASIC STRUCTURE OF A CAD/CAM SOFTWARE SYSTEM

The basic CAD/CAM software system includes the following elements (see Figure 2.7):

1. An *algorithm base*, made up of a set of sub-programs intended to ensure that the various functions are carried out. This base can be considered as the system's 'know-how'.

2. A *design monitor*, which allows different tasks to be performed in sequence, on request. This (see Figure 2.8) controls the data base and algorithm base, as well as the dialogue between operator and computer.

3. A *communication monitor*, which provides for communication between the operator and the computer. The general structure of such a monitor (see Figure 2.9) usually consists of two levels:

(a) *logical units*, corresponding to a functional definition of the dialogue;

(b) *physical units*, which correspond to the communication system.

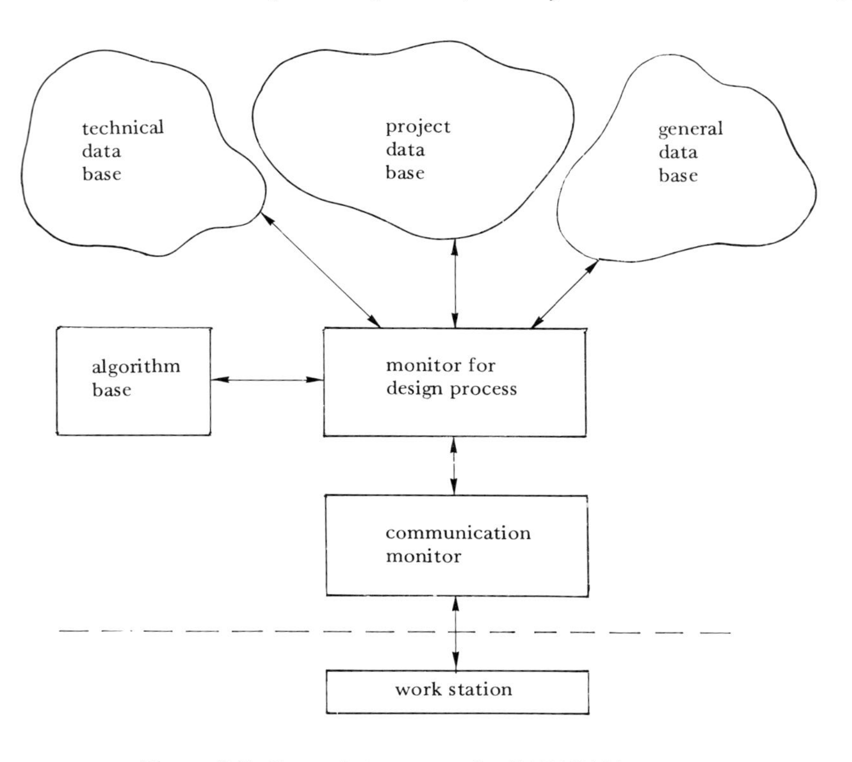


**Figure 2.7.** *General structure of a CAD/CAM system*

The communication monitor provides for dialogue to be carried out by making the connection between the logical and physical units of a system.

4. A set of *data bases*, representing the information necessary to carry out a particular project. The following types of data base can be distinguished:

(a) the *data base of the project in progress*, which contains a representation of the object being designed – this data base will henceforth be referred to as the *model*;

(b) the *technical data base*, which is a collection of technical information on the project, concerning both the design and manufacturing stages (eg data concerning the various machines used in manufacture and their application);

(c) the *general data base*, which contains all the non-technical information on the project; this type of data base is not yet widely used, since it requires the use of completely integrated CAD/CAM systems;

(d) the *data base on previous projects*, contains a representation of objects which have already been designed and can be used for consultation before modification of the model (in designing a new product based on a previous one, for example, or in product improvement).

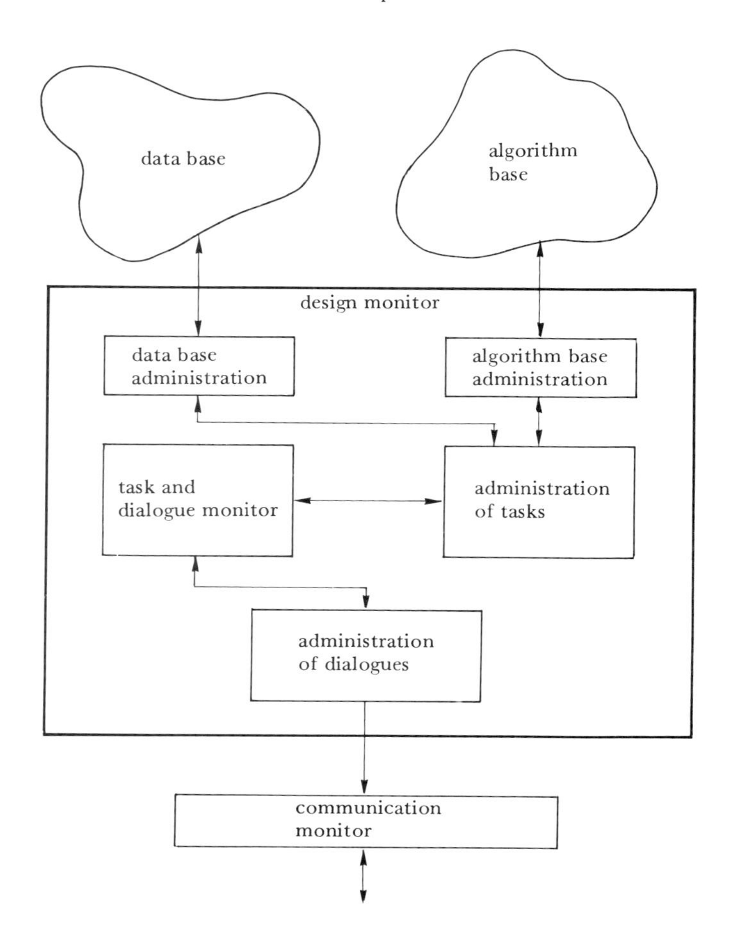


**Figure 2.8.** *The design monitor and its environment*

The following points should be noted: the term 'data base' is used to describe a collection of information, without implying anything about its organization or representation. Thus, a data base can take the form of simple files, or at the other extreme, involve a data base management system (DBMS) of a most sophisticated nature. Although DBMS of standard design have been used in CAD/CAM systems, no DBMS has been designed specifically for use in such systems. The differences between a standard DBMS and the sort of system which would be required for use in CAD/CAM include:

1. The information to be managed is dynamic by nature and changes as the object to be designed is evolved, ie the information develops throughout the design process. The DBMS must thus act not only on the information provided but also on the connecting structures.

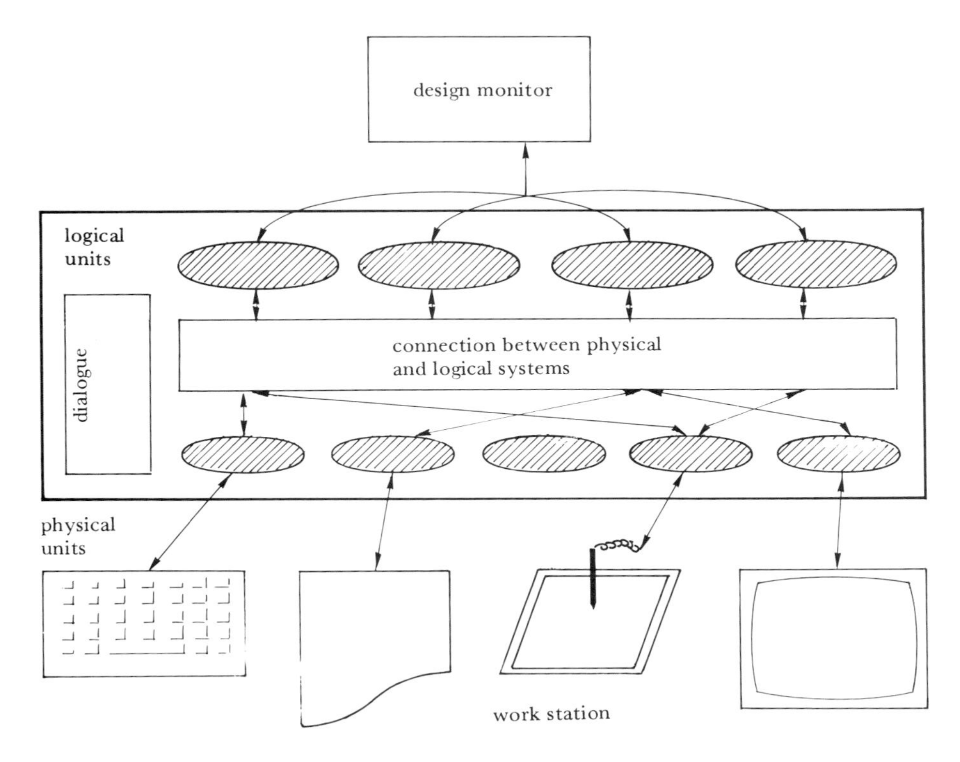


**Figure 2.9.** *The communication monitor and its environment*

2. The amount of information to be handled is large and the description of a single object may comprise several levels of information. For example, the geometric description of an object may be made up of a number of elements, each of which need to be taken into account according to a given criterion, eg the distance between object and observer. The rules for the formulation and description of an object do not correspond to the normal criteria used in DBMS and are more difficult to establish.

It should be emphasized that the central component of any CAD/CAM system is the model, about which all design procedures revolve (see Figure 2.10). This model contains a description of the object (particularly in geometric modelling, which will be discussed further in Chapter 3), and the information required for project management.

The structure used in EUCLID (Matra-Datavision) for project management is illustrated by Figure 2.11, and shows various, highly diverse work zones which can be managed by the same user. The central zone contains the names of projects being carried out (the size of this zone is limited but the space taken up by each project is very small).

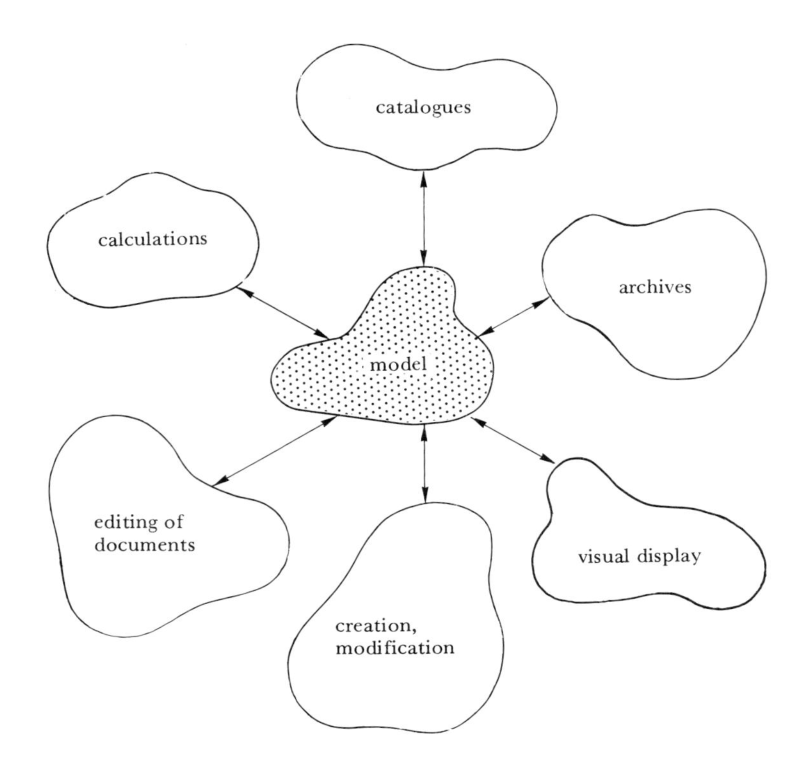


**Figure 2.10.** *Structure of a CAD/CAM system*

Associated with each project name is an information block, which contains the couplets: (*sub-project name, project zone name*).

A project zone may be stored on disk or be transferred on to an external storage device (tape, diskette, etc). Whatever the case, the project zone name indicates the physical input. If a project zone is active, it stays on disk, which allows access to the EUCLID entities stored under a part or entity name in the sub-project. For instance, in Figure 2.11, to start work Paul will input his acronym and indicate which project and sub-project he wants to work on. He will thus be put in contact with the corresponding project zone and will simply need to give the part name for the operations to be carried out in this zone. The use of 'user codes' avoids confusion between different users working on the same sub-project and storing different data.

| *project* | *sub-project* | *part* | *user* |
|---|---|---|---|
| STYLE ROCOCO | ROCOCO BLACK | LITET 1 | PAUL |
| 12 char max | 16 char max | 8 char max | 4 char max |

Figure 2.11 shows the different representation structures and their sequences. The 'MAQ' extension indicates that the information blocks are from the EUCLID data structure, and the 'age' 0 shows that they

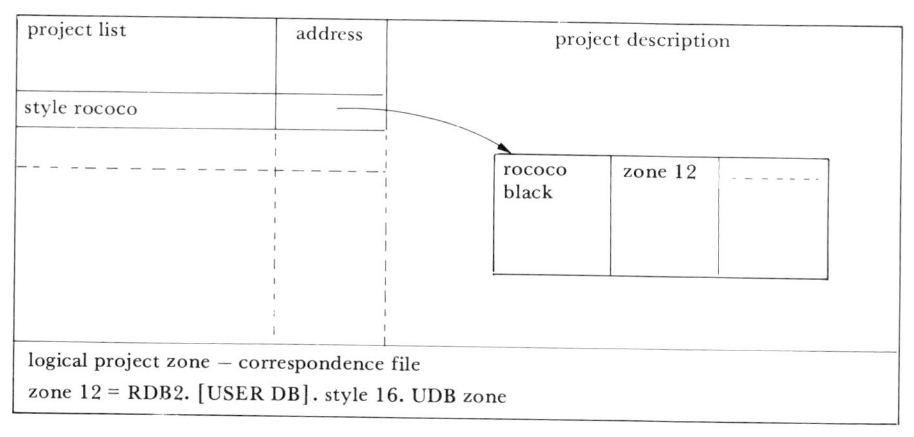


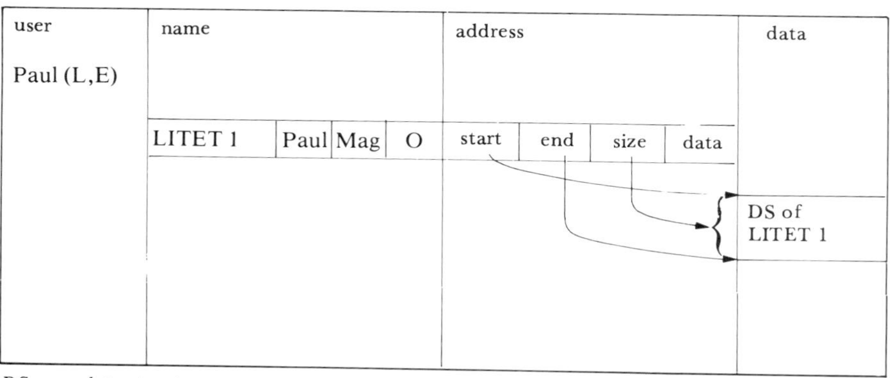


*DS = data structure*
*DB = data base*
*UDB = user data base*

**Figure 2.11.** *Project management – EUCLID structure*

are part of the most recent update of the LITET 1 part. The redundancy of information in the address zone is intentional and makes up part of the data protection system. Some project zones can have the status of standard zones and can be accessed and read by anyone. However, each user has a special zone, called the *user zone*, which contains safeguards, display lists and records of work sessions. At any time the user can store and recall data for his sub-project; but to gain access to data other than his own he must supply the appropriate code. He can also gain access to a standard zone and an external zone and will be able only to recall data which will be coded 'non-modifiable'; depending on the system, a facility which allows the state of reference to the data base to be modified may or may not be accessible to the users. There are, in addition, special facilities which allow the person responsible for the system to rename, reclass and change the order of the objects.

### 2.3.2 INTEGRATION LEVELS

The set of programs which make up a CAD/CAM system can vary in the extent to which it is full or complete, and also in its degree of homogeny. When a CAD/CAM system is first introduced into an industrial set-up a common strategy is to develop programs with the following characteristics:

1. they should correspond to a precise moment in the design process and be designed so as to provide effective assistance at that moment, without any link with other stages;
2. they should be designed independently of each other, with no connection between them, except a manual link, produced using data obtained from another program.

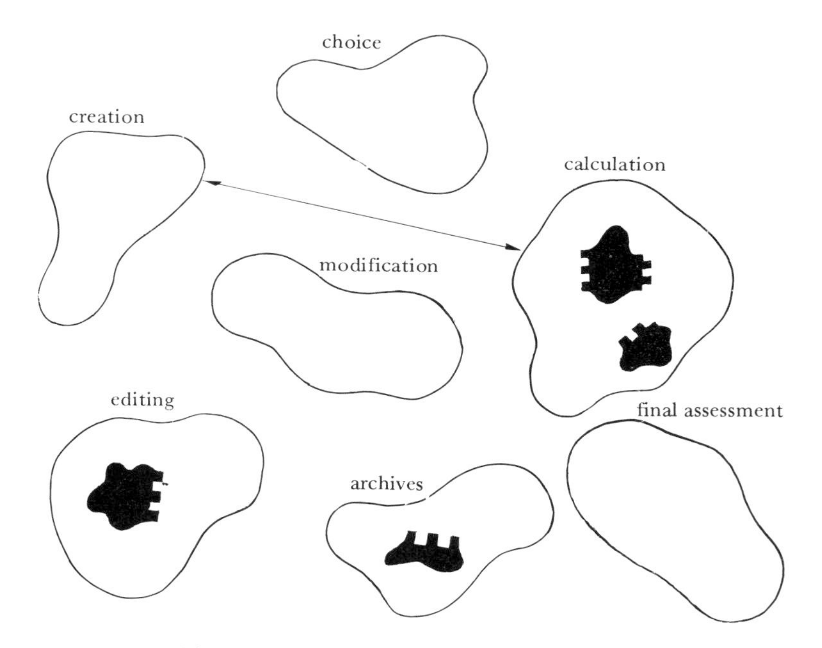


**Figure 2.12.** *Units of unconnected software*

This method of working is shown diagrammatically in Figure 2.12. It corresponds to the acquisition of programs provided by the Sociétés de Service et de Conseil en Informatique, who often use programs which are diverse in nature and well adapted to a particular class of calculation. This structure of unconnected software can be satisfactory in certain cases, but in others there may be a need to combine two programs. In this case, it becomes necessary to ensure that the results from one program can be passed automatically into the data store of another. The second level of CAD/CAM integration is thus attained through

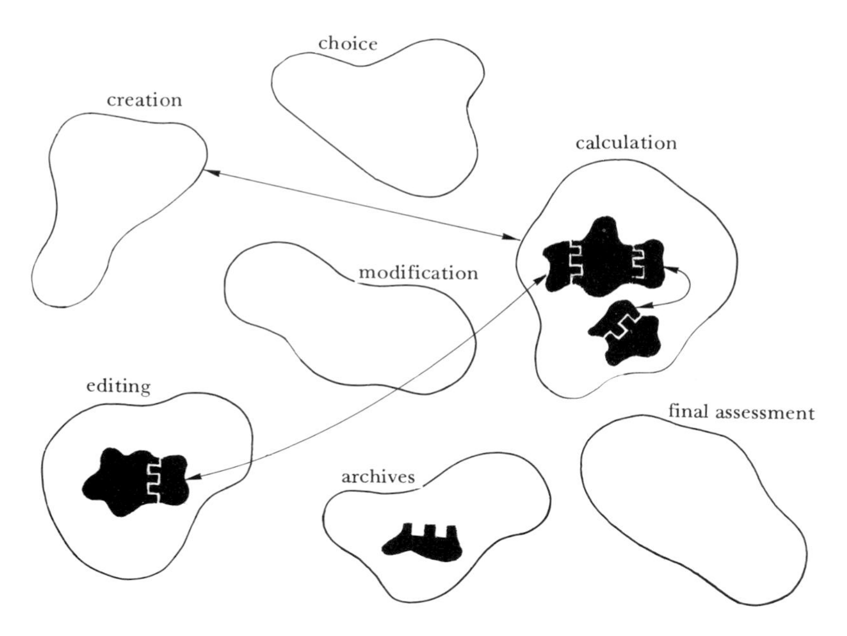


**Figure 2.13.** *Interface writing*

the development of interfaces between programs (see Figure 2.13). These interfaces are programs which, using results obtained in a particular form, can produce the data necessary for forming program sequences and present them in a suitable form.

This technique, which is widely practised in companies which provide processing advice and services, can be explained further. Sometimes it is not possible to write an interface, because the necessary information is not available. A typical problem is that of information retrieval. Information is often output in the form of a list, but it may also be necessary to have data on disk so as to be able to process them automatically. However, this supposes that access to a source program is possible, which would allow the writing commands to be modified. In some cases, a source program is not supplied and therefore such an operation is not possible. This is also the case for operations controlling the preparation of data.

This technique tends to delay the execution of programs, since any sequence formation is preceded by a phase in which the data is transformed from one format to another. Faced with such a problem, the final level of integration may be attempted (see Figure 2.14): a data structure and programs are planned which will allow new modules to be added to the existing unit at any time. To this end, a centralized mechanism can be installed, so that all the requests for information are directed through a master module, which is in sole control of

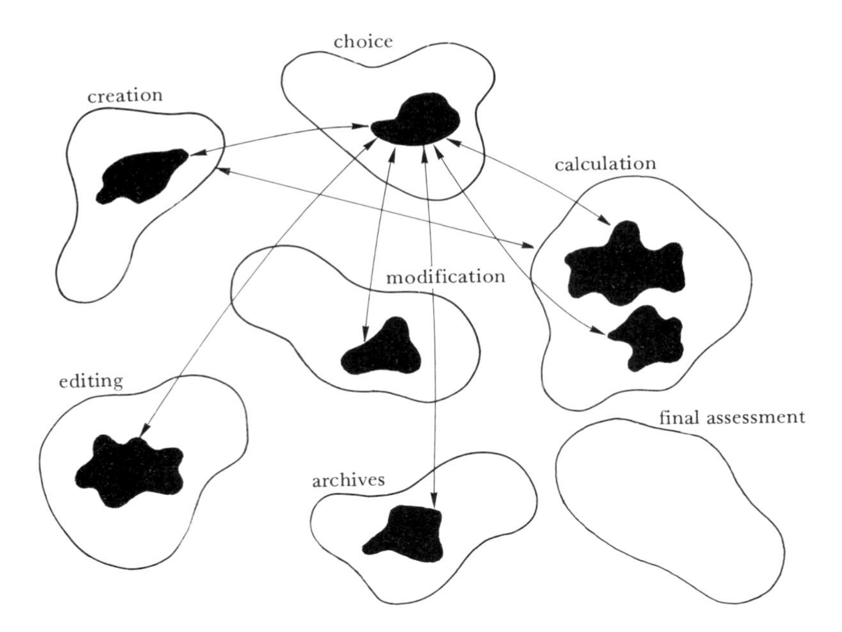


**Figure 2.14.** *An integrated CAD/CAM system*

the various exchange formats. In this situation, a CAD/CAM system constitutes an integral unit in itself, and the problem is to provide, from the outset, rules allowing the core of the system to be formed.

'Turnkey' CAD/CAM systems have been designed on this basis. It should be noted that a CAD/CAM system, whether totally integrated or not, is more effective if its constituent elements are separated into modules (see Figure 2.15), since:

1. efficiently itemized modules facilitate the construction of new functions, simply by regrouping the required programs;
2. the system can be improved by writing new modules which can be added to the algorithm base;
3. the various operations carried out by the system can be performed by several machines, ie by using specialized devices for visual display, modelling, and dialogue or calculation management. Each element then carries out a specific procedure through the application or design monitor (see Figure 2.16) until the project is completed.

### 2.3.3 BASIC STRUCTURE OF CAD/CAM SYSTEMS

The graphic software used in CAD/CAM systems is extremely varied, because the diversity of applications calls for a range of software. It is

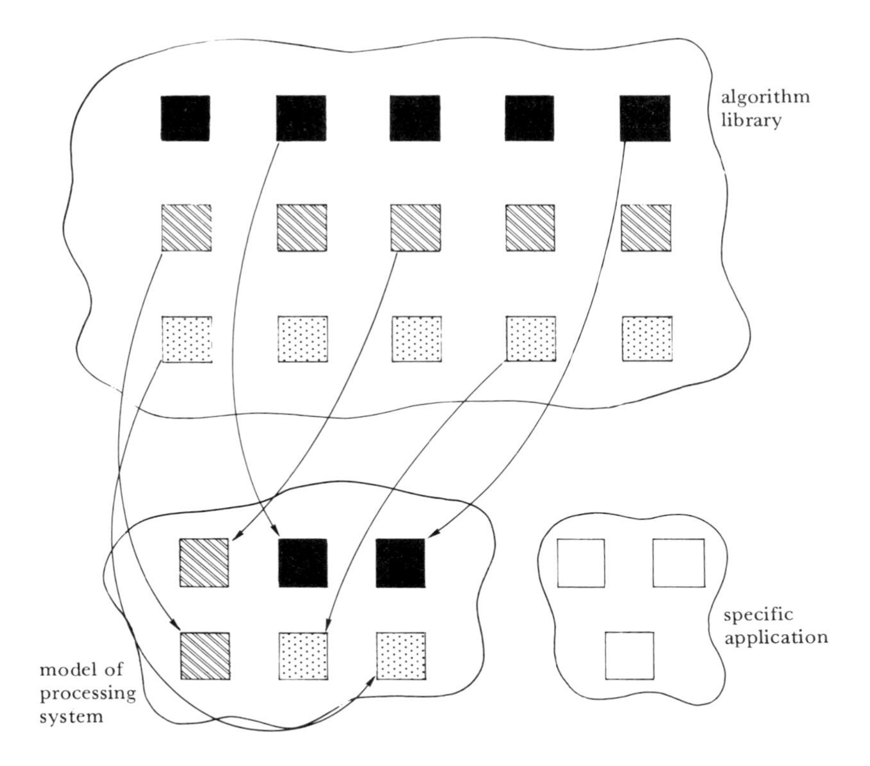


**Figure 2.15.** *A modular CAD/CAM system*

possible, however, to detect major structural similarities and differences which can be used to classify different kinds of software.

Data linked directly to the application are not generally in a form suitable for direct graphic presentation. Consider, for example, an application concerning the installation of an urban transport system. The various points to be served by the network can be represented on a graph, which can take the form of a *connection matrix* (see Figure 2.17).

Using this matrix, a certain number of calculation algorithms can be applied (eg to find the shortest routes). An operator may wish to follow the work process using graphic representation, eg a graph in the form of points joined by a series of arcs.

It thus becomes necessary to progress to a level at which the application data can be handled in such a way as to allow it to be presented in the form of a graph of points, labels (named points) or graphics (to join the various points on the graph). Once this has been achieved, the graphic elements can be processed using graphic software to produce an image on a screen. In the same way, once the image has been produced, the operator may wish to include some information obtained from the graphic representation. It may, for example, be required that the

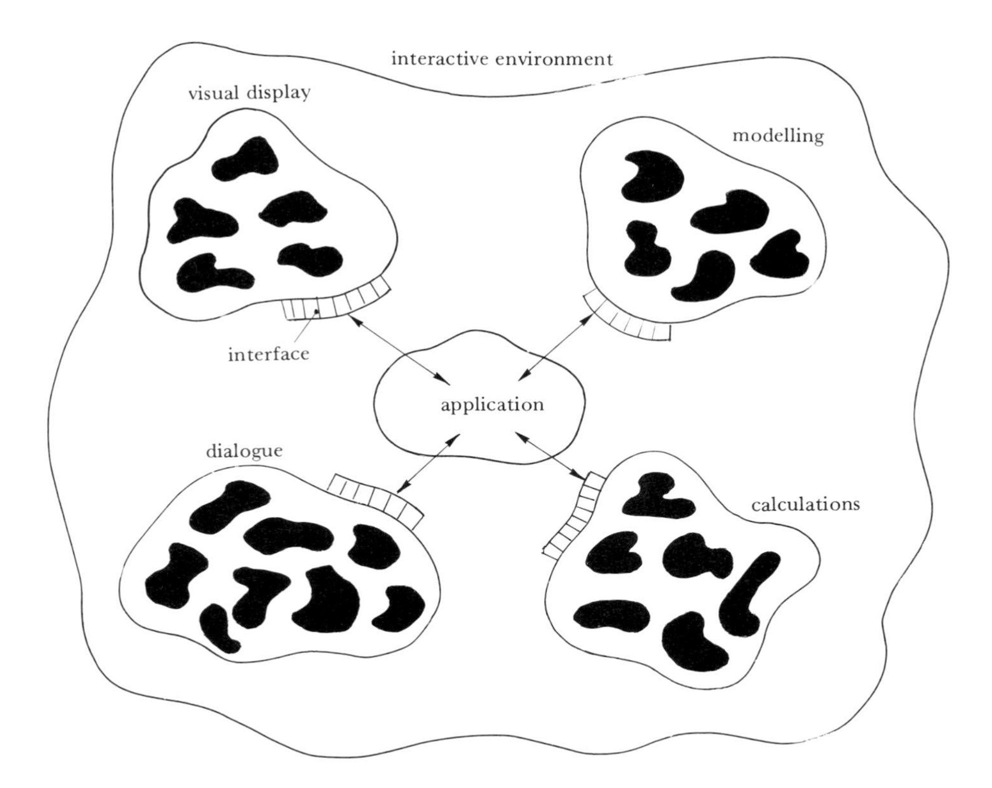


**Figure 2.16.** *Operations separated for sharing between hardware*

calculation program should take into account a point or curve of the graph. At the lowest level this is possible using a coordinate couple (x, y); however, this cannot be directly related to the application program. The graphic software must be capable of transforming this graphic element into another form, so that the point or curve can be identified in the connection matrix and located according to a corresponding line and column index.

Closer study of this operation reveals that interactive graphic software consists of four levels (see Figure 2.18):

1. The *application level*, made up of the program which controls a specific algorithm library for the application and a data base and which is also specific to the application; such data is generally non-graphic.

2. The *description level*, made up of descriptive or modelling software, which uses encoding algorithms and a data structure known as the *scene* or the geometric model data structure. The basic elements of this structure are geometric objects, a view or graphic representation of which can be calculated.

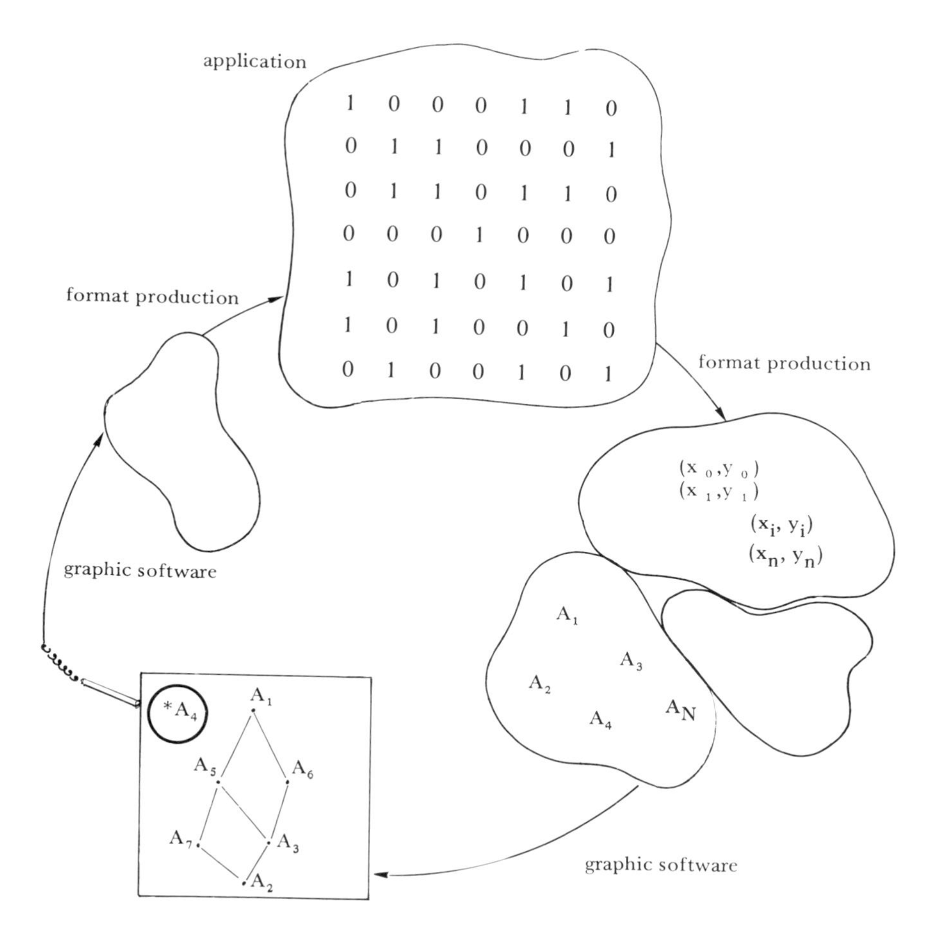


**Figure 2.17.** *The requirements for format production*

3. The *level of preparation for visual display*, comprising:

(a) *decoding*, an operation in which the scene code is transformed into a code specific to a drawing or image. This code is two-dimensional and is generally chosen so as to ensure a degree of independence relative to the application and the hardware – this is referred to as a *graphic file*;

(b) the *page layout*, which allows the various parts of the graphic representation to be arranged on screen. It is at this level, for example, that the windowing mechanism comes into play, moving from the window itself (an area defined by the user coordinates containing the part of the graphic file to be displayed) to the boundary or rectangular portion of screen which displays the contents of the window.

4. The *elementary level*, at which it is possible to change from the preceding code to a code understandable to the machine. The result is a display file of commands which allows effective use of the hardware.

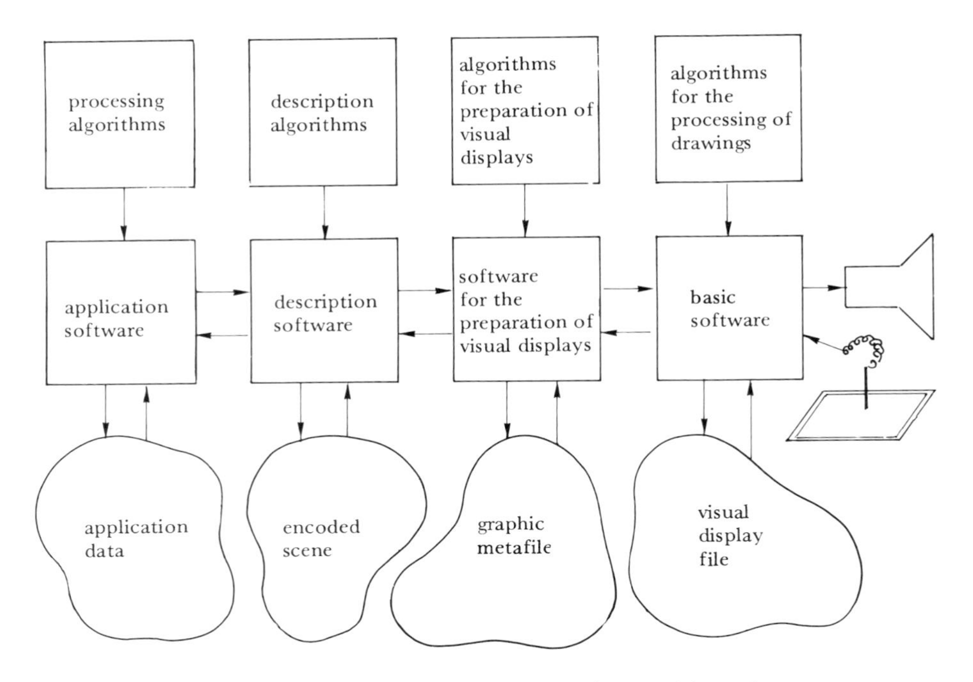


**Figure 2.18.** *General structure of interactive graphics software*

It should be noted that the operations described above can easily be applied to the production of a graphic representation of an object. However, if the hardware is being set up for a particular application, there are far more problems in that many small units of information must be synthesized. This synthesis can be very difficult, particularly when three-dimensional objects are being reconstructed from side views.

This structure is not ideal, and in practice it may become evident that there is insufficient definition between the four levels.

Figure 2.19 illustrates an example of a software structure in which the description level does not exist as a separate entity. This means that if the software is shared between a number of machines, it would not be possible to derive a level at which the geometric model is managed independently. There are two reasons for not adhering to the suggested hierarchy:

1. Efficiency can be increased by combining the calculation stages (see Figure 2.20). A good example is that of geometric transformations. Transformations in on-scene positioning and in page format on screen may be considered to be of the same order. Calculation techniques can be used which necessitate the use of only one transformation for the production of a definitive image. In this way an economy is made in

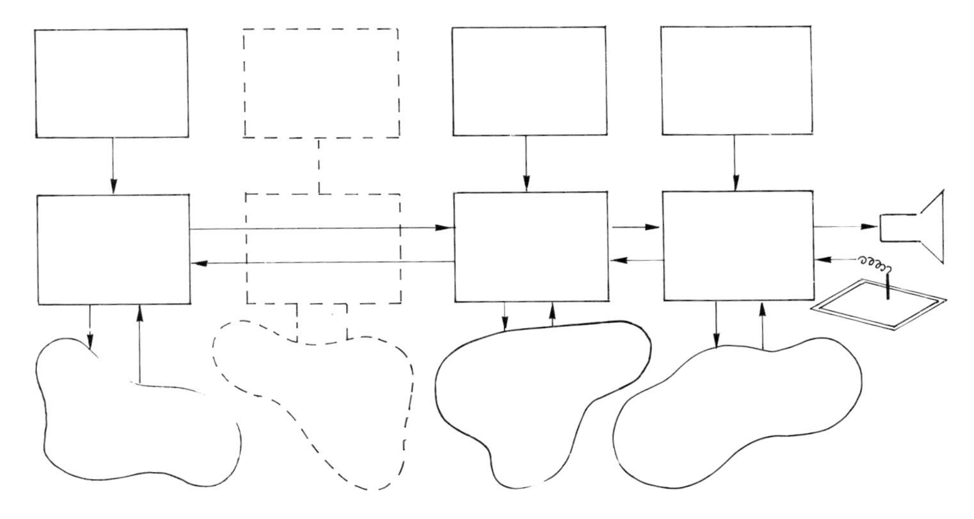

**Figure 2.19.** *Disappearance of the modelling level*

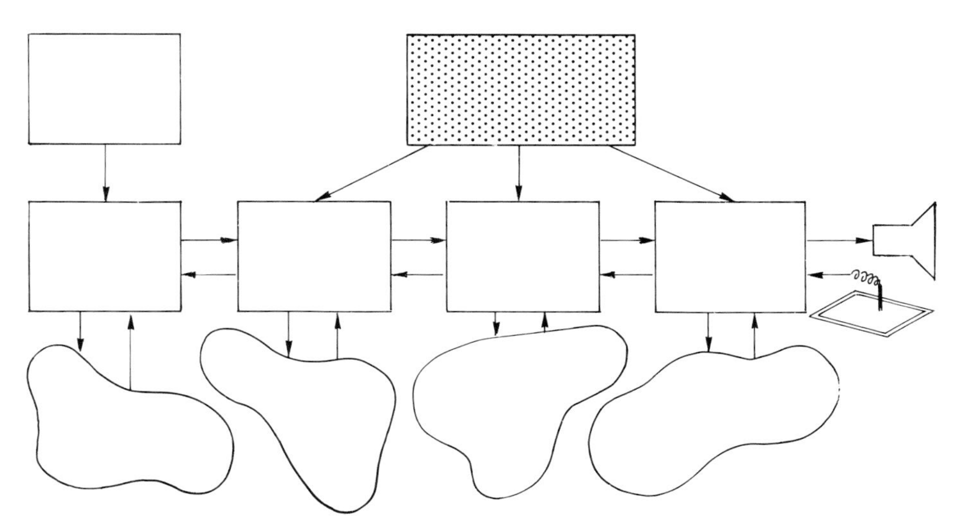

**Figure 2.20.** *Repositioning of algorithms*

the number of processing stages necessary in that each stage results in a partial transformation.

2. Economies can be made in the memory, if one of the data structures is not kept up to date (see Figure 2.21). In this case, each time it becomes necessary to reconsider the elements of a given level the data structure is replaced with a calculation. For example, if a visual display list is not kept up to date (which can occur in terminals with memory tubes or raster scanners), a simple operation to alter the position of the

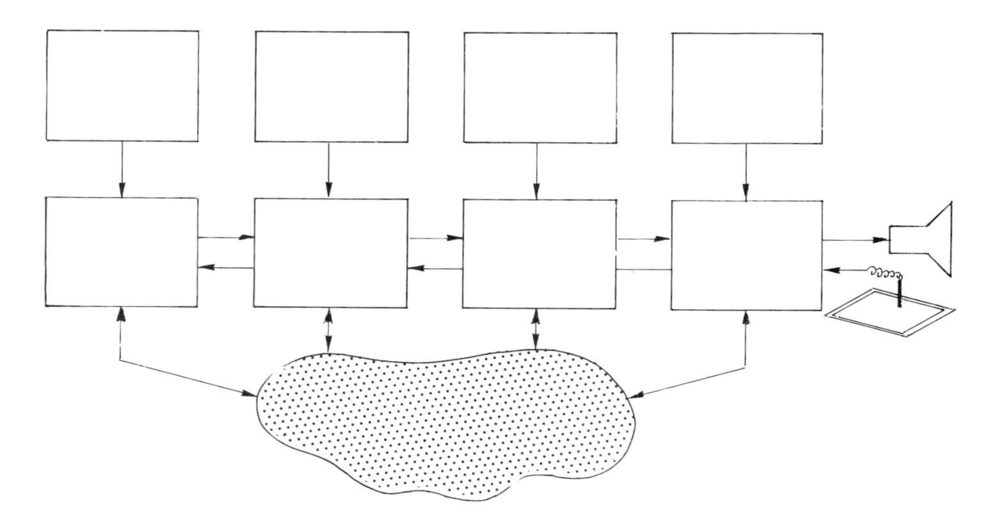

**Figure 2.21.** *Reassembly of data*

image on the screen can result in the entire image being recalculated from the preceding levels, when more efficient techniques could otherwise be used.

The choice of structure of graphic software has a considerable influence on the possibilities available:

1. Rearrangement of the calculation procedures which correspond to different levels, as well as duplication of some data structures could rule out the possibility of dividing tasks between different machines.

2. Data structures which may be considered to be redundant can be erased but this may limit the possibilities for interaction at a later stage, in that moving to higher levels becomes difficult (consider how many systems do not even allow the simple operation of setting information in a page format to be carried out by the operator).

3. If a system is intended to be used in different locations and with a variety of hardware, definition of basic graphic software can become indispensible. Under these conditions, clearly defined separation of the various constituents can be an asset, in that it is easy to tell exactly what each level depends on. This is why the current tendency is to define the following modules (see Figure 2.22):

(a) *modules for geometric modelling*, using various codes, very closely linked to the applications;

(b) *modules for the preparation of visual display*, basically including projection operations and graphic processing of the sort that involves elimination of hidden parts, corresponding to the 'decoding' part;

(c) *basic graphic software*, including page format and elementary

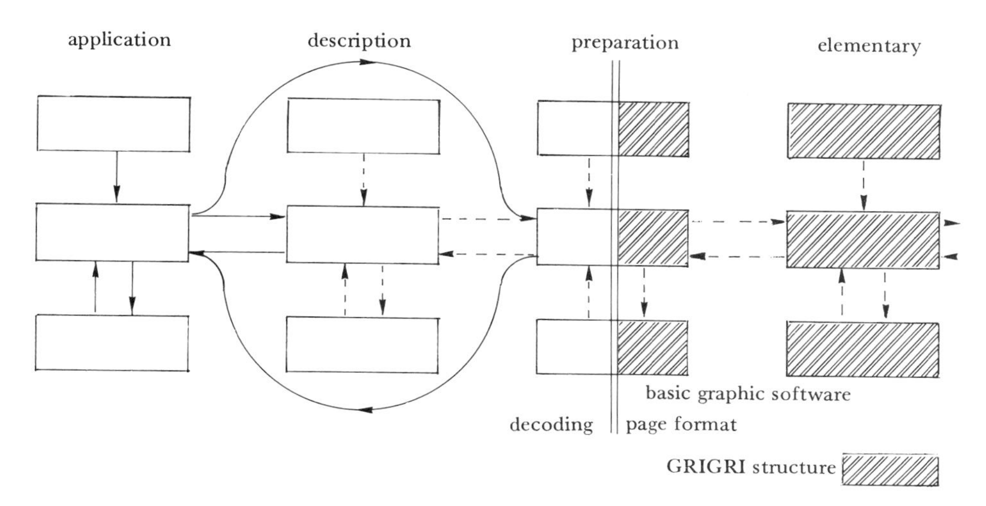


**Figure 2.22.** *An example of basic graphic software*

software. An example of this is GRIGRI, software developed by ENSIMAG and distributed by MICADO, and the norm proposition ISO which is generally known as GKS.

In studying this type of software, the following features can be observed:

1. *A high degree of independence relative to the type of hardware in use*: GRIGRI is structured in two modules, a core written entirely in FORTRAN, independent of the hardware, and an interpreter which manages the terminals (there is an interpreter corresponding to each type of terminal). There are interpreters either already available or in the process of being developed for a certain number of consoles (Tektronix 4010, 4012, 4014, IBM 2250, AFIGRAPH, IMLAC, SECAPA). One of the advantages of GRIGRI is that the application program does not have to be modified in the event of a change of hardware. GKS offers the same type of service through the use of a work station.

2. *Independence relative to the means of dialogue*: while dialogue is being written, the programmer is not concerned with the actual methods being used, rather the choice is left to the operator. Finally, it should be noted that basic graphic software is used to develop experimental versions of CAD/CAM systems, and profit from the facilities which are generally presented in this type of software (particularly for the instigation of dialogue), but that this should be gradually replaced once a fixed version on a specific piece of hardware is required. In this situation, the stages which exist simply to facilitate portability are dispensed with, so that certain characteristics of the chosen hardware can be made better use of.

*Chapter 3*

# Geometric modelling

A model which represents an object either designed or in the process of being designed can contain many different types of data: geometric, technological, etc. This chapter is concerned with *geometric modelling*, or the representation of objects from the point of view of their geometric properties. The geometric model frequently occupies an important place in CAD/CAM applications and is used both during development and manufacture. For example, it is necessary to know the geometric properties in order to model finished parts, or to produce manufacturing plans, or to produce, by more or less automated means, numerical control tapes.

Geometric modelling was first carried out in about 1963, when there were numerous studies made on graphic representation (the basics of most algorithms for the elimination of hidden parts being established before 1972). Specific applications, particularly in the automobile and aeronautical industries, which rely on surface representations, were also considered in those early days. From the 1970s onward, algorithms were improved, and such subjects as numerical control began to be better understood. The first systems used for modelling three-dimensional objects then began to appear, and by the end of the 1970s their industrial exploitation had begun. The specific functions which are now available first made their appearance in these models, basically because of the developments that had taken place in hardware (which allowed animation and the use of colour, etc).

The geometric model of an object is the data processing-based representation of the shapes and dimensions of the object. Too often the image representing the object on a graphic screen is imagined to be the same thing as the model. It would not be true to say, for example, that if a system only allows line drawings to be made, the model cannot be a 'solid' type. In the same way, a two-dimensional model of an object, which can include relational information, is different from a visual display model, which contains vector-type information. It is very common, moreover, to associate the realization of geometric modelling with the interactive use of a graphic terminal.

It will be seen later that a model can be created in a number of ways, which can be based on calculations, for example, as well as on work at the screen. In this chapter, a general survey of models (including the most widely used) and an analysis of their advantages and disadvantages will be made, followed by a more detailed study of the various types of two- and three-dimensional models. Finally, the problems presented by inter-system communication of information and the various methods of using models will be considered.

## 3.1 General points

### 3.1.1 PRINCIPAL TYPES OF MODEL

#### *3.1.1.1 Two-dimensional models*

The earliest models used were two-dimensional which allowed plans to be formed and modified. This type of modelling is still frequently used because it is relatively inexpensive (because of the low degree of complexity of the algorithms and their ease of use) and well suited to the solution of many types of industrial problem. Two-dimensional representation is, however, often inadequate for even a slightly complex object. Using normal techniques (ie without CAD/CAM), plans are used which show the object from various points of view, but when the object is highly complex, it is usually best represented by a prototype model.

#### *3.1.1.2 Three-dimensional models*

A three-dimensional model is intended to show the form of an object in its three dimensions. From the work that has been carried out in this field and also on operational software, it is possible to distinguish three types of three-dimensional model:

1. the 'line' model;
2. the 'surface' model;
3. the 'solid' model.

The *line model* was the first to be developed. It requires only the coordinates (x, y, z) of the points to be plotted and the lines which connect them. Figure 3.1 shows the type of ambiguity that can arise from the use of a line model, because when only the vertices and connecting lines are present, several interpretations can be made of a single model.

The *surface model* allows definition of surfaces and sometimes these may be highly complex. This technique has often been combined with the use of line illustrations to define the surfaces of an object when these cannot easily be deduced using a line model. In some cases, however, this hybrid model (line + surface) is still not sufficient to render

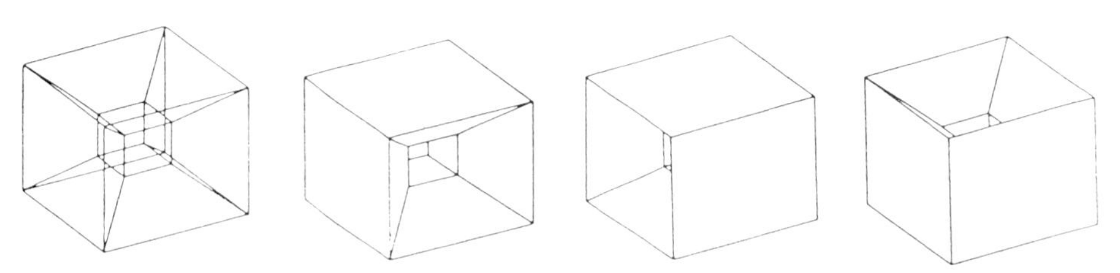

**Figure 3.1.** *Ambiguous representation using line models; several representations can arise from a single model*

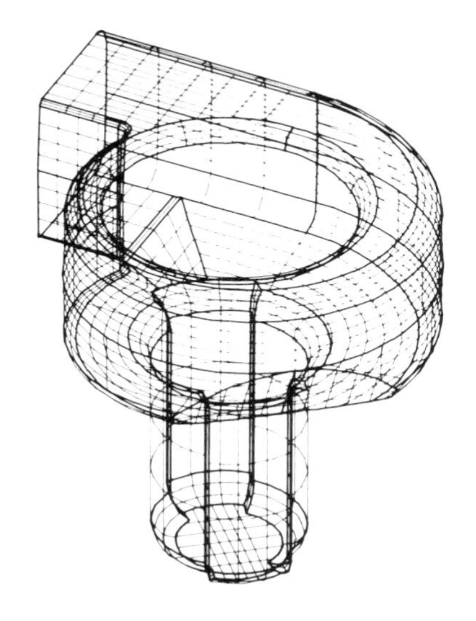

**Figure 3.2.** *Example of a complex shape*

the presentation completely unambiguous, as is the case sometimes when determining which of an object's surfaces define its volume. The surface model fulfils a number of needs in the aeronautical and automobile industries, in particular, in the defining and handling of complex shapes (Figure 3.2). Surfaces can be defined in a variety of ways (planes, rotating surfaces or lined surfaces). Mathematical models for surface approximation are also used (Coons, Bezier, B-Spline). In fact, the various qualities of the mathematical models allow modifications to be made to the appearance of the surfaces based on parameters, of significance for non-mathematical users.

The *solid model* can be used to represent complex objects and provide coherent information, particularly by object recognition. The volume of an object can be enclosed by complex surfaces. Table 3.1 shows the standards of performance of different types of modelling for specific tasks:

| | *line* | *surface* | *volume* |
|---|---|---|---|
| *geometric calculations* (volumes, lengths) | difficult or impossible | difficult or impossible | possible |
| *view generation* (perspectives, front, sides) | guided only | guided only | possible |
| *elimination of hidden parts* | manual | depends on definition of *SURFACE* | possible |
| *cross sections* | guided (intersections and points) | guided | possible (even automatic cross-hatching) |
| *numerical control* | guided | automatic possible | automatic possible |
| *sequence of sides tolerances* | guided | possible | possible |
| *verification of interference* | visual (boxing of objects possible) | visual (not all volumes defined) | possible |
| *object feasibility* | no verification that object can be produced | see *line* | possible (potentially) |
| *measurement* | only distance between points | see *line* plus surface calculations | all, can be exact (potentially) |

**Table 3.1.** *Comparison of different types of modelling*

### 3.1.2 CONDITIONS AFFECTING THE QUALITY OF GEOMETRIC MODELLING

The aim of geometric modelling is the representation of real objects. These objects (in the broadest sense of the word, ie not only manufactured objects but the tools necessary for their manufacture, or robots used on a production line) are real and their modelling must take into account a large number of constraints due to their function, or due to the use of a particular tool. The model is considered to be more accurate the more the conditions relate to the constraints on the real object, its manufacture and function, that are taken into account. For example, a two-dimensional model which simply uses views made up of straight lines and arcs, and without providing the relationships between the views, would be of no great practical use. On the other hand, a model that took account of the fact that the objects represented were three-dimensional would be considered as being of very high quality, at least from a point of view of geometrics (since the constraints associated with the manufacture or application of an object are often difficult to take into account during its design, although this is one of the basic objectives of CAD/CAM).

The conditions which must be fulfilled for high quality geometric modelling to be carried out satisfy the following criteria:

1. any model that can be formed must correspond to a real object (*validity* of model);
2. a model of any real object can be constructed (*power* of model);
3. it must allow calculation of geometric quantities such as volume, etc;
4. it can be used in different procedures (numerical control, scales, calculation of structures).

These imply a certain number of mathematical properties; this has been discussed by Gardan, 1983. It is particularly important that a model should have the following properties:

1. *homogeneity*: a solid must possess internal solidity;
2. *finiteness of dimensions*: a solid must occupy a finite space;
3. *rigidity*: a solid must have an unvarying form, no matter what its position and orientation.

Moreover, the processing system must respect the following conditions:

1. *coherence of operators*: all operations applied to solids must produce solids (Boolean displacements or operations), unless the user makes a specific request to the contrary;
2. *description:* any solid must be able to be represented;
3. *coherence of information*: any point in space must appear in only one solid object at most (ie for any point in space, it must be possible to say whether or not it appears in a solid).

It should be noted that several models can be made of the same object and that different models of objects belonging to the same unit can sometimes be used together – however, this can cause problems of coherence from the point of view of processing. In particular cases, the transition from using different models individually to using them together may never be realized.

There are also a number of other less easily defined qualities, which may be required of a geometric model. These include:

1. *Conciseness*: this depends on the quantity of information necessary to produce a given representation. This consideration cannot, however, be entirely independent of the needs of the processing

involved, and a certain amount of redundancy of information may sometimes assist the efficiency of certain algorithms.

2. *Range of applications*: the model or models must be able to be used for different algorithms and applications (numerical control, studies of bulk reduction, etc). This concept is a vague one, but it is clear that several representations will often be useful (taking into account the concept of coherence). This idea of range availability is very important since it is related to the concept of using the geometric model for a variety of functions (finished parts, calculations, numerical control, etc). The 'availability' of the model cannot be defined in formal terms but can be evaluated from the functions that can be attributed to the model (addition, deletion, modification, etc), which facilitate, to a greater or lesser degree, enrichment of the model and the development of applications using the model.

### 3.1.3 CONSTRUCTION METHODS

Here, the main methods available for creating a model of an object, without taking into account the implied internal representation, will be considered. Only the most commonly used methods will be discussed and this treatment is in no way intended to be exhaustive.

#### *3.1.3.1 Technical drawing*

Technical drawing is the use, with data processing techniques (screens, dialogue, etc), of methods traditionally used by designers. The computer programs allow the user to complete and modify plans, whether in interactive mode or not. The model input simply provides a set of two-dimensional elements (generally made up of straight lines and arcs, see Figure 3.3).

The model only considers the object in terms of the view it provides, and thus has a very poor knowledge of it. If several views are taken, the model does not generally take into consideration the possible relationships between the views and, because of this, any modification to one view must be reproduced by the operator on the others. It should be noted, however, that attempts have been made to provide a facility to recognize a three-dimensional object from several views. This method can be effective when used with simple objects, but is not viable in most industrial applications.

#### *3.1.3.2 Depth, rotation and movement*

Rotating objects and those that can be defined by a view and a depth constitute a particular class of object, which can be described with a

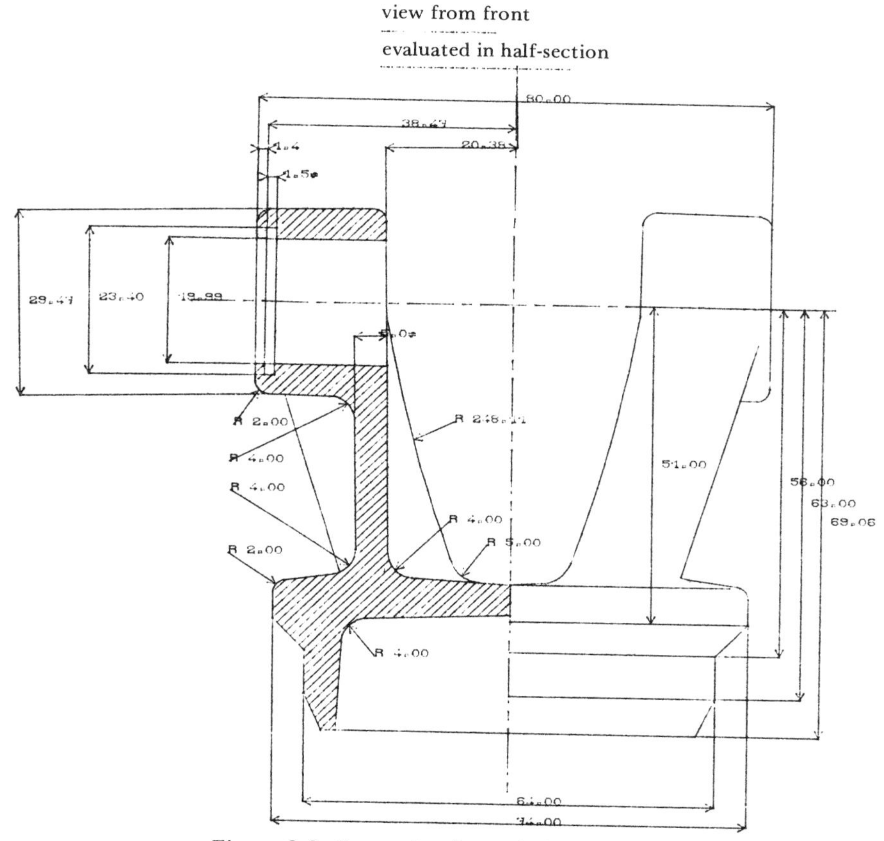


**Figure 3.3.** *Example of a technical drawing*

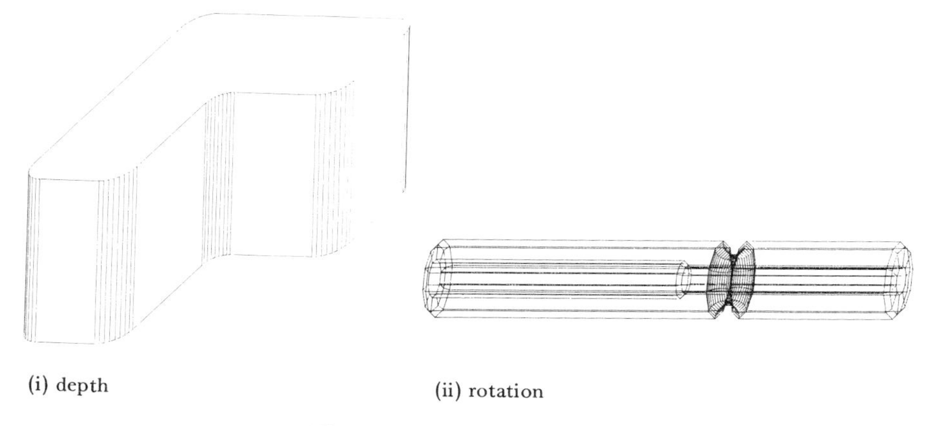

(i) depth

(ii) rotation

**Figure 3.4.** *Depth and rotation*

technical drawing input and the parameters defining the object in space (depth or axis and angle). This is a simple extension of a technical drawing model (see Figure 3.4).

An object can also be defined in terms of an entity (eg a surface or a

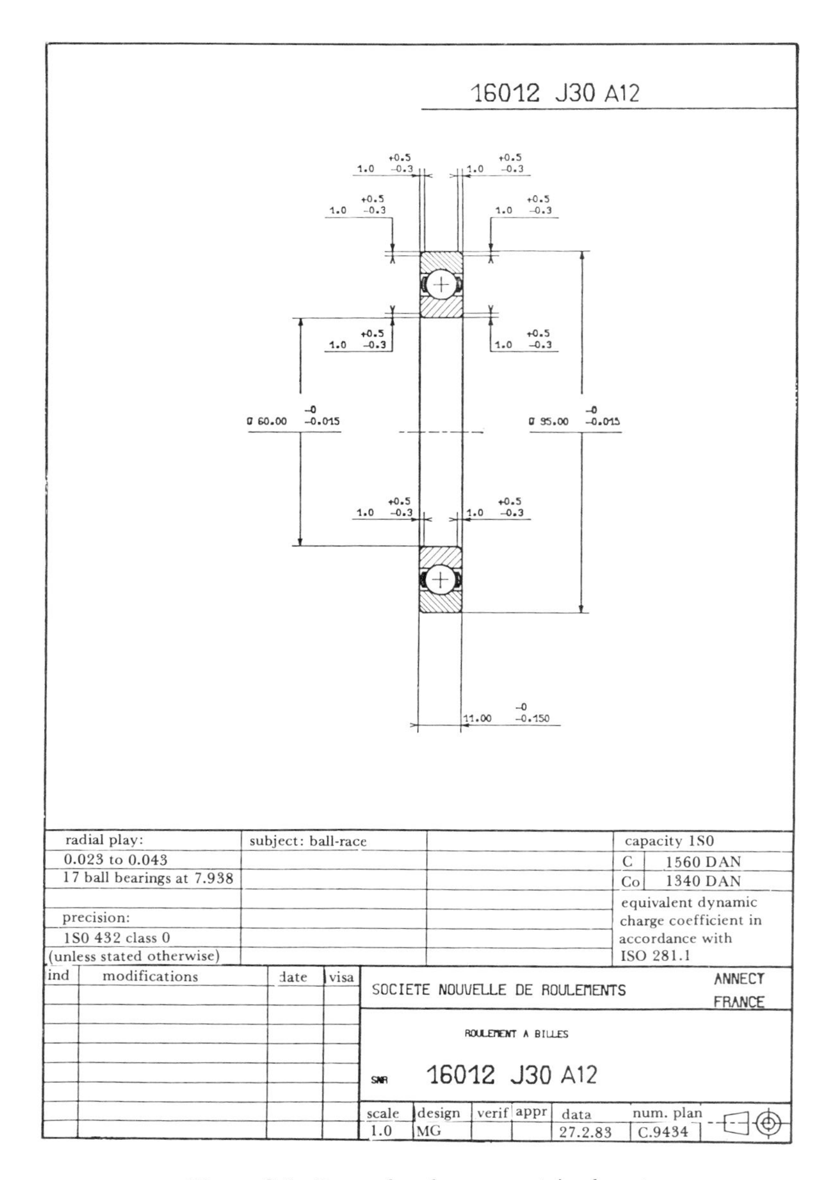


**Figure 3.5.** *Example of a parametrized part*

solid) and a trajectory in space. This method largely arises out of production methods. For example, a machine tool can lift an object with a tool of a specific shape moving according to a given trajectory.

### *3.1.3.3 Parametrics*

The theory of parametrics arises from the concept of families of parts. A family of parts is made up of different entities, which differ from

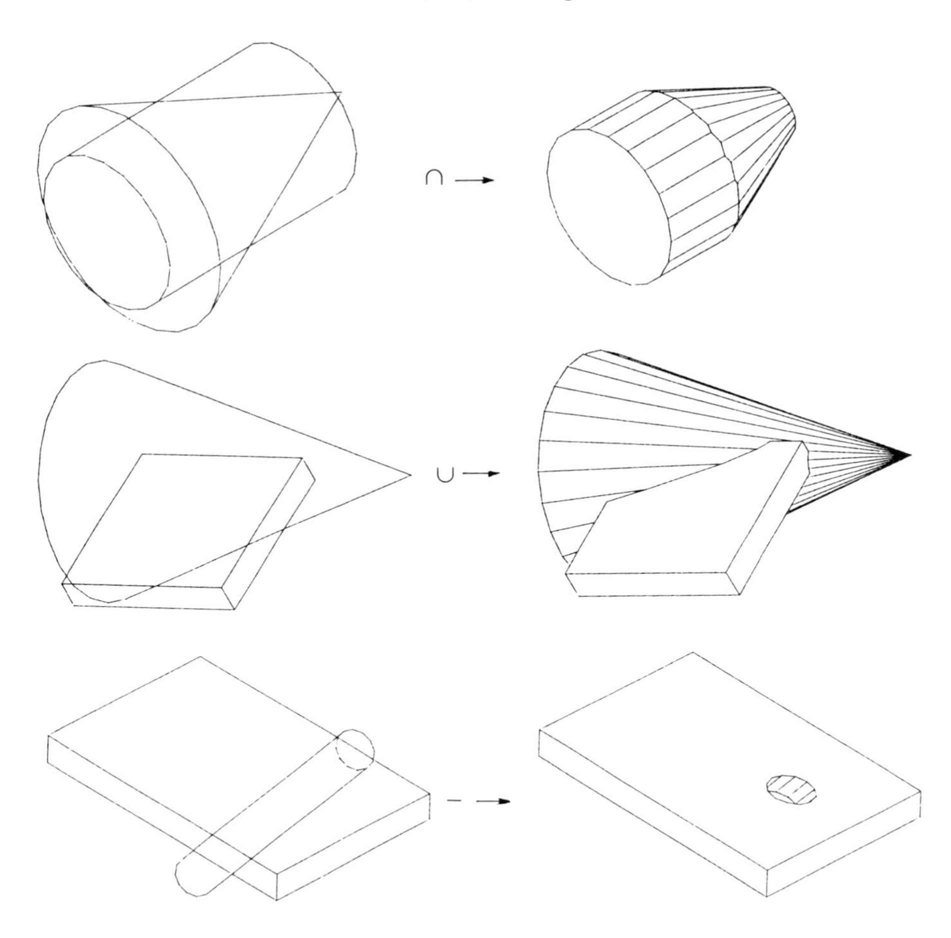


**Figure 3.6.** *Boolean operations: the simple objects on the left combine to form the complex objects on the right*

each other only in the values of certain parameters (geometric, in this case). The input for a particular solid is provided simply by giving the values of the parameters which define the family. The example given in Figure 3.5, which shows a plan for a ball-race, is of a parametrized part. In fact, this plan (part format with dimensions shown) was produced automatically from about twenty parameters supplied by the designer at the keyboard. The program, which was written specifically for this operation, chooses, from the basic tools provided, all aspects of the page format and allows modifications to be made on the parameters which define the plan.

### *3.1.3.4 Construction from primitives*

This method consists of generating complex objects from Boolean operations carried out on more simple objects. The basic objects (or primitives) can be cubes, cylinders, spheres or cones. The operations generally comprise combining, intersecting and erasing (see Figure 3.6) such simple objects. This type of construction has an advantage, in that it produces only acceptable solutions if the semantics of the basic operations are strictly defined.

#### *3.1.3.5 Local modifications*

Some local operations can be carried out using a model, eg modifications to the coordinates of a point on an object. Certain problems of coherence of information can, nonetheless, arise. Figure 3.7 shows a modification carried out on the geometrical structure of a pyramid – changing the position of the vertex. If the vertex is moved down into the base plane, the solid would no longer exist.

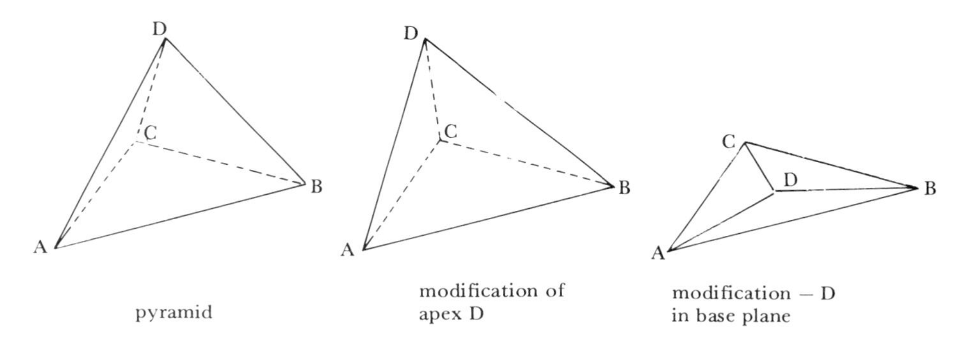


**Figure 3.7.** *If the position of the apex of the pyramid is changed it can take up a position in the base plane, when the solid no longer exists*

### 3.1.4 INTERNAL REPRESENTATION

One of the first choices which presents itself to systems designers is that of representation by data structure (or a data base management system) and/or representation in procedural form. This choice is crucial when the modelled objects are created using a language associated with the model. For reasons of manipulation (visual display, interaction, etc), procedural representation must be converted into a better adapted form, which is in general, data structure form. Procedural representation has the advantage of being compact, and entails less redundancy of data than data structure representation and for this reason provides a certain level of coherence. This problem most often arises in models to be used in interactive units. In parametrized shapes, to mention but one example, a shape can exist in its evaluated form and at the same time in its procedural form. When defining a model, it is very important to specify which data the model must manage. In some cases it may be sufficient to create a model which is very similar to the visual display (lines and arcs, in the case of two-dimensional models; vertices and edges, in three-dimensional models). However, this limits the use of the model. Generally, models are defined in such a way that standard operations can be carried out easily (evaluation, two-dimensional geometric transformations, cross sections, elimination of hidden parts in three dimensions, etc). For some time, model designers have been attempting to provide more detailed information of the modelled object, in order to facilitate highly complex operations, such as modification that takes into account constraints of active parametrization. These concepts are applied differently in two- and three-dimensional models. They imply that the designer's construction methods are stored and can be recognized and reproduced.

The information contained in a model varies widely according to the quality of modelling required. By referring to the four basic levels, the following general principles can be extrapolated:

1. *The two-dimensional model*: these are the most simple models, simply managing visual display-type elements. More sophisticated types associate the elements in a functional way (eg evaluation is associated with evaluated objects, assembled in such a way as to retain the identity of each). Attempts have been made to manage the methods of construction (eg the fact that a circle is tangential to a straight line). The outline of two-dimensional models varies considerably according to application: for mechanical use, graphical information is sufficient; for diagrams, it is possible to manage symbols and their connections (for this type of application, the model is frequently better adapted, since the problem to be solved is specifically two-dimensional).

2. The *line model*: although this is a three-dimensional model, it is not very sophisticated and only two types of information can be stored:
   (a) *topological*: edges depending on vertices;
   (b) *geometrical*: coordinates of points.

3. The *surface model*: models of this type contain only the definition of surfaces. They can, however, vary considerably and designers of models adapted to surface handling use concise methods of mathematical representation which allow interactive handling of complex calculations.

4. The *solid model*: in this, information allowing recognition of empty space is used (empty space may be considered as a particular type of entity). There are two main methods currently in use: the first is the use of a model which recognizes an object by its silhouette. It stores topological and geometrical information, as in the line model, but the information is more complete (the surfaces are known and oriented so as to define an interior and an exterior). The other model is the type

which recognizes an object in terms of the construction methods used to define it. These can be stored either in the procedural form or in the form of a data structure.

In the parts of this book dealing with two and three-dimensional modelling, the effective development of models will be discussed further. Particular attention will be given to solid modelling, an area in which considerable progress has been made recently.

To conclude this general survey of modelling theory, it must be stressed that there is generally more than one single model for any given application. An example which is common to a number of systems is that of the coexistence of a geometrical model, which may be high level (solid, surface, etc), as well as a visual display model allowing the handling of graphic information (display, interaction, etc).

The management of data associated with geometric models has, so far, been carried out using tools created specifically for a particular job. This has the advantage of providing a high level of efficiency in the application of these models, but has the disadvantage of needing a duplication of effort in the development of software. Unfortunately, there are no general systems for the management of data (as there are for general modelling) which are effective for geometrical models. Some characteristics are difficult to take into account:

1. *Management of different objects*: a geometrical model can include graphical information, alphanumerical and even procedural types. Such types of information can be interdependent (eg the formation of labels with corresponding plans).

2. *Dynamic management of schemata*: the relationships in a model are dynamic, because the model is generally constructed and handled interactively, and constitutes a specific design aid. The schema of the model can thus not be pre-specified at the level of the description language and compilation of this schema is not possible.

3. *Management of objects and tables of variable length*: objects of the same type can be of different lengths and these can vary during the design process. For example, tables describing elements of the shape of an object should be either all of maximum length (maximum number of objects in a shape) or of variable length.

4. *Facilities for the extraction (localization) and 'integration' (globalization) of groups of data*: one of the peculiarities caused by interactive use, particularly of graphic data, is that not only is it necessary to extract a part of this data, but also to view it in a more or less detailed manner. For example, to work on an assembly, the designer will 'call up' the shapes of the parts and their functions (contact surfaces, rotational axes, etc), whereas to modify one of the parts, it would be

necessary to see particular details of the part. These facilities for 'extraction' and interactive use of data also make it necessary to be able to interactively name (or modify the name of) an object, so as to be able to gain access to that object by that name at a later date.

## 3.2 Two-dimensional modelling

A two-dimensional model is intended to handle information of the following types:

1. *geometric*: point coordinates, line or circle equations, etc;

2. *topological*: a segment is identified by two points, a contour by its base objects, orientation and intersections, etc;

3. *structure*: a unit is made up of basic elements; this structuring, oriented towards assembly, is often in tree form;

4. *presentation*: this includes evaluation, texts, cross-hatching and various symbols. The presentation of a plan may, for example, be carried out in the form of a two-dimensional model which can include a number of very useful elements, particularly concerning the association of the evaluation with the elevated elements and simple construction methods. It also allows important gains to be made (use of symbol libraries, geometric transformations, etc);

5. *relationship*: a certain number of representations of the relationships existing between elements or units can exist in high level models. These may concern, for example, the geometrical relationships between elements (A is at a tangent to B), or assembly relationships between sub-units (part A is connected to part B in a surface to surface assembly);

6. *visual display*: a two-dimensional model is often very similar to the visual display. This is why information of this type is frequently stored as a two-dimensional model. It may consist, among other things, of different types of line (dashes, full, mixed, etc) for the basic elements, or of more sophisticated concepts, such as levels of visual display or management of views.

### 3.2.1 MANIPULATED PARTS

The manipulated parts of a two-dimensional model can be of various types, depending on the intended application. If the application involves the use of symbols interconnected to a greater or lesser extent, the basic elements retained in the model will be the symbols and connections. In other cases, eg the modelling of mechanical plans, the basic elements will be straight lines and circles. The explanation over is based on two-dimensional mechanical modelling through the medium of technical drawing software, and the examples given in section 3.2.4 will illustrate the variety of models possible.

### *3.2.1.1 Basic objects*

The types of primitive manipulated by technical drawing software are essentially the dot, the segment, the straight line, the arc of circle, a curve created by joining dots, text and outline with, for example, the following definitions:

object: [dot/arc/circle/straight line/curve]
dot: [coordinate pair; visual display level]
arc of circle: [dot; angular pair; radius; display]
circle: [dot; radius; display]
segment: [pair of dots; display]
straight line: [pair of dots; display]
shape: [object; direction of travel; direction of intersection/shape]
curve: [list of dots; type of curve; display]
level of visual display: [total]
display: [graphic mode]
graphic mode: [following mode; level of visual display]
following mode: [representation of coordinates; depth; texture; colour]
representation of coordinates: [broken line; disjointed segments]
depth: [nine possible depths]
texture: [continuous; short dashes; long dashes; dotted; mixed]
colour: [green/red/blue/yellow]
text: [dot; character sequence; text mode; type; size; orientation]
size: [four possible sizes]
orientation: [angle with horizontal]

The entities which cannot be directly manipulated by the user are those concerned with the presentation of the design, in particular, evaluation and cross-hatching.

evaluation: [type; object 1; object 2; coordinate pair; values]
type: [number of objects; valuation]
object 1: [object]
object 2: [object/O]
value: [real]
valuation: [exact value/imposed value]

### *3.2.1.2 Units*

Objects that can be manipulated can be reassembled into units. A unit or the objects which make up the unit can thus be designated. The user can, using dialogue, manipulate an object or several objects simultaneously; or manipulate a unit, several units, or the design as a whole.

### 3.2.2 CONSTRUCTION OF BASIC PARTS

There are basically two types of construction: construction under constraint and construction by geometrical transformation.

#### *3.2.2.1 Construction under constraint*

A construction under constraint can be applied to an object. A constraint is defined as: (type of element to be constructed) (list of constraints), (type of element on which constraint acts).

The operation to be carried out is specified by the choice of object to be constructed, the type of constraint to be applied and the parameters (other objects implied in the constraint and/or values). The establishment of the dialogue will be discussed in detail in Chapter 5. The objects implied by the type of constraint chosen are indicated by the user. The software then processes the determination of the type of these objects (dot, arc, etc) and their parameters. The fact of whether or not the values for the parameters are provided will entirely determine the action taken by the software.

The major types of constraint are as follows:

'passing through $n$ points' ($n = 1, 2, 3 \ldots$)
'tangent to $n$ objects' ($n = 1, 2, 3 \ldots$)
'parallel to'
'making an angle of'
'distance from'.

Moreover, some commonly used constraints may be particularized in the dialogue, eg:

'join'
'bisector'.

There are two possible solutions which would take into account construction under constraint:

1. General solution: this can be divided into two phases:

(a) construction of a system of algebraic equations from the types of constraint, the elements and parameters;

(b) resolution of this system and the values that characterize the desired element belonging to the set of solutions of the system of equations. There are certain disadvantages with this system: the system of equations may be non-linear, in which case simplifying methods, and eventually an interactive method for the determination of an approximate solution, must be used (in general, several methods are used, so that they can be applied in sequence if any become inappropriate). In some cases, one solution must be chosen from several. The designer must thus give a preliminary idea of how the part being constructed is envisaged.

2. Solution by constraint and element: this consists of writing a subprogram by triplet (element to be defined, type of constraint, other elements concerned). The essential advantage of this solution is that it does not involve complex methods of calculation. The process involved in determination of a solution is also easy to apply. Further, it allows a sub-program library to be built up, which can then be used in a number of applications. The main disadvantage is that the addition of a constraint or another type of element involves one or more new subprograms being written. However, this solution is often favoured since:

(a) it avoids the use of interactive methods (which in some cases may be ineffective);

(b) it allows a library of geometric constructions to be created, on which a number of applications can be based.

Consider the following example: the position of a circle tangential to a given straight line is to be found; its radius and the approximate position of its centre are known (Figure 3.8). The approximate position of a point is frequently used as a solution for choosing an object, from a number, all of which respect the constraints. The method used in this process can be explained as follows.

(i) *data*: the following straight line equation is known:

$$Ax + By + C = 0 \quad (1)$$

The circle can be defined by its centre X1, Y1 and its radius R1. An approximate point Xc, Yc, which is close to the centre of the circle, and the radius (R) of this circle are known.

(ii) *method*: the centre of the circle is on a line parallel to that line described by equation (1). Calculations can be made using the equations of the two straight lines parallel to that given by equation (1). The equations are:

$$Ax + By + (-R.\sqrt{A^2 + B^2} + C) = 0 \quad (2)$$

$$Ax + By + (R.\sqrt{A^2 + B^2} + C) = 0 \quad (3)$$

By replacing X and Y by Xc, Yc, it is possible to determine directly which straight line the point Xc, Yc is closer to, and thus which of the two equations, (2) or (3), should be used for the straight line D. The locus of the circle's tangent to the given circle (X1, Y1, R1) is on one of the circles with centres and radii (X1, Y1, R1 + R) and (X1, Y1,

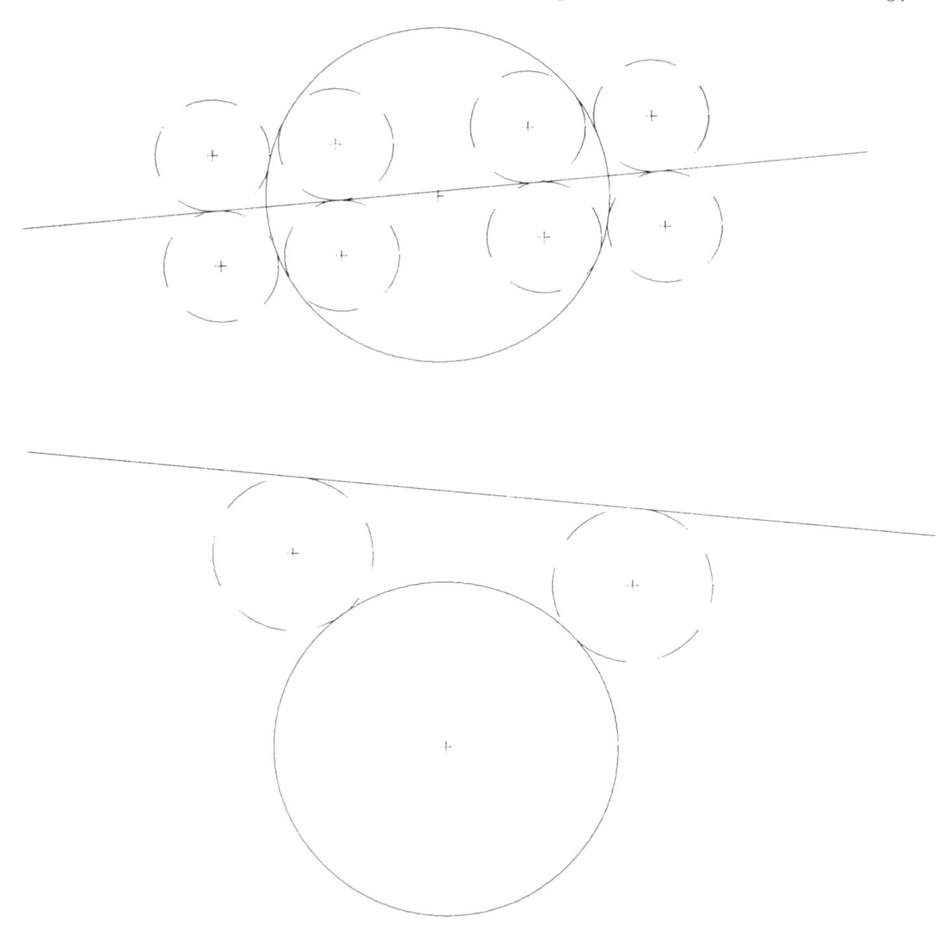

**Figure 3.8.** *Circles tangent to a circle and a straight line*

| R1 − R |). The centre is thus at the intersection of the straight line D and one of the circles. The method chosen involves calculating the intersections of D with each of the circles, using a basic operation which calculates the intersection of a line described by an equation and a circle described by its centre and radius.

All the intersections are stored in a table. Calling the (CLOSER) function allows the point closest to the approximate point Xc, Yc to be found.

### *3.2.2.2 Construction using geometrical transformation*

A set of sub-programs facilitates the construction of matrices defining the different geometrical transformations, and the execution of the operations by matrix multiplication. The use of transformations involves:

```
      SUBROUTINE CTGDCR(A, B, C, X1, Y1, R1, R, XC, YC, IR)
C ***************************************************
C * CIRCLE TANGENT TO STRAIGHT LINE AND CIRCLE       *
C *   INPUT                                          *
C *      A, B, C       STRAIGHT LINE PARAMETERS      *
C *      X1, Y1, R1    CENTRE, RADIUS OF CIRCLE      *
C *      R             RADIUS OF DESIRED CIRCLE      *
C *      XC, YC        APPROXIMATE POINT CLOSE TO    *
C *                    CENTRE OF DESIRED CIRCLE      *
C *                                                  *
C *   OUTPUT                                         *
C *      XC, YC     DESIRED CENTRE                   *
C *      IR         IF IR=1 THEN NO CIRCLE           *
C *                 IF IR=0 THEN CIRCLE IS FOUND     *
C ***************************************************
      REAL XX(4), YY(4)
      C3=SQRT(A*A+B*B)
      C1=-R*C3+C
      C2=R*C3+C
      I=1
C     CHOICE OF STRAIGHT LINE
      IF ((ABS(A*XC+B*YC+C1)).LT.(ABS(A*XC+B*YC+C2))) GOTO 97
      C1=C2
C  &&&& INTERSECTION (A, B, C1) WITH CIRCLE
97    CALL INTDC(X1, Y1, R+R1, A, B, Cl, XX(I), YY(I),
     *XX(I+1), YY(I+1), IR)
C  IR=1 MEANS NO INTERSECTION
      IF (IR.NE.1) I=I+2
      CALL INTDC(X1, Y1, ABS(R1-R), A, B, Cl, XX(I), YY(I),
     *XX(I+1), YY(I+1), IR)
C  IR=1 MEANS NO INTERSECTION
      IF (IR.NE.1) I=I+2
1     XC1=XC
      YC1=YC
      I=I-1
      IR=1
      IF (I.GT.1) IR=0
C  THE CENTRES FOUND ARE IN XX, YY
C  CLOSER FINDS THE NEIGHBOUR OF XC1, YC1
C  AND PLACES IT IN XC, YC
      CALL CLOSER (I, XX, YY, XC1, YC1, XC, YC)
99    RETURN
      END
```

## *Examples from a constraint calculation library (GRI 2D)*

```
SUBROUTINE      CTGDPR(A, B, C, X1, Y1, R, XC1, YC1, XC2, YC2, IR)
      ***************************
      ****   SPECIFICATIONS   ****
      ***************************
             (XC1, YC1) AND (XC2, YC2) ARE THE RESPECTIVE CENTRES
             OF THE TWO CIRCLES WITH RADIUS R TANGENT TO THE STRAIGHT
             LINE (A, B, C) AND PASSING THROUGH POINT (X1, Y1)
             IR = 1 IF NO SOLUTION
      ***************************
SUBROUTINE      CTG2D(X1, Y1, X2, Y2, X3, Y3, X4, Y4, MX1, MY1, R, XR, YR, A1,
                B1, IR)
      ***************************
      ****   SPECIFICATIONS   ****
      ***************************
```

```
            (X1, Y1) (X2, Y2) AND (X3, Y3) (X4, Y4) DEFINE
            TWO STRAIGHT LINES
            (MX1, MY1) IS A WORK POINT
            R IS THE RADIUS OF THE DESIRED CIRCLE – OR ARC
            1) IF IR = 1
               ARC = CONNECTION BETWEEN THE STRAIGHT LINES
            2) IF IR = 2
               ARC IS TANGENT TO THE SIDE OF (MX1, MY1)
            3) IF IR = 3
               CIRCLE IS TANGENT TO THE SIDE OF (MX1, MY1)
            IF IR = 1 IN OUTPUT THERE IS NO SOLUTION
      ***************************
SUBROUTINE        C2PTR (X1, Y1, X2, Y2, R, XR1, XR2, YR1, YR2, IR)
      ***************************
      ****    SPECIFICATIONS    ****
      ***************************
            (XR1, YR1) AND (XR2, YR2) ARE THE RESPECTIVE CENTRES
            OF THE TWO CIRCLES WITH RADIUS R PASSING THROUGH THE
            POINTS (X1, Y1) AND (X2, Y2)
            IR = 1 IF NO SOLUTION
      ***************************
SUBROUTINE        C3PTS(X1, Y1, X2, Y2, X3, Y3, XR, YR, R, IR)
      ***************************
      ****    SPECIFICATIONS    ****
      ***************************
            (XR, YR) AND R ARE RESPECTIVELY THE CENTRE AND RADIUS
            OF THE CIRCLE PASSING THROUGH THE THREE POINTS
            (X1, Y1), (X2, Y2), (X3, Y3)
            IR = 1 IF NO SOLUTION
      ***************************
SUBROUTINE        DPTALP(X, Y, ALP1, ABC)
      ***************************
      ****    SPECIFICATIONS    ****
      ***************************
            (A, B, C) IS THE EQUATION OF THE STRAIGHT LINE
            PASSING THROUGH POINT (X, Y) AND FORMING AN
            ANGLE ALPH1–IN DEGREES– WITH THE HORIZONTAL
      ***************************
SUBROUTINE        EQ2PT(X1, Y1, X2, Y2, A, B, C)
      ***************************
      ****    SPECIFICATIONS    ****
      ***************************
            (A, B, C) IS THE EQUATION OF THE STRAIGHT LINE
            DEFINED BY THE TWO POINTS (X1, Y1) AND (X2, Y2)
      ***************************
SUBROUTINE        INTCC(X1, Y1, R1, X2, Y2, R2, XR1, YR1, XR2, YR2, IR)
      ***************************
      ****    SPECIFICATIONS    ****
      ***************************
            (XR1, YR1) AND (XR2, YR2) ARE THE TWO POINTS OF
            INTERSECTION OF THE CIRCLES (X1, Y1, R1) AND (X2, Y2, R2)
            IR = 1 IF NO SOLUTION
      ***************************
SUBROUTINE        INTDC(X, Y, R, A, B, C, X1, Y1, X2, Y2, IR)
      ***************************
      ****    SPECIFICATIONS    ****
      ***************************
            (X1, Y1) AND (X2, Y2) ARE THE TWO POINTS OF INTERSECTION
            OF THE CIRCLE (X, Y, R) AND THE STRAIGHT LINE (A, B, C)
            IR = 1 IF NO SOLUTION
      ***************************
SUBROUTINE        INTDP(A, B, C, A1, B1, C1, X, Y, IR)
      ***************************
      ****    SPECIFICATIONS    ****
      ***************************
            (X, Y) IS THE POINT OF INTERSECTION OF THE STRAIGHT LINES
            (A, B, C) AND (A1, B1, C1)
            IR = 1 IF NO SOLUTION
      ***************************
```

1. determination of the matrix defining the overall transformation by calling up the definition, transformation and matrix multiplication sub-programs;
2. carrying out matrix vector multiplication for all the characteristic points of the objects to be transformed. For the angles, the calculation which allows them to be reduced to points is applied and then matrix vector multiplication is carried out.

The examples below indicate the types of sub-program that can be used to manage geometrical transformations.

```
C
      SUBROUTINE TRAN2D(T, TX, TY)
C     TRANSLATION IN 2 DIMENSIONS
C     TX, TY TRANSLATION VECTOR
C     OUTPUT T(3, 3) IS THE TRANSLATION MATRIX
         DIMENSION T(3, 3)
      DO 10 I=1, 3
      DO 20 J=1, 3
20    T(I, J)=0.
10    T(I, I)=1.
      T(3, 1)=TX
      T(3, 2)=TY
      RETURN
      END
/*

C
      SUBROUTINE MV2D(T, V)
C        MATRIX–VECTOR MULTIPLICATION
C        RESULT IN THE VECTOR
      REAL T(3, 3), V(2)
      A=V(1)
      B=V(2)
      V(1)=T(1, 1)*A+T(2, 1)*B+T(3, 1)
      V(2)=T(1, 2)*A+T(2, 2)*B+T(3, 2)
      RETURN
      END
/*
```

### 3.2.3 CONSTRUCTION OF COMPLEX ELEMENTS

The composition of basic elements can involve either topological and geometrical concepts, or presentational information.

#### *3.2.3.1 Standard structure*

This involves the indication of a certain number of elements that make up the same unit. This means that such units can be handled as a whole, which may be useful for visual display information as much as for functional information. For visual display, a set of transparent sheets is simulated in such a way that they can be placed together in any order or combination. This allows, for example, the construction outline to be placed on level 1, the definition outline on level 2 and the presentation on level 3. It is thus possible to display the definition and construction outlines without the presentation, or the definition outline and presentation without the construction outline. This can be used as an aid to comprehension (see section 4.3).

For functional structuring, the basic elements are organized into parts (called *groups* or *details* depending on the system). The number of functional structuring levels can be large and are frequently organized into tree form. The main aim is to allow assembly at levels of high or low complexity, which is why the supplementary information is stored with the model, as in the case, for example, of a pivot point and a lever point, where the model may facilitate the installation of these elements (by translation and rotation). Opening the model to non-geometric information, such as assembly types (axis . . . axis . . .) is very important in CAD applications.

### *3.2.3.2 Topological and geometrical concepts*

These are used, to take one example, in the construction of contours. A contour is an ordered list of objects, which can be open or closed.

A closed contour defines an interior and an exterior and may be shaded or be an element of a three-dimensional model (see section 3.3). A contour can be modelled according to the basic elements of which it is formed. An example of this is in GRI 2D, the contours of which include the following information (see Figure 3.9):

1. the number of elements making up the contour;
2. general information on the contour (opened or closed, graphical, etc);
3. the objects making up the contour, with:

(a) the direction of scanning: the objects are scanned in the order defined by their position in the list and each object lies in the direction

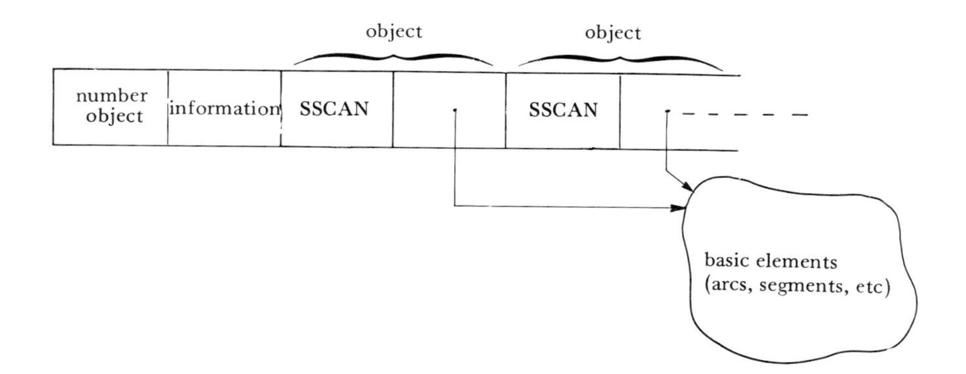


**Figure 3.9.** *Structure of a contour*

defined by (SSCAN) (the direction of the basic element or the opposite direction);

(b) the direction of attempted intersection: when two consecutive objects include at least one circle, the scanning direction SSCAN is not always sufficient to determine the point of intersection. A unit of information (SINTER) is thus added which allows every case of intersection to be taken into account.

When a contour is modelled in this functional form, it becomes necessary to use an algorithm for the preparation of visual display. In the present example, the contour can be evaluated in two ways:

1. by finding a sequence of segments (defined by two points) and arcs (defined by centres, radii and angles) which provide an evaluated form of the contour in the structure of the basic elements of GRI 2D – this form is useful, for example, for making evaluations;
2. by approaching the contour in relation to a polygon, which provides the sequence of its constituent segments – this form more resembles visual display and a general shading algorithm may be used if necessary.

### *3.2.3.3 Presentation information*

Presentation is essentially made up of evaluation, shading and texts. It will be dealt with in section 4.3 and discussed in the light of the fact that it is an aspect of communication graphics. A two-dimensional model is sufficient for this type of information. It is important to determine whether this presentation should be associated with a two-dimensional model or simply considered as a specific graphic technique. The example in section 4.3.1 explains the influence of these concepts on comprehension and dialogue. One aspect of presentation is that it respects extremely strict norms. Because of this, preparation for visual display involves the development of programs to process a wide variety of cases, whilst respecting these norms. In this way the choice between pure graphics and association with the model can be made, whilst respecting a development method such as high level modelling. For example, in Figure 3.10 evaluation of the two points is as follows:

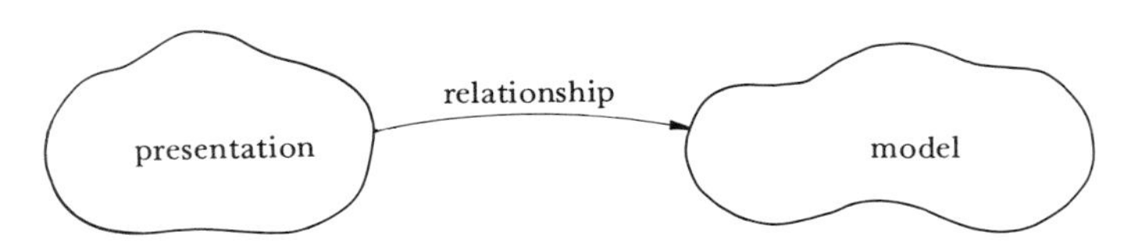


**Figure 3.10.** *Association between presentation and model*

EVAL 2 PTS: F (POINT 1, POINT 2, WORK POINT)

Since the parameters POINT 1 and POINT 2 are pointers directed towards the points of the model, the work point can simply be an approximate point at which the evaluation is made (other parameters of direction or orientation of the text can intervene).

Presentation, when considered as graphic display, is a function of a finite number of parameters, which is associated with a program for the preparation of visual display. For example:

PAFEVAL (X1, Y1, X2, Y2, DIR, XFLC, YFLC, XTX, YTX, ANG, LGTX SEQUENCE)

with:

X1, Y1 start of return line 1
X2, Y2 start of return line 2
DIR direction of return lines (angle)
XFLEC, YFLEC point through which the dimension line passes
XTX, YTX position of text
ANG direction of text
LGTX length of text
SEQUENCE text (sequence of characters of length LGTX)

The PAFEVAL function is intended to prepare the visual display of an evaluation (return lines, evaluation arrows, values, etc). The use of

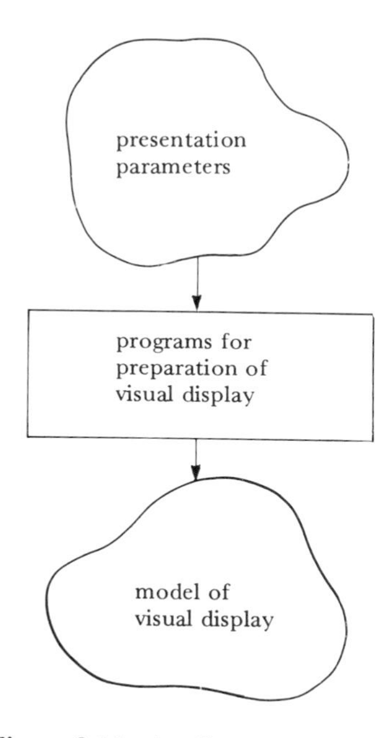


**Figure 3.11.** *Application of graphics*

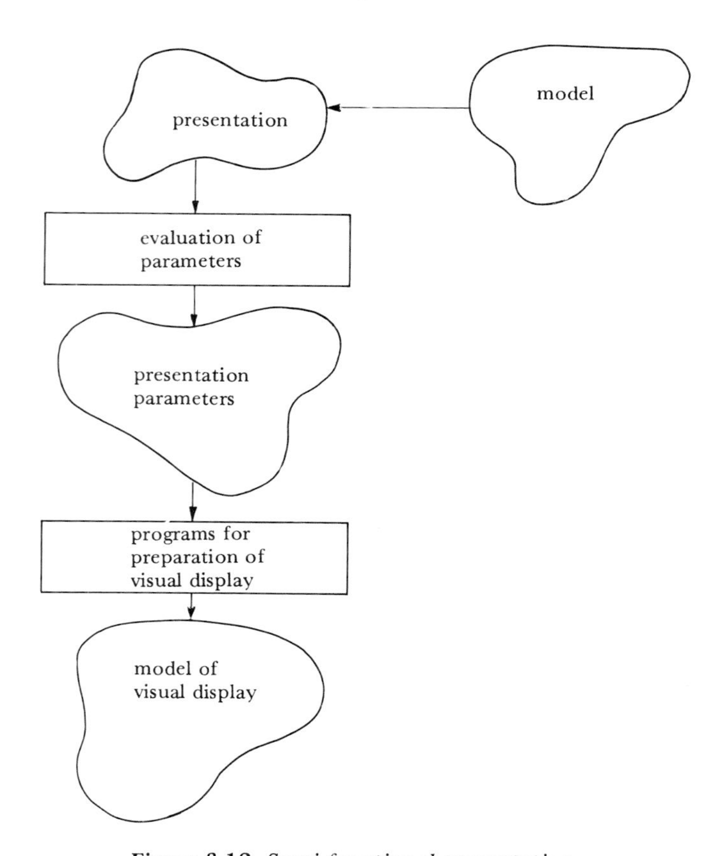


**Figure 3.12.** *Semi-functional presentation*

graphics and semi-functional presentation is illustrated by Figures 3.11 and 3.12, respectively. This general schema permits coexistence of a presentation associated with the model (evaluation with the basic elements, shading with the contour, text with the parts, etc) and a presentation of the graphic types. It should be noted that the library used for the preparation of visual display will tend to include a large number of programs. This is because of the number of symbols that can exist in a norm.

### 3.2.4 EXAMPLES OF MODELS

A two-dimensional model can be used in a number of different ways and the method chosen depends on the processing to be carried out, the aim being to reduce the load wherever possible. The following examples give some idea of the diversity of methods available:

1. encoding using character chains;
2. syntactic encoding using basic vocabulary and grammar;
3. geometric encoding, based on a data structure.

The first two methods will be dealt with specifically in subsequent sections, and the rest of the chapter will be concerned mainly with various aspects of geometric codes.

### *3.2.4.1 Encoding using character chain* (*example used: the Freeman code*)

This allows representation of a discretized line drawing on a dot surface. Discretization means that, for example, a curve is described by a list of small elementary vectors, oriented in eight possible directions (see Figure 3.13).

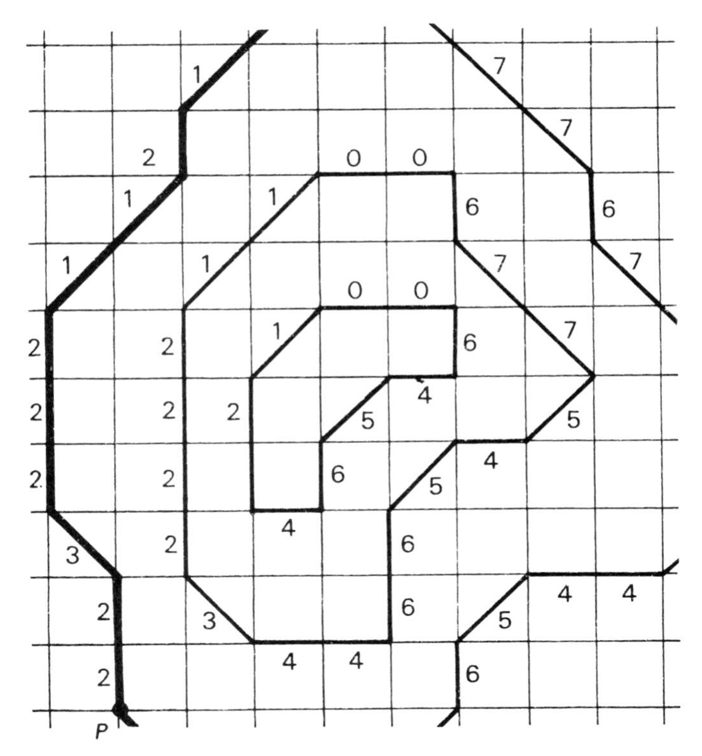


(i) encoding a design element

*P* = starting point

this part of the design would be encoded: 2232221121

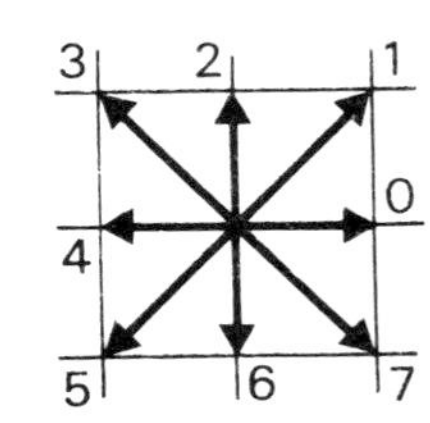


(ii) encoding method

**Figure 3.13.** *Use of the Freeman code*

A chain is an ordered series of links. A link is an elementary vector of length $T(\sqrt{2})^p$ forming an angle $a_i \times 45°$ with the axis, $a_i$ being an integer between 0 and 7, p the value of $a_i$ modulus 2, and T the size of each component. To decrease the length of the code chain, the repetition operators of a single elementary vector are defined. Other operators allow the introduction of elementary transformations and qualitative (name) or quantitative (number of vectors passing through a given core) information. The list below contains the operation codes used by Freeman, 1974:

|  |  |
|---:|---|
| 0400 | end of chain |
| 0401 | the following chain should not be plotted (invisible chain) |
| 0402 | the following chain should be plotted (opposite of 0401) |
| 0403 | indicates that the rest of memory word is empty |
| 0404 | the chain contains the sequence of inverse links 04 |
| 0405XYZ | XYZ is an octal identifier (000 to 777) associated with certain points in the chain |
| 0407UV | the series of UV digits that appear after this code is a numerical identifier, used, for example, to repair a chain |
| 0410 | follows WXYZ digits (not part of encoding chain), allows insertion of comments into description |
| 04111 | same description as for previous code, except that the series is terminated by a special code, which means that the length of the commentary zone does not have to be pre-defined |
| 0413UWXYZ | WXYZ is an identifier for a grid core. This code is used to specify the number of chains passing through this core (U). If U = 0, the number is unknown |
| 0414UVWXYZ | rotation indicator. The following chain has been rotated through U.VWXYZ radians |
| 0415TUVWXYZ | scale change indicator. The following chain has been subjected to a scale change of factor UVXYZ. The other digits are used to specify the transformation exactly |
| 0417UXYZ | repetition of link U a number of times equal to XYZ |
| 0420UN | repetition of link U a number of times equal to the number represented in the (N + 4) digits which follow. Used for long chains |
| 0421TUVWXYZ | repetition of group of TUV digits which follow, WXYZ times |

| | |
|---|---|
| 0422U | colour indication |
| 0423WXYZ | used for contour lines: WXYZ is the altitude of the following chain |
| 0424XYZ | used to represent light intensity, with three digits |
| 0425U | control point for logic sum |
| 0426VWXYZ | forces abcissa x into position VWXYZ |
| 0427VWXYZ | forces ordinate y into position VWXYZ |

The last two instructions enable the starting coordinates of a chain to be fixed, with the rest of the description being made up of vector components (relative coordinates) and not absolute coordinates. The use of this code allows a certain number of calculations to be carried out comparatively easily on the chains to be processed, including: length; surrounding rectangle; reversal in direction of movement; calculation of area defined by a closed chain; moments of inertia in relation to axes or diagonals; determination of shortest chain joining beginning and end of a given chain, such that link codes are arranged in order of increasing size; distance between two points; mirror chain. These operations are widely used in techniques used for processing images and shape recognition. This code is well adapted for use with very irregular contours (those with large numbers of inflexion points and very small curve radii). It is, however, too simple for most of the applications that use interactive infography. In particular, it does not allow images to be described simply, since its primitives are of too low a level, though it (or a derivative of it) is used in many applications involving interactive image processing.

#### *3.2.4.2 Syntactic codes*

The drawings are considered to be graphs of $R^2$. The codes must enable not only the components (vertices and edges) to be found, but also a trace of the structure described in the graph to be retained. To do this, a grammar (G) producing a language L(G), is used. This grammar must:

1. allow a family of graphs to be described with a finite set of signs and rules;
2. allow a structure to be imposed on to the graph which is described using the rules of generation;
3. allow economic encoding of the graph;
4. provide efficient means of handling, analysis and generation of graphs.

The grammar models used to describe a family of graphs can be classified into three categories (Azema, 1975): chain grammars, structure grammars and graph grammars.

*Chain grammars* produce linear expressions describing the graph by using binary and unit operators. Let G be a graph, then G = (S, A), where S is the set of vertices and $A \in S \times S$ the set of lines. If $A \in A$, then $a = (o_a, e_a)$, where $o_a$ is the origin of a and $e_a$ the extremity of a. A set of values $v(a) \in V$ is associated with every line of the graph. To describe the graph, a certain number of operations, known as *concatenations* (a series of interdependent operations) are described. The characteristics of composition, indicating for each concatenated object the new origin and extremity, can then be defined. The best known example of this, described by Shaw, 1967 is given here. The rules adopted by Shaw are as follows:

1. $a_1 + a_2$: $e_{a_1}$ and $o_{a_2}$ become confused, the new origin is $o_{a_1}$ and the new extremity is $e_{a_2}$;

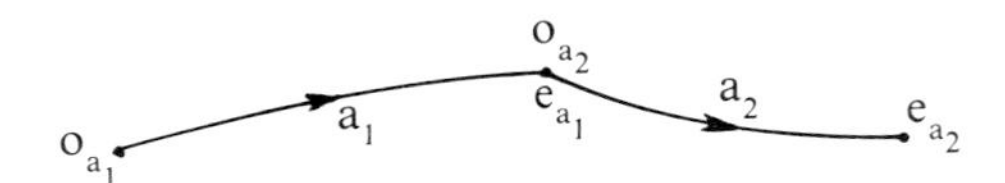


2. $a_1 \oplus a_2$: $o_{a_1}$ and $o_{a_2}$ become confused, the new origin is $o_{a_1}$ (or $o_{a_2}$) and the new extremity is $e_{a_1}$;

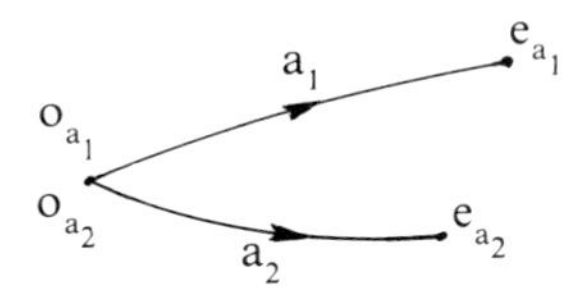


3. $a_1 - a_2$: $e_{a_1}$ and $e_{a_2}$ become confused, the new origin is $o_{a_1}$ and the new extremity is $e_{a_1}$ or $e_{a_2}$;

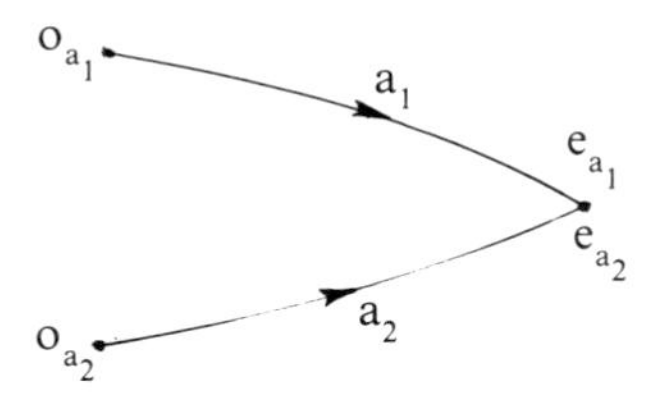


4. $a_1 * a_2$: $o_{a_1}$ and $o_{a_2}$ become confused, as do $e_{a_1}$ and $e_{a_2}$; the new origin is $o_{a_1}$ (or $o_{a_2}$) and the new extremity is $e_{a_1}$ (or $e_{a_2}$);

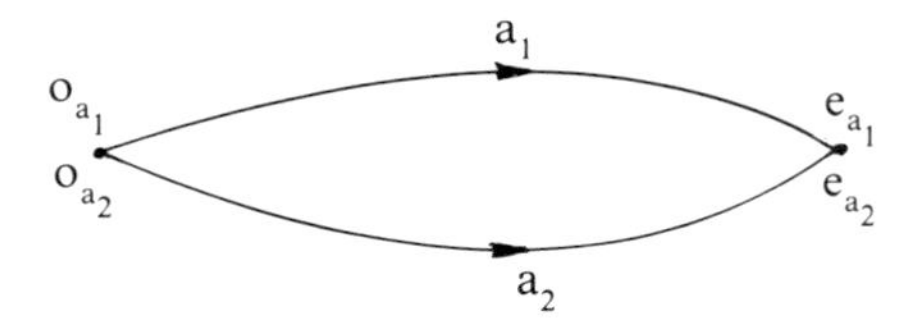

5. $/a_1$: this operator exchanges the origin and the extremity.

The following chain:

$$(((((/a_2) + a_1)*a_3)*(/a_1))*(/(((a_1 + a_2)*(/a_3)) + a_2)))$$

represents the graph in Figure 3.14. For a given graph, there is no unique representation; any graph can be described with this type of expression. The operators /, + and ⊕ are adequate for this. The others were introduced to help in the processing normally associated with this type of representation, ie the analysis and recognition of shapes.

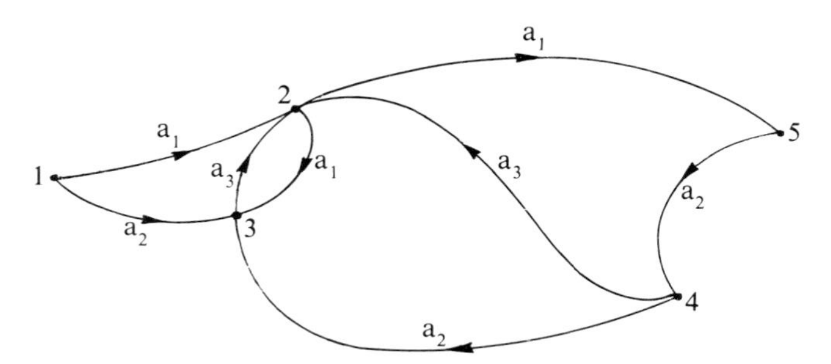


**Figure 3.14.** *Example of a graph*

*Structure grammars* show not only the way to describe the graph, but also supply, in the production rules, the way to construct it. The primitives used can no longer be assimilated into the graph, because instead of simply using the notion of the beginning and end of lines, as many connection points as necessary are used. In terms of structure grammars, the end symbols represent the primitives and the other symbols represent the high level components of the design. The description of the concatenations of the various parts of the drawing is given by an extension of the production rules: after the end and non-end symbols, to the right and left, a list of connection points is added, to form a table of correspondence between the connection points on the right and those on the left.

Consider the example described by Gips, 1975, concerning the generation of drawings for non-figurative art, or recognition of three-dimensional scenes from two-dimensional representations. To achieve these aims, shape grammars were used; the following example is one which allows an outline known as a *snow flake* to be produced. To form this outline, Gips used two grammars, one classical, in which the outline is obtained by substituting the rules sequentially, one by one, and another requiring substitution of different rules in parallel. Using this method, a design is not constructed in a single part of the visual display surface but simultaneously in several parts. The grammar resulting from sequential construction of the design is:

$$SG7 = \langle V_T, V_M, R, I \rangle \qquad V_T = (—) \qquad V_M = (\circlearrowright)$$

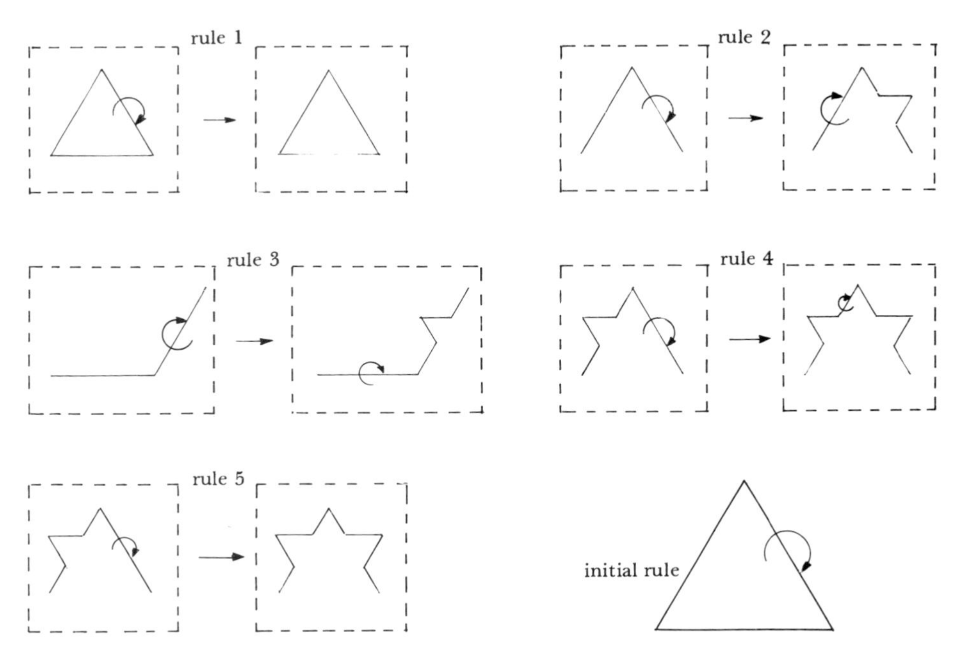


An example of substitution is shown in Figure 3.15:

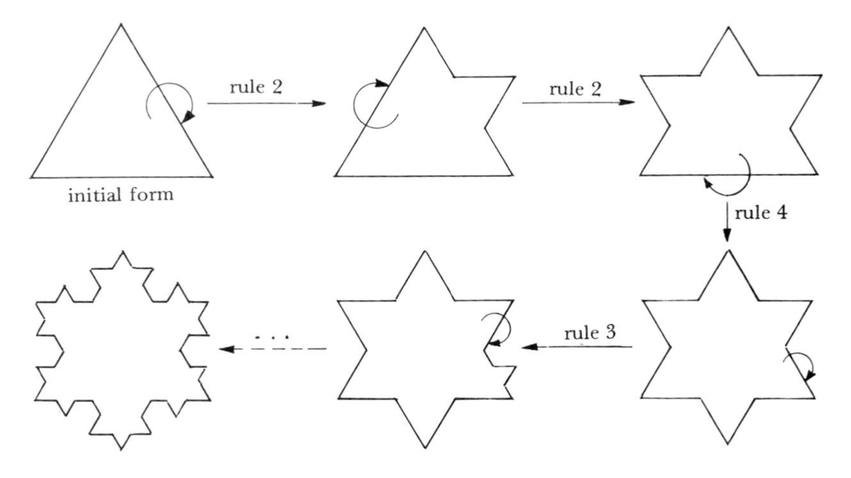


**Figure 3.15.** *Example of sequential substitution*

The parallel grammar is:

$$PSG6 = \langle V_T, V_M, R, I\rangle \qquad V_T = [—] \qquad V_M = [\curvearrowright]$$

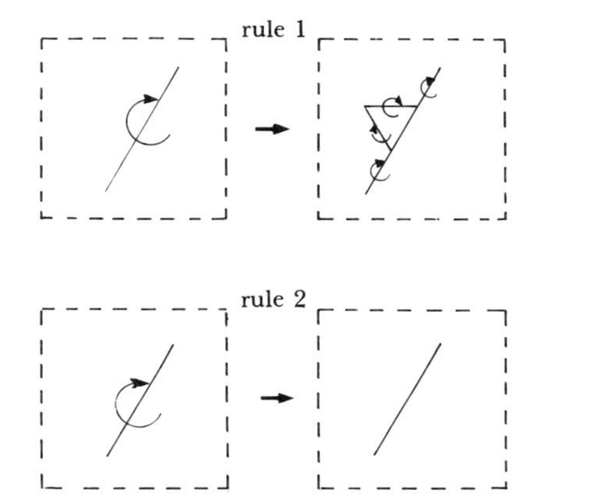


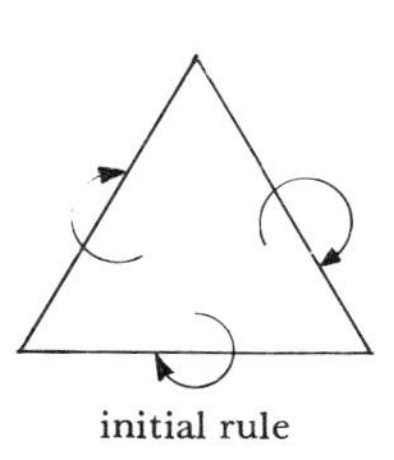


An example of substitution is shown in Figure 3.16.

*Structure grammars* (or shape grammars) are extremely interesting in that the description of the graphs is more synthetic (because the primitives chosen are of a higher level) and the grammar exactly provides the way of constructing the graph, which is not the case in chain grammars.

The final type of grammar is *graph grammar*, with which graphs can be produced directly (with the application of a production rule) by replacing one sub-graph with another. The starting axiom is a set of initial graphs. Each graph has its points and lines labelled, with the labels being elements of the end and non-end vocabulary. In any production rule, there are:

1. two graphs, the left hand graph having at least one point or one line labelled with a non-end symbol;
2. a set of nesting rules and conditions for the application of the rule.

The example described is commonly used in the determination of molecular formulae (see Azema, 1975). In this case the elements of end vocabulary are not only atomic symbols (graph labels) but also labels showing the degree of linkage (1, 2, 3, etc). The non-end elements of vocabulary are only labels for the points: $M_1$, $M_2$, $M_3$, $M_4$, $M_0$. The initial graph is $M_0$. The production rules are as follows:

a) $\overset{M_1}{\bullet} \longrightarrow \overset{M_{i+1}}{\bullet} \overset{1}{\text{———}} \overset{M_1}{\bullet} \qquad 0 \leqslant i \leqslant 3$

b) $\overset{M_1}{\bullet} \longrightarrow \overset{M_{i+2}}{\bullet} \overset{2}{\text{———}} \overset{M_2}{\bullet} \qquad 0 \leqslant i \leqslant 2$

c) $\overset{M_1}{\bullet} \longrightarrow \overset{M_{i+3}}{\bullet} \overset{3}{\text{———}} \overset{M_1}{\bullet} \qquad 0 \leqslant i \leqslant 1$

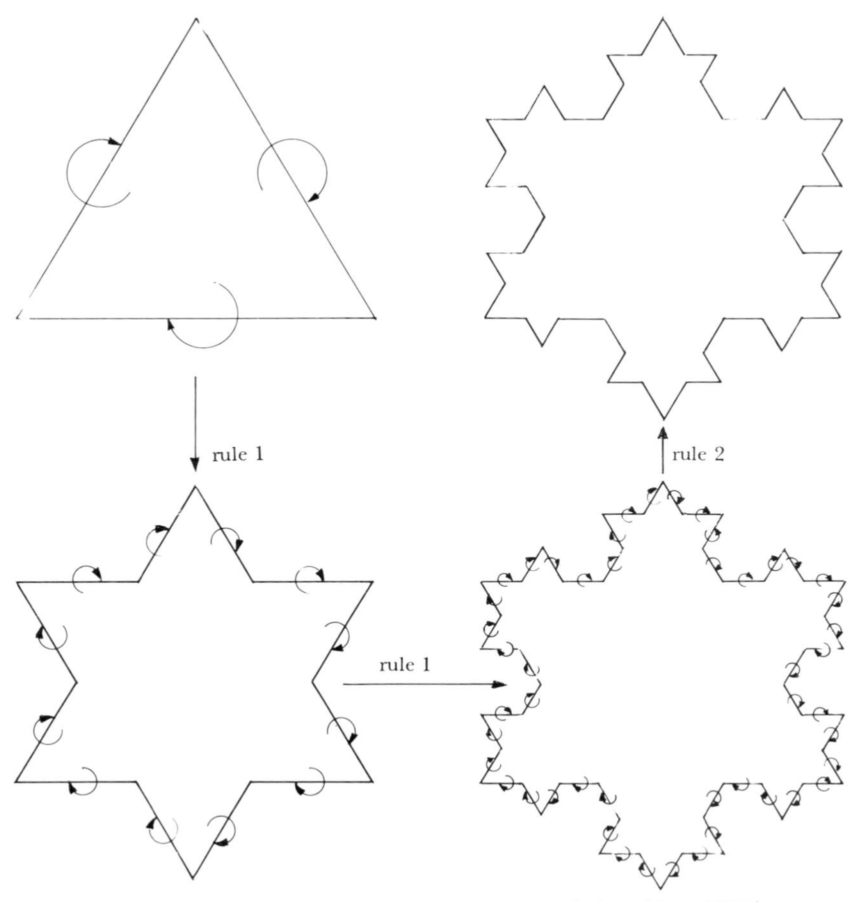


**Figure 3.16.** *Example of parallel substitution (after Gips, 1975)*

There are no application conditions, but there are nesting rules:

1. The point on the right hand part labelled $M_{i+1}$, $M_{i+2}$ or $M_{i+3}$ is the same as the single point on the left hand side.
2. The point labelled $M_1$, $M_2$ or $M_3$ is a new point.

d) $M_i$ $M_j \longrightarrow M_{i+1}$ 1 $M_{j+1}$ 1 i 3

e) $M_i$ $M_j \longrightarrow M_{i+2}$ 2 $M_{j+2}$ 1 i 2

f) $M_l$ $M_l \longrightarrow M_4$ 3 $M_4$

The condition for the application of these rules is that the points on the left hand side should not be closely related in the graph to be derived. The nesting rules show that a new line is created between the two points and their labels become those of the right hand side. Also:

g) $M_1$ H/Li/Na/F/Cl atoms of valency 1

h) $M_2$ Be/Mg/Ca/O/S atoms of valency 2

i) $M_3$ B/Al/Ni/P atoms of valency 3

j) $M_4$ C/Si/Ti atoms of valency 4

An example is shown in Figure 3.17:

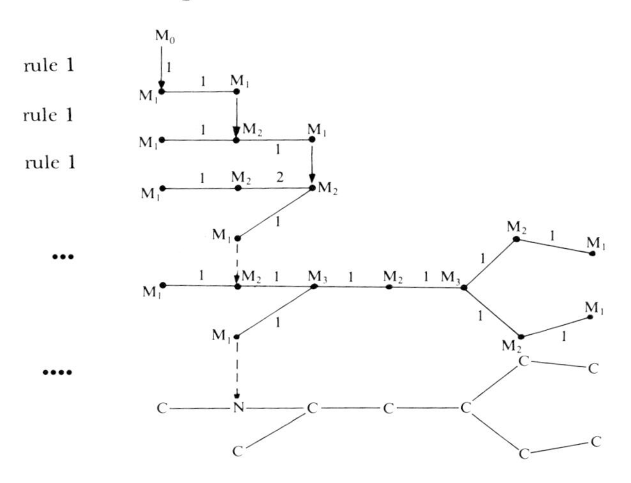


**Figure 3.17.** *Example of derivation of a chemical formula (after Azema, 1975)*

Graph grammars have been used in the development of algorithms which enable certain graph properties to be processed: recognition or production of particular types of graph, problems of planarity or isomorphism, card coding, etc. It appears that graph grammars are well adapted for certain types of application. They are more useful than the Freeman code, but still inadequate for the establishment of software enabling the construction of grammars, dependent on the application concerned, in any automatic mode. The necessary techniques are not yet available, and so the majority of systems use geometric encoding, which will be discussed in the following section.

### *3.2.4.3 Examples of geometric codes*

Three types of model will be discussed: a model used for visual display; two models used for the description of two-dimensional scenes mainly for use in mechanics and technical drawing and finally a model that can be used for the description of schemata.

*Model for visual display*

The model described below is created with graphic software using the GRIGRI base. The basic elements are: coordinate pairs, graphic characters and messages. A *section* is a set of basic *elements*. To define a section, the following must be specified: the number of elements it contains, the list of abcissae and the list of ordinates. These coordinates are defined in the user's set of coordinate axes. A section of text is defined by: the number of characters it contains and the chain of characters from which it is formed. A *figure* is a set of sections (of points and of text). The sections belonging to a single figure are defined in relation to the same coordinate system for the user. A *mode* is a set of graphic characteristics associated with a section. It permits graphic interpretation of the elements of the section, eg the texture, colour, size and orientation of the characters. A *name* can also be given to the sections (correlation). This name may be common to sections of different figures, which allows a structuring level to be added. The window and the boundary allow definition of space imposed by the user and the final space on the screen, respectively. The model has two levels:

1. the *core* level: the role of the core is essentially to communicate with the application;
2. the *interpreter* level: the role of the interpreter is to manage the screen and the associated dialogue (or the tracer, if it is a tracer interpreter).

Communication between the application and the basic software is carried out for coordinate elements and texts through tables declared in the application, the basic software of which will recognize the addresses. Figure 3.18 shows the structure of these tables. The core retains:

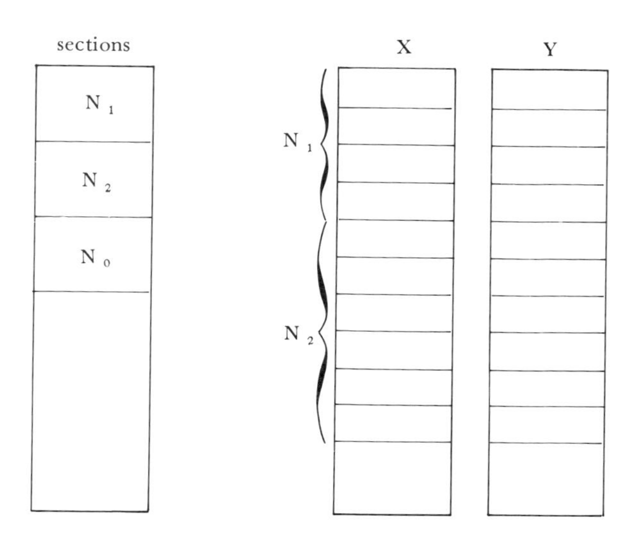


**Figure 3.18.** *Communication application – GRIGRI*

1. a table of figures: figure name and addresses of tables defining the figure;
2. a table of windows and a table of boundaries (name, abcissa and ordinates of bottom left and top right corners);
3. a table of modes associated with the figures and sections with, eg figure name, section name, associated correlation, graphics, etc.

The interpreter retains:

1. a table of sections displayed with their names, correlations, pointers and lengths in the display list;
2. a table of displayed messages with message numbers, pointers and lengths in the display list (with another table of zones reserved for the introduction of values) (Figure 3.19).

For some terminals, the interpreter must retain supplementary information, specific to the hardware. The data structures described above are present in all interpreters. It is clear that the concept of the pointer does not have the same meaning in all cases, as:

1. it can be an address in the buffer memory (if there is one);
2. if the terminal does not use a buffer memory, the pointer refers to the display list simulated by the software.

*Model for technical drawing*
Consider the example of the GRI 2D model described by Gardan, 1983 (Figure 3.20). The original aims of the model handled by GRI 2D were:

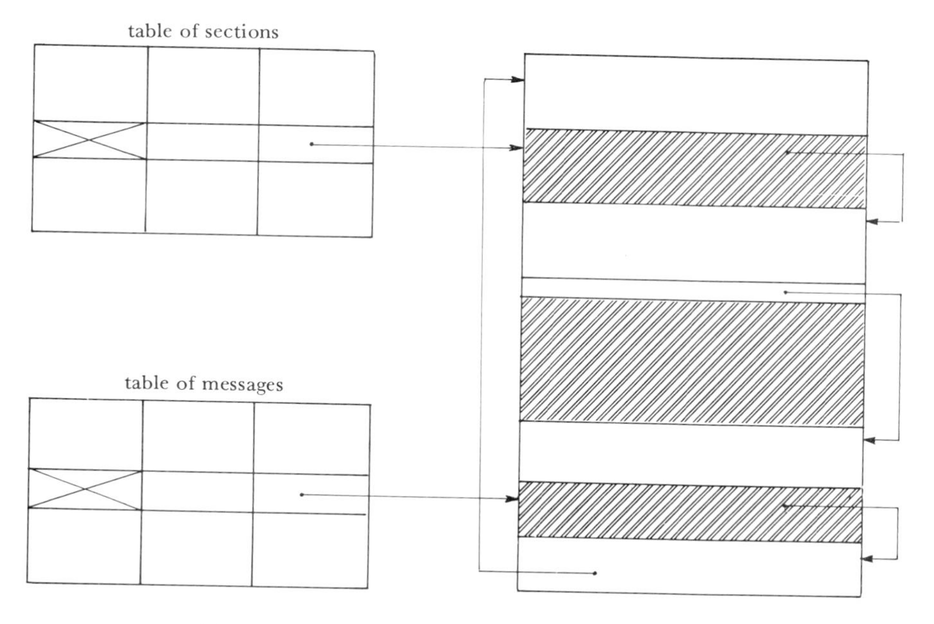


**Figure 3.19.** *Internal structure of an interpreter*

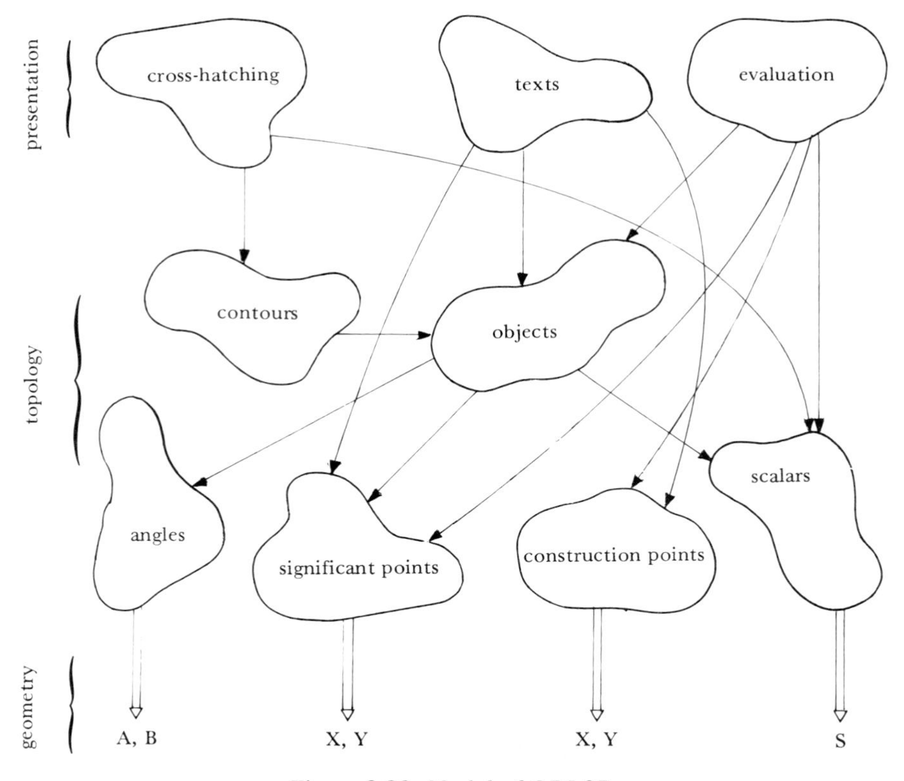


**Figure 3.20.** *Model of GRI 2D*

1. to take into account a maximum number of functional aspects of the drawing;
2. to allow a connection to be made with the applications, and thus with the functional links between the applications and the geometric data.

The following types of information can be manipulated:

1. *Geometrical information*: concerns the points (PO), the values of angles (PA) and the scalars (R) for the radii, distances, etc.

PO (X, Y)
PA (A, B)
R (r)

2. *Topological information*: the structuring of the drawing is based on a large amount of topological information, with the following notation:

segment or straight line = SG
arc or circle = CE
contour = CO
} basic objects OB

SG (POi, POj)
CE (POi, PAj, Rk)
CO (OBi, information)

For a contour, the complementary information indicates (for each object) the direction of movement, and one element of information concerning the intersection (since in the case of an intersection between a straight line and a circle or between two circles, there are two points of intersection). This intersectional information can be determined according to the direction of movement ('first' or 'second' point of intersection).

3. *Presentation information*: the model retains the functional link between the presentation and the objects concerned, and the following notation is used:

cross-hatching = HA
specification = CT
text = TX
HA ((COi, i = 1, n), R1, R2)

where R1 is the angle and R2 the distance between cross-hatching lines (it should be noted that R1 and R2 can be defined by the user or by the type of cross-hatching).

CT1 (Tn (OBi, POj, Rk)) specification of object
CT2 (Tn (OBi, OBj, POj, Rk)) specification of two objects
CT3 (Tn (OBi, OBj, POj, Rk, OBp)) complex specification (direction according to an angle or the direction of a segment of straight line; where Tn is the type of specification)
TX = (POi, chain, OBj)

A purely graphical presentation can, however, be used with a semi-functional presentation if a schema equivalent to that described in section 3.2.3.3 is used. This means that the model of the presentation in GRI 2D can appear in a semi-functional form, as described above, or in an evaluated form corresponding to the parameters of the functions used in the preparation for visual display. These functions always use the evaluated model. The model can arise from a purely graphic presentation, for example, because it is calculated from an external program or from the semi-functional model, which will only be re-evaluated if the modifications affect the two-dimensional model.

4. *Structural information*: with each basic object (OB), an element of structural and functional information (set, sub-set . . .) is associated:

PART (OBi)

With each basic object (OB) and each point (PO), an element of visual display information (level of visual display) and graphic information (type of line) is associated:

TYPE (POi)
LEVISU (OBi)
GRAPH (OBi)

□ Extension of the capacity of technical drawing software:
GRI 2D retains many associations between the elements in its model. It 'forgets', however, the design logic of the user. If, for example, the user draws a tangent to two circles, the information 'tangent to' is dumped as soon as the geometric construction is calculated. In order to retain this information, a structure of the type shown in Figure 3.21 must be managed. These points are taken into account in PARAM 2D (Gardan, 1983). Using this method, the family of parts can be formed in a totally interactive mode, and thus the writing of programs can to a large extent be avoided. This type of modelling, which is very similar to the construction methods, can be compared to certain three-dimensional modelling methods, such as the construction tree (see section 3.3). Nonetheless, it should be noted that:

1. the model retains the construction logic and the user must 'construct' a model by taking into account the intended modifications:

2. the management of parameters linked to existing elements in the model requires the use of generalized input graphics (see section 5.3.2);

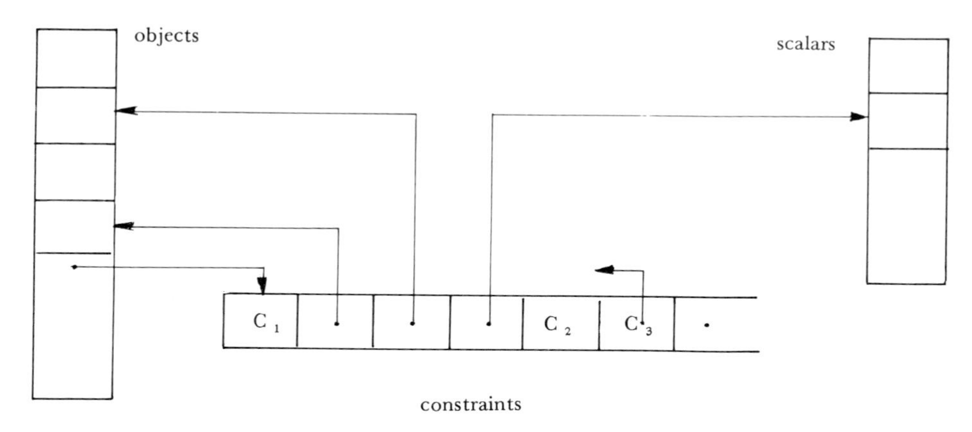


**Figure 3.21.** *Construction modelling (simplified)*

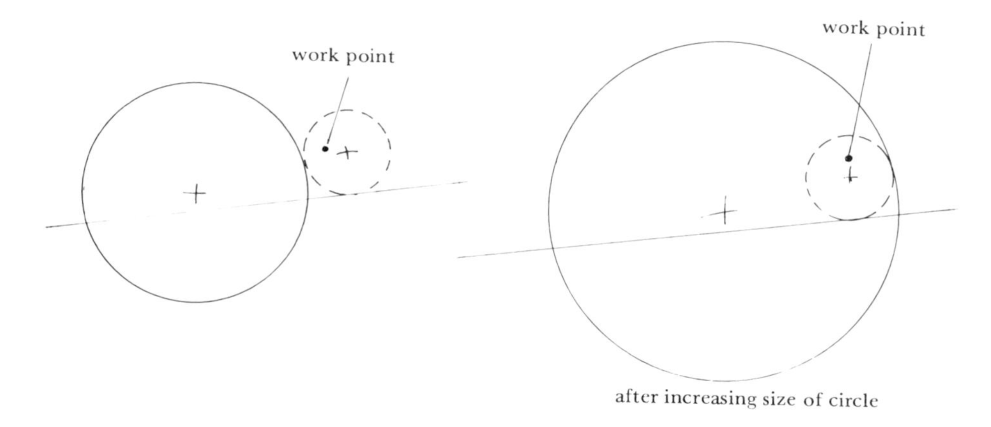


**Figure 3.22.** *Incoherent modification*

3. the connections between values or the definition of variables also require a generalized graphic input;

4. logical encoding of the constructions is often necessary: Figure 3.22 shows that if in the construction of a circle (tangent to a circle and a straight line) it is decided to retain the coordinates of the 'work' point (which allows the right circle to be chosen) as an absolute value, the result after modification cannot respect the logic of the construction. Information of the type: 'the circle to be formed is to the right of the segment, outside the circle and to the right of the perpendicular leading from the centre of the circle to the segment' must be retained. A form of encoding which takes into account the direction of movement of the elements allows this type of information to be managed.

□ Other possible extensions:
Information similar to the construction methods can also be useful for the management of, for example, assembly.

*Other modelling possible for mechanical use*
In a mechanical plan, the three traditional views are made up of contours. If all the projections of the object on the three reference planes are drawn, the contours remain closed. For reasons of clarity, a certain number of hidden lines are eliminated and the resulting view is made up of contours, some of which are open and some closed. It is possible, therefore, to form a model of the type defined below. The contours are described by lists, recording information which includes (Figure 3.23):

1. X, Y – coordinates of a point (or pointer to a coordinate table);
2. T – texture of the line terminating at this point;

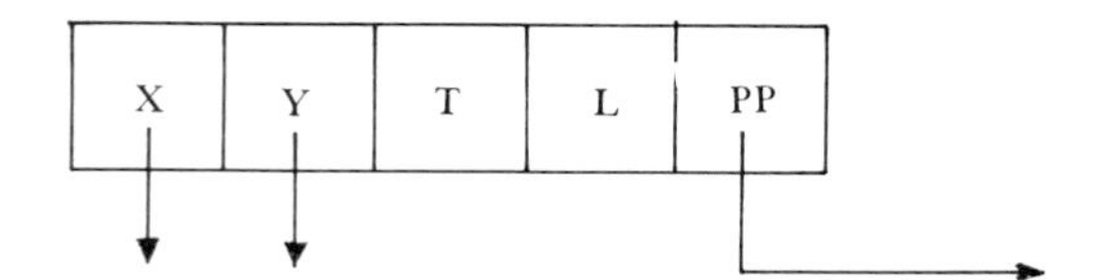


**Figure 3.23.** *Description of contours*

3. L – type of line joining the preceding point to this one (0 if it is the first point); if this line is not straight, a pointer can be used to determine its parameters (eg the radius);
4. PP – pointer to the point following the contour.

Other information can also be included, eg a pointer to the coinciding points (ie points with the same coordinates in different contours). This type of structuring has the advantage of processing the contours as elements of the drawing, and with the structure of the list defining a contour, it facilitates modifications of the 'deletion or addition of points in the contour' type. On the other hand, the concept of elements (arcs, segments) is not really used in this method, and the specification of an angle between two segments must be made according to the respective extremities of the segments.

*Simple schema model*
Consider a very simple schema, the application of which consists of positioning symbols of fixed dimensions and creating links between them. The model defined in Figure 3.24 is characteristic of this. The positioned symbols are defined by coordinate pairs which allow the presence of a symbol to be located in the schema (this can also apply to more complete information, such as a transformation matrix in situations in which the symbols can be rotated). The definition of the symbols is not specified in the schema, because it can be carried out in various ways:

1. either by retaining the coordinates of the points (in a given system) that define a symbol;
2. or by knowing the symbol by a procedure defining it.

The links are identified by their type (possibly with a technological connotation) and the symbols concerned (with the numbers of connections in cases where several connections can be made with one symbol). This association means that during modification of a symbol (or its movement) the graphics of the link can be produced automatically. The establishment of visual display consists, first of all, of interpreting the symbols with their location and then creating the links.

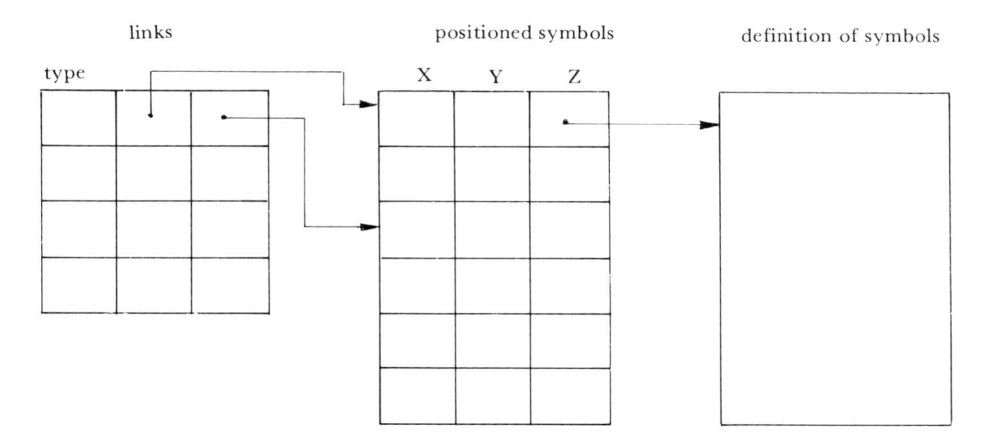


**Figure 3.24.** *Simple schematic model*

## 3.3 Three-dimensional modelling

### 3.3.1 AIMS

Software for three-dimensional modelling is designed to allow the creation and use of a model of an object in three-dimensions. The different types of model – line models, surface models and solid models – have been discussed. A solid model is essentially a hybrid of the other two. In this section, software for solid three-dimensional modelling, which can also be used to model complex surfaces, will be described.

A number of the features of technical drawing software can, or should be, useful for three-dimensional modelling; in particular, interactivity, applicability and independence of hardware and dialogue methods. The choices which are made in three-dimensional modelling software depend to a large extent on the intended application. Although processing associated with technical drawing software is relatively cheap and the models produced correspond to the same general criteria, three-dimensional modelling software is quite different.

Some processing methods can be very costly (elimination of hidden parts, cross-sections, etc) and depend on the choice of model, which may be very complex. It may be simple, for example, to decide that a surface model is the best to use for adaptation to the shape of car bodies, but it is still necessary to choose the best adaptation. The choices involved in three-dimensional modelling vary with intended application. After consideration of the diversity of elements that can be manipulated, two main types of solid model will be discussed: the *limit model*, broadly similar to graphics, and the *construction tree model*, which attempts to integrate the highest levels of knowledge concerning design. It is important to stress the diversity of possible models and the flexibility in their use. As the design logic is being ever more completely and efficiently modelled, the models are often close to the method of construction employed by the final user. The different construction methods will be discussed later, with examples of the mathematical modelling (where applicable) and algorithms used, in particular for transfer from a model close to the construction method to one close (by limits) to visual display. Finally, a number of examples of models will be described.

### 3.3.2 MANIPULATED PARTS

Manipulated parts are far more varied than those involved in two-dimensional modelling. In general, two-dimensional elements (points, lines, etc) are taken into account by three-dimensional software. The basic elements are as follows:

*level 0 elements*: *two-dimensional elements*
- points
- straight lines and segments
- circles and arcs of circle
- curves
- contours

*level 1 elements*: *surfaces*
- planes
- lined surfaces
- rotating surfaces
- twisted surfaces

*level 2 elements*: *solids*
- cylinders, cones, prisms, etc
- any polyhedron
- any solid

Using these elements, various sets can be formed.

### 3.3.3 INTERNAL REPRESENTATION

If the various types of internal representation used for 'solid' geometric models are analysed, two major modes can be distinguished (leaving aside the methods specifically adapted for a particular application, for example, for use with parametrized parts, in which the internal representation is the set of dimensional parameters, or the logic defining it):

1. *representation using limits of the object*: the model comprises the limits of a solid, eg its faces, edges and vertices;

2. *representation using a construction tree*: the non-terminal nodes represent the operators, the 'leaves' represent the basic objects (or possibly the surfaces).

Before analysing these modes of representation, it should be noted that representation of a solid may be carried out by enumerating occupied positions in space. This is sometimes simplified to an assembly of simple boxes 'stuck' together. This type of representation is not without disadvantages. It is extremely demanding of memory and so can only be used for certain types of application; also the 'sticking' operation of two boxes can be considered as a union of the boxes. This breakdown can, however, be useful in the calculation of finite elements. One of the advantages of this type of representation is that it is always easy to tell whether a given point belongs to a solid or not, whereas this operation is complex when attempted with other forms of representation.

### *3.3.3.1 Representation by limits (eg with polyhedrons)*

This type of representation can be explained with reference to a set of faces, limited by their edges, which are themselves limited by their vertices. Three types of information are involved:

1. *Geometric information*: eg the coordinates of the vertices and the equations of the edges or faces. This information is often stored in homogeneous representations, thus avoiding problems of mismatched capacity and allowing both the interior and exterior of the solid to be determined for a given face. The cabling of certain operations is also made easier. The main disadvantages are the large memory capacity required and lengthy calculation time.
2. *Topological information*: if geometric information alone is retained representation is incomplete, except for convex objects. For this reason, information which allows the topology of the object to be assessed is also stored.
3. *Ancillary information*: this information includes certain important elements such as colour of the surface, degree of transparency of a face, etc. Information of this nature is important in visual display.

The topology and geometry are often well separated. This separation makes it possible, for example, to carry out a translation by multiplying the coordinates of the vertices by the translation matrix without modifying the topology. It is clear, however, that topology and geometry are not independent. A representation may become inaccurate following modification of the geometry, eg movement of the vertex of a pyramid towards the base surface.

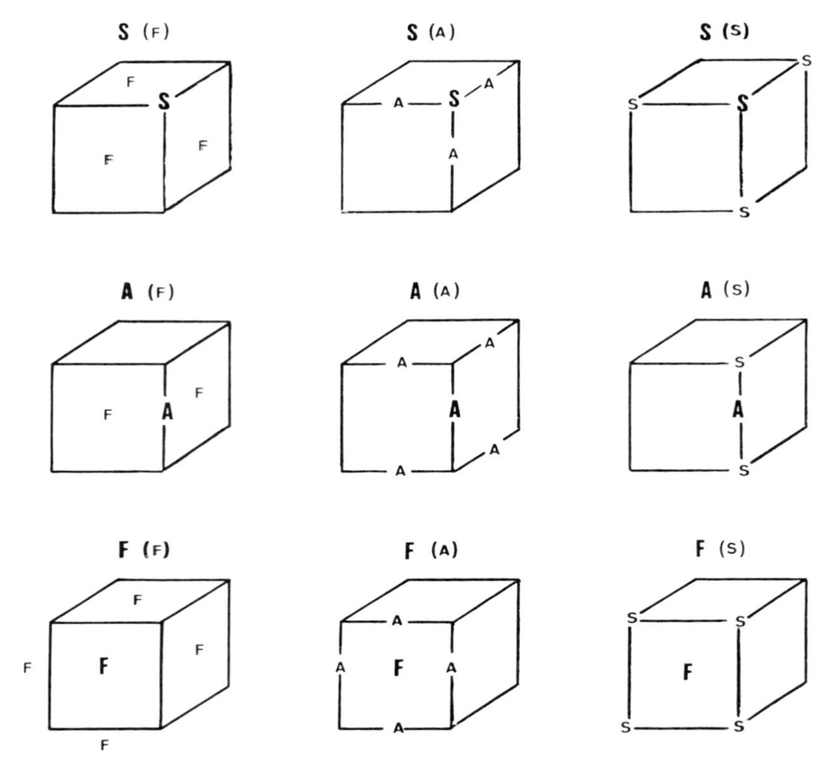


**Figure 3.25.** *Topology (nine relationships of a polyhedron)*

Figure 3.26 shows two examples of modelling by limits. In example 1 it can be seen that geometry/topology separation is complete, since it includes a table of values containing all the scalars, allowing the geometry to be determined. Also the face adjacent to each face for each edge allows the realization of A(F) and F(F) to be facilitated. Example 2 shows an extremely low level model, which retains only the edges and the vertices (line model). Other limit models are discussed in section 3.3.5.

### *3.3.3.2 Representation using a construction tree*

This type of representation is generally used only with set-forming operators. It can be defined as:

---

Figure 3.25 shows that the topological and geometric information retained may be redundant to a greater or lesser extent – the degree of redundancy being chosen as a compromise between the space occupied and the time required to reconstitute (or calculate) the dumped information. This choice is, however, related to the work to be carried out on the model. For example, in a line drawing it is extremely useful to know how the vertices should be connected and it is essential that information concerning the relationships of the vertices (A (S), for example) is retained.

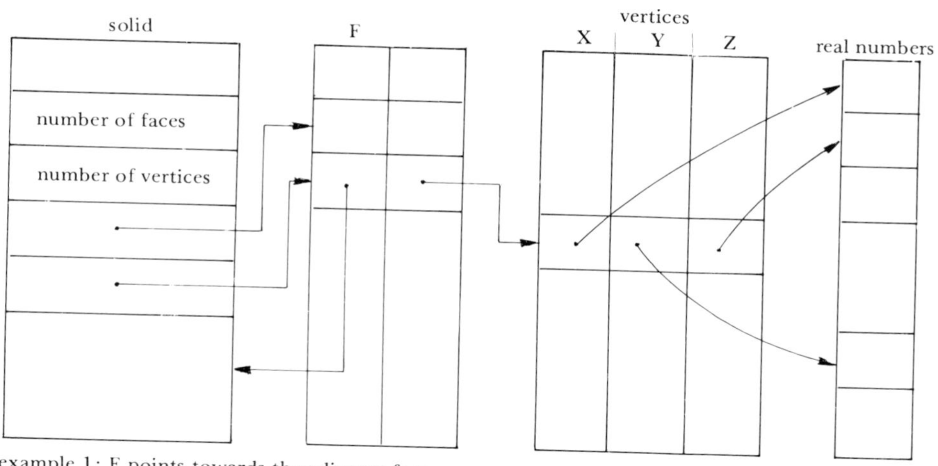


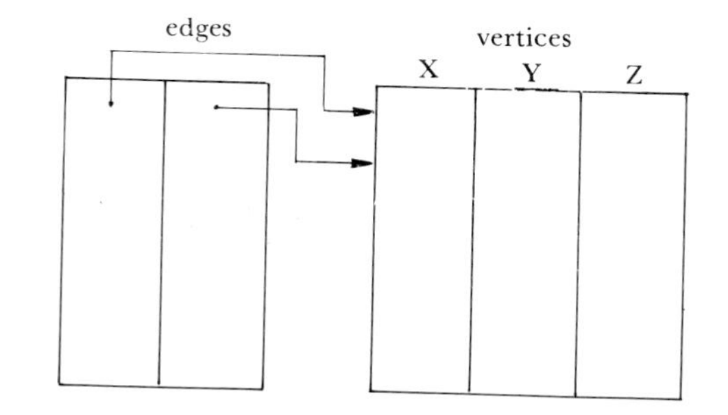


**Figure 3.26.** *Example of limit models*

(construction tree) = (basic object) (construction tree) (operator node) (construction tree) (placing node) (placing arguments).

This type of representation is often more complex than a binary tree, because some of the sub-trees can be shared (a hierarchy is evident). The representation can go as far as the primitive solids and sometimes as far as half-spaces. Figure 3.27 shows that a box can be represented as the regular intersection of six flat half-spaces and can be defined as: a flat space is a set (P: $f(p) \leqslant 0$), where P is a point in E3 and $f = 0$ defines a flat surface ($ax + by + cz + d = 0$). The use of primitive solids makes these properties easier to verify. With a half-space, the 'limited' property must be verified (this concept can, of course, be extended for use with surfaces which are not flat). The use of a known number of primitives means that the validity of the construction can be verified at the syntactic level.

Generally the following operators are taken into account: association, intersection, difference and geometric transformations. These operators,

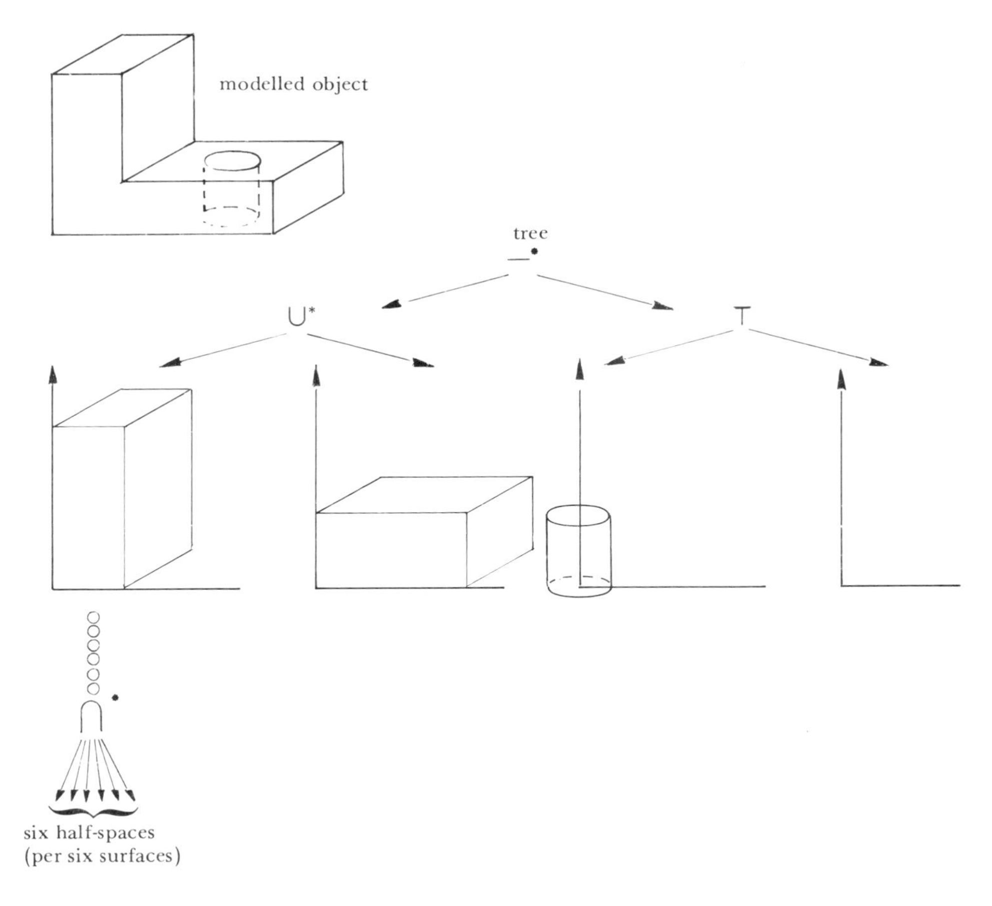


**Figure 3.27.** *Construction tree*

which are said to be *regularized*, must be processed so that an operation on two solids will not produce a 'degenerated' solid (eg if two solids are tangential to one face, the result of their intersection is not one face, but nil). The following advantages and drawbacks are often encountered with this form of representation:

1. It must be evaluated before any display takes place; this often involves using a representation closer to the display (often a representation by limits) in parallel to avoid extra calculation.
2. If the basic objects are solids and the operators are correctly defined, every evaluated object is sure to be a solid.
3. It allows the functional aspect of the construction to be retained and can thus be used for design purposes. If the construction tree is not retained, and representation by limits is adopted immediately, some operations become impossible, eg see Figure 3.28: object **C** is to be constructed using operation A ∪ B. If the first

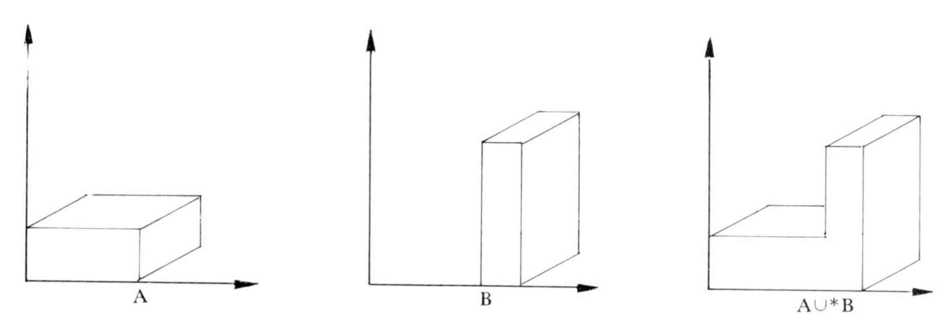


**Figure 3.28.** *Example of association*

placement of B relative to A is incorrect and it needs to be moved by a distance X, then if the construction tree has been retained and it need only be re-evaluated, or if only the representation of C by its limits has been retained, the whole operation must be repeated.

Representation using a Boolean operation tree, which appears to be most appropriate, can present fundamental problems (other representations can give rise to similar problems):

1. Evaluation of a representation, eg used in the transfer from this model to a visual display model; this concerns the use of Boolean operations in data processing.
2. Evaluation of characteristics which may be necessary for a given processing procedure, eg determining whether or not a point P belongs to a solid S. This may be extremely difficult, if not impossible, without preliminary evaluation of the model.

Some models contain information concerning the method of construction used. If an object is constructed from a contour and a depth (or a rotation), the model can retain this information and families of parametrized objects can be produced.

The last type of model to be considered here is the *hybrid model*, which can be used with objects modelled in different ways. For example, a hybrid model made up of 'a construction tree and polyhedral solids' is quite commonly encountered. In this hybrid, a 'construction tree' type model has leaves which are either primitive solids (cylinders, boxes, etc) or a limit representation of non-primitive solids. In the same way, if *extruded* objects are added, the leaves can also represent objects derived from a contour and a depth, or a contour and a rotation. With hybrid models, it is usually necessary to homogenize the model to make the operations easier to use. This is why representation is often of a low standard, as is limit representation.

### *3.3.3.3 Conversion between models*

No model is better than all others for all purposes. For example, although the construction tree enables a certain level of parametrization to be carried out, it is unsuitable for visual display because it must be evaluated. The use of hybrid models (because objects are constructed, used and modelled in different ways) raises the question of whether or not it is easy to transfer from one model to another.

Figure 3.29 shows the algorithmic potential for two by two transfer of the most commonly used models: spacial enumeration, 'extrusion', limits and construction trees. The solid lines indicate an 'exact' transfer and the broken lines represent an approximation. Since certain types of model (eg 'extrusion') have fewer applications than others, there cannot always be conversion algorithms operating in two directions. As can be seen in Figure 3.29, any model can be converted to a 'limits' model. This is very easy when moving from 'depth-rotation' to 'limits' representation, but is more difficult (due to the complexity of the algorithms) when moving from a construction tree to limits or from enumeration to limits (see section 3.3.4). In this situation, the faces belonging to a single 'basic box' are found and these constitute the external faces.

It is also possible to pass from any model to the spacial enumeration model by using an approximation which will depend on the precision of the enumeration.

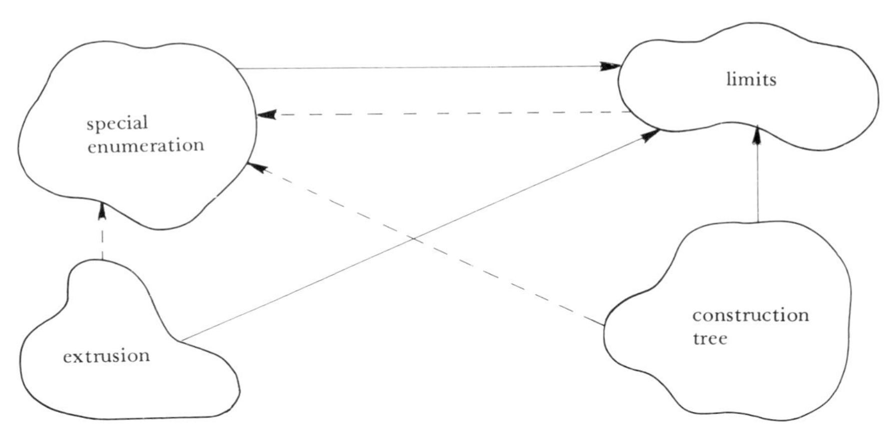


**Figure 3.29.** *Conversion between models*

## 3.3.4 METHODS OF CONSTRUCTION

The techniques that can be used for creating objects are extremely varied. Those described below are the most commonly used for the formation of surfaces and solids.

### *3.3.4.1 Construction of curves and surfaces*

In the construction of complex surfaces (*skew surfaces*), the definition of the elements on which they are based can be obtained by a variety of methods (numeration, photogrametry, etc) or calculations (aerodynamics, etc).

A curve can be formed by:

1. curve fitting;
2. curve deformation (moving points, modifying polynomials);
3. a curve parallel to a given curve, at a fixed or variable distance in a plane;
4. open or closed contours created from segments and arcs of circle in a plane;
5. conics (ellipses, parabolas, etc);
6. intersections of surfaces;
7. joining two curves.

A surface can be formed by:

1. curve fitting;
2. deformation of a surface;
3. a generator curve moving along a trajectory curve;
4. a surface parallel to a given surface at a fixed distance;
5. the joining of two surfaces.

Objects produced in industrial contexts are frequently complex in form and their production often involves complex calculations, eg aerodynamics. The computer representation of these objects enables simple methods to be formulated which allow such objects to be easily manipulated, using such techniques as modification and display, etc.

Many types of surface are processed in CAD/CAM. Some can be represented by equations. This section deals with complex surfaces, which appear often in automobile and aeronautical applications as well as in design processes in which complex surfaces need to be created and modified whilst respecting the criteria of continuity. This arises in calculations or in the automatic creation of information used in production (numerical control). There are important constraints involved: curves and surfaces must be modelled in such a way as to allow the user to 'see' them and to modify them (whilst respecting the design criteria of the user) in an interactive mode. Designers of systems have therefore attempted to design data which is both economical and easy to use for the production of processing results.

Some qualities are fundamental, including:

1. *Overall and local control of the shape*: whether in relation to curves or surfaces, a local modification must only affect the local area (or the curve or surface unit). These modifications are generally made

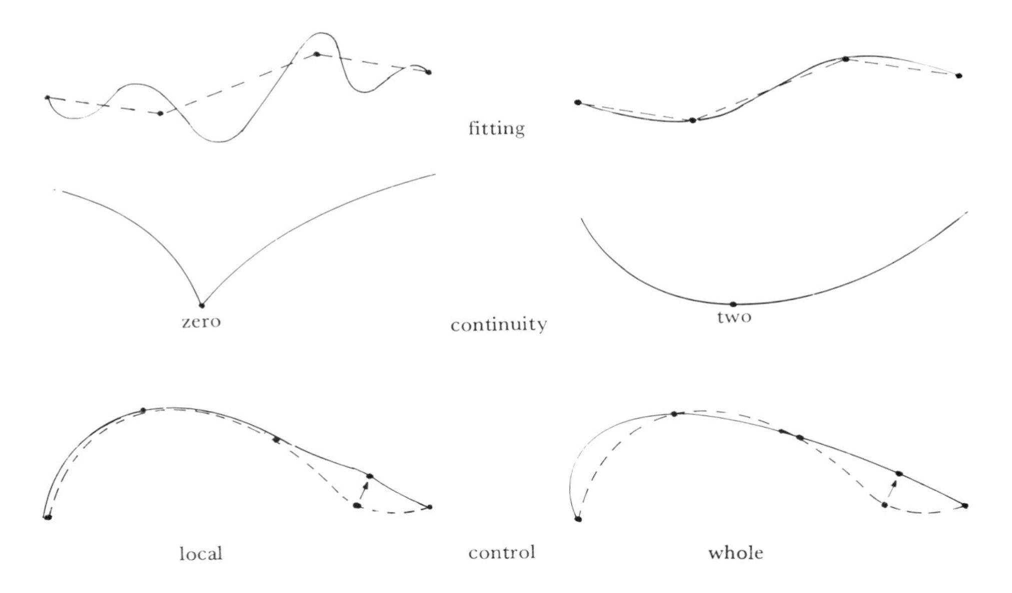


**Figure 3.30.** *Properties of curves*

using control points (points through which a curve passes, or which allow the shape of the curve to be controlled). Overall control may be difficult when the designer wishes to carry out very precise adjustments on a specific part of the curve or surface.

2. *Quality of fit*: one of the basic qualities of modelling is that it should provide a 'smooth' curve or surface and one, in particular, which does not oscillate about the control points (see Figure 3.30).
3. *Continuity*: a shape is generally described by several curves or surfaces. The designer may wish these to be tangential to the points of contact (first-order continuity), or even want them to conform to the same curve (second-order continuity).

The most commonly used method for modelling curves or surfaces is the *parametric method*. In this, a curve can be represented using a parameter, and a surface represented using two parameters. A point is represented as a vector, thus:

$$P(u) = [x(u), y(u), z(u)] \quad \text{for a curve, and}$$

$$P(u, v) = [x(u, v), y(u, v), z(u, v)] \quad \text{for a surface.}$$

The parametric equation can define a curve or surface in a precise manner; eg a circle is defined by:

$$P(u) = [xo + R \cos u, yo + R \sin u]$$

Curves and surfaces can also be defined using approximations, usually polynomial.

The constraint of defining a shape using a number of surfaces imposes the definition of *patches*. A patch is a part of the space enclosed by four curved boundary segments. Continuity problems arise when patches are to be joined. A patch can be defined thus:

$$P(u, v) = [x(v, u), y(u, v), z(u, v)]$$
$$\text{with:} \quad u \in (0, 1), \quad v \in (0, 1)$$

The following equations define the four curved boundary lines:

$$P(u, 0), P(u, 1), P(0, v) \quad \text{and} \quad P(1, v)$$

The two most commonly used methods are the Bezier and B-Spline methods.

*Representation of curves*
A Bezier curve is defined according to the control points p, so:

$$p(u) = \sum_{i=0}^{n} p_i B_{i,n}(u)$$
$$\text{with: } B_{i,n}(u) = C^i_n u^i (1 - u)^{n-i}$$
$$C^i_n = n!/i!\,(n - i)!$$

A B-Spline curve is defined by:

$$P(u) = \sum_{i=0}^{n} p_i N_{i,k(u)}$$
$$\text{with: } N_{i,1}(u) = 1 \quad \text{if } a_i \leqslant u \leqslant a_{i+1}$$
$$= 0 \quad \text{if not}$$
$$N_{i,k}(u) = \frac{(u - a_i)\, N_{i,k-1}(u)}{a_{i+k-1} - a_i} + \frac{(a_{i+k} - u)\, N_{i+1,k-1}(u)}{a_{i+k} - a_{i+1}}$$

The values of $a_i$ allow the relationship between u and the control points to be chosen. This choice is generally close to non-periodic B-Spline curves for modelling open curves, and to periodic B-Spline curves for modelling open curves.

The mathematical aspects of curve modelling have been discussed by Barnhill and Riesenfeld, 1974. For the purposes of this discussion, the basic differences between Bezier and B-Spline curves arise from the fact that B-Splines allow the definition polygon to be strictly adhered to and, above all, that the curve is not corrupted except around the vertices (because of the local character of the approximation), whereas modification of a control point in a Bezier curve puts the whole of the curve's definition in doubt.

*Representation of surfaces*
These are defined in the same way as curves, ie:

$$\text{Bezier:} \quad P(u, v) = \sum_{i=0}^{n} \sum_{j=0}^{m} P_{i,j} B_{i,n}(u) B_{j,m}(v)$$

$$\text{B-Spline:} \quad P(u, v) = \sum_{i=0}^{n} \sum_{j=0}^{m} P_{i,j} N_{i,k}(u) N_{j,1}(v)$$

The properties are the same as those for curves.

#### *3.3.4.2 Extrusion*

Using the contours described in a plane with two-dimensional operations, the user can define solids in a variety of ways:

1. depth: S = F1 (C, P, D, L)

The reference contour C is placed in plane P (plane z = 0 by default) and a second contour is created by a translation of contour C according to director vector D and of length L.

2. rotation: S = F2 (C, A)

Using contour C (open or closed) the solid formed by rotation about axis A is created.

3. contour joining: S = F3 (LC, LP, LR, LS)

LC is the list of contours to be joined. If LC(I) is the ith contour, LP(i) is the surface in which it is to lie and LR(i) is the direction of the contour.

4. pierced depth: S = F4 (LC, D, L)

This type of construction is similar to the ‘depth’ example. The method used is identical, with LC(1) as the ‘exterior’ contour and the succeeding contours (LC(2) . . . LC(n)) the ‘interior’ contours, of the holes.

5. generalized extrusion

The preceding examples illustrate the creation of solids from rigid contours moved through simple trajectories (the solid is made up of the set of points ‘scanned’ in the surface defined by the contours). The first extension of this technique is to take a surface which is defined by rigid contours and to make it follow a trajectory of a required complexity. The use of this technique in the construction of an exhaust pipe is shown in Figure 3.31. It should be noted that this method can give rise to non-coherent objects (see Figure 3.32).

A larger scale extension is made possible using non-rigid objects (surfaces or solids) with a complex trajectory. The basic objects can thus be deformed according to the relevant laws and this, combined with the trajectory, can facilitate the creation of complex objects. This method is used in some systems (ACRONYM; see Brooks, 1981) in association with the idea of generalized cones (see Figure 3.33).

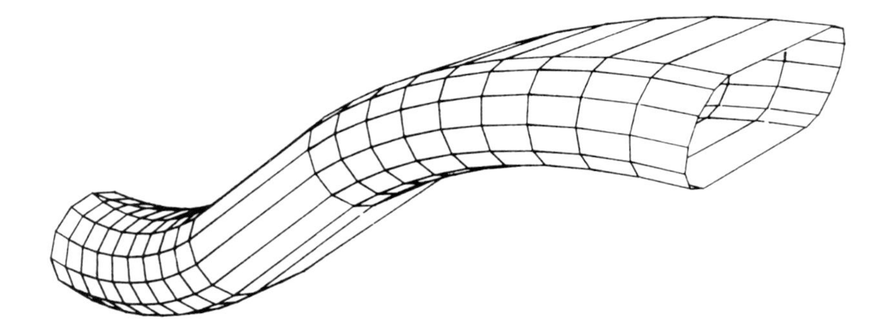

**Figure 3.31.** *Design for an exhaust pipe*

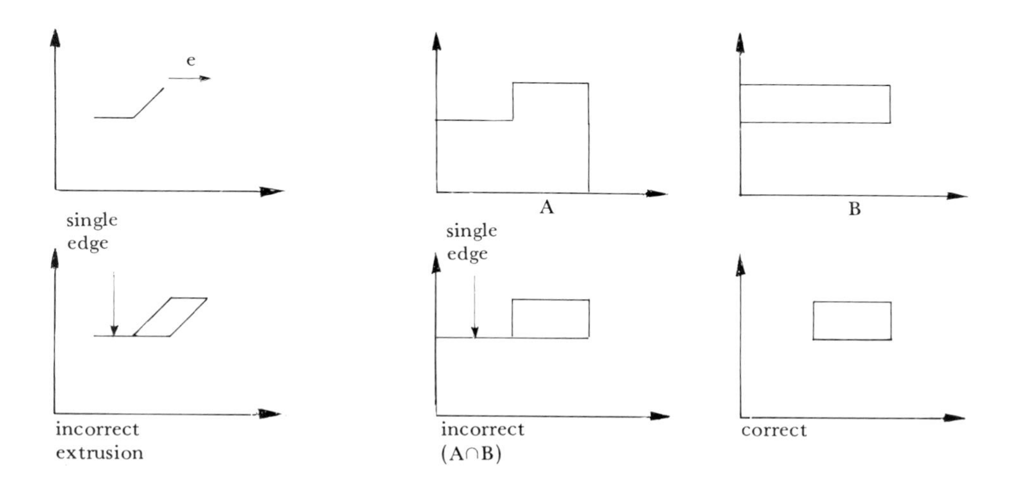


**Figure 3.32.** *Incoherent results of operations*

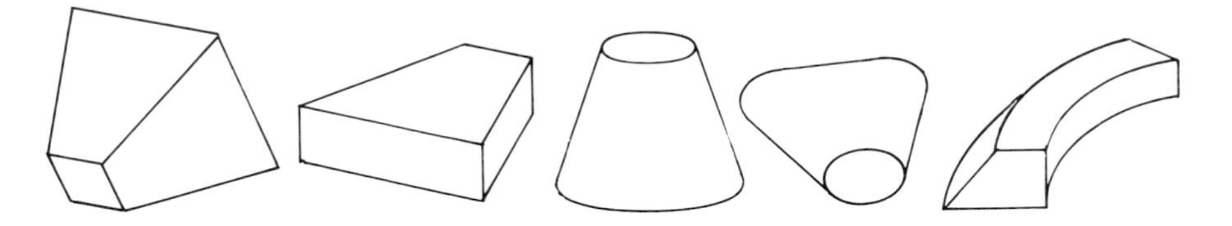

**Figure 3.33.** *Generalized cones*

The model can maintain the various construction parameters, eg the contour address, the contour plan, the director vector and the vector length for a solid obtained by depth. This information can be used for a number of operations, including the creation of families of solids. It is, however, remote from graphics and it is necessary to use algorithms to create information having some graphical character, similar, for example, to a limit model.

An example of a change of a model (in which the construction parameters are maintained) into a visual display oriented model, is given below. This involves transforming the model of a joined contour-type object (in which the list of contours LC is known) into a *facet model* (cf. GRI 3D in section 3.3.5.2). A solid is thus defined as being limited by: the first contour, the last contour and for two consecutive contours LC(i) and LC(i + 1). A facet (not necessarily flat) is created, from two objects of the same rank in each contour (the first object of each contour LR(i) and LR(i + 1) and the direction of each object with contours LS(i) and LS(i + 1) are known). Essentially, the idea is to make the objects correspond; three different situations can arise:

1. A segment Si, k of contour LC(i) corresponds to a segment Si, j of contour LC(i + 1). The facet is thus made up of four lines joining the points: beginning (Si, k), beginning (Si + 1, j), end (Si + 1, j), end (Si, k), beginning (Si, k).
2. An arc of circle Ai, k of contour LC(i) corresponds to an arc of circle Ai + 1, j of contour LC(i + 1). To obtain the facets whose sides are the segments, the two arcs of circle are broken down into an equal number of segments (*polygonization*). The segments correspond to each other in pairs, and each pair of segments is then subjected to the operation described above.
3. An arc of circle Ai, k of contour LC(i) corresponds to a segment Si + 1, j of contour LC(i + 1) or vice versa. To obtain the facets, the arc of circle and the segment are broken down into an equal number of segments, and the operation defined above is then performed.

This transfer from construction model to facet model imposes a definition of parameters, such as the factor of arc polygonization, or of the number of meridians in a solid formed by rotation. If the model allows these operations to be carried out and does not simply retain the facet presentation, these parameters can be defined according to need (low level of precision for interactive use, high level of precision for plan output). It should be noted that the validity of the objects constructed (the qualities of a good model) is taken into account at the algorithmic level of construction. Any object constructed according to one of these methods is thus considered valid (assuming that the construction algorithms are correct).

### *3.3.4.3 Local operations*

Consider an object modelled in the form of [faces, edges, vertices]. Its structure accords to the Euler-Poincaré formula:

$$V - E + F - L = 2(P - H)$$

where V = number of vertices; E = number of edges; F = number of faces; H = number of holes; P = number of distinct parts of object and L = number of loops inside the faces not connected with the exterior contour of the faces.

Various combinations of faces, edges and vertices can be added to or deleted from the structure (topology), whilst retaining the ability to verify this formula. Local operations (or Euler operations) involve carrying out additions to and deletions from the topology. These are facilitated by the separation between geometry and topology.

The operations defined below are Euler operations:

CAS: construction of an edge and a vertex ($A = A + 1, S = S + 1$)
CAF: construction of a face and a vertex ($F = F + 1, A = A + 1$)
CFFST: construction of two faces and deletion of a hole ($F = F + 2, T = T - 1$)

### *3.3.4.4 Boolean operations*

These operations allow solids to be constructed from basic solids or possibly from half-spaces (see Figure 3.34). The model can maintain this information using a construction tree (see section 3.3.3); however, the tree must be evaluated to obtain a limit model that approaches the quality required for graphics. If the leaves of the construction tree are considered as basic objects, the evaluation consists of:

1. approaching the basic objects with the chosen limit representation;
2. evaluating the construction tree by carrying out the operations and 'climbing', ie with each node (designating an operation) it is possible to associate a similar solid until the solid which results from the tree is formed (standard algorithmic processing of a tree).

These operations are quite complex and are expensive to carry out because they require numerous comparisons to be made. Some of the aspects to be taken into account are considered below in an example

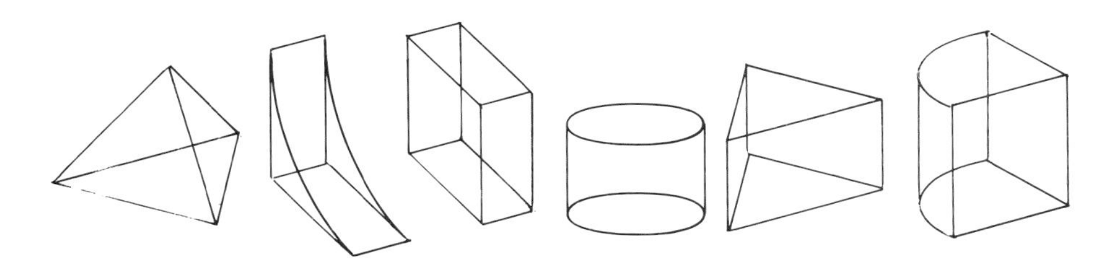

**Figure 3.34.** *Simple shapes (after Braid, 1974)*

concerning the joining of two solids (A and B), the faces, edges and vertices of which are known. First consider a specific case in which two objects, A and B, have faces placed in juxtaposition (sticking operation). In this case, once a pair of faces that touch has been determined, the operation is local to these faces and their adjacent faces, and all the edges of the resulting object remain parts of the edges (or complete edges) of the original objects. Now, let $F_A \in A$ and $F_B \in B$ be two adjacent faces. The algorithm is originated by two basic processes:

1. Each edge of $F_A$ is compared with each edge of $F_B$. When two edges intersect, they are broken up and a new vertex is formed. This vertex is marked as being common to $F_A$ and $F_B$. If the edges are superimposed, or if they intersect at an existing vertex, the vertices concerned are also marked as being common.
2. The edges, both complete and broken, are then assembled. Overall, when two contours intersect, the edges (complete or broken) are added by passing from $F_A$ to $F_B$ each time a common vertex is encountered, until the new contour is closed.

In the general case, each edge and each face of A and B must be compared using edge/face comparisons. To avoid unnecessary comparisons, as many as possible are eliminated using filters (eg by using the sphere test which consists of comparing the faces of an object with the sphere surrounding the other object). Overall, the algorithm functions in the same way as in case 1, ie:

1. by breaking up the edges if necessary and marking the common vertices; however, the structure to be managed and the tests to be applied are more complex;
2. by reassembly, which allows the faces of the resulting object to be created.

It must be stressed that this whole presentation hides many problems, in terms of the basic operations (eg processing all possible face–edge intersections using high performance algorithms), as well as at the reassembly level, in which the number of cases to be processed is significant. Many specific cases must be tested in Boolean operations. Figure 3.32 shows, for example, that the result of the intersection of two faces can be an edge. Thus, the intersection of two objects can produce a face. The algorithms must be written so as to ensure coherence, so that, for example, two solids produce a solid.

### 3.3.5 EXAMPLES OF MODELS

In this section a number of three-dimensional geometric models will be discussed, in order to illustrate the concepts described.

### 3.3.5.1 *A solid model*

EUCLID is a CAD/CAM software package including a 'solid' type model (see Matra Datavision Report, 1982; Brun, 1983). The first version of EUCLID, developed in 1970, was organized around a data structure in the central memory which was common to all the algorithms; it was presented as a symbiotic language, which extended the capacity of FORTRAN in algorithmic geometrics. The current version has been completely reshaped (EUCLID-80).

The 'virtual models' of EUCLID-80, constructed with the help of algorithms working in a data structure, are stored in a data base in the form of rehouseable blocks. These data base entities are 'exact', ie a circle is really a circle, and a rotational surface is encoded as such, whereas the algorithms work in a data structure on a set made up of an exact describer and a polygonal or polyhedral approximation. To find the point of contact, the exact descriptor is used, and to draw a circle, its polygonal approximation is used. Depending on the accuracy of the approximation, the result will be graphically 'pleasing' to a greater or lesser degree, and the time of execution will vary.

The work mode for which EUCLID-80 is best suited is an interactive graphic technique organized around a data base and containing the EUCLID data structure and geometric algorithms. The use of the EUCLID language provides a rapid and easy method of installing a CAD system; the basic interactive system is also written in EUCLID. This method of organization allows immediate use of polyhedrical algorithms for visual display or solids algebra, without excluding the possibility of subsequent development of these algorithms for the processing of exact descriptions stored in the data base.

It is possible to interactively construct an exact model, with a suggestive but inexact drawing, and to store it in the data base. During data base retrieval, a greater degree of precision can be requested, and the drawing will be accurate, with calculation time (which would interfere with the interactive work) no longer presenting a problem – particularly since it can be carried out by deferred processing which can even be performed overnight.

The 'data system plus language' unit is based on the creation and manipulation of a new type of variable: *the geometrics*. The geometric has the same number of bits as the floating point number – 32, 36, 48, or 60 bits, depending on the machine. For reasons of portability, the basic structure corresponds to 32 bits and allows forms containing up to 16,000 points to be created.

The EUCLID data structure is based on a set of tables and encoding, decoding, exploring and extracting functions. From the point of view of logic, the data structure is made up of information blocks and pointers between the blocks.

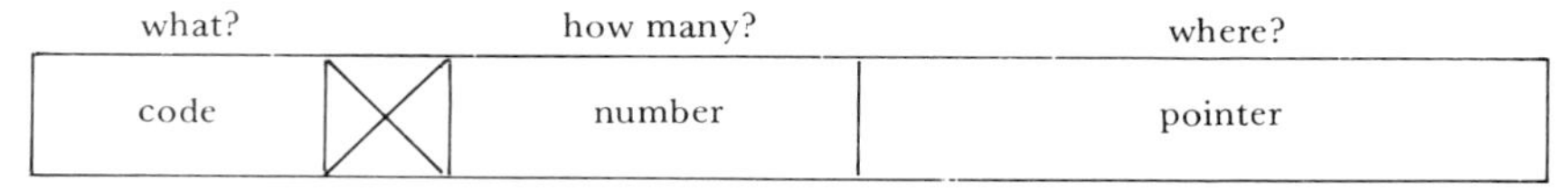


**Figure 3.35.** *EUCLID geometry*

A *geometric* is a word containing three basic pieces of information: a *code*, a *number* and a *pointer* (see Figure 3.35). The geometrics form a tree structure in which the number of levels can vary enormously. The exploration functions can be used in nested explorations (pseudo-recursion):

□ Start of exploration of *item 1*

*IEL* = number of *item 1* element in progress

Start of exploration of *item 2* (can be identical to *item 1*)

*IEL* = number of *item 2* element in progress

End of exploration of *item 2*

□ End of exploration of *item 1*

The overall structure can be schematized as shown in Figure 3.36. The double lines represent the main paths. Depending on the code, the pointer indicates the table of geometric elements (code: Fig as in Figure), the table of connections (code: Lin as in Line), or directly to the tables of coordinates (code: Pnt as in Point) (see Figure 3.37).

The development of the *figures of figures* allows a set to be compared progressively and without a theoretical limitation. The stack of interactive elements acts as a host language and provides access to all the elements created. In EUCLID programming, the role of this stack is devolved to the FORTRAN variables situated on the left of the '=' sign in EUCLID order. The connection between data structure and data base is ensured by a geometric with a special code, the *administrator*. Chaining of the type illustrated in Figure 3.38 is applied. It should be noted that there are named elements which are not stored. They have no associated transformation and complete the interactive elements to make up the interactive host language. When storing a figure including an administrator, it is sufficient to store its name and associated transformation, which shows the movement relative to the position of the part referred to in the data base. In this way the unity of the data base is ensured. The technological properties are stored in an independent table and can be created or modified *a posteriori* using simple functional operations, which, however, can give rise to structures with complex hierarchical properties.

A pointer to the 'father' allows the list of properties specific to the element to be completed by properties common to the set. In the table

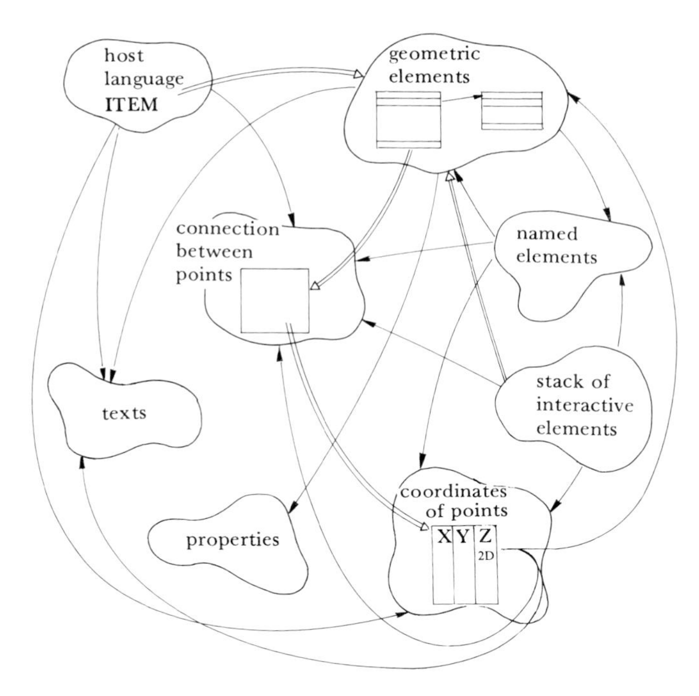


**Figure 3.36.** *Data structure*

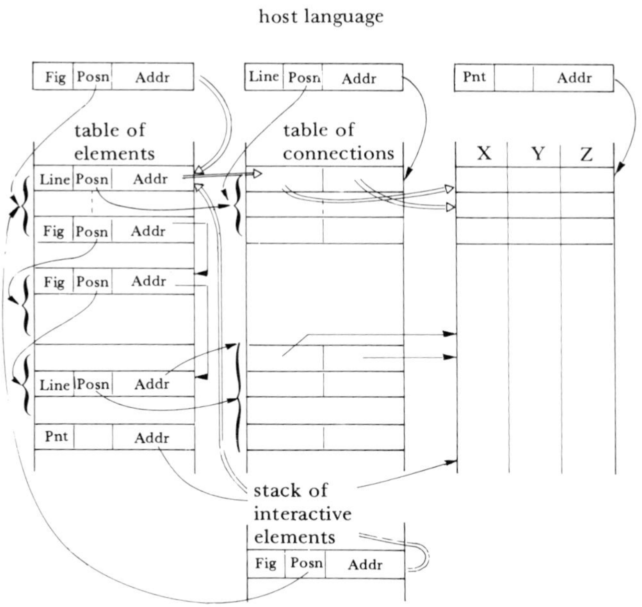

host language

Fig Posn Addr
Line Posn Addr
Pnt Addr
table of
elements
table of
connections
X Y Z
Line Posn Addr
Fig Posn Addr
Fig Posn Addr
Line Posn Addr
Pnt Addr
stack of
interactive
elements
Fig Posn Addr

**Figure 3.37.** *Schematic representation of the main pathway inside the data structure*

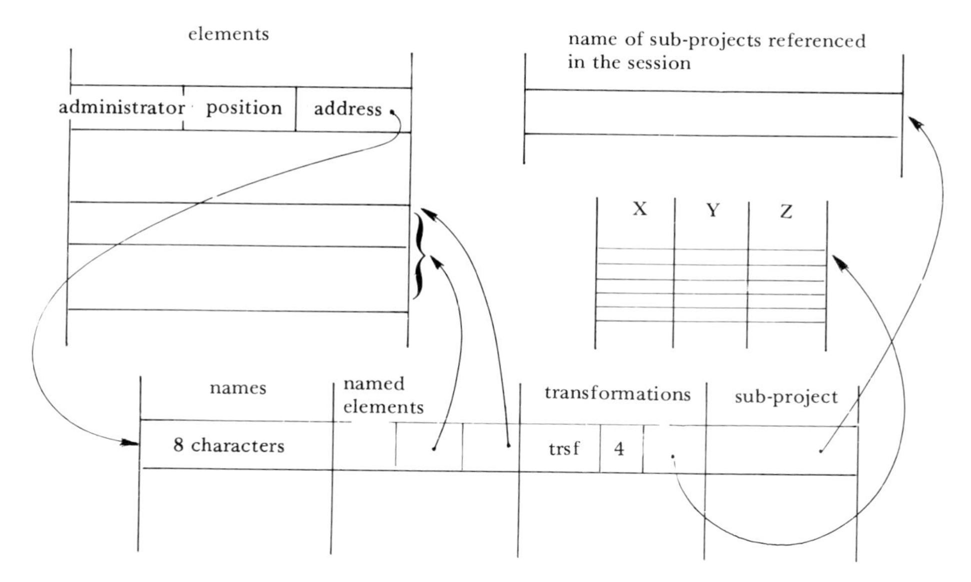


**Figure 3.38.** *Chaining the 'table of elements-table of names'*

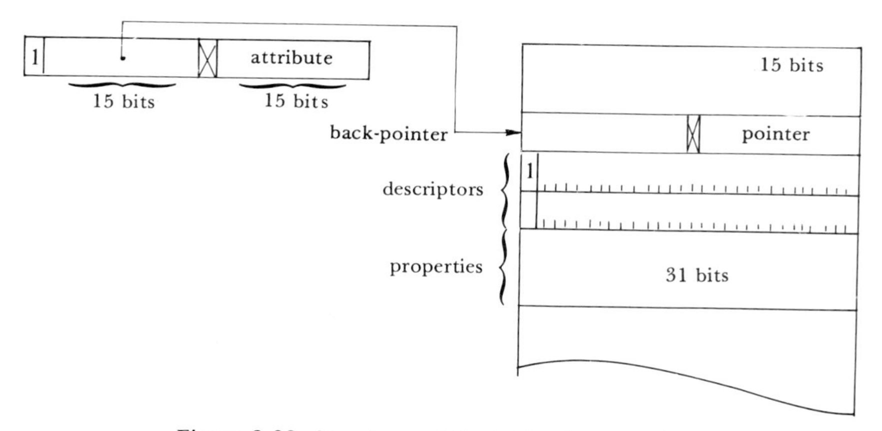


**Figure 3.39.** *Structure of the table of properties*

of properties (Figure 3.39), there is a header which shows the types of application encoded for this model (15 possible types), a pointer follows, and this allows undefined properties to be added during the initial encoding, as well as chained words which specify the properties attributed (1 bit per type of property).

A EUCLID text is processed as a special geometric. This points to a table of bytes in which the characters of the alphanumerical chain which comprise it are stored. This enables the formation of two-dimensional graphic symbols and enables them to be positioned by simple placement of special points which use the 'Z', or third coordinate, which is free in two dimensions, to point to the symbol created before.

### *3.3.5.2 Integration of models*

In this section the main characteristics of GRI 3D are described, mainly to show the diversity of models that can exist in conjunction with one another, since GRI 3D is a prototype, and not all of the functions described are operational (Gardan, 1983). The models are illustrated in Figure 3.40. The advantage of storing the construction methods has been noted. Objects constructed using contours (derived from the GRI 2D model), for example, are retained in their generator form. In this way, an object which is known by a contour and a depth could give rise to a family of objects, the parameters of which are the definition of the contour (the shape of the contour can be parametrized, either interactively or by language) and the depth.

The *visual display model* (see Figure 3.41) is limited by facets (flat or uneven). It consists of:

1. *for the geometry*:
   (a) coordinates of the points PE (X, Y, Z);
   (b) equations defining the surface on which each facet is based;
2. *for the topology*: sufficient information is presented to facilitate the use of algorithms, and the model retains:

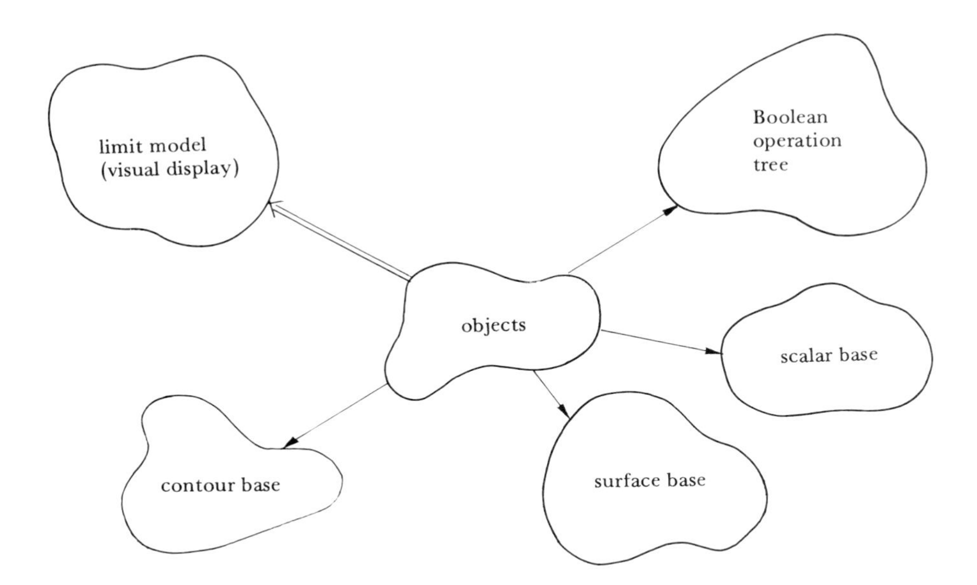


**Figure 3.40.** *Schematic model of GRI 3D*

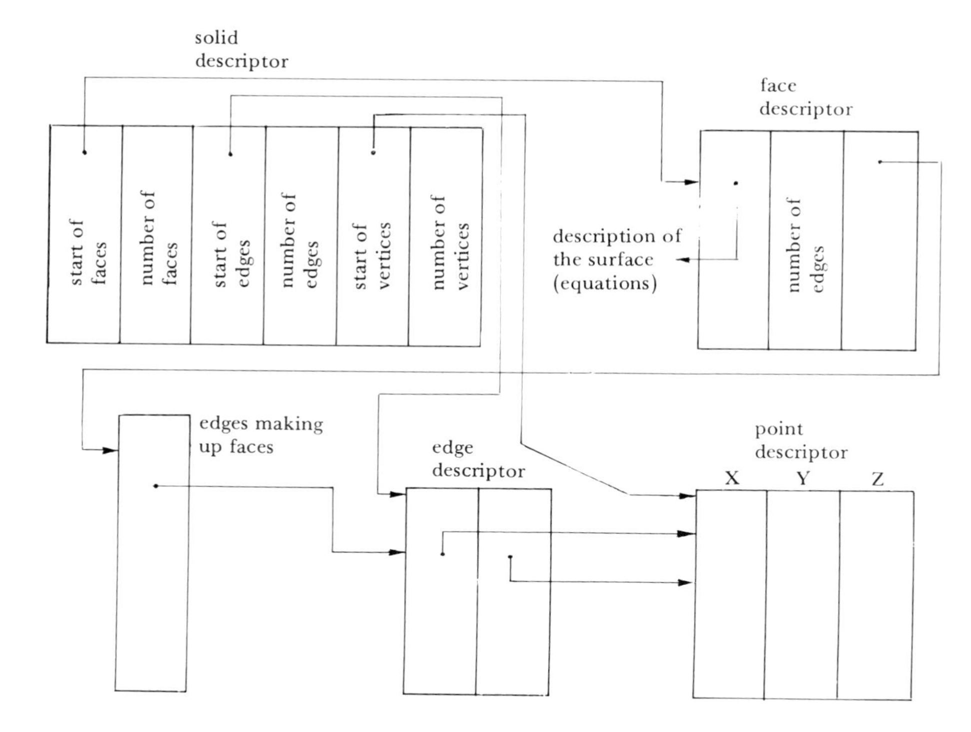


**Figure 3.41.** *Visual display model GRI 3D*

(a) A (S) edges as a function of the vertices;
(b) F (A) facets as a function of the edges;
(c) O (F) object as a function of the facets.

The topology is represented by an oriented graph. The contour of a facet is oriented such that the side of the facet on which the material of the modelled object lies is evident. The objects considered in this model have a property whereby one face determines the 'material' side and the 'empty' side:

$$(x, y, z)/f(x, y, z) \leqslant 0$$

The *solid descriptor* allows the following to be recognized:

1. the start of the description of the faces limiting the solid in the face descriptor;
2. the number of faces;
3. the start of the description of the edges;
4. the number of edges in the solid;
5. the start of the description of the vertices;
6. the number of vertices in the solid.

The *face descriptor* contains:

1. the address of the surface geometry description;
2. the address of the geometry of the edges of which it is made up;
3. the number of edges of which it is made up.

The *edges* which make up a face are contained in a table which addresses the edge descriptor containing the points of origin and extremity for each edge.

The *edge descriptor* points to the point coordinate description table. With the encoding conventions, it is possible to take into account, the fact that an edge of a given face is not covered in the direction recognized by the edge descriptor, but rather in the opposite direction (the Moebius rule can be managed).

### *3.3.5.3 Mathematical representation*

To avoid the excessive combinations caused by the representation of many different entities (lines, circles, surfaces, solids, etc), some systems, such as SYSTRID 1 (Massabo *et al.*, 1979), are based on a single mathematical representation. This mathematical representation can be, for example, a polynomial approximation, ie two-dimensional in a ($i = 1, 2$) or three-dimensional ($i = 2, 3$) referential:

1. a *point* is defined by $P = [p^i]$
2. a *part of a curve* is defined by $C(u) = C^{i\alpha}\, b\alpha(u)$
   $$u \in (0, 1), \alpha = 1, \alpha \text{ maximum}$$
3. a *part of a surface* is defined by $S(u, v) = S^{i\alpha\gamma}\, b\alpha(u)\, b\gamma(v)$
   $$u \in (0, 1), \quad v \in (0, 1)$$
   $$\alpha = (1, \alpha \text{ maximum}), \quad \gamma = (1, \gamma \text{ maximum})$$
4. a *solid* can thus be defined by the set of surface sections delimiting it, with, for example, the normal for each surface oriented towards the exterior of the solid: $V = (S_k\,(u, v)/k = 1, n)$.

The polygons form a vectorial space for which several bases can be used. The basic advantage of this method of modelling entities is, of course, that it uses uniform processing for all entities. On the other hand, some entities must be approximated in order to be modelled (as is the case for circles, for example); methods such as the method of least squares can be used.

### *3.3.5.4 Basic methods simplified*

A model based on simplified elements can be useful if the problem under consideration involves positioning a number of solids. This is the case in architectural design of buildings. A building can be

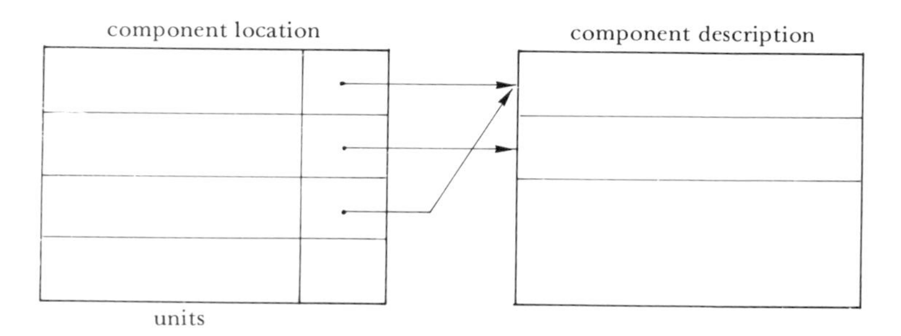


**Figure 3.42.** *Model based on component parts*

processed as if it were an assembly of boxes. This provides a model of the same type as the schema model, with an overall structure as shown in Figure 3.42. The description of a component will include, in the case of a building, information of the following type:

1. *The dimensions*: will show the space occupied by the component. This information can be used to verify the occupation of space and supplementary information can show which components can be combined with others.
2. *The presentation*: since all the components are approximated to boxes, it is possible to include views of the modelled object for each side of the box, eg the ARC system.

The description of the unit contains information necessary for the positioning of the components.

## 3.4 Communication between systems

Generally models created by one system cannot be used directly in another system. It has been shown that transfer from one type of model to another is not always possible. On another level, the use of data supplied to a CAD/CAM system A by another CAD/CAM system B is often required. This is the kind of constraint frequently met with by subcontractors to large companies (for example, automobile manufacturers) who use different CAD/CAM systems. The subcontractor would receive information from the company transmitted to him in computerized form. To cope with this, he must either buy each type of system used by the companies with which he works (a solution which is too costly to be feasible), or make use of means available for using the data provided by each company in conjunction with his own system.

This problem was solved a number of years ago when interfaces were developed for use between various systems. These interfaces were costly to develop, and still more costly to produce in relation to developments in systems and system requirements. Some businesses produced data structures instead with varying degrees of success, which made possible communication between systems. These constraints have given rise to a need to use a type of norm which allows communication to take place between systems with different origins (ie hardware and software). From the user's position, this norm makes it possible to:

1. use systems produced by different companies, and thus provide a degree of independence;
2. communicate both with clients and suppliers without any difficulty.

For the supplier this 'norm' can help enlarge his market. One way of facilitating this is to replace the step-by-step method of development shown in Figure 3.43 by a 'normalized' structure, in which, for each system, it would simply be a question of using a pre- and post-processor (see Figure 3.44). The second solution is the one adopted by Initial Graphics Exchange Specification (IGES). Without going into the details of the IGES, the main aspects of what could become a recognized norm can be summarized as follows. The basic unit of the IGES information structure is the *entity*, and the main types of recognized entity are:

1. *geometric entities*: points, lines, arcs, ruled surfaces, parametric entities, etc;
2. *notational entities (presentation and explanation)*: dimensions, evaluations, texts, presentation symbols, etc;
3. *structural entities*: relationships which may exist between the elements defining the product (groups, etc).

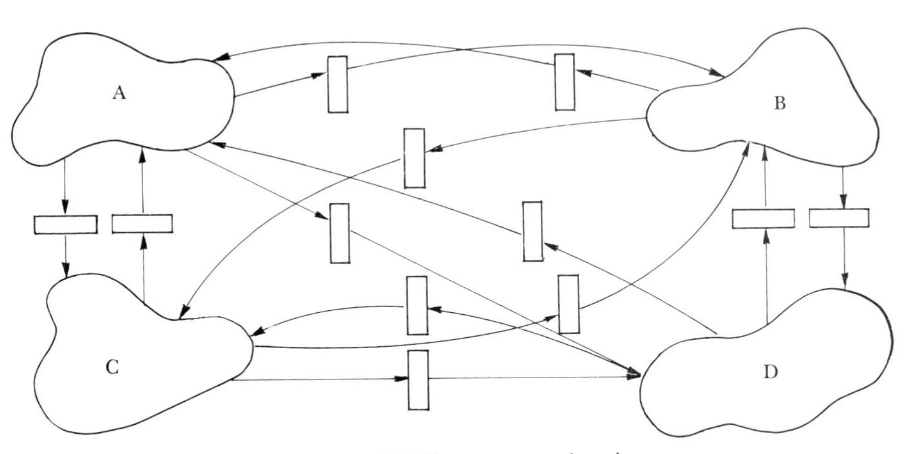


to establish communication between N different systems in pairs, N(N-1) interfaces are required; the addition of a new system requires 2N interfaces to be written

**Figure 3.43.** *Direct communication between systems*

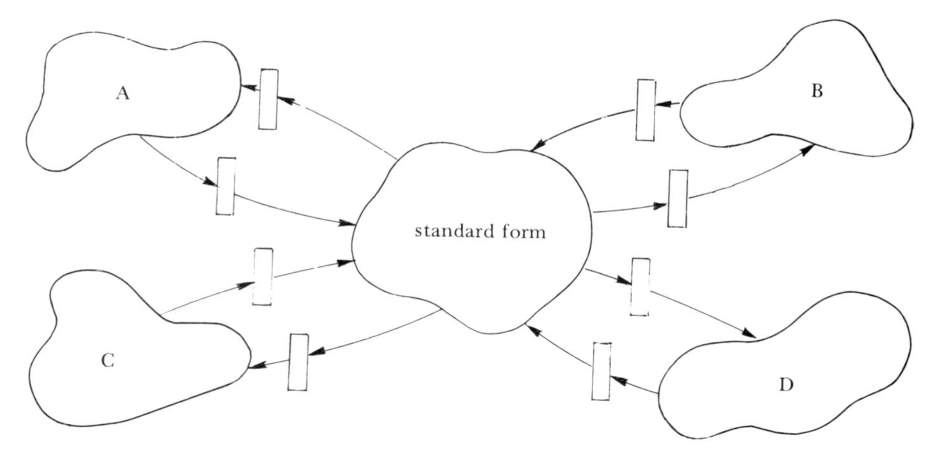


to establish communication between N systems in pairs, 2N interfaces are sufficient; addition of a new system requires only a further two interfaces (each pre- and post-processor can be associated with a model of its definition)

**Figure 3.44.** *Standardized communication between systems*

The format of these entities is independent of the application. The most important step in defining the IGES was to determine the entities to be taken into account with their format. Each entity is made up of a *repertoire* (of fixed length) and *parameter data* (of variable length). An IGES file is made up of 80 recorded characters, with the letter in column 73 identifying the membership of the recording (eg 'D' indicates that it belongs to the repertoire). The types of data recognized by the IGES are integer and real numbers, character chains, pointers – which are useful for showing that there is supplementary information in the file (eg from the repertoire to the data); or to reference an entity with another entity – and language instructions (character chains defining macro-instructions). Moreover, a free format can be used.

Overall, an IGES file contains:

1. '*Starting*' *section*: (S in column 73) this contains an introduction which can be read directly by the user (ASCII).

2. '*Whole*' *section*: (G in column 73) this contains information describing the pre-processor and the information a post-processor requires in order to handle the IGES file (eg the number of bits in the exponent and the mantissa with real, simple or double precision, the identification of the emitter system, the number of the IGES version, definition of the space, etc).

3. '*Repertoire*' *section*: (D in column 73) this contains information common to all entities in the file, and pointers to data sections or other repertoires.

4. *'Data' section*: (P in column 73) the contents of this varies with the entity:

(a) *geometric*: with the number of the entity (eg 100 = arc, 112 = spline, etc), state information (view, transformation matrix, depth of line, etc), geometric information (coordinates of the centre of an arc, starting and finishing points of an arc) and pointers (to properties and other entities, etc);

(b) *annotation*: with the number of the annotation, state information and pointers (to the entities and properties, etc);

(c) *visual display*: two entities (view and drawing) allow the visual display and the model to be separated. A view entity contains the vision cube, the chosen projection, etc; a drawing entity allows the equivalent of an industrial drawing plan to be produced from the result of 'view' operations;

(d) *structural*: the aim is to establish logical relationships between the entities. In particular, it is possible to define a new entity as a function of other entities from macro-instructions, in which the instructions for allocation (LET), definition (SET), repetition (REPEAT) and reference to other macro-instructions (MREF) are possible;

5. *End section*: (T in column 73).

Analysis of the IGES suggests that since this is a first attempt, it is hardly surprising that the IGES is unable to solve all problems. As with any norm used in this context, the use of the IGES means extra processing time. The designers of the IGES based the system on the state of the art at the time, and thus took into account only 'line' modelling and some aspects of 'surface' modelling. The question now arises of how a defined norm can keep pace with a technique such as CAD, which is developing so rapidly. (The situation is analogous to that of the CORE graphic norm, which encountered problems in taking task type terminals into account.)

Methods other than those used in the IGES can provide some communication between systems. It should be noted, for example, that GKS contains a concept of a graphic file (*metafile*). This file, although not part of the norm, has a normalized content and can be associated with certain attributes. It can thus be used as a link between different systems, although this is limited to the graphic aspects (at the level of preparation for visual display).

## 3.5 Use of models

A geometric model, as such, is not generally the final output of a CAD/CAM system. A model can be the result of a certain number of actions (calculations or interactive construction, for example) and can be used for a variety of functions, including simulation and plan output. However, given the complexity of the models and the operations to be performed (elimination of hidden parts and Boolean operations, for example), a CAD/CAM system is generally based on an established geometric model. Once this model has been selected according to the relevant criteria, it is associated with complex operations which are programmed in one definitive version. One of the essential qualities required of software for geometric modelling is that it should be 'open'.

A number of methods can be used to provide access to the model. In particular, it is possible to define primitives which can be called in a high level programming language, such as FORTRAN or PASCAL. These primitives will be called in the same way as sub-programs, and their parameters can be used to specify the data. The high level language used is frequently of the compiled type, which requires compilation and editing of the links during use. On the other hand, the full potential of the language can be used, because no modification or restriction is made. Some examples of the access operations to GRI 2D are shown below [each parameter has its type (E = integer, T = table, C = character) and mode (E = input, S = output, M = mixed) shown in parentheses].

```
MODULE
          UACGRO
FUNCTION
          ACCESS TO CURRENT VALUES OF GRAPHIC
          ATTRIBUTES OF SIMPLE GRI 2D OBJECTS
CALL
          CALL UACGRO (TEXTUR, THICKN, IO)
                 TEXTUR (E, M) TEXTURE OF OBJECTS
                               1- SOLID
                               2- DOTTED
                               3- SHORT DASH
                               4- LONG DASH
                               5- MIXED
                 THICKN (E, M) THICKNESS OF LINES
                               FROM 1 TO 3
                 IO (E, E) TYPE OF ACCESS
                           =2 TO BE MODIFIED
                           =1 TO BE READ
                    NO ACTION IF ERROR IN PARAMETERS

MODULE
          GRACIR
FUNCTION
          DISPLAY OF GRI 2D CIRCULAR
CALL
          CALL GRACIR (E, E) CIRCULAR REFERENCE TO A FILE
```

MODULE

UADOBJ

FUNCTION

ACCESS TO STRUCTURE OF OBJECTS (SEG, ARC, CIR)
TO READ OR MODIFY GRAPHIC ATTRIBUTES OF
THESE OBJECTS

CALL

```
CALL UADOBJ (TEXTUR, THICKN, TYPOBJ, IRFOBJ, IO)
        TEXTUR (E, M) TEXTURE OF LINE
                      1- SOLID
                      2- DOTTED
                      3- SHORT DASH
                      4- LONG DASH
                      5- MIXED
        THICKN (E, M) THICKNESS OF LINE
                      FROM 1 TO 3
        TYPOBJ (E, M) TYPE OF OBJECT TO BE PROCESSED
                      1- SEGMENT
                      2- CIRCLE
                      3- ARC
        IRFOBJ (E, M) REFERENCE OF OBJECT
                      <=0 ON RETURN=PROBLEM !
                      =0   NON-VALID REFERENCE
                      =-1 NON-VALID TYPE
                      =-2 NON-VALID TEXTURE
                      =-3 NON-VALID THICKNESS
        IO (E, E)     TYPE OF ACCESS
                      = 0 TO BE MODIFIED
                      = 1 TO BE READ
```

MODULE

UCRARC

FUNCTION

CREATION OF AN ARC IN ARC STRUCTURE OF GRI 2D

METHOD

THIS MODULE TRANSMITS THE GEOMETRIC ATTRIBUTES
OF AN ARC. THE GRAPHIC AND LOGIC ATTRIBUTES ARE
THE CURRENT VALUES ASSOCIATED WITH THE ARCS

CALL

```
CALL UCRARC (IRFPOI, RADIUS, ALPHA1, ALPHA2, IRFARC)

        IRFPOI (E, E)     REFERENCE OF CENTRAL POINT
                          OF THE ARC
        RADIUS (R, E)     RADIUS OF THE ARC
        ALPHA1, ALPHA2   (R, E) ORIGIN ANGLES AND EXTREME
                          ENDS OF THE ARC TAKEN IN POSITIVE
                          TRIGONOMETRICAL DIRECTION
        IRFARC (E, S)     REFERENCE OF ARC CREATED
                          <=0 NO CREATION
                          =0   NO SPACE
                          =-1 NON-VALID IRFPOI REFERENCE
```

```
MODULE
              UCRSEG
FUNCTION
              CREATION OF SEGMENT IN SEGMENT STRUCTURE OF GRI 2D
METHOD
              THIS MODULE TRANSMITS THE GEOMETRIC DESCRIPTOR OF
              A SEGMENT MADE UP OF THE REFERENCES OF THE TWO
              EXTREME POINTS OF THE SEGMENT. THE GRAPHIC AND
              LOGIC ATTRIBUTES ARE THE CURRENT VALUES ASSOCIATED
              WITH THE SEGMENTS
CALL
              CALL UCRSEG (IRFP1, IRFP2, IRFSEG)

                   IRFP1, IRFP2 (E, E) REFERENCES OF THE TWO POINTS
                                THAT FORM THE EXTREME ENDS OF
                                THE SEGMENT
                   IRFSEG (E, S) REFERENCE OF SEGMENT CREATED
                                <=0 NO CREATION
                                =0  NO SPACE
                                =-1 NON-VALID IRFP1 REFERENCE
                                =-2 NON-VALID IRFP2 REFERENCE
```

It is also possible to extend, syntactically and semantically, an existing programming language: this involves integrating geometry into the programming language. The result is that new types of variable are added to the types of variable already in the system. For example, in FORTRAN a geometric type variable is added to the integers, real numbers, and all the others. The format of the geometric variable depends on the implantations. In EUCLID, for example, a geometric variable may be effected by:

Cl = circle (A, B, C)

with A, B, C being geometric types. The circle can henceforth be recognized by its name Cl. The concepts used here may imply syntaxes which are not recognized in the host language, eg the number and types of non-fixed variables. Thus a circle may be defined by:

Cl = circle (A, B, C)
A, B, C are geometric types (three points)

Cl = circle (P, S, R)
P and S are geometric types (centre, surface)
R is a real type (radius)

Cl = circle (C, R)
C is a geometric type (centre)
R is a real type (radius)

This total integration into a high level programming language means that all the possibilities of the chosen language can be used. It can also impose limitations connected with the language itself. In FORTRAN, for example, the number of characters in a geometric variable is limited to six (this does not cause any problem), and these names may not start with I, J, . . . N, since these are translated entirely by FORTRAN. If the symbiosis between the high level language and the geometry is carried out thoroughly (ie by respecting the syntax of the host language), no modification of the compiler will be made (thus ensuring optimum portability), and will not be necessary, apart from an interface between the user commands and the FORTRAN program, to manage, for example, a list of variable length.

A specialized language can be used (usually of an interpreted type), created according to the circumstance. These languages may superficially resemble high level languages but are generally more limited from the point of view of the functions, and obviously oriented towards geometric modelling.

The types of data involved could be:

1. *scalar*: numerical value;
2. *chain*: character chain;
3. *vectors and matrices*: allowing representation of directions or geometric transformations;
4. *object*: basic geometric object (point, line, arc, etc);
5. *group*: set of geometric objects, etc.

The calculation functions are generally complete (—, +, *, /, etc) with classic syntax (A = B, A = B − C, etc). These operators can have an unusual meaning when the operands are of the geometric type. For example, A − B can mean the Boolean difference A and B if A and B are solids. Specific functions are also added (eg LONG (A) calculates the length of object A). Basic objects can be created using primitives: BOX (parallelipiped), CYL (cylinder), SPH (sphere), etc with the following type of syntax: CYL (base, axis, radius), where:

*base*: vector giving coordinates of the centre of the base of the cylinder;
*axis*: vector giving the axis of the cylinder;
*radius*: scalar giving radius of the cylinder.

Complex objects can be created using the instructions, thus:

OBJECT: CYL 1 = CYL 1 ((0, 0, 0), (0, 0, 4), 2) +
SPH 1 ((0, 0, 2), 4)

OBJECT is the union of the cylinder CYL 1, with the centre of its base at the origin (height 4 and radius 2) and the sphere SPH 1 with centre (0, 0, 2) and radius 4.

The commands are specific to the management of a model, eg display of an object, translation of an object, rotation of an object, or calculations relating to the model (mass, surface area, etc). Whatever type of language is chosen, its application can provide access to the model for reading or writing, and allow the construction of programs which may be highly complex. This is why the first use that was made of geometric models was in conjunction with batch processing. The user would program an application to create and modify the model, with the only outputs available being on to paper. The use of conversational alphanumerical keyboards gave rise to dialogue by messages and inputs of values, allowing a certain degree of interactivity to be associated with CAD/CAM applications. The use of these systems was simple, because the input of alphanumerical values was the only result of the dialogue.

Creating information for a model in interactive mode at a work station gives rise to many problems. Consider the definition of geometric shapes by language. It is clear that it will be necessary to carry out the following operations in interactive mode:

1. *choose an action*: type of object, type of constraint, . . . (MENU);
2. *give values*: these can either be exact (entered alphanumerically) or linked to the model (thus able to 'recognize' elements of the model);
3. *indicate objects*: these can either be 'named' (entered alphanumerically) or 'shown' (identification);
4. *indicate points*: these can either be explicit (by coordinates) or shown on the design (as intersections of two segments).

These interactivity constraints have lead to the development of programming environments that allow interactive techniques to be used. This type of environment also includes the set of tools described previously, as well as means (eg PRIMITIVES) of managing the interactivity. The primitives given below are dialogue primitives linked to GRI 2D and primitives linked to GRIGRI. For example, when using a menu, the choice of one or several functions from a set, to influence the conduct of the program, can be activated by the function: MENU (NB, LIST, TRETURN), where: NB = entire variable specifying the repetition factor; LIST = literal, constant or variable chain specifying the list of functions among which the user makes his choice; this chain is limited to 256 characters; and TRETURN = table of integers containing either numbers entered directly by the user or numbers associated with the designated functions.

The display is made, if at all, during the request for interaction in the following way. The names of the functions appear one under the other, starting from the top right-hand corner of the screen. They occupy a maximum of 1/9th of the width of the screen and disappear at the end of the menu activation. If a reply is incorrect, a new entry is requested. The graphic inputs (identification and coordinates) can be described by:

MODULE ENTGRA

FUNCTION

PROCESSING MODULE FOR GRAPHIC INPUTS. GRAPHIC INPUTS ARE THE COLLECTION OF COORDINATES AND/OR THE IDENTIFICATION OF OBJECTS VISIBLE ON THE SCREEN

METHOD

IF THE USER SPECIFIES COLLECTION OF COORDINATES THE MODULE SENDS THE COORDINATES FROM THE CURRENT USER SPACE, WHICH HAVE BEEN ENTERED WITH THE RETICULE, THE KEYBOARD OR TABLET.
IN THE CASE OF IDENTIFICATION, THE MODULE SCANS THE GRI 2D DATA STRUCTURE AND SENDS THE FIGURE NUMBER AND CORRELATION OF THE OBJECTS IDENTIFIED, TAKING INTO ACCOUNT THE VARIOUS CONSTRAINTS IMPOSED BOTH DURING THE CALL (SEE VARIABLE SIGN) AND BY THE USER DURING INTERACTION

APART FROM THE CONTROL CHARACTERS COMMON TO ALL INTERACTIVE FUNCTION, THE FOLLOWING VALIDATIONS CAN BE USED:

FOR ACQUISITION OF POINTS
- R COLLECTION WITH NO PARTICULAR CONSTRAINT
- V COLLECTION OF A POINT BY VERTICAL PROJECTION ON THE PRECEDING POINT
- H COLLECTION OF A POINT BY HORIZONTAL PROJECTION ON THE PRECEDING POINT
- X COLLECTION OF A POINT BY CALCULATION OF THE INTERSECTION OF TWO LINEAR OR CIRCULAR OBJECTS

FOR IDENTIFICATION
- I IDENTIFICATION WITH NO PARTICULAR CONSTRAINT
- P IDENTIFICATION OF A POINT
- C IDENTIFICATION OF A CIRCULAR OBJECT
- L IDENTIFICATION OF A LINEAR OBJECT
- M SEARCH FOR FOLLOWING OBJECT OF THE SAME TYPE AS THE OBJECT PREVIOUSLY IDENTIFIED

CALL

CALL ENTGRA (NB, IND, TX, TY, FIGN, ITFIG, ITCOR)

NB : MIXED INTEGER, CONTAINING IN INPUT THE MAXIMUM NUMBER OF ACQUISITIONS PERMITTED IN OUTPUT. IT CONTAINS THE NUMBER OF INPUTS REALLY EFFECTED. THE VALUE 0 IS STRONGLY DISCOURAGED

IND : INPUT INTEGER CONTAINING THE NATURE OF THE DESIRED ACQUISITION
= 1 COLLECTION OF COORDINATES
= 2 IDENTIFICATION OF OBJECT
= 3 IDENTIFICATION OR COLLECTION

TX, TY : REAL OUTPUT TABLES CONTAINING THE USER COORDINATES OF THE POINTS COLLECTED

```
FIGN     :  INPUT INTEGER CONTAINING POSSIBLE
            RESTRICTIONS ON THE IDENTIFICATION
            OBJECTS
            = 0     NO RESTRICTIONS
            = VAL   CONSTRAINTS ARE IMPOSED ON
                    THE TYPE OF OBJECT. IF THE
                    1 ST BIT OF THE CODE IS EQUAL
                    TO 1, ANY TYPE 1 OBJECT IS
                    IDENTIFIABLE.
            HERE IS THE LIST OF THE TYPES OF
            OBJECT:

              1   CIRCLES, ARCS
              2   SEGMENTS, STRAIGHT LINES
              3   POINTS
              4   CONTOURS
              5   CROSS HATCHING
              6   EVALUATIONS (GEOM.
                  DEFINITION)
              7   EVALUATIONS (ALPHANUM.
                  DEFINITION)
              8   TEXTS
              9   ARROWS

ITFIG    :  TABLE OF OUTPUT INTEGERS,
            CONTAINING, IN THE CASE OF
            IDENTIFICATION, FIGURE NUMBERS OF
            THE OBJECTS IDENTIFIED

ITCOOR   :  TABLE OF OUTPUT INTEGERS WITH
            EITHER 0 IN THE CASE OF COLLECTION,
            OR THE CORRELATION NUMBER OF
            THE OBJECT, IN THE CASE OF
            IDENTIFICATION
```

To summarize, the application of a model can be of:

1. *batch processing type*: the programs enable a model (the subsequent use of which is not defined) to be created;
2. *conversational type*: the parameters, generally alphanumerical, can be provided conversationally;
3. *interactive type*: the tools allow the model to be displayed and manipulated in a totally interactive manner.

Generally, the programming methods and a certain number of tools (allowing the model to be used by an operator who is not trained as a computer specialist) are associated with a geometric model. It is thus common for a model to be formed by calculations before it is modified interactively. Models with associated dialogue tools can be of great use.

## 3.6 Conclusions

There has been considerable progress in geometric modelling recently. Solid modelling is still being developed. It must again be stressed that this chapter has been concerned, not with visual display, but with modelling. The distinction between the two is frequently forgotten.

It appears that the problems that remain unsolved are connected with concepts of integration, and possibilities of managing several types of model in one system. A geometric model is frequently very effective for modelling an object, but in most cases, a very large number of objects must be modelled. This clearly poses problems, since the number of objects to be handled strongly influences the performance of some algorithms, as is the case with the elimination of hidden parts. The fundamental constraint appears, however, with management of graphic and non-graphic data, for example, in the management of an assembly, in which the evaluation chains and statistics must be allocated.

It is clear that the use of different models, with computer representations specific to each supplier, presents problems of compatability between systems. This is particularly important for subcontractors. A certain amount of work has been carried out to introduce procedures for information exchange between systems, but the solutions available are of a low level in relation to the improvements brought about in the quality of models.

CAD/CAM systems which manage geometric models have, up until the present, retained this model as '*the model of the object*', restricting themselves on occasion to models similar to visual display models. The integration of geometric data into a larger and more complete model of an object, from the point of view of physical properties, is one of the important developments to be expected in the future. This integration will make use of software tools (data base management systems adapted for CAD/CAM) and the evolved hardware which should then be available (terminals, local networks, multi-microprocessors, etc). The management of models of an object will allow an integrated approach to CAD/CAM, from design and planning of an object, through to its manufacture and use.

*Chapter 4*

# Visualization techniques

## 4.1 Different types of graphic representation

To fully understand the problems posed by certain types of graphic representation, it is useful to create a number of classifications. The technical progress made in the last few years, both in hardware and software, now provides access to all the graphic techniques currently in use. An object can be represented in a number of different ways, according to the design stage reached. This is illustrated in Figure 4.1, which shows the different steps taken during construction of a group of buildings:

1. positioning the buildings on the site, using simple schematization for the installation of the blocks;
2. perspective view of a group of buildings;
3. schema of a living unit, with symbolic representation showing some elements of furnishing;
4. plan of an apartment;
5. plan showing the functional definition of an apartment, based on the requirements of the occupants.

The need for graphic software functioning on different levels is clear: the positioning of a building on a site is a pure two-dimensional exercise, whereas the view of a group of buildings demands processing of a three-dimensional scene. In the same way, it is easy to appreciate that the program used for visual display of a plan is quite specific to this application, and thus constitutes a particular module. The other graphic representations all use the same basic graphic unit: the line. This is not adequate if, for example, a realistic representation of the site and buildings is to be produced – in this situation it is necessary to use colours and coloured dots to create an illusion of a photograph of a real site. This distinction leads to a clear differentiation between the two types of graphic representation:

1. *line drawings*, which are basically made up of straight lines, and sometimes conics, arcs, circles or ellipses;
2. *pictures*, which are made up of a number of simple points (pixels)

positioning the buildings on the site

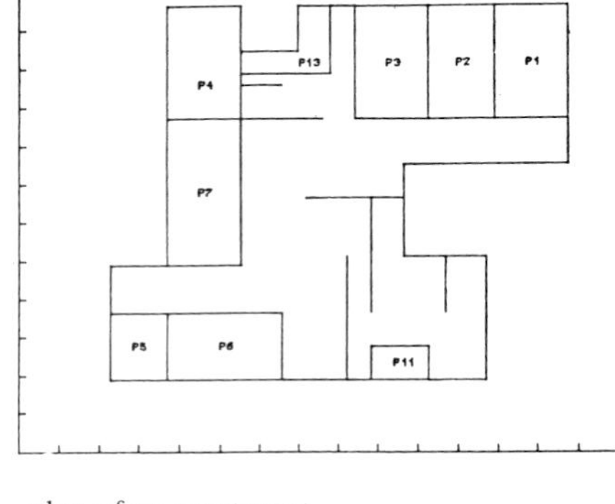


plan of an apartment

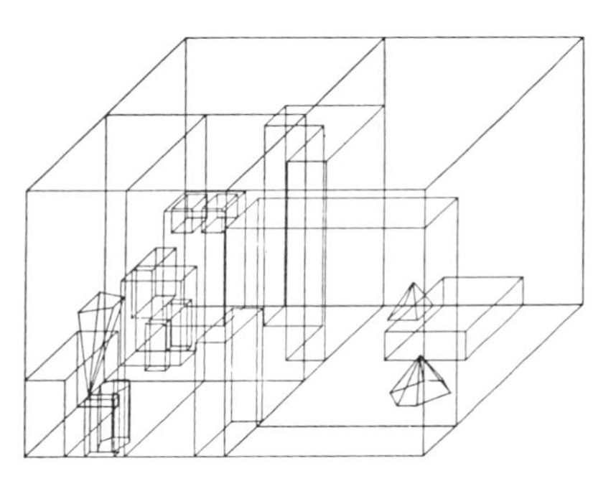

schema of a living unit

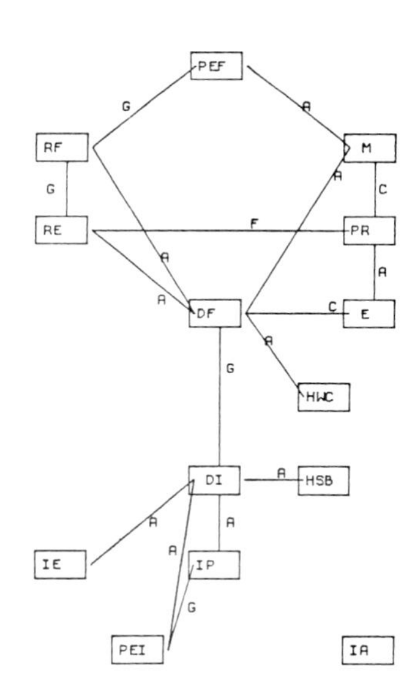


graph showing the functional definition of an apartment

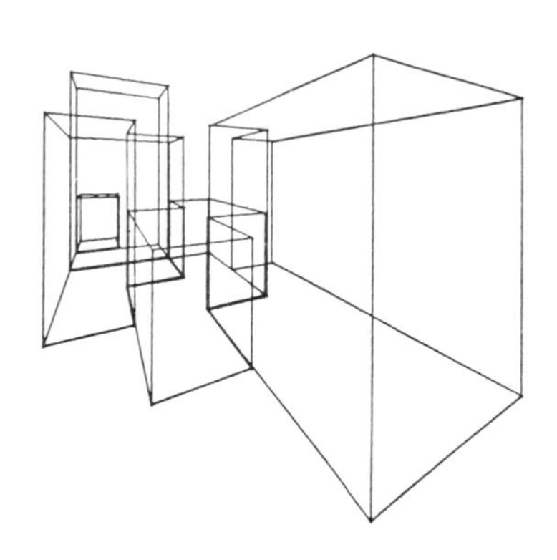

perspective view of a group of buildings

**Figure 4.1.** *Different representations of an object*

which correspond to an elementary square addressable on a graphic screen. By allocating a colour to each of the points on the screen, areas of colour can be built up, and a graphic representation based on dots can be produced.

These two types of representation can be associated with specific types of hardware for visual display, and there are two corresponding types of screen surface which relate to them:

1. *surfaces for line drawing*, used in calligraphic plotting and tracers;
2. *dot surfaces*, such as those used in television screens or electrostatic scanners.

This fact suggests that the two types of hardware are opposed and mutually exclusive, in that the display techniques are not similar. However, if a high quality image is not essential (particularly during the design process), a certain degree of independence relative to the hardware is possible.

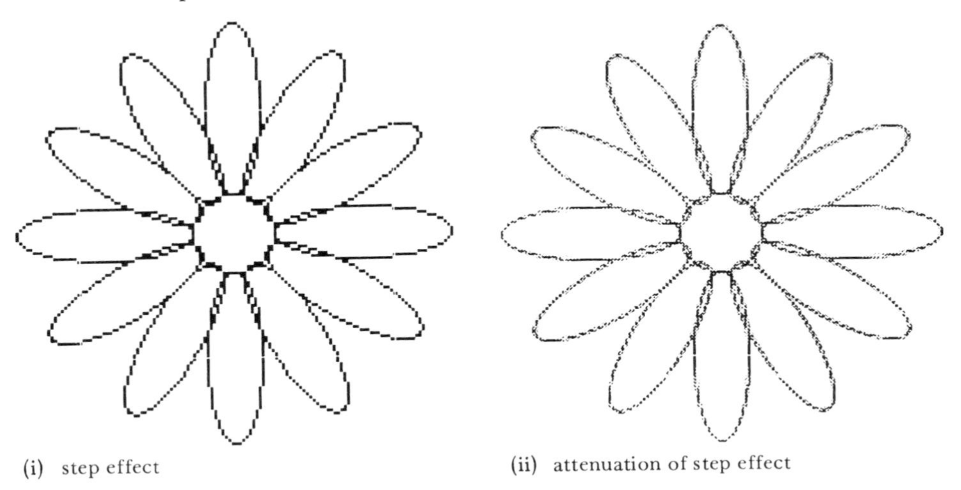

(i) step effect (ii) attenuation of step effect

**Figure 4.2.** *Attenuation of the step effect*

Any line drawing can be displayed on a raster screen. The main problem with this type of surface is that the resolution is often poor, and step effects become obvious when straight lines are displayed. This fault can, to a large extent, be attenuated using a few tricks of calculation (see Figure 4.2), and can effectively be overcome if high resolution screens are used. If only a few colours are needed, and if the particular colours are not significant, these representations can be simulated on vector screens, using cross-hatching to show the areas of colour (see Figure 4.3). If monochrome representation, with different levels of grey, is adequate, they can be simulated even on a screen

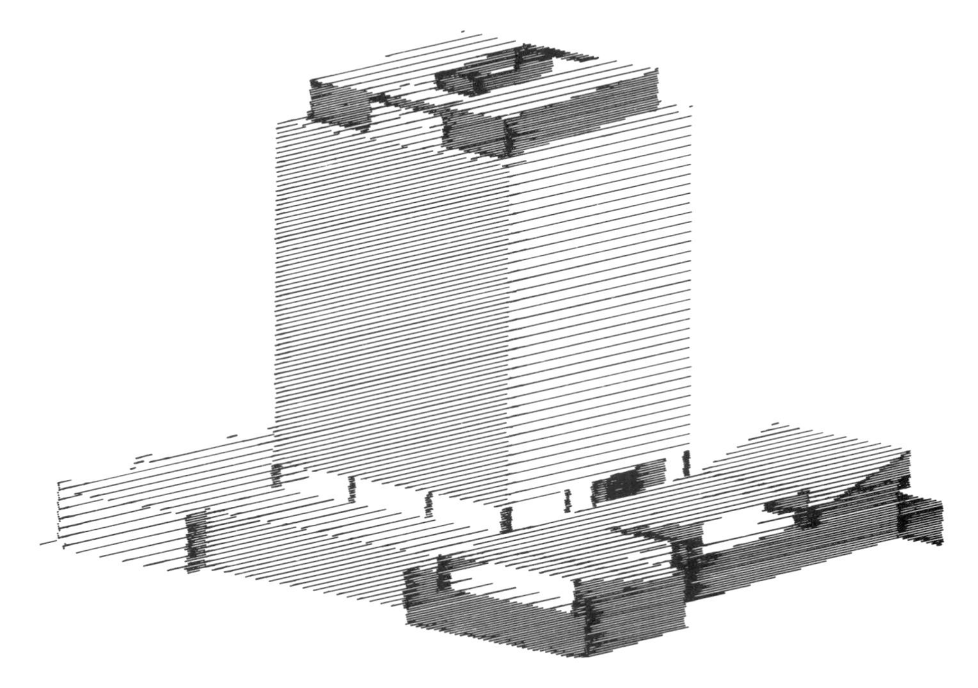

**Figure 4.3.** *Simulation of colour using cross-hatching*

which only provides an on/off facility for the dots (see Figure 4.4). However, some applications cannot be carried out; for instance, if perfect plans are to be produced, only vector screens will supply perfect lines, or if realistic pictures are to be produced, a high quality raster screen must be used.

### 4.1.1 TOOLS OF GRAPHIC REPRESENTATION

The tools of graphic representation can be grouped into:

1. *construction graphics*, with which objects to be processed and modified can be defined;
2. *comprehension graphics*, with which the relationship between objects or their properties can be clearly explained;
3. *communication graphics*, which allow the designer to engage in a dialogue with the machine in order to establish the documents intended for interested personnel (clients, research departments, etc).

Figure 4.5 illustrates the roles of these different types of graphic techniques:

1. construction graphics establish a link between user and machine;

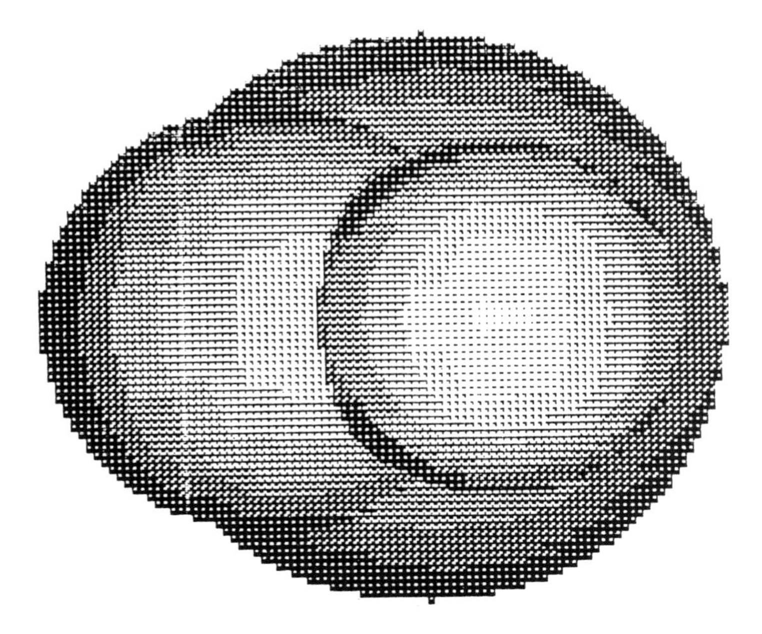

**Figure 4.4.** *Simulation of levels of grey*

2. comprehension graphics establish a link between the computer and the designer;
3. communication graphics establish a link between the interested personnel.

The interest in studying these categories of representation is clear, even though in absolute terms their application is closely connected, and the software involved is not totally separated. Visual display algorithms are adapted to the models which process the objects. A particular external aspect can thus be due to very different calculation techniques, depending on the complexity of the model. Moreover, depending on the modelling primitives, the graphic representations that can be calculated will not always achieve the same degree of completion in a given time.

The main characteristic of technological development in recent years has been the development from a relatively poor, schematic representation, based on line drawings, to a more sophisticated version which makes use of all the potential for graphic expression, based on the control of all the graphic parameters, starting with models that take into account light effects.

Two areas can be distinguished:

1. The use of *false colour*: ie the relatively arbitrary association of a colour with the value of a given parameter. The variations in this

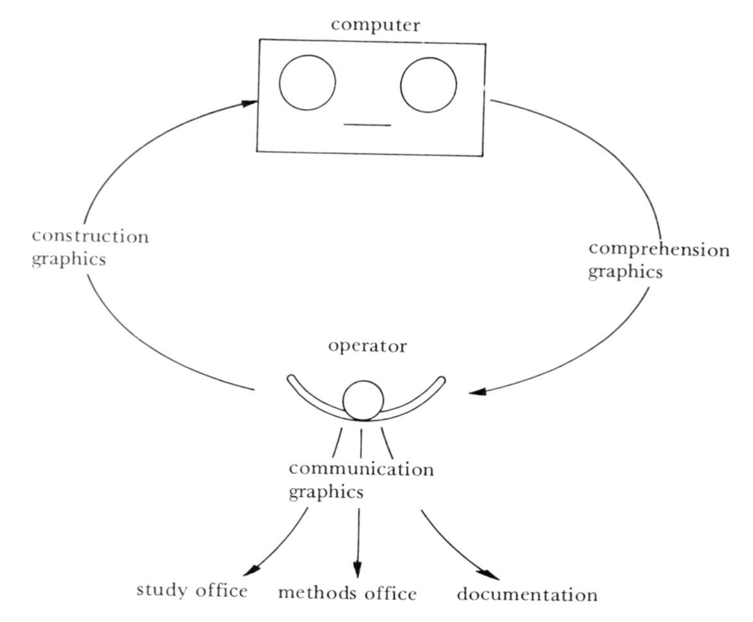


**Figure 4.5.** *The roles of the different types of graphic technique in CAD/CAM*

parameter are shown by variations in the colour (or level of grey) which enables the critical thresholds to be distinguished in a mass of data. This technique is useful in mechanical simulations, or with schematic representations of kinematic chains, in which the distribution of stress applied to the parts (eg to torsion bars) or, in fluid mechanics, the rate of flow can be assessed.

2. The use of *realistic images*, with which a three-dimensional object can be rendered on the screen in a realistic manner: the simplest versions of this technique correspond to standard representation of three views. Even though the use of more elaborate techniques, such as perspective projection, has allowed better representations of objects to be made, only the elimination of hidden parts and the simulation of light effects have lead to the production of images which are easy for the user to interpret. The development of realistic images has been through the following stages:

(a) line representations with isometric or true perspective projection;

(b) line representations with elimination of hidden lines (currently the most common technique);

(c) picture representation with elimination of hidden surfaces and consideration of the light source by the model which shows shadows on each face (but without taking into account other faces, so no shadows which result from the other faces are shown), calculation of reflection, etc;

(d) consideration of the behaviour of light by taking into account transparency, opalescence and translucence, etc;

(e) influence of the nature of the surface of an object (smooth, grained, uneven) on the reflections;

(f) calculation of textures, to take into account the geometric motifs or variations in colour due to the nature of whatever covers the surface of an object.

All these techniques have now been mastered and are in use, for instance, during the production of many advertising films and animated drawings produced by computer. At present, the best finished images from the point of view of realistic representation require hours of calculation on VAX type computers, to such an extent that some film production companies have acquired CRAY 1s to help produce such pictures quickly. These types of image can, however, also be created using current CAD/CAM systems — as the colour plates included between pages 144 and 145 prove.

## 4.2 Comprehension graphics

### 4.2.1 BASIC REPRESENTATIONS

Comprehension graphics give sets of data describing the object or group of objects being designed a true visual meaning. Using various graphic representations, the designer can access the progress of the work at any time, and using the software can gain access to any scene required. This type of software must allow the organization of the different elements in the image to be seen, analysed and understood. The available commands can be classified into the following categories:

1. Commands for the *composition* of the scene to be observed: these allow the initial scene to be defined and a sub-set to be extracted in order to simplify it, or else a scene to be created and studied using cross sections.
2. Commands for *positioning* in space, to permit variation in the angle of observation: the operator can request rotation about the three coordinate axes, specify an observation point or give the values of the three Euler angles.
3. Commands for *scene presentation*, allowing the observer to choose a mode of observation with orthogonal projection, or perspective projection with possible elimination of hidden parts.
4. Commands for *scene analysis*, allowing information concerning the dimensions and composition (vertices, faces, etc) to be obtained.
5. Commands for the *modification of the scene*, allowing incorrect values (vertex coordinates, colour, order or faces, etc) to be modified.

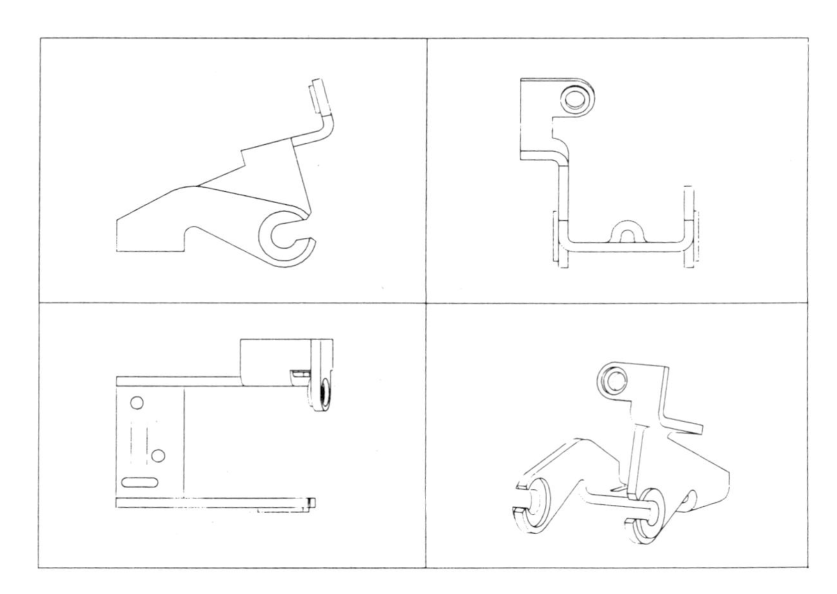

**Figure 4.6.** *Four views of an object*

It should be noted that no mention has been made of the possibility of modifying the structure of the scene itself. The only operations allowed are geometric transformations, which do not affect the data structure. No element of the description can be added or suppressed; this is reserved for construction graphics. This illustrates the fact that software can be unconnected (the comprehension software has no information concerning the construction of the scene, and has no way of modifying it) or else closely linked (which permits highly interactive work to be carried out). This relates to another choice concerning the structure of the visual display system, and each solution has its advantages and disadvantages.

To these commands are added those for establishing a page format, which allow different views to be displayed on the screen at the same time, so that they can be studied simultaneously. Figure 4.6 shows four views of the same object; this allows simultaneous analysis of the arrangement of the elements involved. The commands for page format can make a part of the scene to be observed correspond to an area on the screen. The basic mechanism is known as *association of a window with a viewport* (see Figure 4.7): the *window* is a section of the user space and the *viewport* is a section of the screen space. This mechanism can provide two complementary work modes:

1. simultaneous screen display of several views of one object, or of different objects, to aid visual comparison;
2. change of scale in one part of the graphic representation, to allow

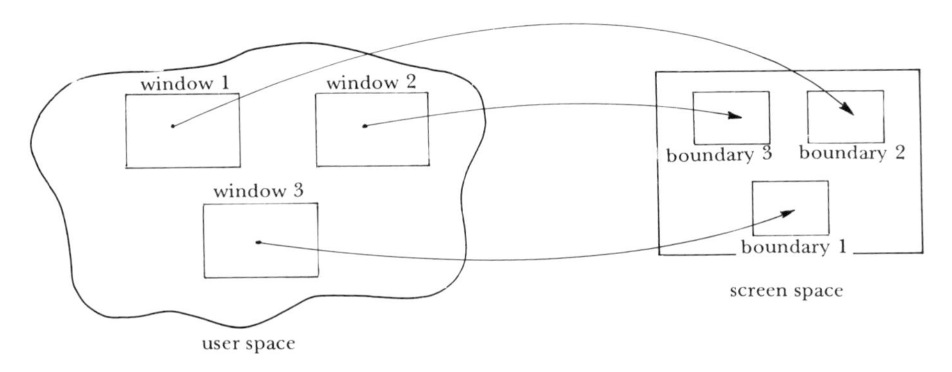


**Figure 4.7.** *Association of a window with a viewport*

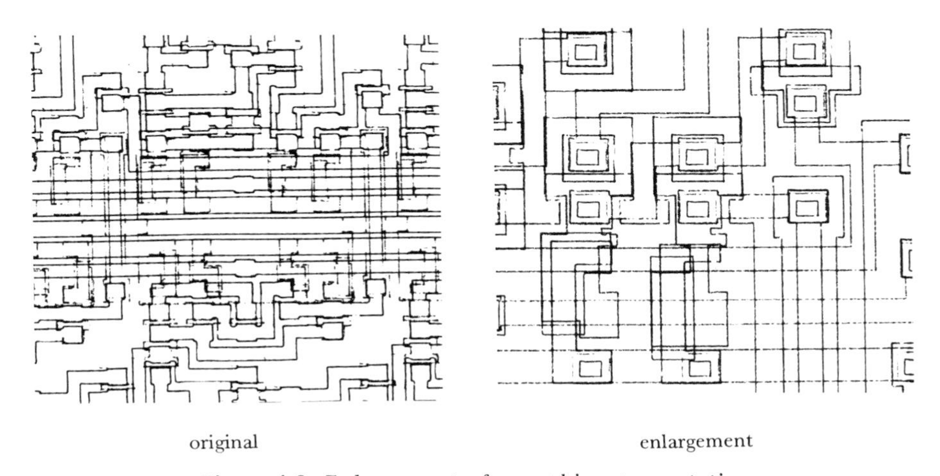


**Figure 4.8.** *Enlargement of a graphic representation*

details to be observed more closely (see Figure 4.8). This technique is used when the designer wishes to see a part of a scene in detail – particularly useful at the modification stage. The use of judiciously chosen windows and viewport helps to overcome the disadvantages of having a small screen relative to the size of the objects or plans.

There are several variations on the page format system: the layout of the screen can be fixed, either by the system (eg four boxes, used successively in a predetermined order) or at the discretion of the operator, who can design the page format interactively.

The format of the contents can be determined at each request for visual display by the designer, or can correspond to standard representations. Thus, the presentation of three views is generally the result of a single command (see Figure 4.9). In some systems a repertoire of

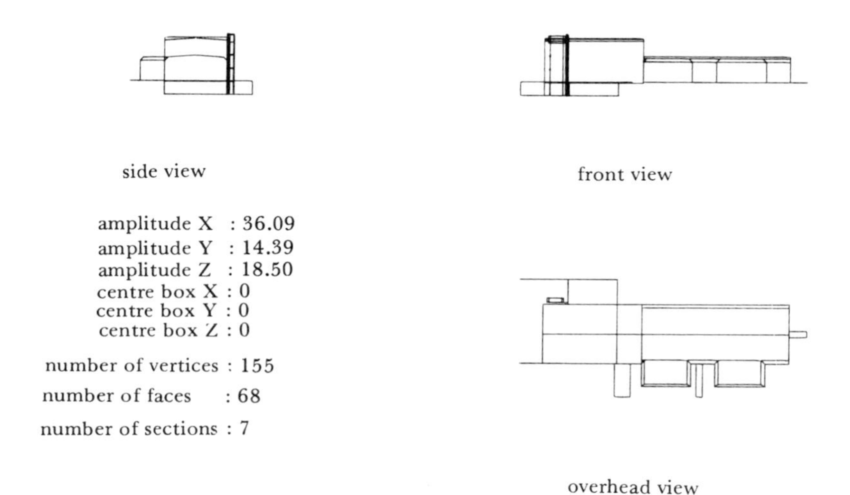


**Figure 4.9.** *Representation of three views of a building*

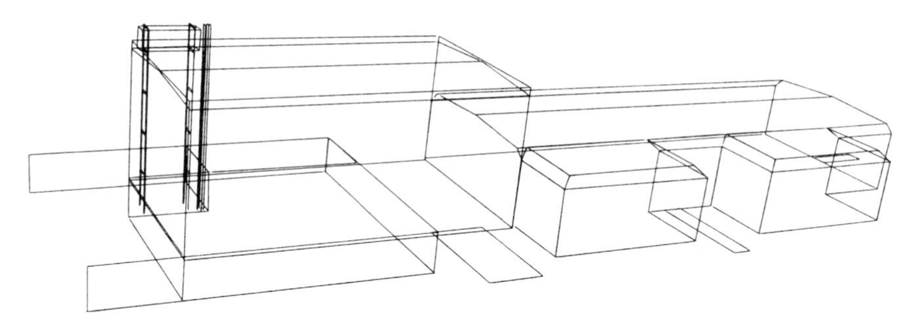

**Figure 4.10.** *Line representation of a building*

views can be composed, which correspond to the information data on the position, orientation and mode of representation for a given object. In addition to the standard types of representation, the operator can thus define a number which are specific to him (eg the same object seen from different predetermined angles). Each presentation is obtained using a single command, which replaces the data of all the commands stored by the system.

The starting point for visual display calculations is the geometric model. Depending on its complexity, this model can be the basis for the development of simple or complex graphical representations. Thus, a 'wire-frame' model, made up only of vertices and lines, will only provide data for a line drawing type representation, in which all the vertices are shown (see Figure 4.10). The comprehension commands can assist interpretation of this type of representation, by allowing the observer to view an object from various angles (see Figure 4.11)

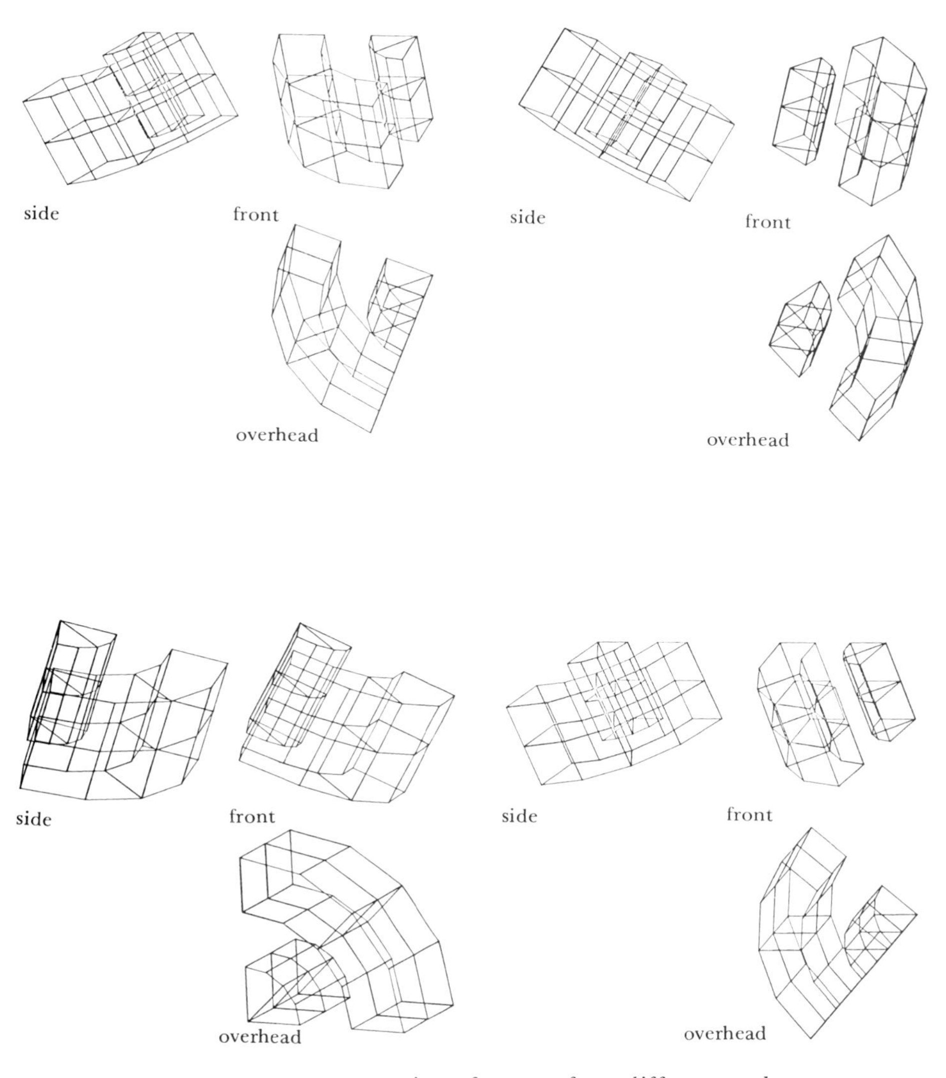


**Figure 4.11.** *Representation of a scene from different angles*

or by providing specific graphic techniques. It is possible, for example, to use perspective projections which give an appearance of depth (see Figure 4.12). Consideration of spatial positioning can also be made easier by cutting a segment at its point of intersection with another segment, situated in front (see Figure 4.13). This technique is often impracticable because of the extent of the calculations involved, and because the image presented becomes cluttered and thus confusing to view. The wire-frame type representation is very widely used, for several reasons:

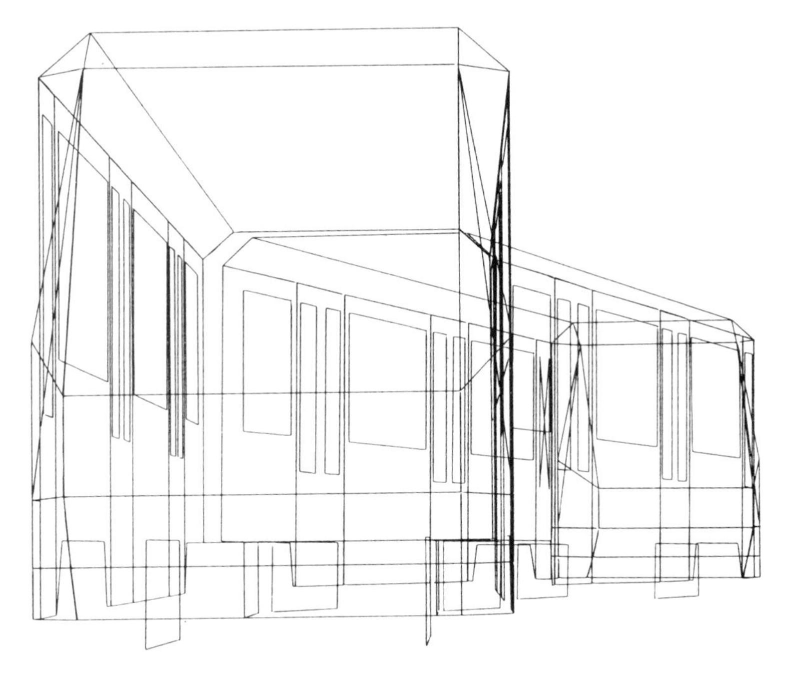

**Figure 4.12.** *Effect of perspective*

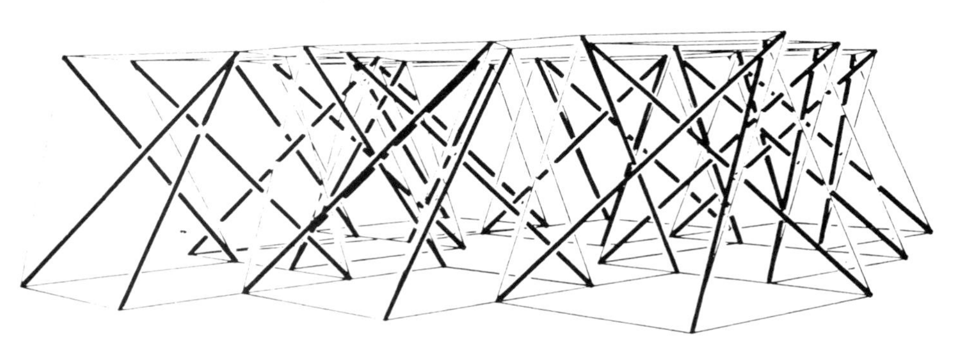

**Figure 4.13.** *Representation of a double spatial surface with squared links*

1. it is easy to calculate and representations can rapidly be produced on the screen;

2. it can be used in most modules, both for skew surfaces (see Figure 4.14) and flat facets – it is always possible to calculate edges from a high level geometric model, eg starting with a scene made up of flat surfaces, a line representation can be derived by either:

(a) tracing the edges bordering the facets; this can be performed quickly, but has the disadvantage of displaying an edge as many times as it acts as the border of a face – this repetition is time consuming

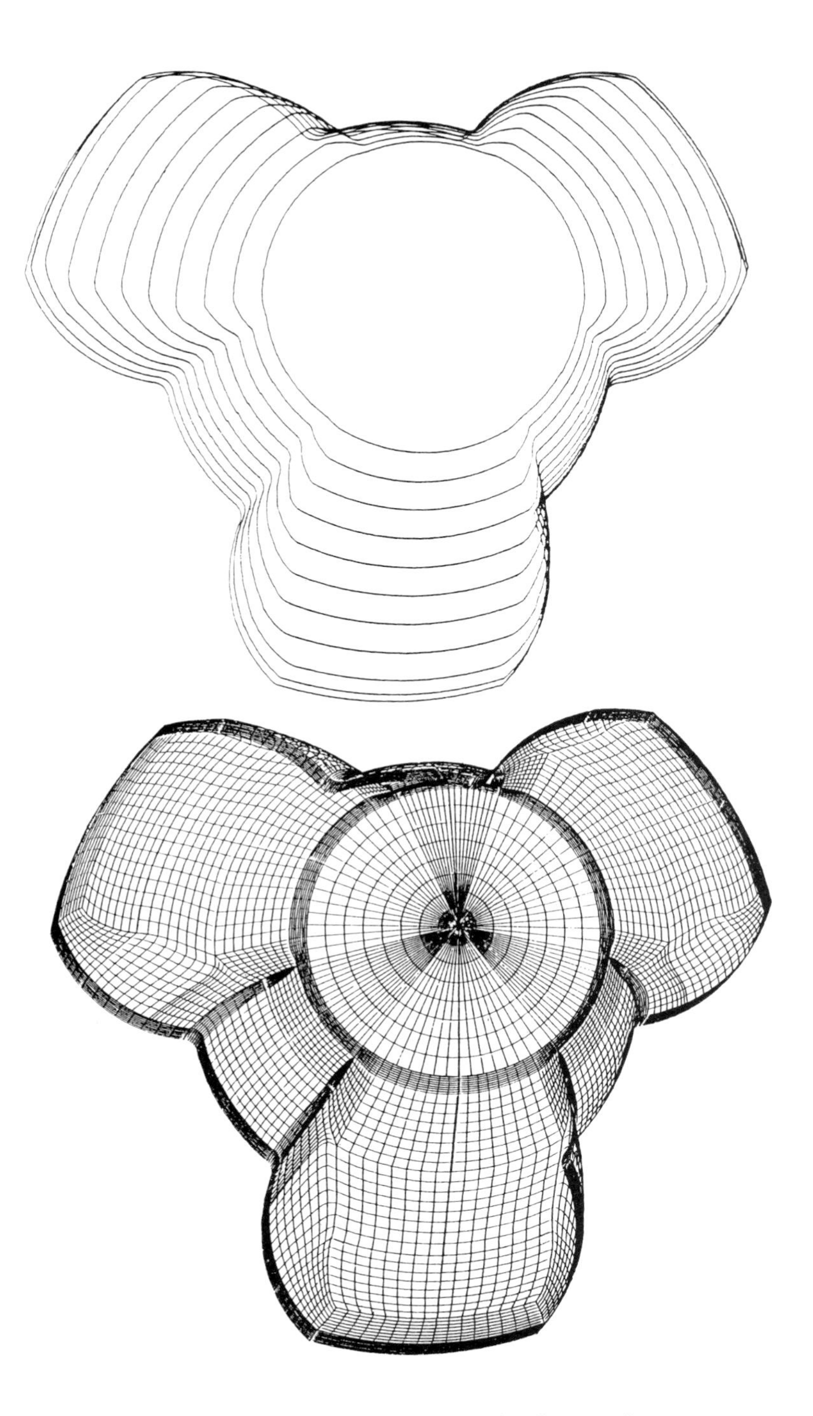

**Figure 4.14.** *Representation of a skew surface*

and can give rise to undesirable optical effects (some lines are displayed more brightly than others, for example); or

(b) changing from a facet model to a line (or wire-frame) model by extraction of the edges making up the facets, verifying that a given edge does not appear more than once.

If it is absolutely necessary to simplify the scene, comprehension software can be used to manipulate the structure of the object by allowing the designer to display only a sub-section of the scene, using data chosen using a selection criterion. The building shown in Figure 4.10 is a detail from the group of buildings shown in Figure 4.15. This facility is probably one of the most important benefits of using a computer. The designer can work on the part of an object of interest at a given moment, or extract the elements linked by logic (eg the elements of a circuit), which not only reduces the amount of information displayed, but also makes what is displayed more legible. The operator can thus at any time concentrate on the most significant part of a display.

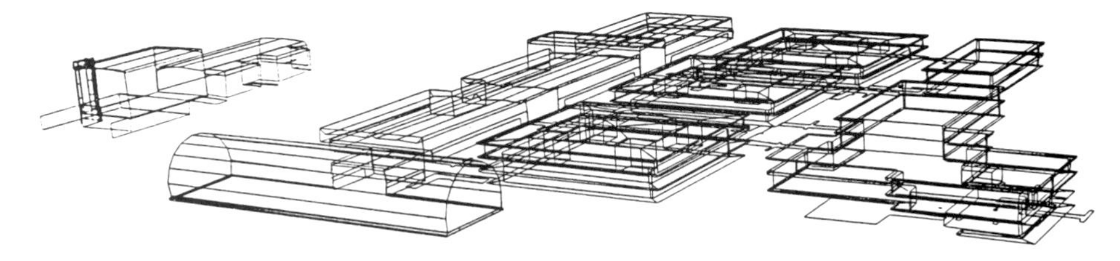

**Figure 4.15.** *Group of buildings*

Another way of handling the structure is to present break-down views (see Figure 4.16). In this technique, the various elements of an object are arranged in such a way as to show all the parts clearly and according to the organization or layout of the parts, so that the overall operation of the object can be more easily understood.

For example, a section can be specified in the following way (see Figure 4.17):

1. the object is presented from three viewpoints (or, if the operator requests it, one or two);
2. the operator indicates, on the plan, the shape of the surface of the cross-section, which is assumed to be orthogonal to the surface being viewed;
3. the operator indicates the half-space in which it is located; the contents of this half-space must (it is assumed) be deleted.

Figure 4.18 shows an example of an object viewed in section. It should be noted that this is a line representation and does not show

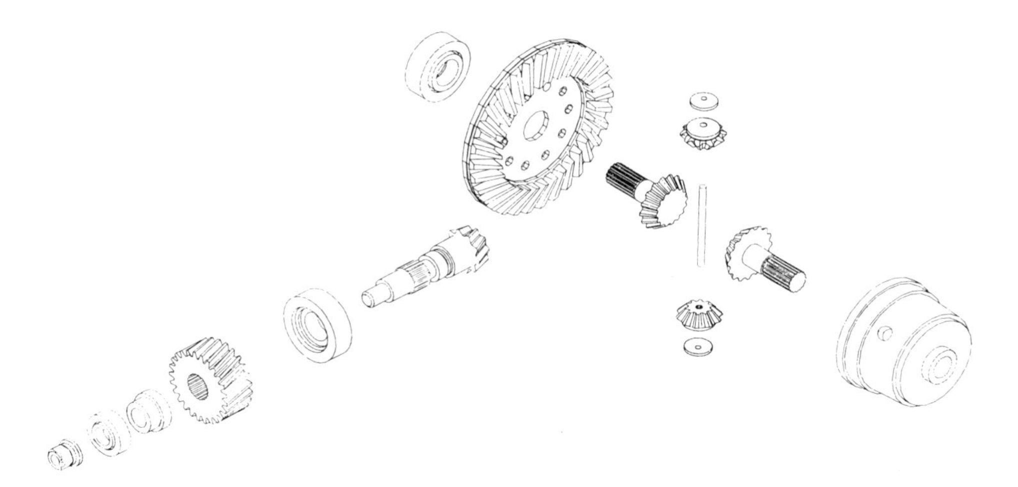

**Figure 4.16.** *Presentation of a break-down view*

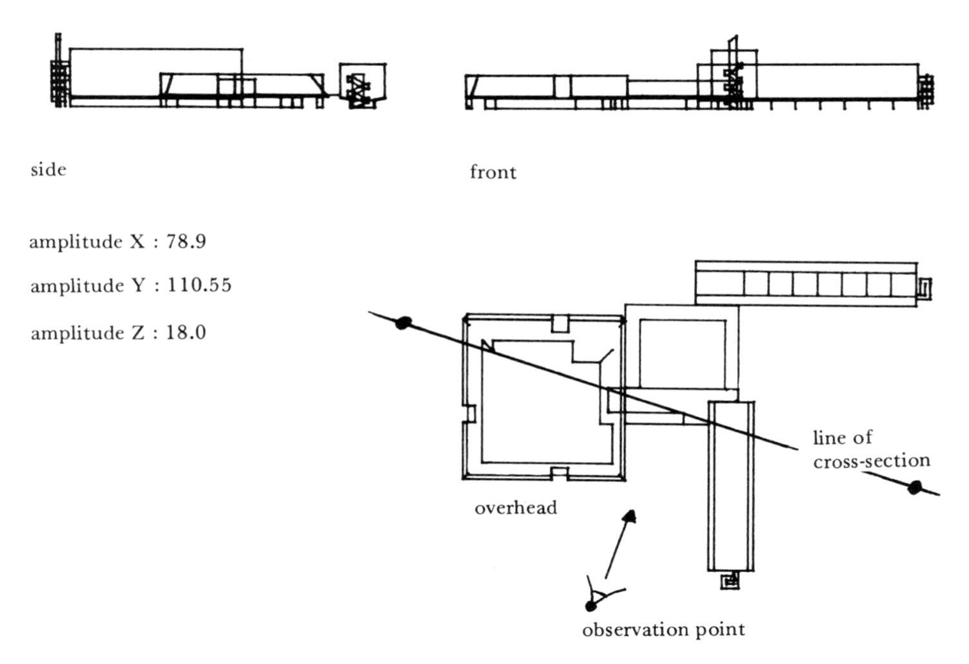


**Figure 4.17.** *Defining the surface of a cross-section*

whether the object is solid. The faces that have been cut are reconstituted, so that cut off edges are not shown and the faces are not left open (see Figure 4.19). The faces defining the scene can be divided into three categories:

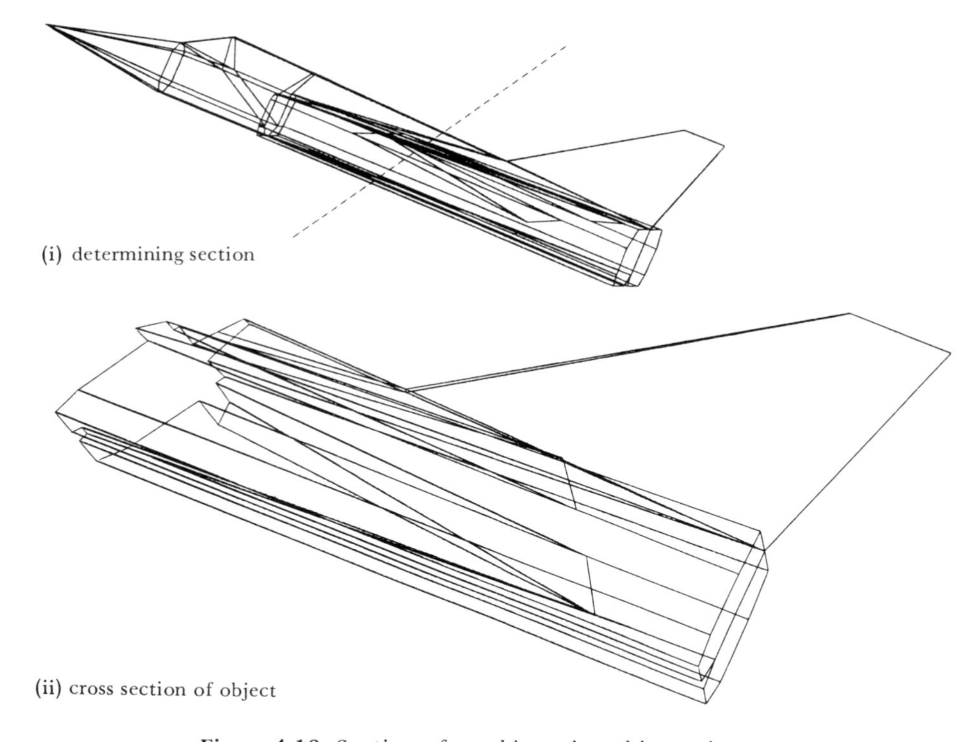


**Figure 4.18.** *Section of an object viewed in section*

*viewpoint

line of section

(i) facet to be cut

(ii) cut lines

(iii) reconstructed facet

**Figure 4.19.** *Section of a flat facet*

1. faces contained entirely within the half-space that includes the viewpoint – these must be deleted;
2. faces contained entirely within the half-space that does not include the viewpoint – these are shown as they are;
3. faces intersected by the cut plane; these must be studied so as to determine which part is contained in the half-space to be projected – the intersection of the face with the surface of the

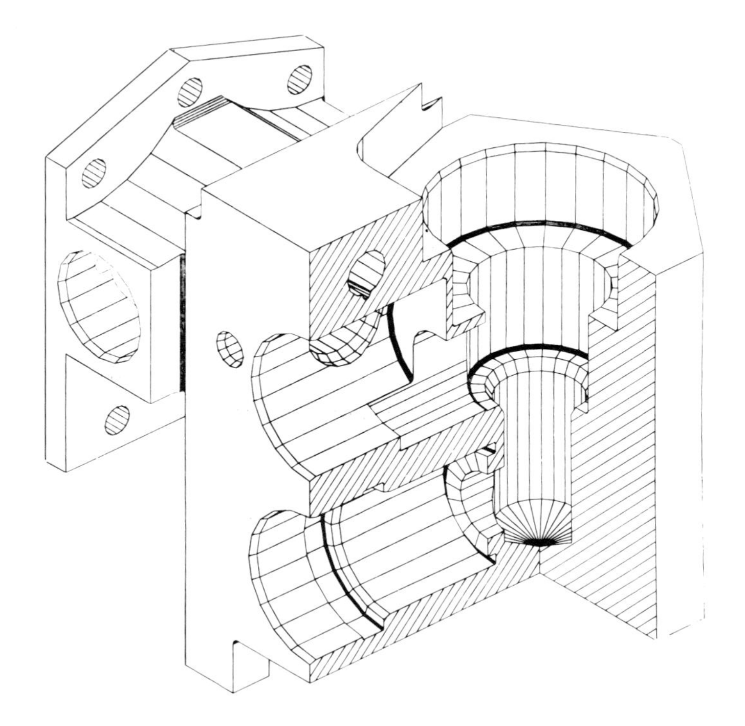

**Figure 4.20.** *Section through a solid*

section must be calculated, ie the lines which are cut by it must be determined, and the cut face closed with the appropriate lines.

Figure 4.20, on the other hand, shows a cut-away section in which the internal surfaces are shown using cross-hatching. In this type of graphic representation it is necessary not only to recreate the faces which have been cut, but also to create new ones corresponding to the surfaces revealed by the section. The algorithm required for this type of display, though very useful, is difficult to introduce. Figure 4.20 also shows the use of a style of representation in which the parts hidden from view are deleted. However if a scene is complex, line representation is not sufficient to show the relative positions of the faces which make up an object. It thus becomes necessary to use a style which takes into account the fact that some surfaces are opaque: the observer will thus only see a sub-group of the faces (or parts of faces) which are closest to his viewpoint, with the others hidden. Some of the techniques for eliminating hidden parts are described in the next section.

### 4.2.2 ELIMINATION OF HIDDEN PARTS

Studies concerning objects in which there is an elimination of hidden parts have constituted a major part of the research work carried out recently in the area of infography. Many algorithms have been produced. Representation, with elimination of hidden parts, of objects with polygonal facets is no longer considered a fundamental problem. Packages producing extremely realistic representations are currently available, and machines capable of processing several thousand facets in real time have now been developed. Using different approaches various types of algorithm have been developed. Rapidity of calculation is not the only criterion that can determine the choice of algorithm. Four types of algorithm will now be discussed in order to show the diversity of approach that can be applied and the various standards of performance that can be expected from each.

#### *4.2.2.1 The Galimberti and Montanari algorithm*

The first algorithms were intended to produce an exact solution for the calculation of the elements to be deleted, by using a geometric approach to the problem. This is the case with the Galimberti and Montanari algorithm, in which each edge belonging to a scene is considered, and its position compared with each of the facets which meet at that edge (see Figure 4.21). Three situations can arise:

1. The edge is situated entirely in the half-space containing the observer and delimited by the surface containing the facet; this edge is entirely visible relative to this facet.
2. The edge is situated entirely in the half-space which does not contain the observer. It is necessary to establish whether it is hidden (either partially or totally) by the facet itself; this involves determining the position and projection of the edge relative to the projection of the contour of the facet, and to determine whether it is situated outside (*visible*), inside (*hidden*), or partly outside (*partly visible*).
3. The edge is situated across both half-spaces – it should be cut in two and each of the parts obtained treated according to which of the methods described above is most suitable.

Using this method, only the visible parts of the edges are retained and analysis is continued using the other facets. The analysis is ended either when all the facets have been subjected to consideration, in which case the edges which remain visible are displayed, or when no edges are visible. This technique can only produce line drawings, because the interior of the facet is not taken into account. However, the images obtained are of very high quality (because of the precision of the calculations and the potential for making full use of vector screens and calligraphic plotters). The calculation time can be rather long, in that the basic algorithm is of a complexity which is a function of the square of the number of facets in the scene, whether visible or not.

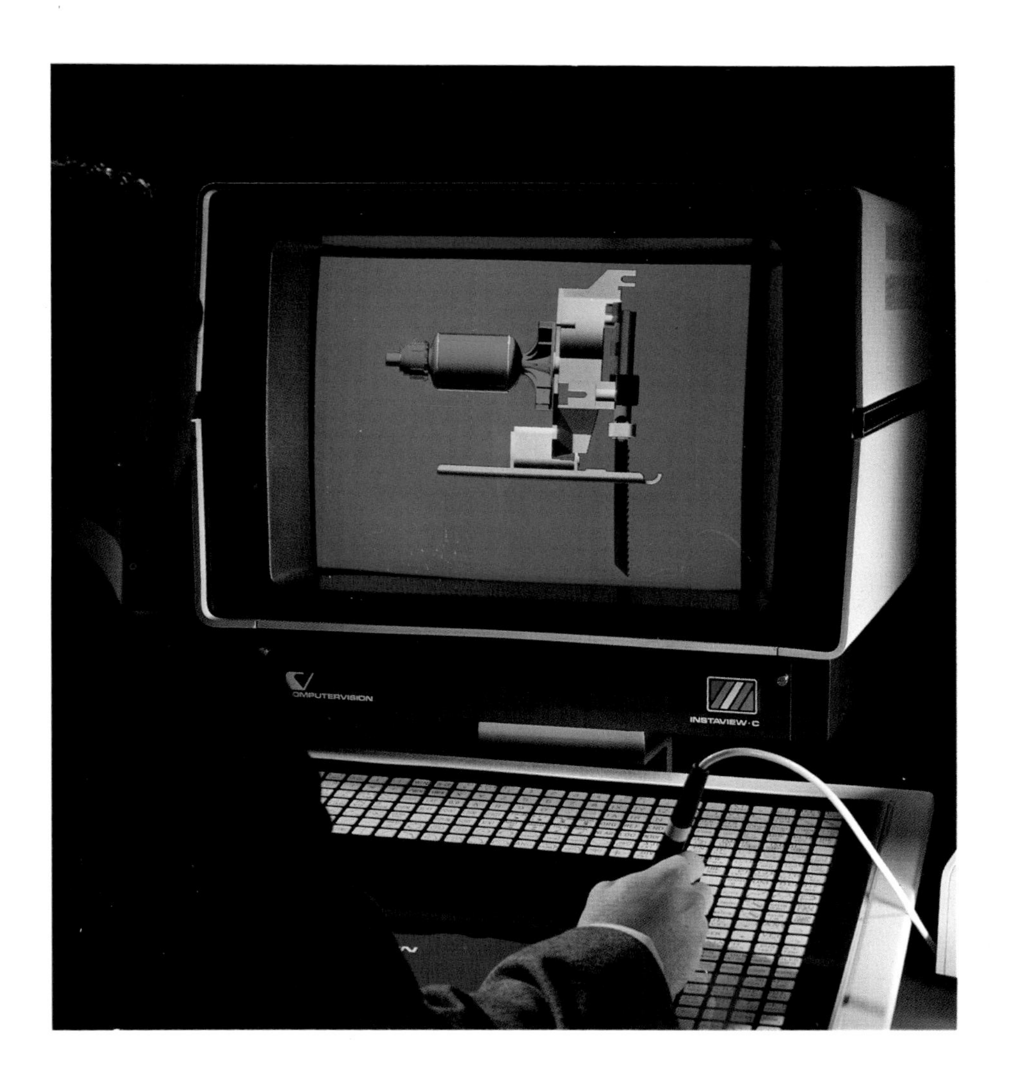


*An internal view of a jig saw (Computervision)*

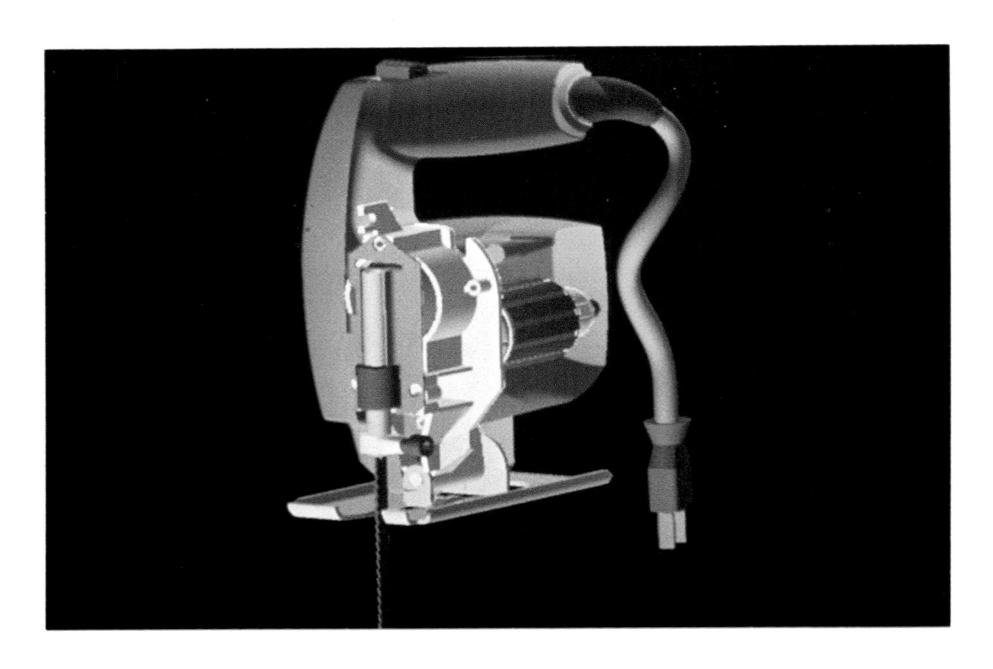

*A cut away view of a jig saw (Computervision)*

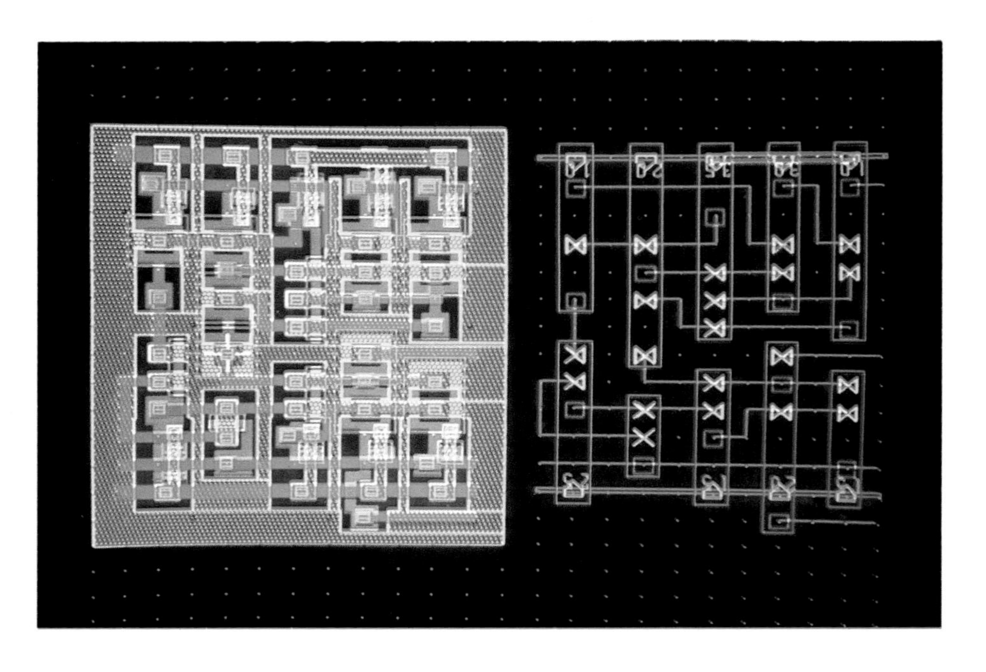

*A view of an integrated circuit (CNET, Grenoble)*

*A view of a bit brace (Control Data-Synthavision)*

*A view of a drive shaft (Control Data-Synthavision)*

*An exploded view of an object (Computervision)*

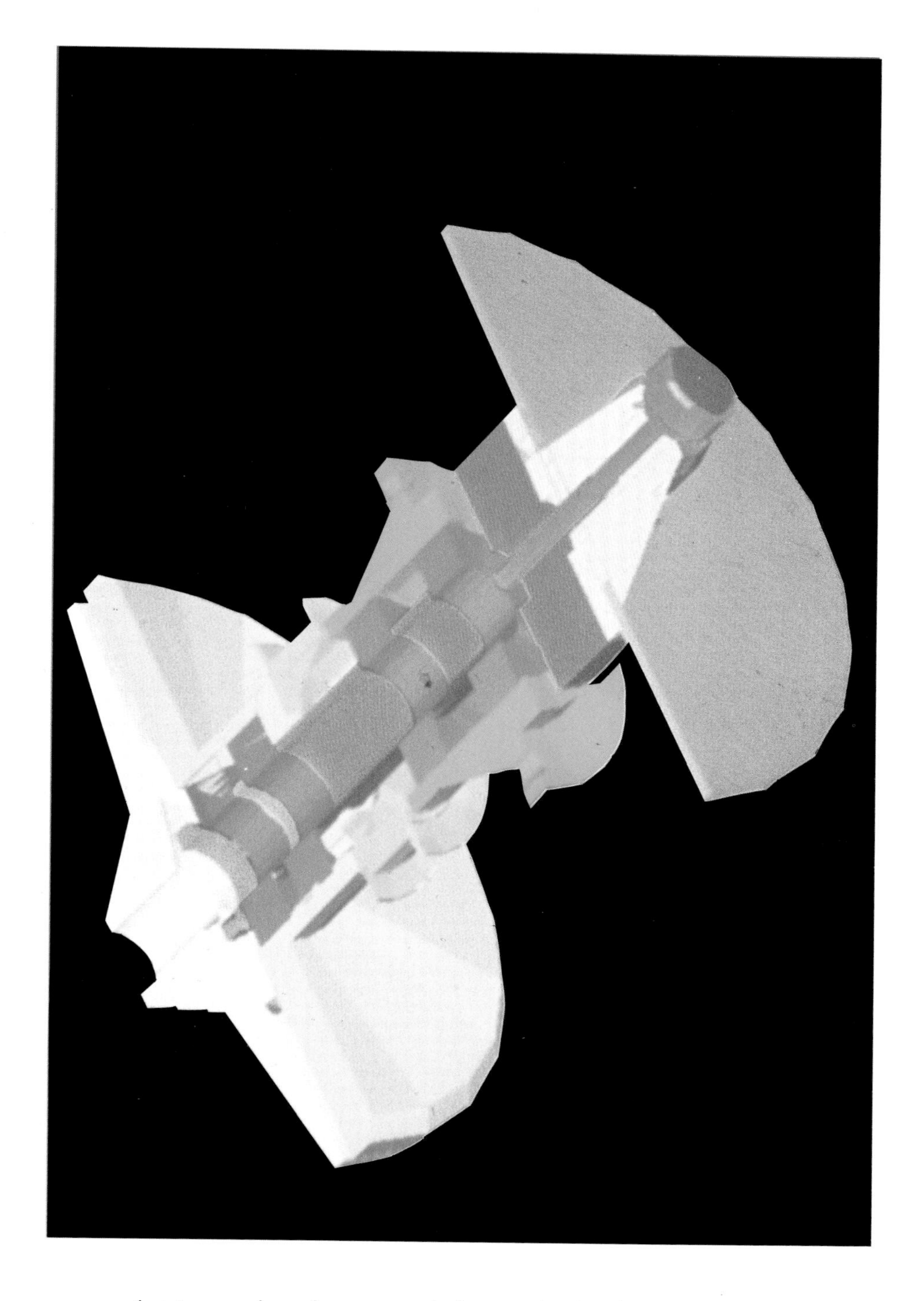

*A cut away view of a camera wind-on mechanism (Matra Datavision)*

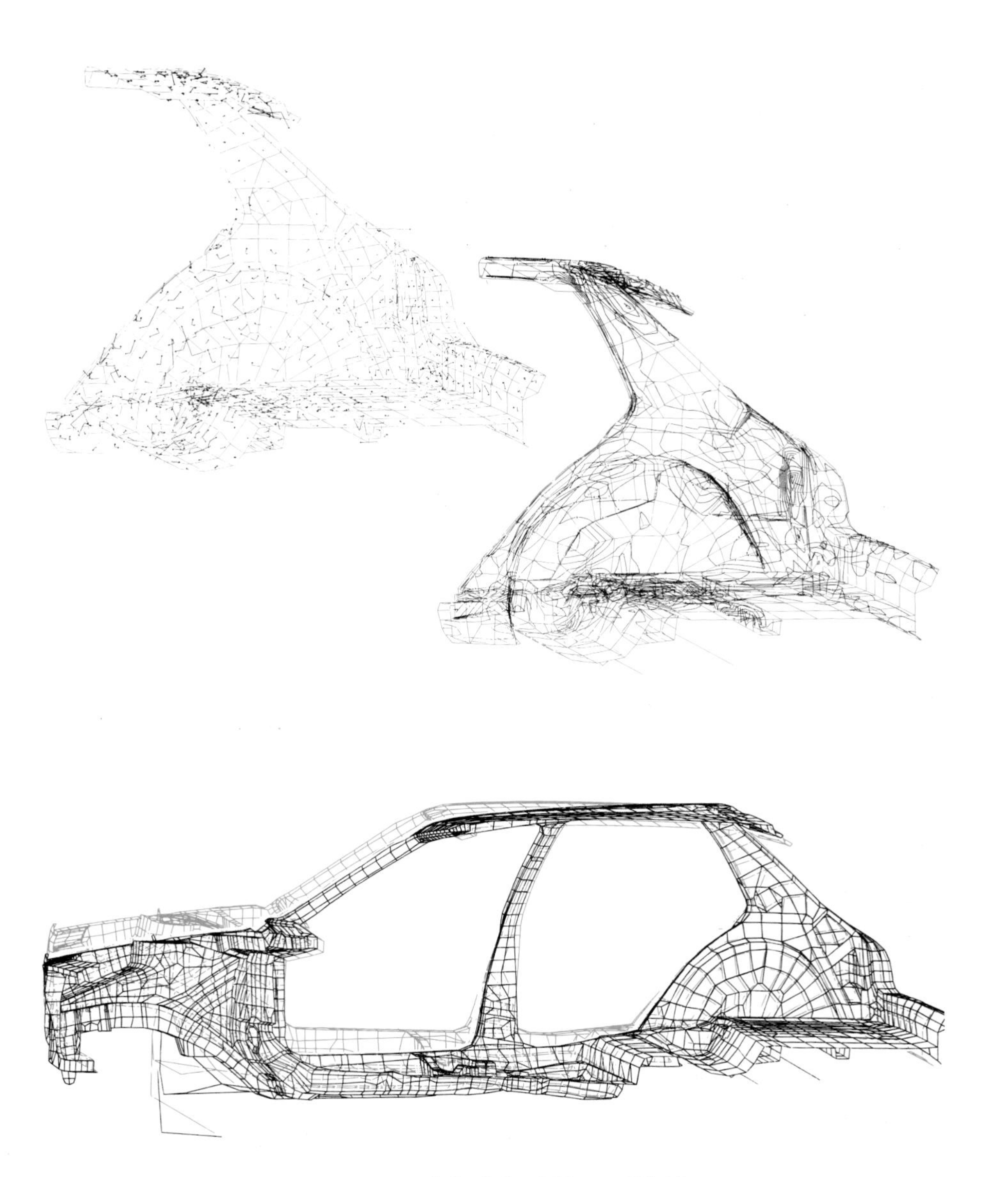

*A line model of the 205 car (PSA)*

*A complete view of the 205 car (Computervision)*

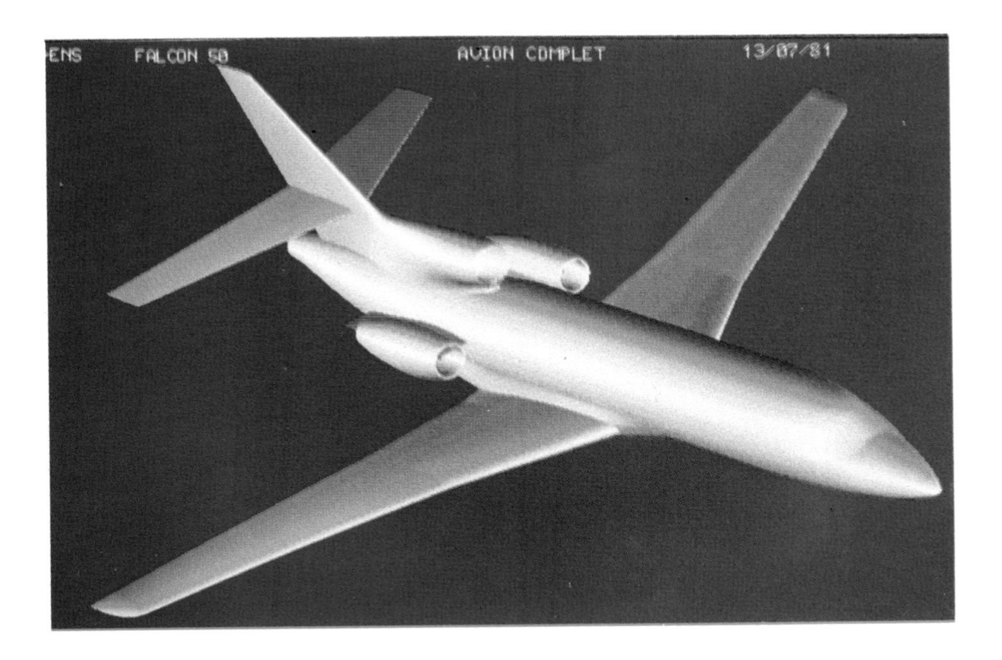


*A complete view of a Falcon 50 aeroplane*

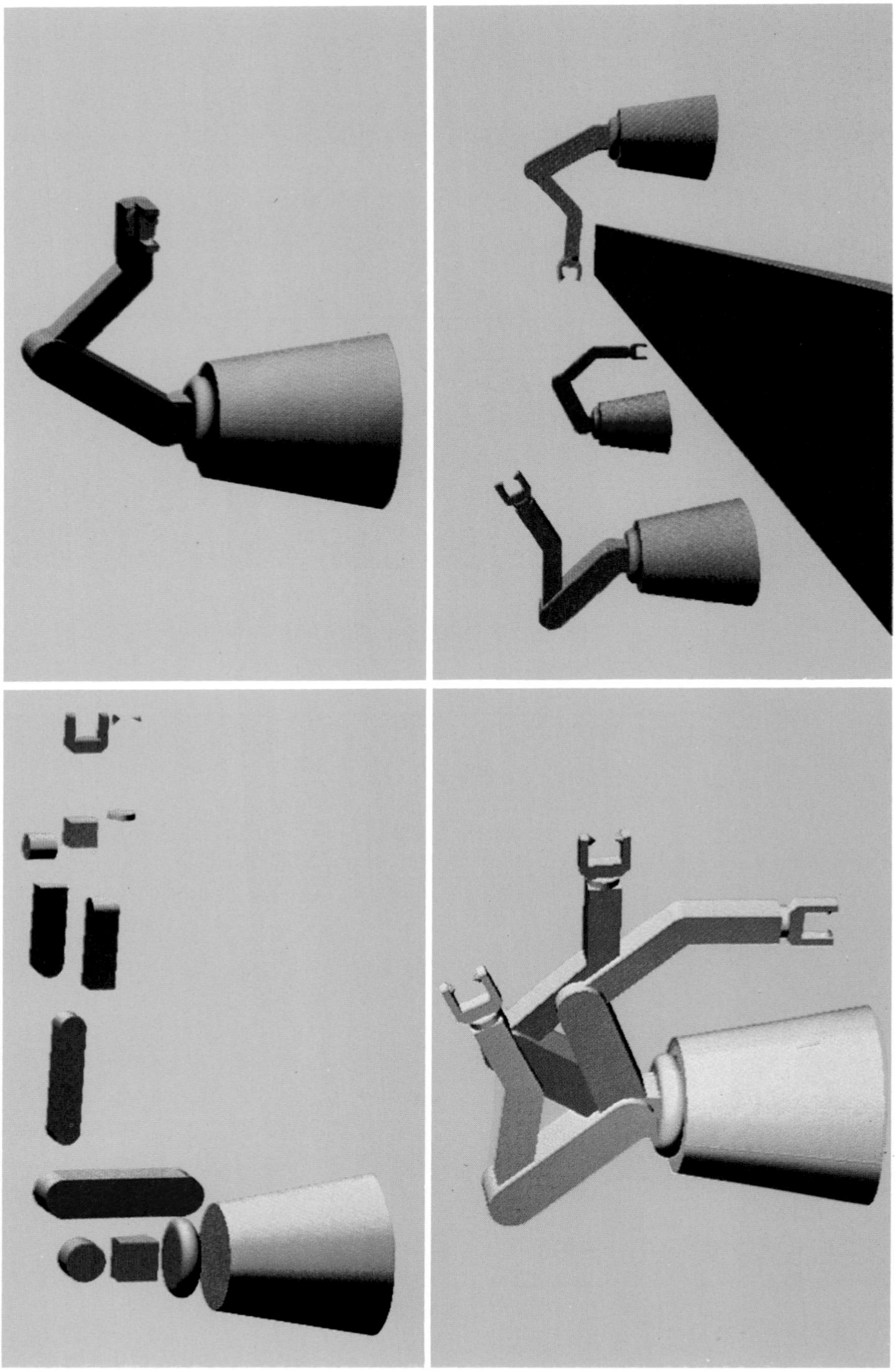

*Several views of a robot (Control Data-Synthavision)*

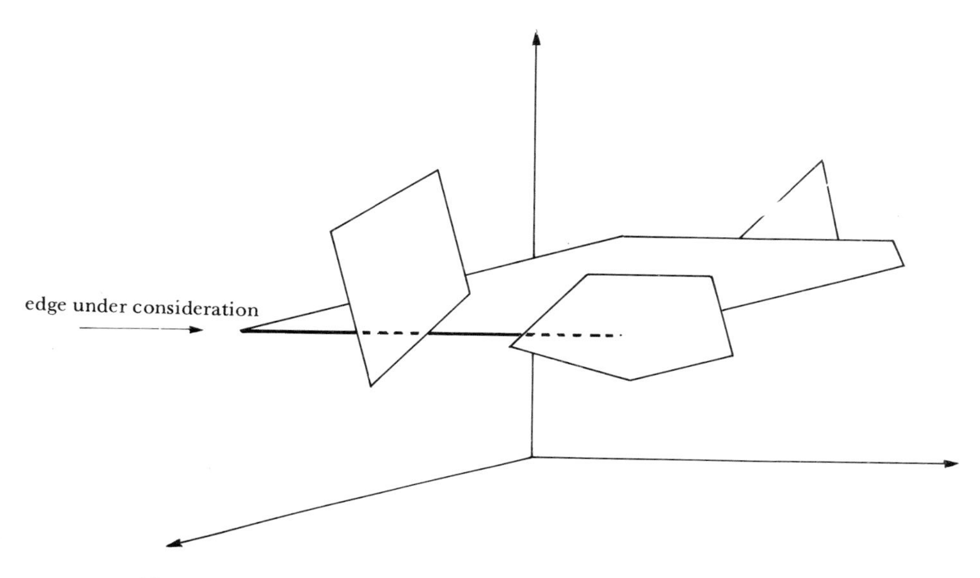


**Figure 4.21.** *Principles of the Galimberti and Montanari algorithm*

Attempts have also been made to design algorithms to provide approximate solutions, by making use of the fact that the resolution of a screen is limited, and that there is no advantage to be gained in going below the limit of resolution because it will not be possible to represent the calculated details with sufficient precision.

#### *4.2.2.2 The Warnock algorithm*

One of the first algorithms incorporating this approach was the one developed by Warnock. It is based on the following principles:

1. In a space defined by a 'tube' with rectangular section, a number of situations can be recognized and represented on the screen. If the scene contained in the tube does not belong to any recognized situation, the tube is then divided into four sub-spaces, based on the initial section divided into four sub-sections. Each of these four (new) tubes is then studied in turn. The recognizable situations are such that more and more detailed studies of successively smaller spaces will allow them to be recognized with increasing certainty. A situation may consist of either an empty tube, or a single facet.
2. The division process is stopped when the size of the section of the tube is the same as that of a single dot on the screen. Whatever the complexity of the scene contained in this tube, only a single dot can be displayed, and it is therefore pointless to continue to break down the image further.

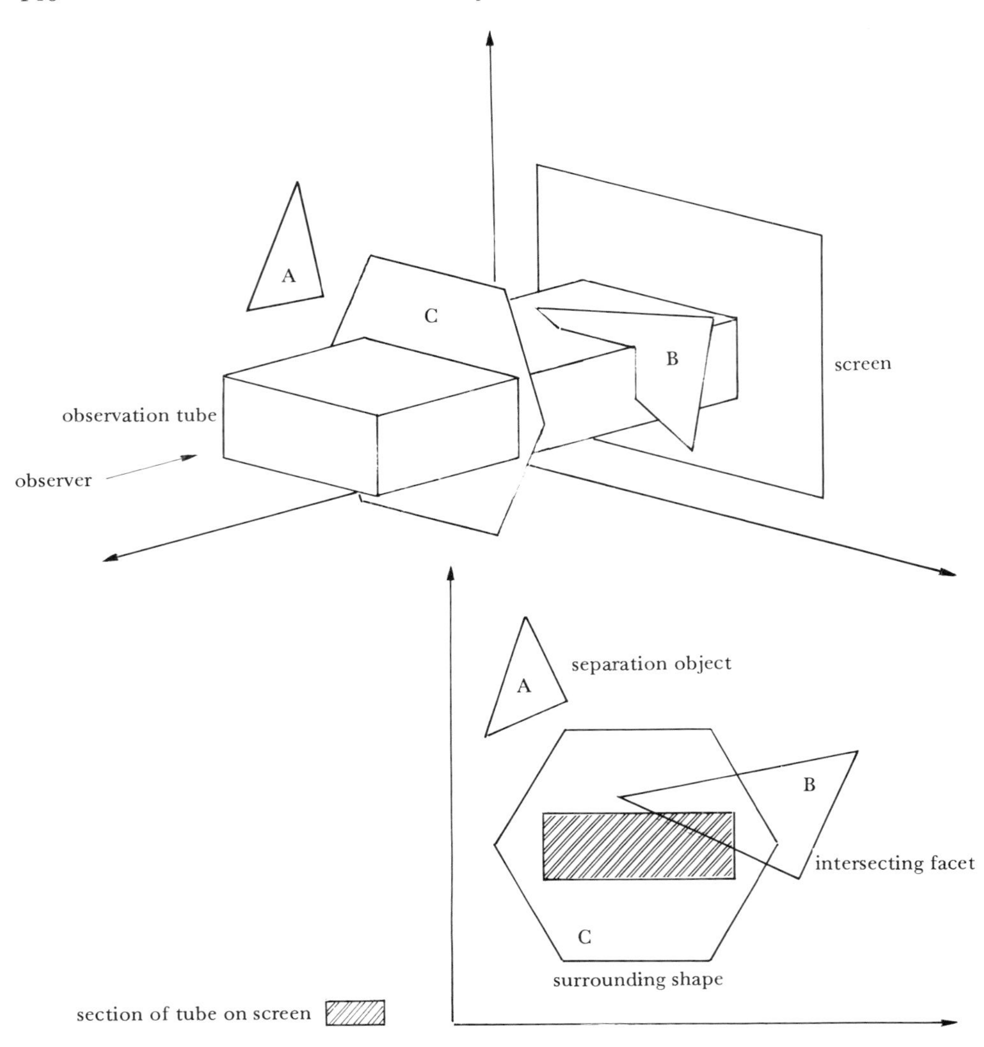


**Figure 4.22.** *Principles of the Warnock algorithm*

A large part of the Warnock algorithm consists of determining the spatial position of each facet relative to the observation tube. The facets can be divided into three categories (see Figure 4.22): *separated facets* (entirely outside the tube), *intersecting facets* (with at least one edge inside the tube) and *surrounding facets* (with the tube entirely inside). This last category plays a vital role in the Warnock algorithm: a surrounding facet is always the first to be sought in the observable space, since if one is present it hides everything inside the tube. Depending on whether a line drawing or a more sophisticated picture is to be produced, the result will be different: in the first situation, there will be nothing to draw, whereas in the second, the portion of the screen that corresponds to the tube is filled with the same colour as the surrounding face.

This implies that the Warnock algorithm can be used for producing both line drawings and pictures. However, the quality of representation produced using this method is not the best, in that the relatively arbitrary cuts which are made to 'understand' the scene can give rise to undesirable optical effects. On the other hand, the reduction in calculation time is considerable: the complexity of this algorithm is directly proportional to the complexity of display. Thus, at least in theory, the more hidden parts there are, the faster the algorithm can complete the calculations. It should be noted, however, that this approach has been largely abandoned (at least for use with flat facets) in favour of the two algorithms described next.

#### *4.2.2.3 The Watkins algorithm*

The most commonly used algorithm at present is probably the one proposed by Watkins. The starting point is an adaptation of the process used with television scanning terminals (*raster screens*), ie a picture is constructed line by line. Watkins had the idea of dividing the scene up with a series of parallel planes perpendicular to the surface of the screen and passing through each scanning line – these are called *scanning planes*. Each scanning plane determines a set of straight lines which indicate the intersection of the faces with the scanning plane (see Figure 4.23). To create a picture, these sets of lines are considered in each scanning plane and their positions relative to an observer are determined. The line segments situated in front hide all or part of the segments behind them. The parts of the line segments visible to the observer are thus drawn on the scanning line. By studying all the scanning planes, the set of lines that result can be presented as an image with hidden parts eliminated.

The Watkins algorithm is particularly well suited for taking into account the play of light on a facet, as well as various other effects of light, including transparency. There are many variants on this idea, and this algorithm was the first to be hard-wired into a synthetic image generator. One interesting variation involves keeping a summary of points at which an edge changes its state of visibility up to date during study of the facets. For as long as the state of an edge (which may initially be visible) does not change, only the line of intersection of the facet to which it belongs is displayed. If a change in state occurs (ie if the edge is no longer visible), the line segment joining the previously stored point and the point at which the state changes is displayed. In this way the apparent contours of the facets can be drawn, and line drawings, pictures and pictures with emphasized contours can be produced.

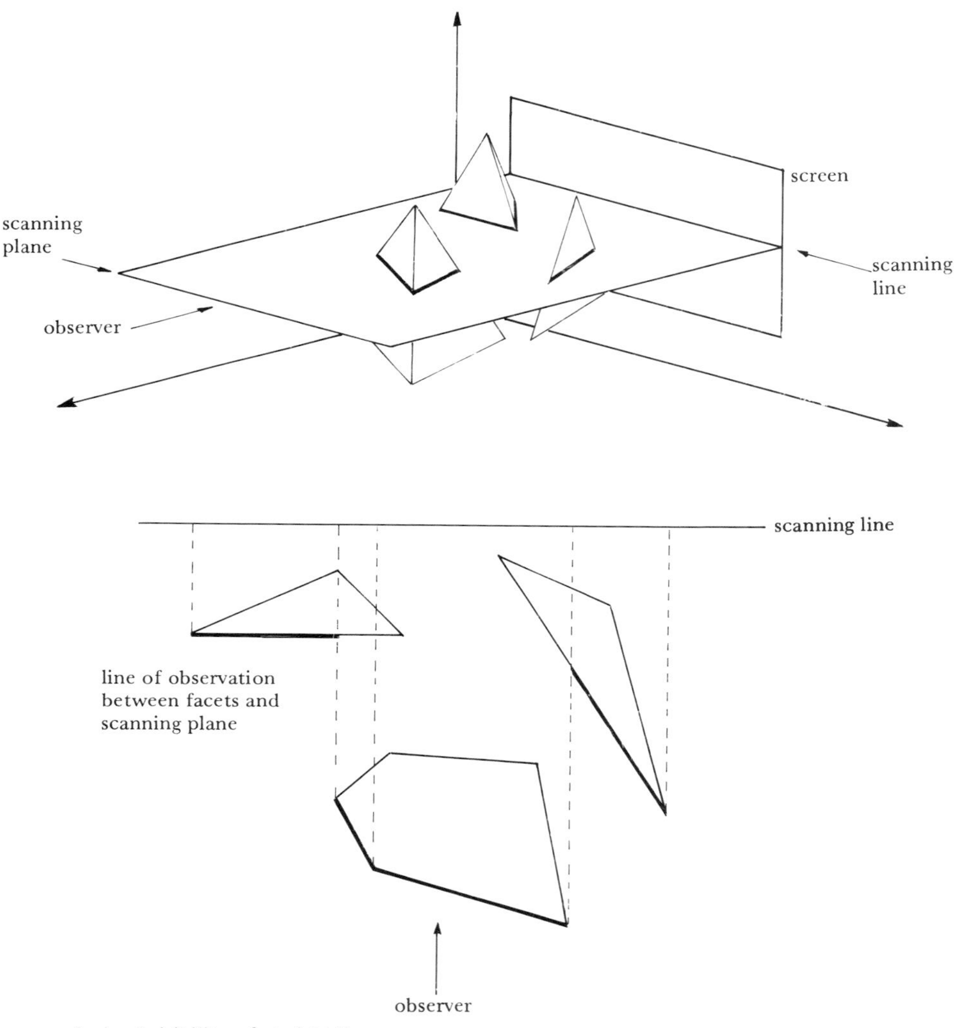


**Figure 4.23.** *Principles of the Watkins algorithm*

Horizontal scanning also allows simulation of several levels of grey on calligraphic plotting screens. Figure 4.24 shows an example of this type of simulation, in which the facets have been shaded using horizontal lines (picture simulation) and the visible edges emphasized. One of the main advantages of the Watkins algorithm is its generality, but a disadvantage lies in the fact that to be effective it requires the use of a relatively elaborate data structure, which makes programming a rather delicate and difficult procedure.

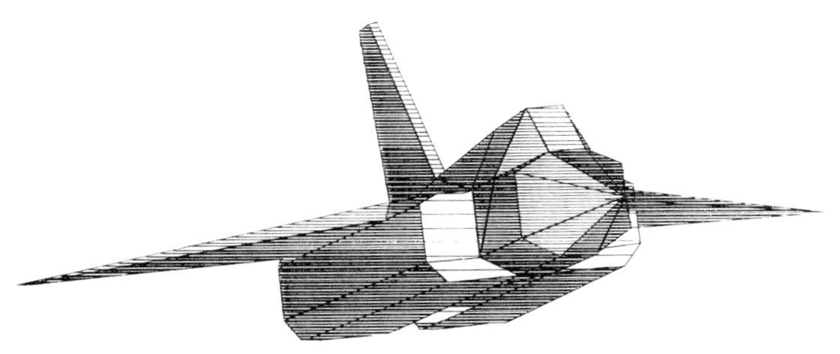

(i) presentation using emphasized lines and colour simulation

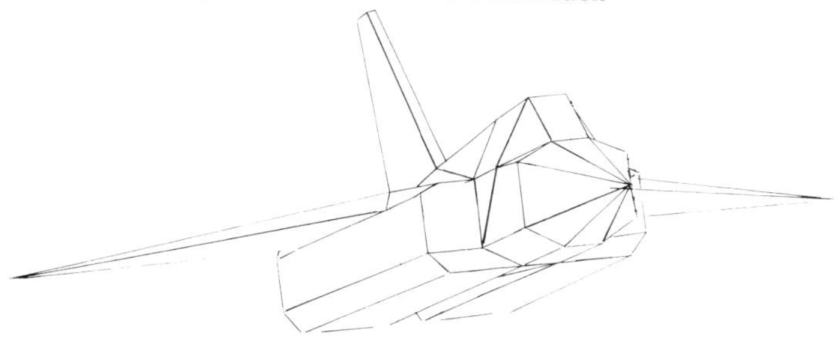

(ii) presentation using line drawing – errors caused by imprecise calculation are evident

**Figure 4.24.** *Line and picture presentation using the Watkins algorithm*

### *4.2.2.4 The algorithm of Newell, Newell and Sancha*

The last of the algorithms to be considered here is one based on an extremely simple idea (see Figure 4.25), in which it is supposed that the facets can be placed in order relative to each other, with the face furthest from the observer (nearest the screen) as number one, and the face nearest the observer (furthest from the screen) as the last. To obtain the correct picture, number one is displayed first on the screen, followed by number two, etc. Two possible situations may arise:

1. The surface covered by the new face has no contact with the surface covered by the first. This means that the two facets do not hide each other.
2. The surface covered by the new face covers all or part of the surface already displayed. This means that the new face hides all or part of the preceding face. Thus, either the common part can be replaced (if the new face is opaque), or a combination of the colour already displayed and the colour of the new face can be displayed (if the new face is transparent).

The apparent simplicity of this algorithm should not conceal the real problem: organizing the faces into order (although theoretically it can be carried out with a complexity of the order of Nlog N) is

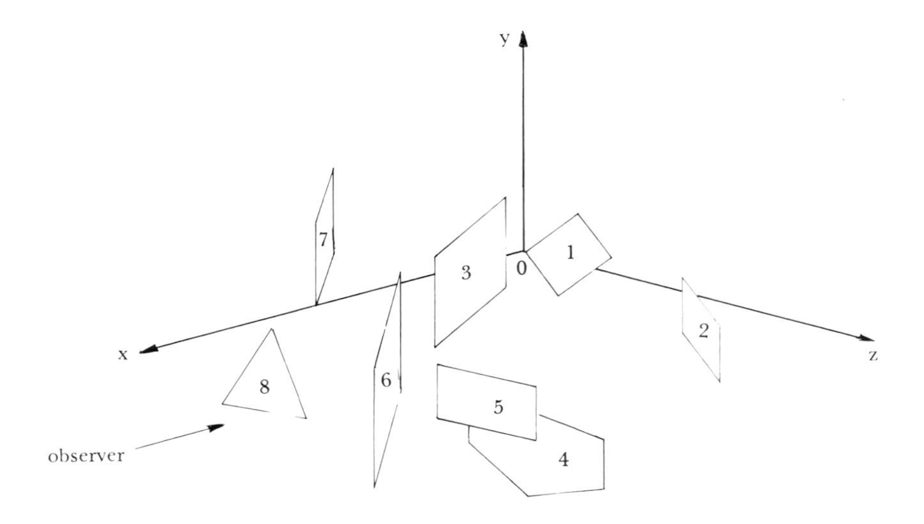


the faces are numbered in order of their decreasing distance from the observer

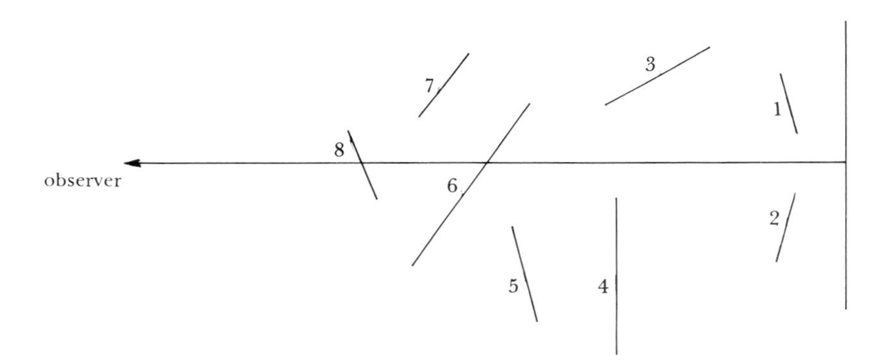


line of faces in a plane parallel to x0y

**Figure 4.25.** *Principles of the algorithm described by Newell* et al.

delicate and complex and can be problematic when two faces hide each other, as happens for example, when facets intersect. The use of the method is increasing, both because of the recent appearance of terminals that directly process the display of facets with priority, and because of the possibility of combining colours during the construction of an image. Thus, the most realistic images are produced using the algorithm proposed by Newell *et al.* Further, it is possible to produce line drawings with this algorithm, although the quality is rather poor (because the display is formed point by point) and without any real potential for improvement (see Figure 4.26).

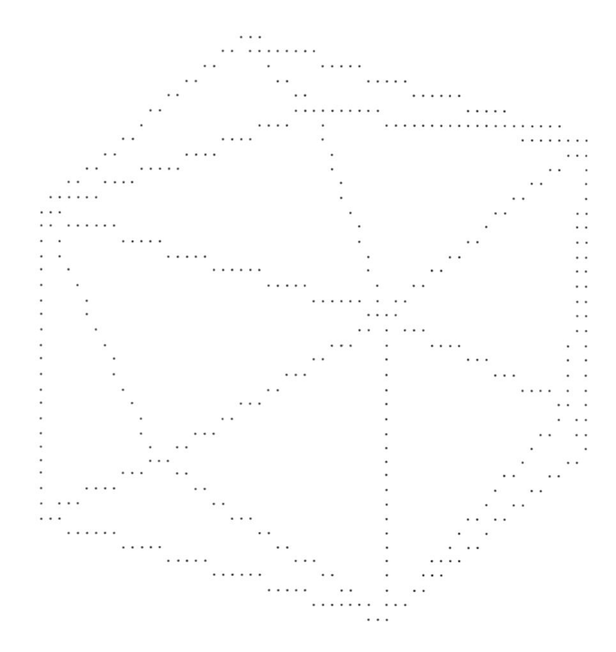

**Figure 4.26.** *Point by point representation*

| | *Galimberti and Montanari* | *Warnock* | *Watkins* | *Newell* et al. |
|---|---|---|---|---|
| *elements of the scene* | solids (edges common to a maximum of two faces) | faces, polygons, planes | faces, polygons, planes (edges common to maximum of two faces) | faces, polygons, planes (quadrilaterals) |
| *processing of intersecting faces* | no | yes | yes | yes (no drawings) |
| *precision of calculation* | poor | depends on screen | depends on screen | depends on screen |
| *quality of drawing* | very good | average (depends on level of tests) | good | bad |
| *quality of picture* | – | average | good | very good |
| *complexity of programming* | average | average | very complex | average |
| *memory size (in words)* | 3*NBSOM + 31*NFFACES | 3*NBSOM + 37*NBFACES | 3*NBSOM + 33*NBFACES + 512 bytes | 3*NBSOM + 40*NBFACES 512 × 512 bytes |

**Table 4.1.** *Characteristics of the four algorithms*

By comparing the characteristics of these algorithms, it is possible to decide which one would be most suitable in a given situation. If high quality of drawing or picture is the most important criterion, the following considerations should be taken into account:

1. For very precise drawings, eg mechanical drawing, use of the Galimberti and Montanari algorithm is must suitable. In most cases it would be better to use this algorithm only for definitive outputs on to a graph plotter, and to use another type for the preparation of the drawing on a screen. The exact solution produced as a result, can be reused with a two-dimensional model. This technique is extremely useful if a functional specification is to be added to a graphic representation. Algorithms with approximate solutions cannot be used to provide this facility.

2. If line drawings are all that is needed, the Warnock algorithm is best used, as its usefulness is proportional to the complexity of the scene.

3. The Watkins algorithm is useful in that it allows drawings of a fairly high quality, as well as very realistic pictures, to be obtained. However, its programming requires considerable care.

4. The Newell, Newell and Sancha algorithm is useful because of the simplicity of the programming required. It is particularly useful for processing reflection or transparency problems, which can sometimes be crucial (eg in the glass manufacturing industry). It can also be extended for use with analytical surfaces.

In processing terms, these algorithms require a large memory capacity. The increasing use of microprocessors is giving rise to the use of limited capacity memories, with recourse, if necessary, to secondary memories. It is therefore clear that algorithms developed on limited-memory processing devices will be at a disadvantage from the point of view of performance, because of the frequent exchanges involved between primary and secondary memories. In considering the effectiveness of these algorithms, it is extremely difficult to compare their performances since:

1. If such comparisons were to make any sense, the program considered would have to be of the same technical level. This level depends on the programming language and the method used and, more importantly, on the degree of sophistication of the application of the algorithm itself. For example, improvements may be made which are not specific to the algorithm used, but are associated with one of them more than others. Consider, for example:

(a) the use of priorities between objects, allowing only those objects or elements of objects likely to influence each other to be compared. If, for example, an observer is standing looking down the middle of a street, it is obvious that the buildings on the left can have no influence on those on the right. Thus, there is no point in comparing the facets of these two groups with each other. This setting of priorities can be made during the creation of the geometric model;

(b) when an interior and exterior can be determined (in solid objects), it is possible to orient the facets such that a normal, pointing towards the exterior, can be associated with them. Under these circumstances, it is possible to eliminate all the faces such that their normal is directed away from the observer: then they cannot be seen. In this way the number of facets to be processed can be reduced considerably;

(c) concepts of coherence can be used, such as the probability that, in a given position, the structure of an object is not particularly distorted. Calculations can be made based on the previous ones, so long as the modifications are not radical, or if they are, that this does not occur often. For example, with convex solids it is possible to determine in advance the positions in which a change in appearance takes place. Thus, so long as the position held is between two key positions, there is no need for extensive recalculation. Only if a key position is reached will a complete recalculation become necessary.

2. A set of tests which are 'neutral' with respect to the algorithms being tested is indispensible. The significance of this is that it is not known what makes an algorithm process one set of data more rapidly than another, since the concept of scene complexity is not completely understood. The behaviour of algorithms in relation to scenes is also relatively unpredictable, with a given type of scene responding better to a particular type of algorithm for no apparent reason. This is a subject into which research must be carried out, since a full understanding of these concepts would certainly lead to improved algorithms.

#### *4.2.2.5 Skew structure models*

The processing of geometric models using skew surfaces is not so well advanced. Even though pictures or drawings of objects formed from such surfaces can be displayed (see Figure 4.27), the algorithms used have not yet been perfected (unlike those used with facets). One of the most widely used techniques, that of the *Z-buffer*, will now be considered.

The idea is very simple: imagine that from each pixel on a screen, a perpendicular line is produced (see Figure 4.28). These will eventually pass through different squares of the scene. The altitude of each of these points of intersection is calculated, and the maximal altitude (relative to the screen) is recorded by constant updating. When the altitudes of all the points of intersection for a given line have been

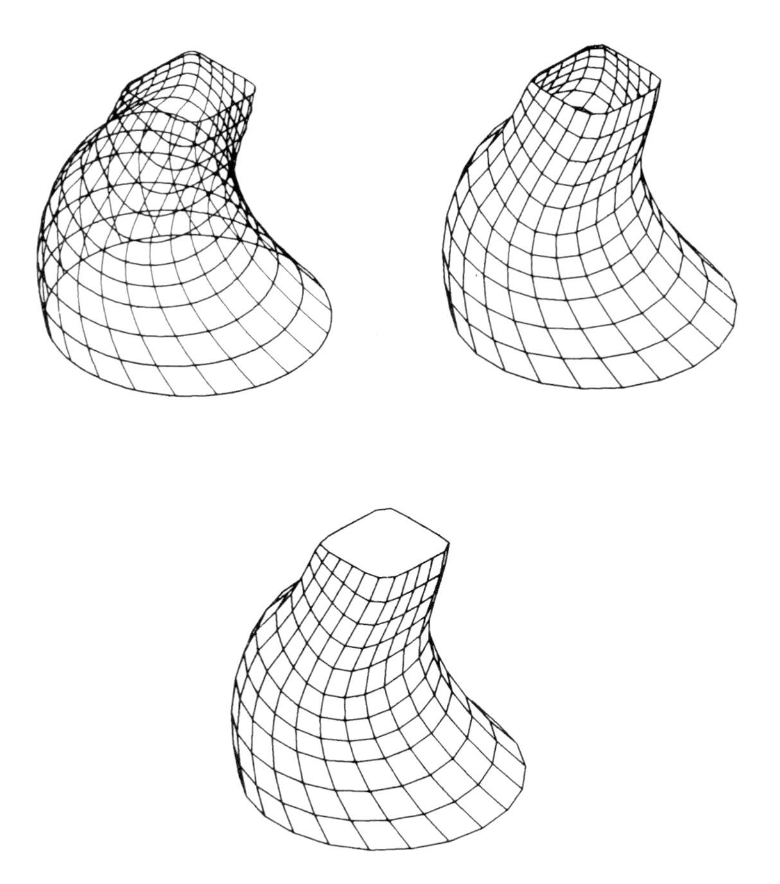

**Figure 4.27.** *Various representations of a skew surface*

calculated, the maximal altitude recorded represents the altitude of the point nearest the observer. All that remains is to display the colour associated with this point.

In practice, the process is usually carried out in the opposite direction, ie a square is projected on to the surface of the screen. If the square covers more than one pixel, it is divided into smaller squares (see Figure 4.29), until only a single pixel is covered. At this point, the altitude of the basic square is noted, so that the maximal-Z can be updated for this point. This technique is relatively slow, however. The problem is that the techniques that could theoretically be used are impeded by the fact that very different functions are used to approximate the squares on a skew surface, and these functions vary in their degree of compatability with the calculations involved for the elimination of hidden parts.

To conclude this survey, it should be noted that current research

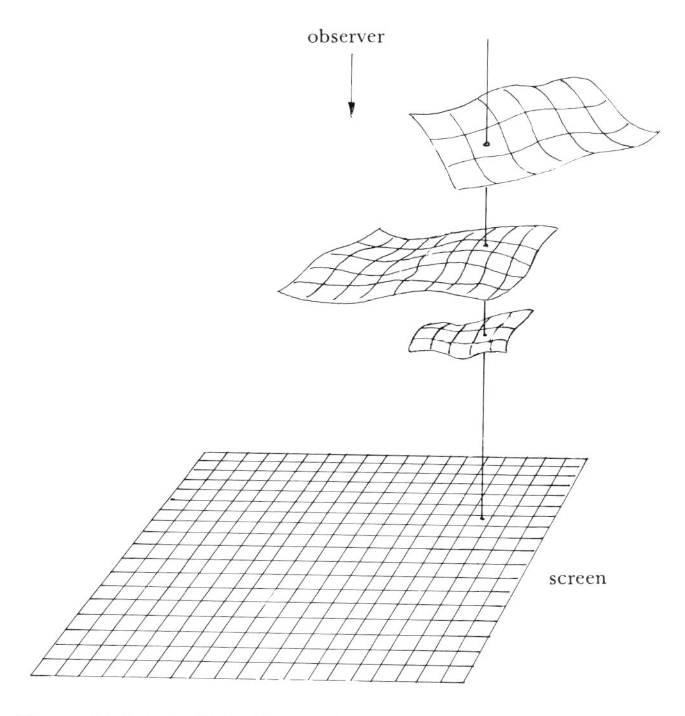


**Figure 4.28.** *The Z-buffer method applied to skew surfaces*

tends to favour algorithms that are capable of processing different families of objects equally well, eg flat facets and solids, or flat facets and skew surfaces. More interest is being taken in complex scenes involving objects of different types, eg landscapes (skew surfaces) and buildings (flat facets).

### 4.2.3 ANIMATED GRAPHICS

One of the fundamental advantages of graphic visual display is that it enables the operation of a mechanism to be simulated, so that the role and interaction of all the elements can be studied using a virtual model. This type of simulation can be used to draw graphs of the development of each parameter as a function of time, and can also be used to show the different positions of parts as they change with time. This technique can also be used to produce a sequence of pictures, each one corresponding to an evaluation of different positions at a given time. Several modes of visual display are used:

1. Images that correspond to different sequences are produced on the same input medium, using superimposition. Figure 4.30, illustrating a robot arm at three different positions, was produced in this way.

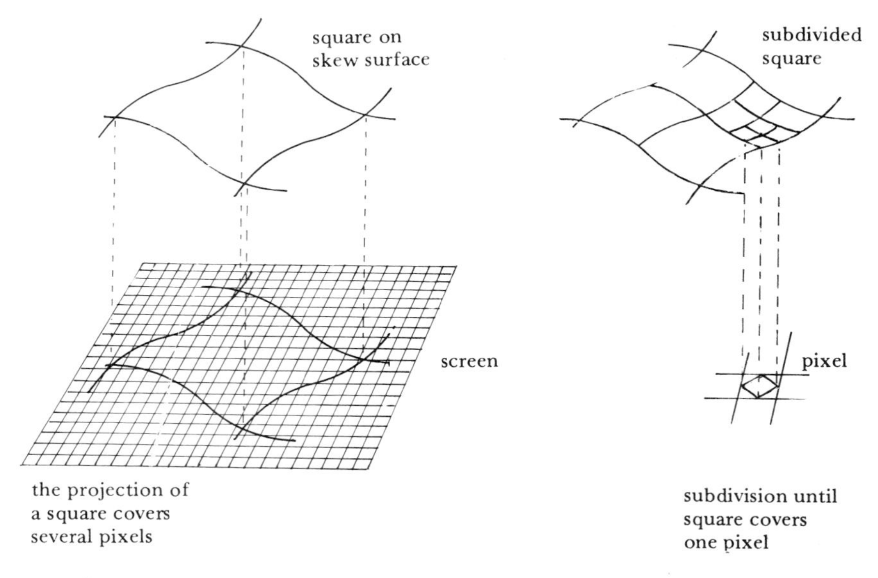


**Figure 4.29.** *The use of the Z-buffer method by subdivision of squares*

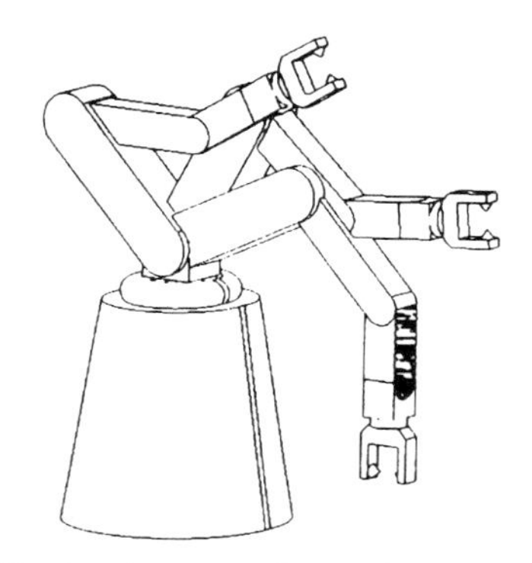

**Figure 4.30.** *A robot arm shown in three positions*

2. Images that correspond to different sequences are produced using different input media for each picture. This process may be chosen for a variety of reasons:

(a) the image is too detailed, and thus illegible – for example, Figure 4.31 shows a car wheel in several positions; it would be impossible to derive much information from these drawings should they be superimposed;

(b) an impression of movement is to be produced: continuous animation can be produced if the calculation time is sufficiently short and providing a suitable screen is used. The operator will be able to view the parts on the screen, and will be able to judge their movements relative to each other. Alternatively, stop-frame animation can be used,

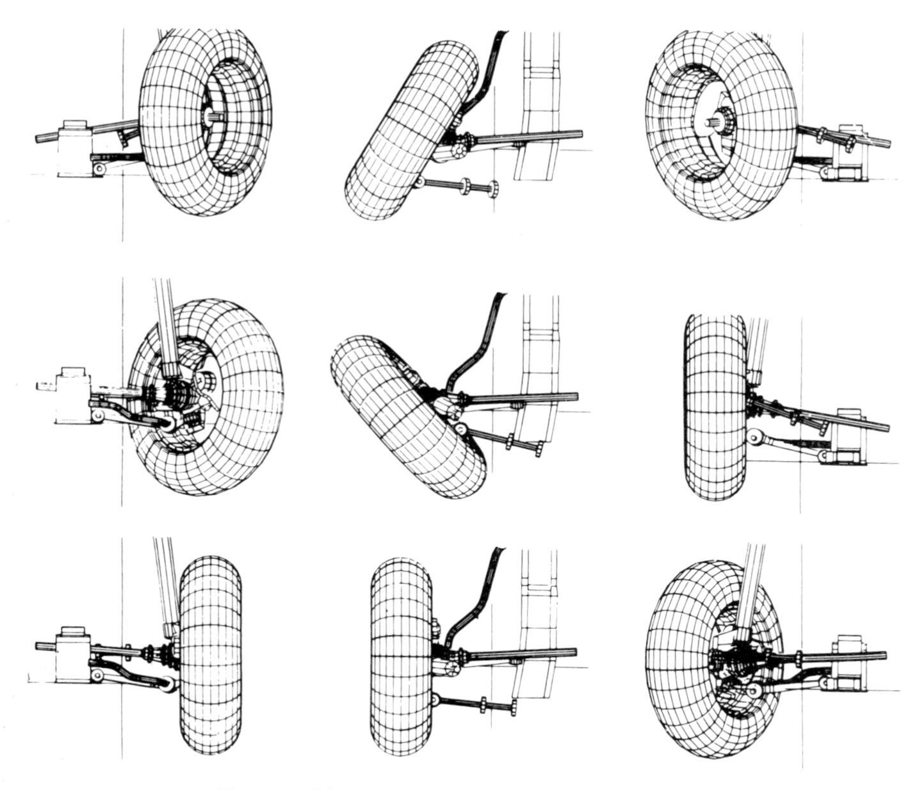

**Figure 4.31.** *Several positions of a car wheel*

by photographing the sequence of movements image by image and then projecting the film obtained.

The importance of these animation techniques is considerable. They can be used in a number of areas; however, they require relatively powerful calculation capacities, either because the kinematic study of the objects involves the solution of relatively complex equations, or because the speed of calculation needed to provide continuous animation is very high. If the animation is needed to take place in real time, ie if the time which elapses between the display of two images is the same time that would elapse in reality between the attainment of the two positions, the calculation capacity required will be even greater. This is the case with flight simulators, in which realistic images must be presented in real time to allow the pilots to develop the necessary reflexes.

## 4.3 Communication graphics

The main characteristics of communication graphics is that they must be carefully constructed, to prevent any possible ambiguity in interpretation. Those who use documents produced in this way cannot always ask the designer to elucidate any points which may be less than completely clear. The production of a plan must, therefore, be based on the national or international standards used in a particular profession. The production process can be divided into two phases (see Figure 4.32):

1. The production of graphics: it must be stressed that a simple copy of a screen display is generally inadequate. It can be supposed that the algorithms that allow plans to be produced are based on the same object models as those for display, but that they may be fundamentally different to the algorithms used for display in dialogue mode. For instance, the output of plans using a graph plotter can take a considerable time (several minutes), and it is not inconceivable that algorithms for plan production could process batches of plans, say overnight.
2. The presentation of the plan, ie the specifications, cross-hatching, the positioning of captions, labels and boxes: this process could be carried out in dialogue mode, possibly with approximate values, with the final positioning being carried out in deferred mode.

The user can use symbols (whether normalized or not) in two ways:

1. By using standard symbols provided by the system (eg axes, diameters, etc): the symbol is simply requested and is automatically positioned on the drawing. The list of symbols can generally be augmented by writing corresponding sub-programs.
2. By the interactive creation of symbols: the operator builds up a library of symbols, which are subsequently used in the same way as the standard symbols.

Texts can also be positioned in dialogue mode; the operator designates the intended position and the desired orientation, and provides the chain of characters to be displayed and the necessary graphic indications (inclination of characters, type of line, etc). It is essential that the presentation should not simply be a set of lines and characters displayed in addition to the normal graphics, but should be functionally associated with the objects being presented. This concept is demonstrated in Figure 4.33, in which two objects (similar to connecting rods) are created, evaluated and then shaded. Following rotation (effected by the designer as a result of calculation), the position of one of the connecting rods is modified. If the presentation is not functionally associated with the objects, the result obtained will be that shown in Figure 4.33(ii) and the designer will have to re-evaluate and re-shade the surface. If, on the other hand, the presentation *is* associated with the objects, the result obtained, without intervention by the operator, will be that shown in Figure 4.33(iii).

Evaluation between two points (A and B) and calculation for the

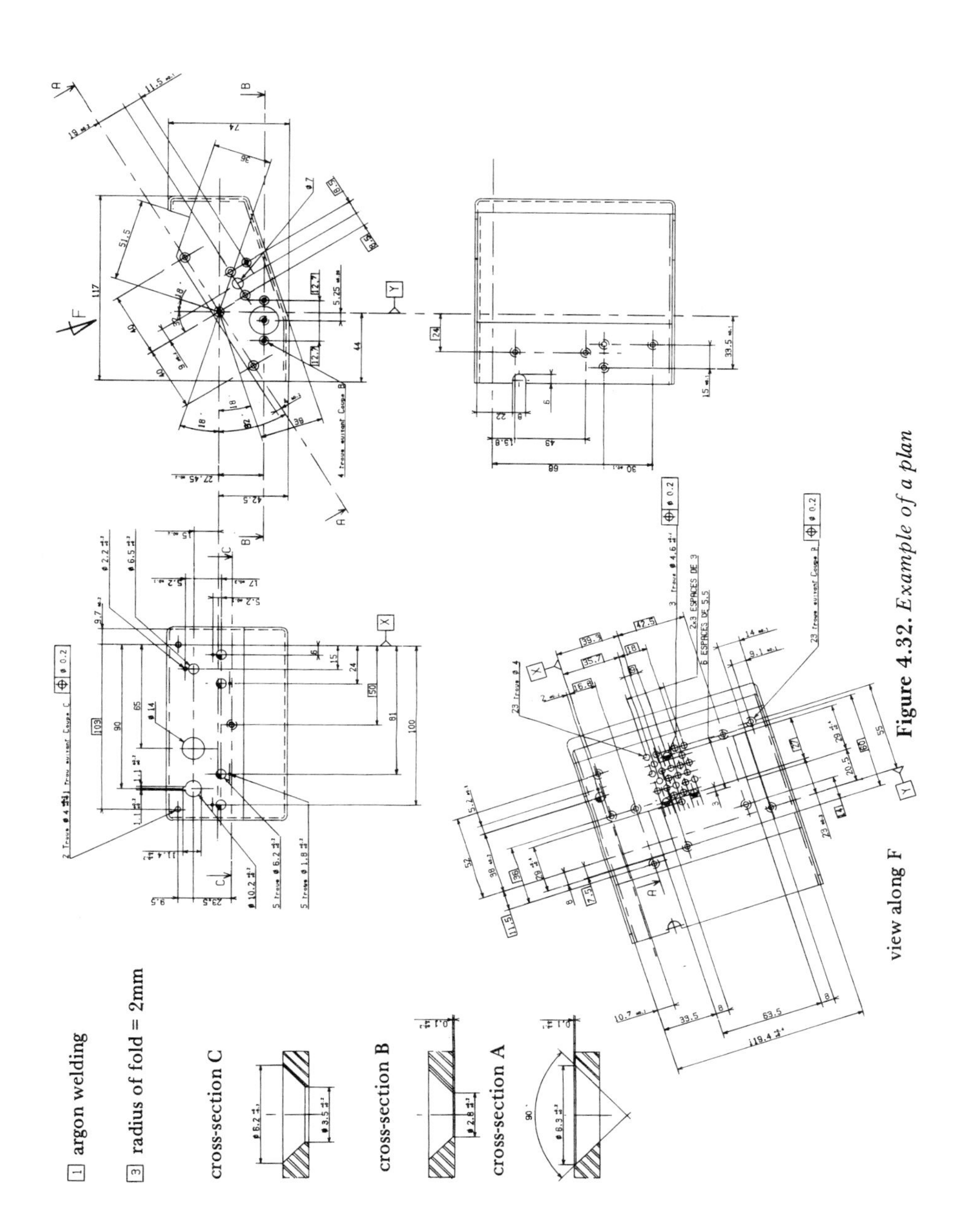


**Figure 4.32.** *Example of a plan*

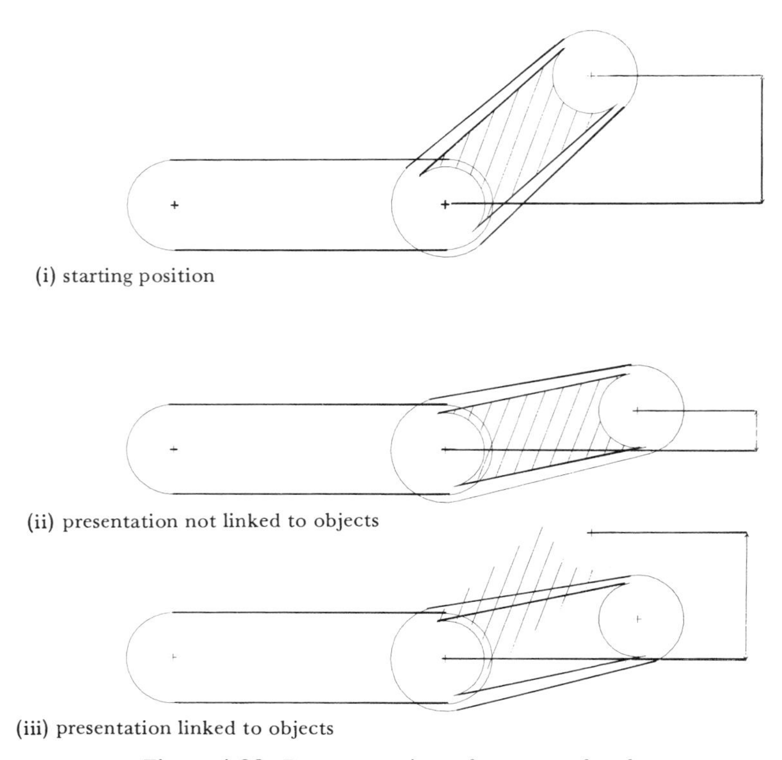

(i) starting position

(ii) presentation not linked to objects

(iii) presentation linked to objects

**Figure 4.33.** *Representation of connected rods*

production of graphics representing the reminder lines and the arrow after a movement of B is performed by the evaluation software. In the same way, the cross-hatching can be positioned if it is known on which contour it is based, and whatever its position. To aid the designer, a number of functions for the establishment of a structure have been introduced; these can be applied at two levels:

1. *The visual display level*: which allows a graphic representation to be organized as if it were made up of a number of transparent sheets, which can then be manipulated at will. Different levels can be used to separate different types of line. Thus, the construction lines can be placed on level one, the definition lines on level two and the presentation lines on level three. By a simple manipulation of these levels it is possible to view only those lines which are of interest at a given moment (see Figure 4.34). This concept can give rise to extremely interesting functions, such as the association of several views of the same object. Being able to use the same lines, whether for construction or as reminders for different views, allows the characteristics of these views to be linked. Modification of the construction or definition

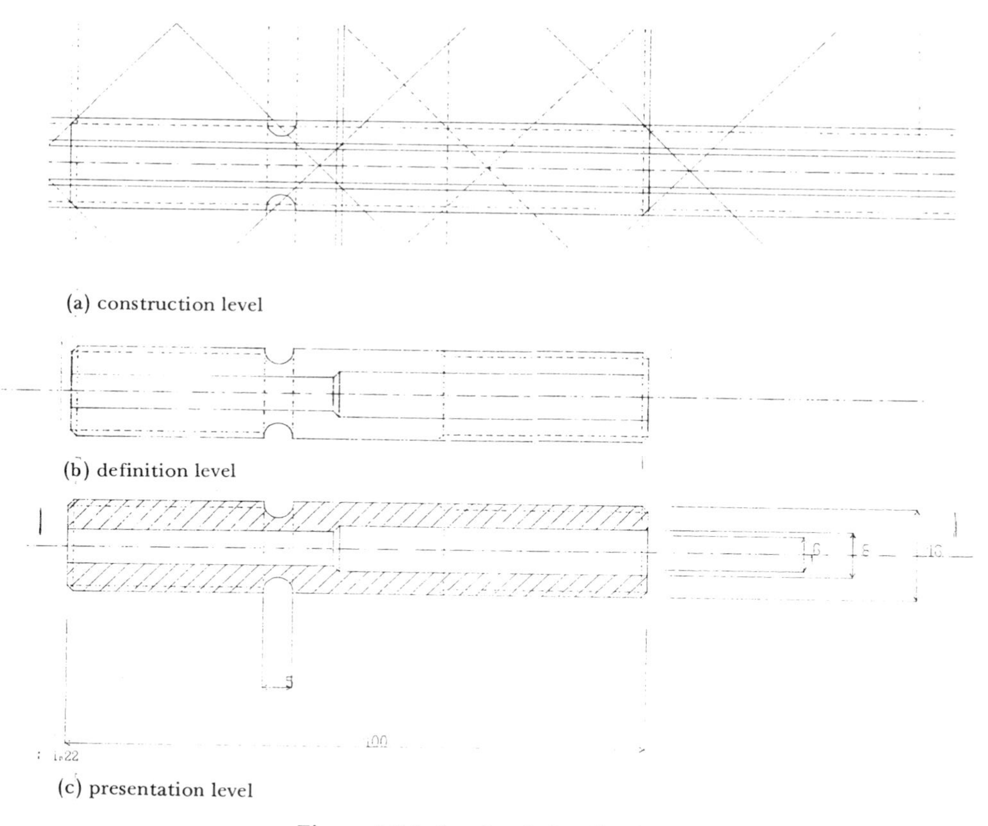


(a) construction level

(b) definition level

(c) presentation level

**Figure 4.34.** *Levels of visualization*

lines based on one view will have an immediate effect on the other view or views.

2. *The structural level of the plan*: it is sometimes possible to manage several levels of objects, by which method parts can be created and manipulated. Management is frequently carried out in tree form, and allows the concept of level of detail to be introduced. A single object can thus be represented with a degree of detail relative to the level.

If the evaluation to be developed concerns a number of objects, the following operations must be carried out:

1. the element or elements to be evaluated must be identified;
2. the evaluation must be positioned or indicated;
3. the value must be calculated automatically;
4. the user must be able to modify the value and its position;
5. the display of texts in any area of the screen is possible.

By identifying the objects to be evaluated, many cases can easily be processed, eg:

1. *evaluation of an object*
   circle (diameter)
   segment of straight line (length)
   point (coordinates)

2. *evaluation of two objects*
   point to point (by specifying an angle)
   point to arc (by specifying an angle and one side of the arc)
   point to segment (automatic)
   segment to arc (plus sides of arcs)

If the approximation position in which the evaluation is to be placed is known, the 'presentation' data structure will contain, for one evaluation:

1. an evaluation code;
2. the object or objects evaluated;
3. the coordinates of the approximate position at which the evaluation arrow is to appear;
4. the indicator specifying whether the evaluation must be calculated or has been provided by the user;
5. the value of the evaluation.

A sub-program can be used to process each element of this structure and calculate the corresponding drawings. A certain number of specific evaluations must be positioned, including:

1. the distance between two points;
2. the evaluation between two points following a direction defined by an angle, a line parallel to a given line or a line perpendicular to a given line.

Some CAD systems can be used to calculate automatically the page layout of some evaluations, leaving the designer to specify the points for evaluation. This type of facility is extremely useful, but involves relatively lengthy calculations, and it is sometimes necessary to make adjustments to the page layout obtained. However, there is still a need for the use of interactive modification tools.

This discussion can be concluded by stressing two points:

1. Presentation (evaluation, texts, shading, etc) is a basic means of communicating information in businesses concerned with design and manufacture processes. The plan (or set of plans) is often held to be the only valid source of information. The most important information is contained in the presentation and it is common, especially in mechanical work, to use evaluations which are precise, even though the

**Figure 4.35.** *Representation of a building*

drawing itself is inaccurate. The presentation must thus be based on strict norms relating to the graphics. For this reason, although an evaluation system may be highly detailed (and may include semi-functional concepts), it may be of little use for communicating information if the graphics do not relate absolutely to the norm. Graphics of this type require the use of complex visual display algorithms, particularly because of the number of examples to be processed – tolerances, text orientation, verification that the evaluation lines do not cut through the text, etc.

2. Although valid information concerning an object is contained in a model, a plan is considerably more important for the communication of certain types of information between clients, suppliers and subcontractors. It seems likely, however, that the widespread use of CAD/CAM and of interactive graphic techniques will produce a tendency to consider plans simply as presenting a particular view of an object. Already, information is frequently exchanged in the form of computer files containing parts of design models. The presentation of object representations in conjunction with traditional plans is proving extremely valuable in some professions. Figure 4.35 shows a representation of a

building. This type of document is quite commonplace and is becoming increasingly indispensible, because of the wealth of information it contains; this is often of less interest in relation to the manufacturing plans than to the object itself. This is particularly true of the automotive industry, where the picture of the car can be of help to the designer, but is certainly of far greater interest to the potential purchaser.

*Chapter 5*

# Dialogue techniques

## 5.1 General points

Dialogue between computer and operator occurs in the form of an exchange of information (see Figure 5.1):

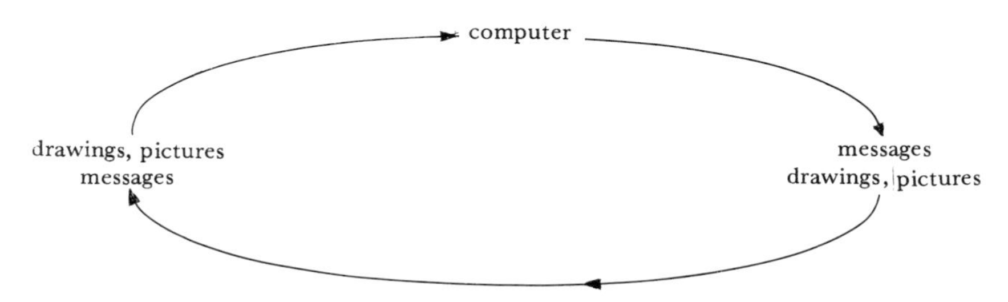


**Figure 5.1.** *Dialogue between operator and computer*

The computer transmits messages, alphanumerical information and drawings or pictures, ie graphic information. This information reflects the state of the machine at a given moment, and is intended to present to the designer the situation he must analyse and understand. The operator gives commands (messages) to the computer and provides it with alphanumerical or graphic data.

It should be noted that in most dialogue techniques, most of the information passes from the operator to the computer, which then reduces the symmetry of the dialogue. In Chapter 4, the visual display techniques involved in dialogue in machine to operator functions were discussed. This chapter is concerned solely with techniques that allow the operator to indicate the task required. The operator acts on:

1. the *program*, using an operation for choosing the desired course of action from the range of possible actions that can be carried out at a given moment; this is called *consulting the menu*;
2. *the data*, by introducing alphanumerical values, introducing drawings or pictures (sets of coordinates) and by designating objects by their graphic representation; this is known as *identification.*

Two of these four basic functions, the menu and the introduction of alphanumerical values, are not essentially graphic. The use of communication devices connected to a visual display console can, however, allow them to be practised quite effectively. A number of techniques which correspond to each of these functions will be discussed.

The main problem with interaction is the need for cooperation between the four data structures described in section 2.3.3. These four structures represent, in effect, the same thing, in that it is possible to consider what appears on the screen as being equivalent to the view through a window of the model of the object being designed. When the operator indicates an action to be performed, he can address different levels for a variety of reasons. There are, however, certain rules that must be observed:

1. In all cases, any modification of a structure must be reflected at the lower levels. If the modifications carried out at the application level must appear in the graphic representation, the operator may have to intervene only in the scene (the geometric model). Thus, any change in position in the scene will be shown on the screen.

2. In some cases, the modifications carried out on a structure must not be shown at a higher level. For example, if an image is simply to be re-framed, or if a caption is to be added, it is desirable that these modifications are carried out at the lowest level possible, without having recourse to the application, but also that these modifications should not have to be taken into account by raising the information to higher levels.

3. In some cases, the modifications carried out on a structure must be reflected in the higher levels. This arises each time action in the graphic representation is intended to symbolize action in the data structure of the application. For example, to delete an element from an integrated circuit, it would be necessary to identify the element to be deleted on the graphic representation of the circuit, leaving the system to make the connection with the representation of this element in the data structure of the application. This can be further complicated because:

(a) the techniques used to structure the various groups of data are very diverse (tables, lists, rings, etc) and locating or exchanging information involves the use of programs making it possible to move from one structure to the next;

(b) two types of relationship are represented in these structures: (i) *logical connections*, reflecting the structure of the application; (ii) *descriptive connections*, used to help encoding (cutting into sub-scenes, sub-designs, etc).

Thus, it is important to provide mechanisms that ensure independent access to each structure and connection between the different structures. The standard method currently in use consists of giving the processed elements structured names, which are kept up to date and are transmitted from one level to another. Two main types of structured name are used:

1. names with one or two levels, with which an object made up of sub-objects on the same level can be processed (typical standardized graphic software);
2. tree-type names, with which objects can be structured into trees of any number of levels. The operator then manipulates the trees or sub-trees.

This problem (naming procedures and object structuring) is crucial to dialogue, and has still not been overcome.

## 5.2 Elementary techniques

Here some of the techniques used for carrying out the functions described in Section 5.1 will be discussed, with reference to various communication devices.

### 5.2.1 USE OF A LIGHT PEN

#### *5.2.1.1 Menu*

The set of commands available at a given moment is displayed on the screen (see Figure 5.2). The operator then brings the light pen close to the screen and points at the command he wishes to have executed. Once the light from the selected command is detected, the action of the light pen causes an interruption with which is associated the coordinate pair (x, y) of the point. The display zone of the menu is made up of rectangular blocks of equal dimension, each containing a command. It is then a simple matter of finding the block containing the coordinate pair of the point, and to deduce which command has been selected.

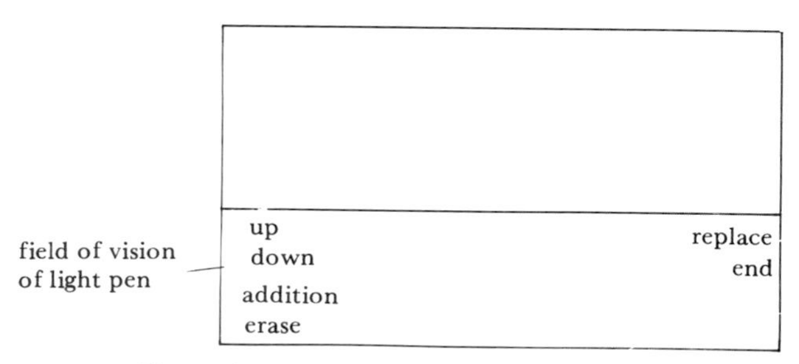


**Figure 5.2.** *Use of a light pen on the menu*

This technique has the following advantages:

1. the list of available commands is displayed clearly;
2. a position on the screen can be indicated easily;

but there are several disadvantages:

1. part of the screen may be obscured by the hand of the operator (inconvenient in some applications);
2. part of the screen must be reserved for the menu, thus restricting the amount of space available for other displays;
3. the physical effort of moving the arm can become tiring.

Nonetheless, this technique is very widely used.

### *5.2.1.2 Introduction of alphanumerical values*

The standard method involves displaying the letter of the alphabet and the figures 0 to 9 on one part of the screen. To make up a value, the operator successively designates the different characters of which it is composed. However, this technique is tedious and is rarely used in practice.

### *5.2.1.3 Collection of coordinates*

The nature of the problem changes in a situation where a position on the screen which is not necessarily lit must be designated. One technique that is fairly standard involves covering the whole screen with characters so that the operator can specify one of them. The main drawbacks to this method are that:

1. the original image disappears, and is replaced by a curtain of characters;
2. the level of precision obtained is very poor, since the coordinates are obtained from the character specified, and characters can cover about 60 points on the screen;
3. access cannot be gained to all the positions on the screen, because the character grid is usually fixed.

An extension of the light pen method involves the use of a luminous symbol, eg a cross (see Figure 5.3):

1. The cross is drawn point by point, starting from the centre each arm is drawn successively.

2. To start with, the cross is displayed in any position on the screen; its appearance activates a response of the system to a request for a collection of coordinates.

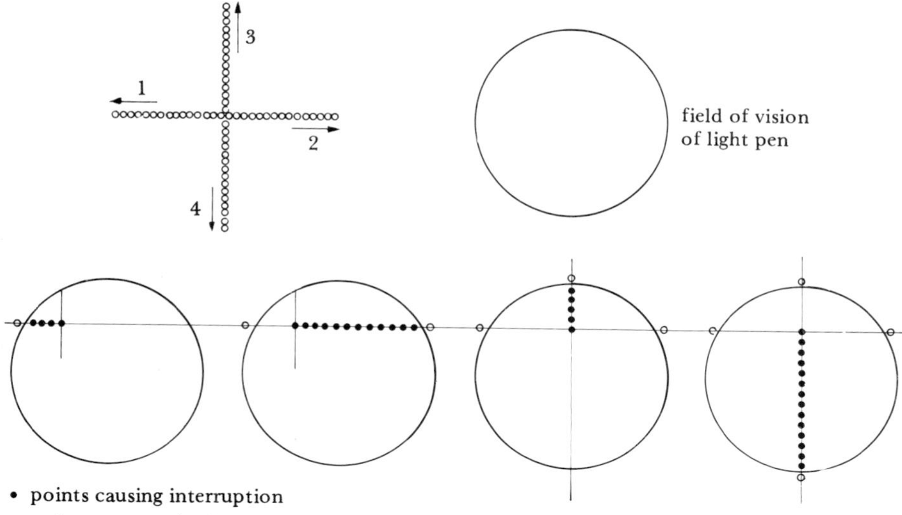


**Figure 5.3.** *Extension of the use of a light pen – the luminous symbol*

3. When the operator brings the light pen close to the cross, part of the cross falls within the field of vision of the photo-electric cell. Each point detected causes an interruption, and this fact is used to 'follow' the movements of the light pen. During generation of each arm of the succeeding cross, only the points detected by the light pen, that is those which cause an interruption, will be displayed. Generation of an arm will be ended when the first point which does not cause an interruption is encountered, ie the first point outside the field of vision. The coordinates of this point are noted, and another arm of the cross is then formed. When the four arms are complete, the new centre of the cross is calculated using the recorded coordinates of the extreme points. This has the effect of recentring the cross in the field of vision.

4. The cross remains stationary for as long as the light pen is still. As soon as the operator moves the pen, the operation for recentring the cross will be activated and the cross will be generated according to the movement of the pen. It is important that the speed of movement does not exceed the speed of the calculations for recentring. In practice, given that the calculations apply to about fifty points, the time required is relatively short, and the speed at which the hand moves can be fairly rapid.

This technique requires an extremely powerful means of calculation, since it is based on the recognition of a large number of interruptions. It has been calculated that, in some interactive systems, more than

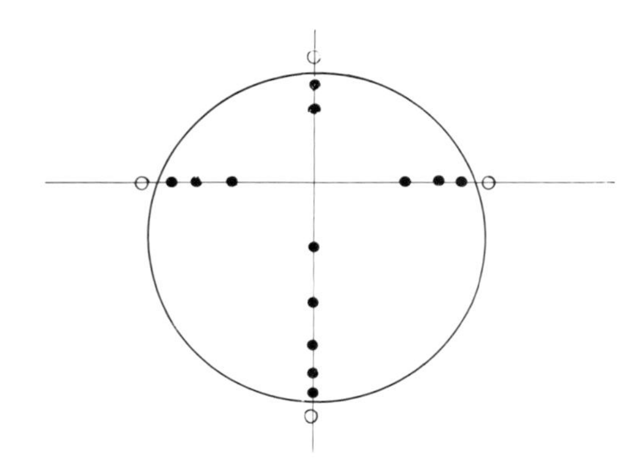

**Figure 5.4.** *Logarithmic tracking*

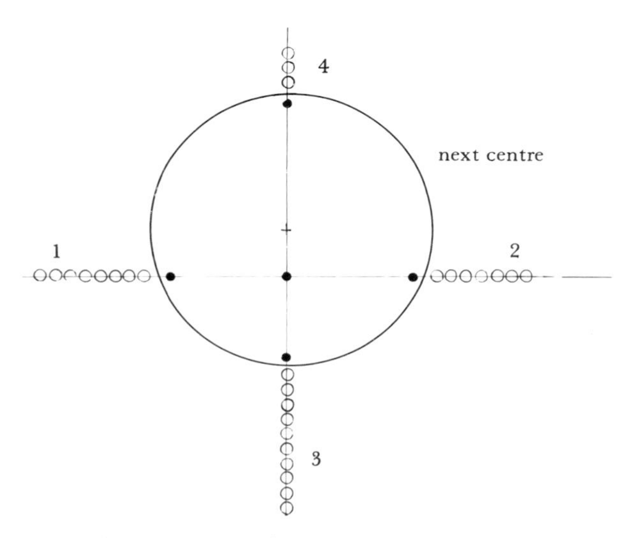


**Figure 5.5.** *Tracking towards the centre*

half the calculation time is spent tracking the luminous symbol. It is not surprising, therefore, that a number of techniques have been developed which reduce the number of interruptions necessary. Here are a few examples:

1. *Logarithmic tracking* (see Figure 5.4): instead of plotting points at regular intervals along the arms of the cross, they are formed at intervals of decreasing size, eg by multiples of two. Thus, the number of points is reduced and the required point can be found more quickly, with an approximation being made at the outset, and a more detailed evaluation made as the field of vision is approached.

2. *Tracking towards the centre* (see Figure 5.5): instead of drawing the

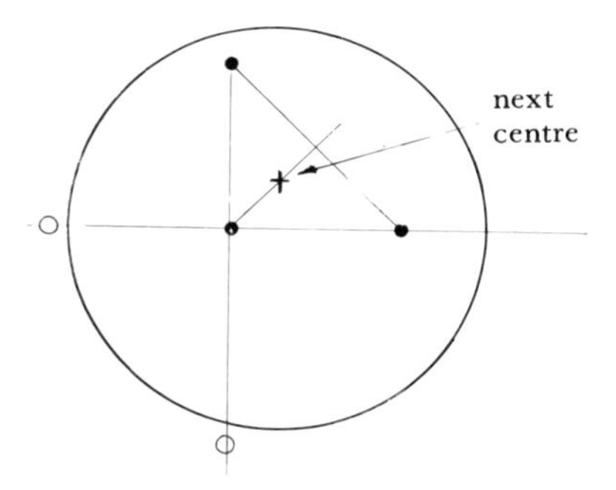


**Figure 5.6.** *A simplified cross*

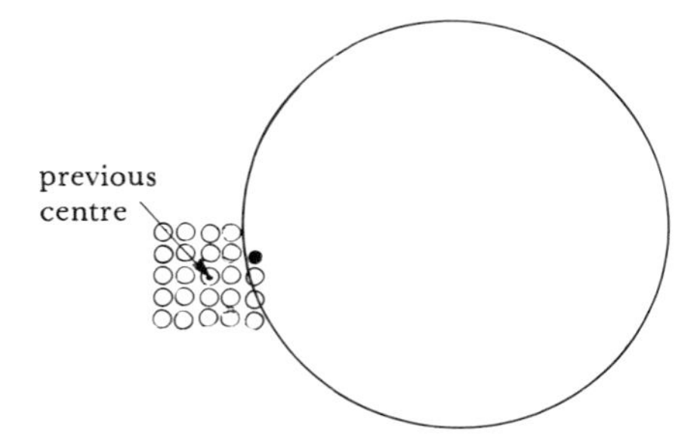


**Figure 5.7.** *Spiral tracking*

cross point by point starting from the centre, the extremity of each arm is used as a starting point. The first point on each arm to cause an interruption is found, and the cross recentred accordingly. Given that in this technique the centre of the cross is never displayed in the field of vision, sighting is rather difficult. For this reason the centre of the cross is usually displayed simply as a guide to the operator. A maximum of five points would cause interruption during each recentring operation.

3. *Use of a simplified cross* (see Figure 5.6): in this technique a symbolic cross is used, made up of only five points (the extremities of the arms and the centre). To recentre the cross, an average of the coordinates of the points detected (those which cause an interruption) is determined. This type of method effectively reduces the number of interruptions to be processed in following the movements of the pen. However, the speed at which the pen can be moved is reduced, because the small number of points used in forming the cross increases the risk of its being lost by the light pen.

4. *Spiral tracking* (see Figure 5.7): in this method, the tracking symbol is formed by a single point. When a request is made for collection of coordinates, the point is displayed and moved along a spiral path,

based on the points next to the positions adjacent to those previously touched upon. The spiral grows until the point enters the field of vision of the light pen. An interruption then occurs and the search is reactivated from that point. This technique clearly involves the smallest number of interruptions. The main drawback is that it requires the operator to sight using not the centre of the light pen, but with its outer parts.

It should be noted that all these techniques have been enhanced by the incorporation of 'movement prediction'. The basic idea is that movements of the pen are anticipated by using the history of previous movements. The calculation of the position of the new centre of the cross can become complicated by considerations related to the speed of movement, the preferred direction and other parameters.

By taking advantage of the facility for tracking a luminous symbol on the screen, it is possible to make use of the techniques for collection of coordinates. Designation of a part of the screen by the operator is carried out as follows (see Figure 5.8):

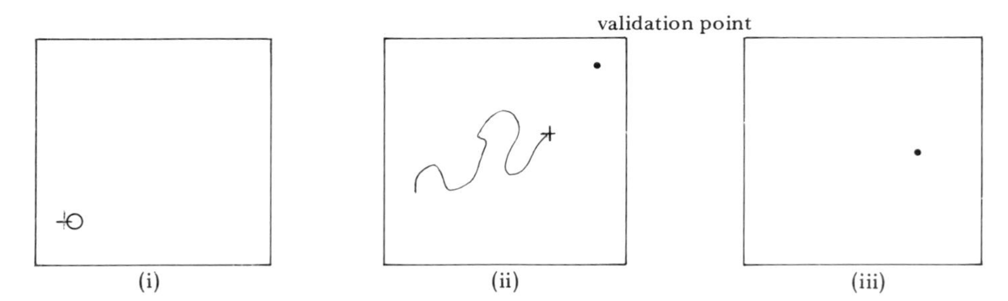


**Figure 5.8.** *Collection of coordinate points*

1. when the request for collection is made, the luminous symbol appears – the operator finds it by using the light pen;

2. the operator moves the light pen in the direction of the area of interest; the different positions of the cross are not recorded;

3. once the required position is reached, the operator must validate it by indicating to the system that it is to be retained as being definitive. This involves the use of a validation method, of which there are several types:

(a) the cross can be abandoned by rapidly moving the pen away from the screen so that it is lost by the light pen – a convention has been established which states that if the cross is stationary for one second, it is in its definitive position (this technique can be rather exacting);

(b) a luminous point can be used which is displayed in the corner of the screen when the cross has changed position. When the operator is satisfied with the position of the cross, an indication of the validation point is made with the light pen, and the coordinates of the centre of the cross are recorded. In practice, the validation function is carried out using a function button.

A number of coordinate collections can be combined, for example, by continuously recording the movements of the tracking symbol so as to form free-hand lines. It should be stressed that it is very unusual to make use of free-hand lines on the screen because of the low level of precision.

To illustrate these techniques consider the following examples.

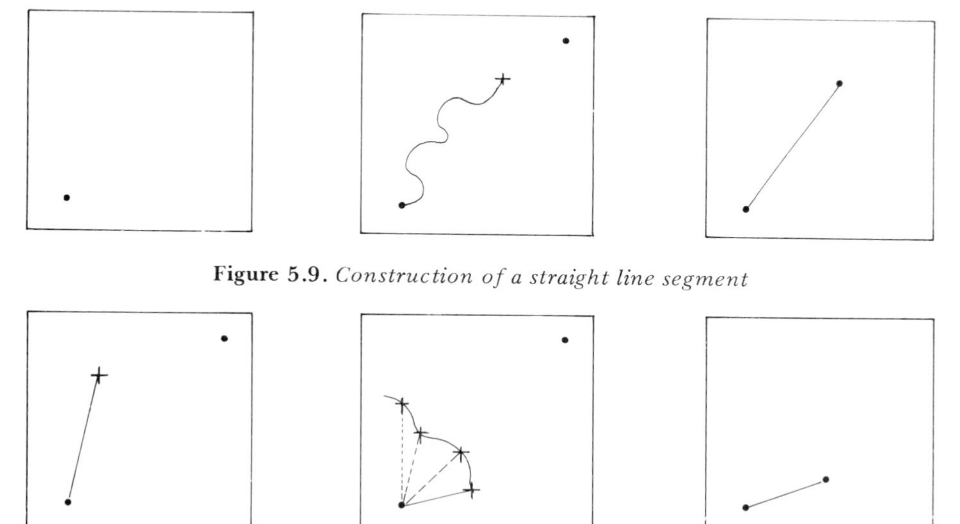

**Figure 5.9.** *Construction of a straight line segment*

**Figure 5.10.** *The elastic band technique*

To draw a straight line segment, the operator starts by designating the first position on the screen. The tracking symbol appears and the operator moves it to the required position, without the intermediate positions being recorded (see Figure 5.9). Once the second position has been determined, designation of the function point activates the display of the entire segment. To make the positioning of certain types of line easier (eg a straight line segment tangential to an arc of circle), the *elastic band technique* is sometimes used. This consists of systematically joining the first extremity of the segment to the instantaneous position of the cross. Thus, the operator can adjust the line of the segment with precision. The deformations of the segment according to the position of the tracking symbol are similar to those of an elastic band when under varying tension – hence the name of the technique (see Figure 5.10).

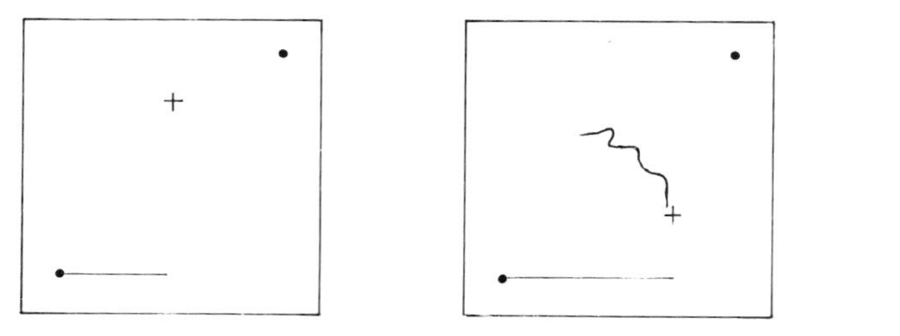

**Figure 5.11.** *A horizontal constraint*

Other techniques for the control of the luminous symbol make use of servo-control of its movement in a given direction. For example (see Figure 5.11), to draw a horizontal line segment, the operator designates the first extremity, then requests the use of, for instance, an elastic band technique, whilst exerting servo-control over the line that is to remain horizontal. To achieve this, the system retains only the abcissa from all the movements of the cross, the ordinates having been fixed during the positioning of the first extremity. A verticality constraint can, of course, be applied, or it can be requested that the movement take place in a given direction, with the movements of the cross being plotted in that direction.

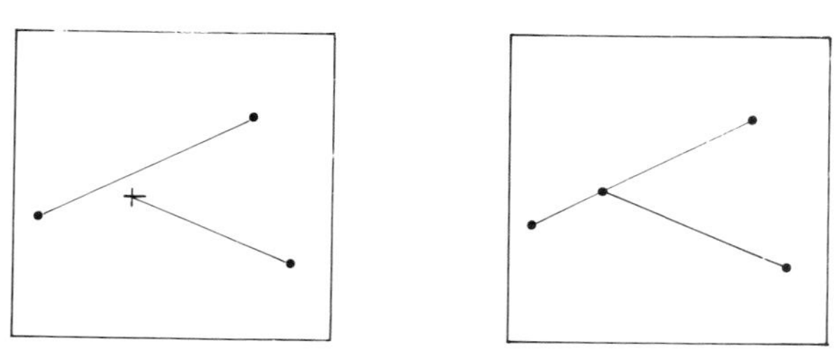

**Figure 5.12.** *A proximity constraint*

Another type of constraint which is frequently used is that of proximity. The problem to be solved is the low level of precision in sighting with a light pen. If an extremity of an existing line segment is to be designated exactly, or if two segments are to be joined, it is most important that the tracking symbol can be moved near to the desired entity; the computer will then automatically calculate the coordinates required. For example, Figure 5.12 shows a scene where an operator has placed the extremity of a segment being created close to an existing segment. This choice is validated using a function point, and the system automatically calculates the required coordinates or, in other words, the point of intersection of the two vectors. This all takes place as if the straight line segment had a zone of influence comprising two parts (see Figure 5.13):

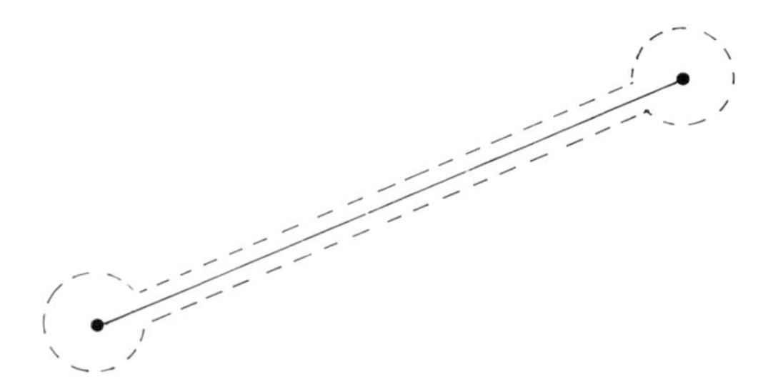

**Figure 5.13.** *The zone of influence of a segment*

1. a circle surrounding each extremity: any point falling within one of these circles is supposed to designate the extremity of the segment which constitutes the centre of the circle;
2. a rectangle surrounding the body of the straight line segment: any point falling within this rectangle is supposed to represent a point in the segment itself (eg the nearest point, or the point of intersection of two segments).

In practice, only very approximate calculations are made, as illustrated by Figure 5.14:

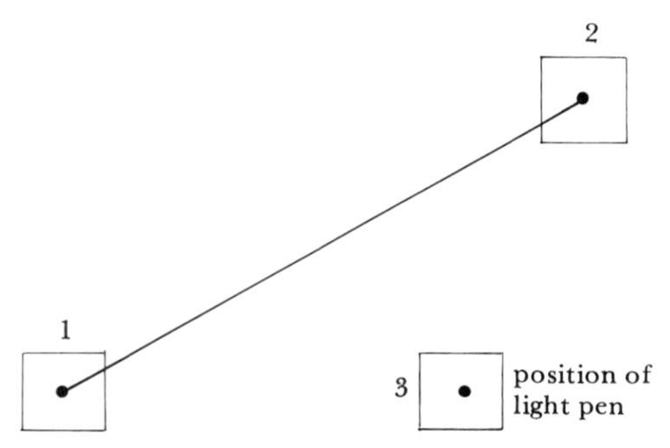


**Figure 5.14.** *Identification of a segment*

1. each of the two extremities is surrounded by a very small square, with sides parallel to the axes. The object is to determine whether or not the point corresponding to the position of the light pen is inside one of the two squares – if it is, the processing is terminated;
2. in the opposite situation, the point which represents the position of the light pen is surrounded by a very small square. The object is to determine whether or not the square is crossed by the segment under test – if it is, the point is connected to the segment just processed;
3. the above method is applied to all the straight line segments which

make up the figure, until a segment which corresponds to one of the two preceding criteria is found.

The following comments can be made on the techniques summarized over:

1. It is clear that testing with squares involves, of necessity, a slight degree of error. The size of the zone defining the margin of influence is, however, so small that the error is almost negligible.
2. This technique implies the existence of a record of all the straight line segments displayed at a given moment. In machines with structured buffer memories, this record exists in the visual display list and can be located easily. In other systems, a virtual display list must be kept up to date.
3. This technique can be extended for use with other graphic primitives, such as character shapes.

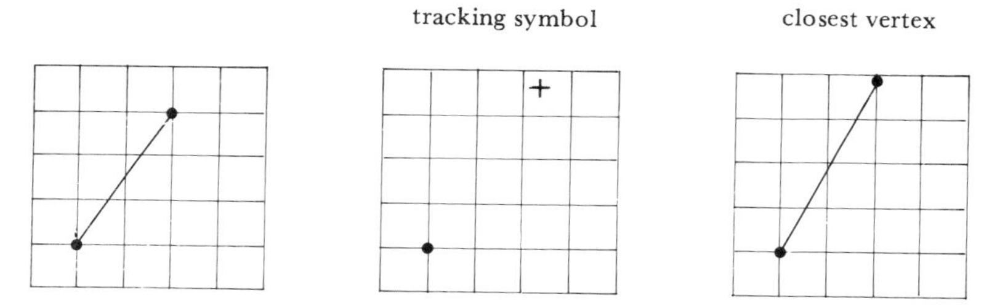


**Figure 5.15.** *Using a grid for tracking a point*

Another similar technique involves the use of various types of grid, which allow any system of coordinates to be formed on the screen. The operator can construct the straight line segments of interest by basing the lines on the vertices of the grid (see Figure 5.15). Use of this technique is frequently completed using a proximity constraint, which associates any point on the screen with the closest vertex of the grid. In this way, the operator has total control over the design.

### *5.2.1.4 Identification*

The operator designates a graphic element, present on the screen, with the help of the light pen (see Figure 5.16). The problem that arises for the system is that of finding a link between the graphic element and its equivalent in the data base of the application. As stated earlier, this link is formed by a structured name. The association is made with the help of correlation tables, which establish a relationship between the structured names and the positions of the graphic elements in the buffer memory (see Figure 5.17). During the interruption brought about by the light pen, the address of the graphic instruction is

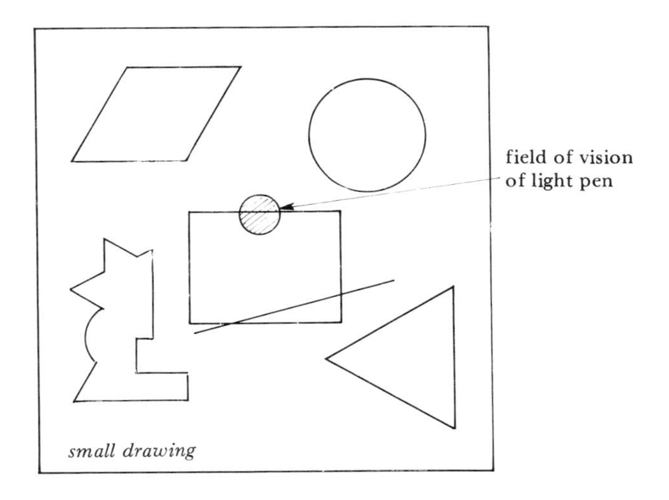


**Figure 5.16.** *Identification on the screen*

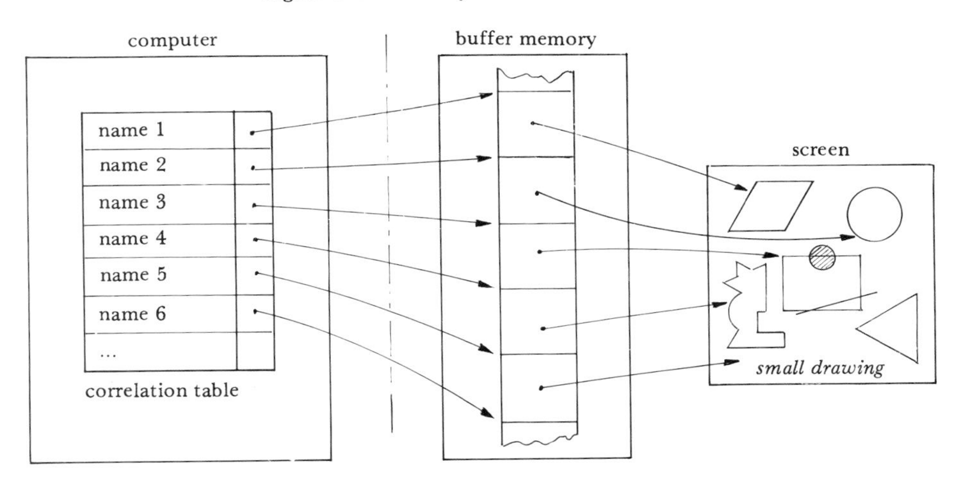


**Figure 5.17.** *Use of a correlation table*

transmitted to the computer, which then searches through the correlation table. This search is very rapid, since it generally involves only a small number of elements. If the terminals are not equipped with a structured buffer memory, the techniques mentioned previously are used to solve the proximity constraints.

### 5.2.2 USE OF AN ALPHANUMERICAL KEYBOARD

There is no great difference in the techniques used with a keyboard terminal when used in a conversational system, apart from the fact that the characters which are typed are displayed on the screen in the

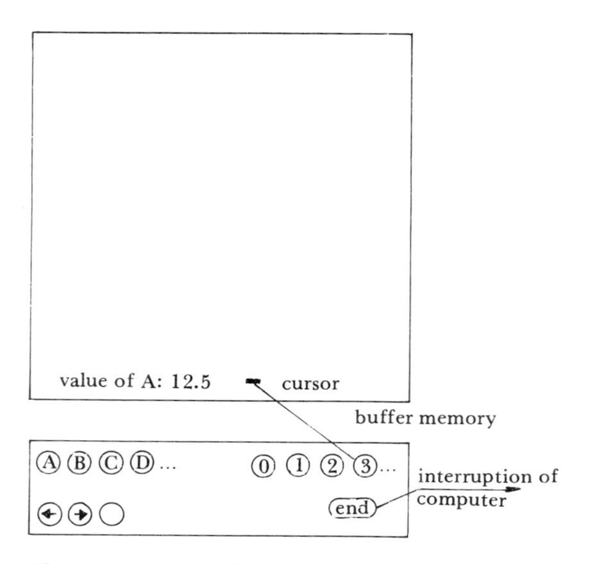


**Figure 5.18.** *Use of an alphanumerical keyboard*

position indicated by a cursor, which moves across the screen as the characters are displayed (see Figure 5.18). The various possible uses of such a system will be summarized here.

*5.2.2.1 Menu*

The name of the command is typed directly by the operator.

*5.2.2.2 Introduction of alphanumerical values*

The alphanumerical keyboard is used to carry out this function.

*5.2.2.3 Collection of coordinates*

In general, collection is carried out using the data in the list of numerical values corresponding to the set of coordinates introduced into the machine. This is a lengthy and exacting process, and is usually avoided except when using very precise coordinates which are fixed in advance and which cannot be rendered precisely by any other means.

Another technique, which is used relatively little, consists of guiding the movements with a tracking symbol by typing appropriate characters. For instance, 'U', 'D', 'L' and 'R' are used to move the symbol up, down, to the left and to the right, respectively. These movements are by a number of screen units, determined in advance, and this can be varied to accelerate or retard the movements. The facility to repeat a character if the key is depressed and held is not generally available.

#### *5.2.2.4 Identification*

These functions are not implemented simply by the operator giving the name of the entity of interest. Indeed, it is often the case that these names are not known since:

1. the number of elements on the screen is too great for the operator to know the names of all of them; there can be thousands of components in an electronic system, for example, and it would be quite impossible to identify each by name;
2. the processing system is often responsible for creating names, in order to ensure that the links required by the designer can be made – these names are often peculiar to the CAD/CAM system.

In practice, an alphanumerical keyboard is not used for identification, except for guiding the symbol, as described across (though this is very rarely used).

### 5.2.3 USE OF A FUNCTION KEYBOARD

#### *5.2.3.1 Menu*

This is the application for which function keyboards are best suited. A function is associated with each key, so that when one is depressed the number of the key indicates the function. Two possible situations can arise:

1. *segments of the menu cannot be lit up by the program*: in this situation, there is only a limited number of keys and their use may cause problems for the operator in choosing one to press;

2. *the keys can be lit up by the program*: this guides the operator in the choice of keys. It is possible to visualize the level at which the operator is working, by the keys which are lit up. Figure 5.19 shows a hierarchized menu, in which each function (figure, drawing, end figure, etc) is associated with a key number. If it is assumed that the keyboard used has 20 function keys, a schematized sequence for the use of menu commands can be constructed as follows:
(a) at the outset, only key 1 is lit up and corresponds to the figure command;
(b) if the operator presses this key, keys 2, 3 and 4 will light up (as indicated by the three closed circles in the diagram);
(c) below each keyboard the name of the command requested by the operator is displayed.

It should be noted that the following choices are made during installation:

1. Elements of the same level are placed at the same level on the

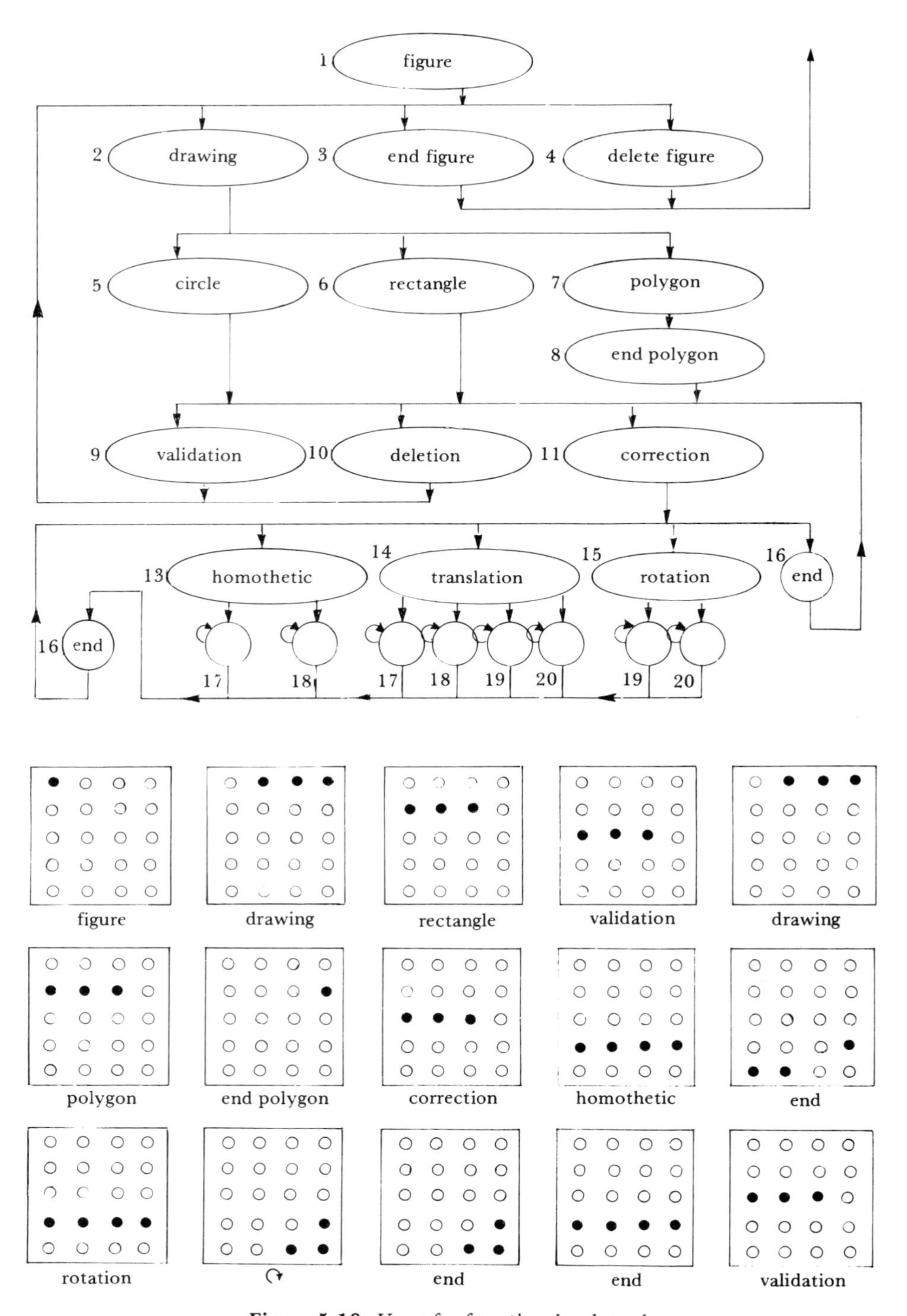


**Figure 5.19.** *Use of a function keyboard*

function keyboard. Thus, the operator immediately knows what stage has been reached in the menu tree.

2. The keys which correspond to functions of the same type are adjacent. For example, the four keys which correspond to a translation command are adjacent. In this way, the operator will find different aspects of the same function in the same place. This arrangement makes it easier to learn how to use the function keyboard, and means that it can be used without the operator needing to look for a particular key.

#### *5.2.3.2 Introduction of alphanumerical values*

Logically, it should be sufficient to modify each function key with a letter of the alphabet and a number. In practice, this is never done. There are a few examples of values which are frequently used (eg standard rotation values, commonly used constants, etc) and which would justify the modification of function keys but, as a general rule, the function keyboard is not used for this type of operation.

#### *5.2.3.3 Collection of coordinates*

Usually, function keyboards are rarely used for this type of operation, except for instance, where the keys are used to guide a symbol on the screen. This only occurs with keys that allow the command to be repeated for as long as the key is depressed – a technique most commonly used for moving the cursor.

#### *5.2.3.4 Identification*

Function keyboards are only rarely used for such an operation, typically for guiding a symbol (see above).

To summarize, the function keyboard does not appear to be particularly useful, except for use with the menu function. It should be noted that although the function assumed by this type of device is not graphic, it is almost exclusively used with graphic consoles. The reason for this is unclear.

### 5.2.4 USE OF A GRAPHIC TABLET

#### *5.2.4.1 Menu*

The response to a request made using a graphic tablet takes the form of a coordinate pair (x, y), which represents the position of the pen on the tablet. There are two ways of using such a device:

1. An indication of the position of the pen is displayed on the screen

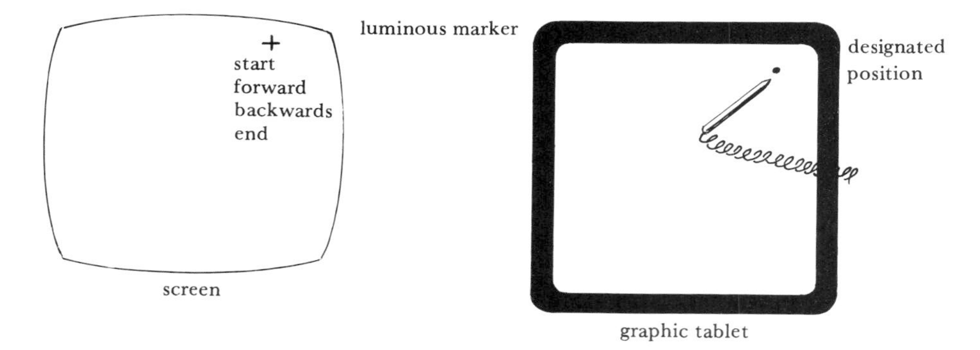


**Figure 5.20.** *Indirect selection*

in the form of a light marker which moves according to movement of the pen. A menu can be displayed on the screen, and a command selected indirectly by moving the light marker along the chosen command. Once the position has been validated, the same type of menu processing is used as with the light pen (see Figure 5.20).

2. The choice is made directly on the tablet, without reference to the screen. This is the approach that will be discussed now.

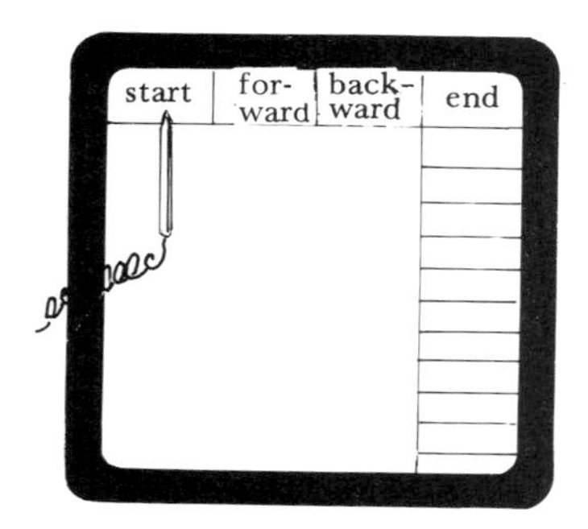


**Figure 5.21.** *A positional menu*

There are two methods by which menus can be formed: positional menus and real-time symbol recognizers. In positional menus, it is as if the tablet were divided into small boxes (see Figure 5.21). To designate a command, the pen is pointed at the required box, and the system automatically makes the association between this position, the box indicated and the corresponding command. This technique can be divided into two types:

1. *static menus*, in which the positioning is fixed on the tablet. There are disadvantages with this type of menu in that sometimes the work zone is disturbed and the continual exchange between the work zone and the menu zone is restricted;

2. *dynamic menus*, in which positioning can vary over a period of time. This method allows the operator to move the menu zone during a session, alerting the system with a specific command. In relatively short menus (with few commands) which are frequently used in a particular stage of work, the menu can be moved as though it were positioned around the point of the pen, and thus follows its movements. The static menu technique is by far the most widely used, although the use of symbol recognizers is also quite widespread. Some CAD/CAM systems make almost exclusive use of it, the general idea being as follows:

(a) to give a command, the operator draws the corresponding symbol on the tablet (see Figure 5.22);

(b) in real time (ie at the same time as the operator draws the symbol), the system calculates the different coordinates, analyses them and determines the symbol which has been drawn, and thus the function associated with it.

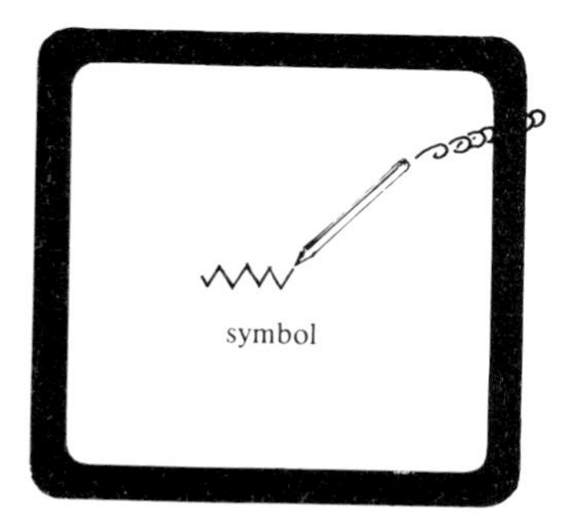


**Figure 5.22.** *Recognition of symbols*

Apart from this aspect of the technique, real-time symbol recognition also has ergonomic aspects:

1. it allows a single surface to be used for drawing and giving commands, thus avoiding the need for several devices;
2. it allows dialogue to be personalized, by adapting the symbols and the manner in which they are presented to the user.

A real-time symbol recognition system must respond quickly, have a very high recognition rate (of the order of 98%) and be sufficiently flexible to allow fairly considerable variations in writing. The main components of this type of system are:

1. a *dictionary of symbols*, allowing the different shapes used by an operator to be described;
2. a *symbol reading module* which processes the data from the tablet into the form required by the dictionary;

3. a *classification algorithm* which compares the data from the tablet with the shapes in the dictionary, in order to recognize the character input.

*Symbol dictionaries* contain a codification of all the characters to be processed. This codification involves a certain number of characteristics by which each symbol can be recognized. Extremely diverse techniques have been used to ensure this. For example, a symbol can be described by data concerning the straight line segments of which it is composed. The number of segments and the coordinates of the extremities of the modelled symbols are recorded. The identification of the symbol drawn by the operator is made by comparing the segments drawn with the segments of the model, eg by calculating the distances with the smallest squares. However, this technique has two disadvantages:

1. a long time is required for calculation;
2. the degree of flexibility for the shape being drawn is very small, which is extremely inconvenient for the operator.

| | | |
|---|---|---|
| 1111 | 0111 | 0011 |
| 1101 | 0101 | 0001 |
| 1100 | 0100 | 0000 |

encoding the zones

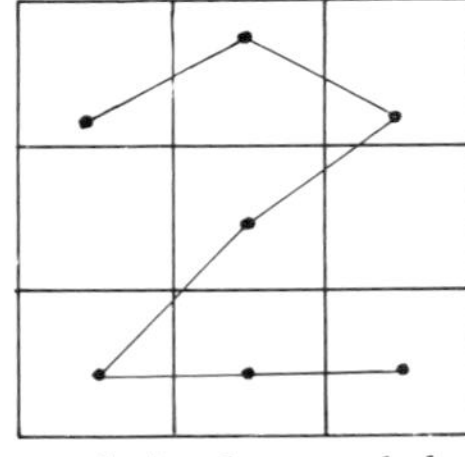

symbol to be encoded

signature 1111 0111 0011 0101 1100 0100 0000

**Figure 5.23.** *Principles of Ledeen encoding*

A very different approach has been developed by Ledeen, who was primarily interested in the topology of symbols, in which a symbol is surrounded by a rectangle and then divided into nine parts (see Figure 5.23). Each line of the symbol is stored in the dictionary in the form of the series of vertices of which it is made. Each vertex is encoded by the number of the part of the rectangle in which it lies. Thus, only the parts through which the lines pass, and not the exact positions in the parts, are recorded. Consequently:

1. the space required to encode a set of symbols is smaller than in the previous example;
2. the shapes accepted for input can be somewhat irregular, since the exact positions in the parts of the rectangle are not used. There is, however, a greater risk of confusion between two symbols which, although different, may follow similar paths through the rectangle.

In practice, this problem does not arise, because the symbols can be chosen freely.

If there are several lines, the signature of each of the lines plus a supplementary signature (made up of a code indicating the centre of the line at the centre of the rectangles surrounding each line) are recorded. It can be seen that Ledeen encoding is designed to be easy to use. Its updating is straightforward, and subsequent development of the dictionary is allowed for. Moreover, the search is made by comparing the signatures of the input lines with those stored in the dictionaries – this process is quite rapid.

Libraries of symbols can be divided into two types:

1. *static libraries* which cannot be modified;
2. *dynamic libraries*, in which the contents can be changed at will either during the creation phases, in which the operator forms a repertoire of symbols, or during use of the recognition facility. For example, statistical information on the frequency of appearance of each symbol (and thus on the probability of its use) is automatically updated, so decreasing the risk of ambiguities.

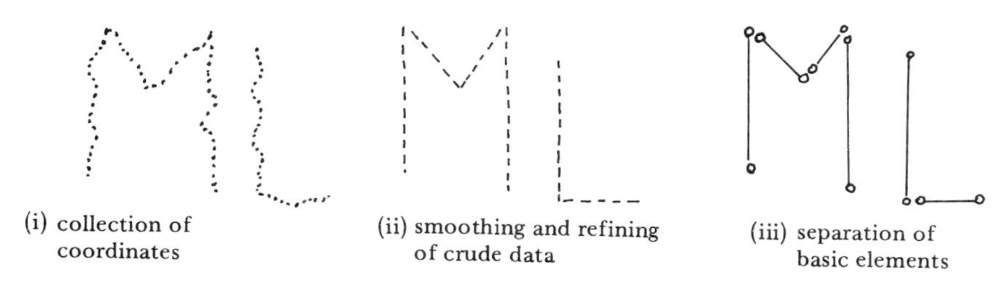


**Figure 5.24.** *Symbol reading*

The *symbol reading module* has the role of collecting coordinates transmitted via the tablet, smoothing and reducing them and of breaking down the sequence of points into the terminal elements used in the dictionary (see Figure 5.24). For example, the symbol reader will be responsible for determining the straight line segments and differentiating the lines. This module has an extremely important role, since it prepares for the recognition phase, and because the processing envisaged must be carried out in a very small time interval.

The *classification module* also plays an important role, in that the rate of recognition and the flexibility possible in the shape of the symbols depends on it. There are several methods of classification in use, some of which make use of artificial intelligence techniques with the introduction of concepts such as recognition of the general context in which the command is made, or teaching frequently used sequences to an operator. The object is to improve the rate of recognition, whilst if possible, taking into account the work methods of the operator.

### *5.2.4.2 Introduction of alphanumerical values*

There are two main types of technique available:

1. Division of the surface (or part of the surface) of the graphic tablet into a symbolic keyboard, relating letters of the alphabet and/or numbers to virtual boxes arranged over the surface (see Figure 5.25). The introduction of values is carried out by designating the required boxes using a pen. This technique is used mainly when the boxes can be associated not only with single characters but with key words, which considerably reduces the time taken for writing.

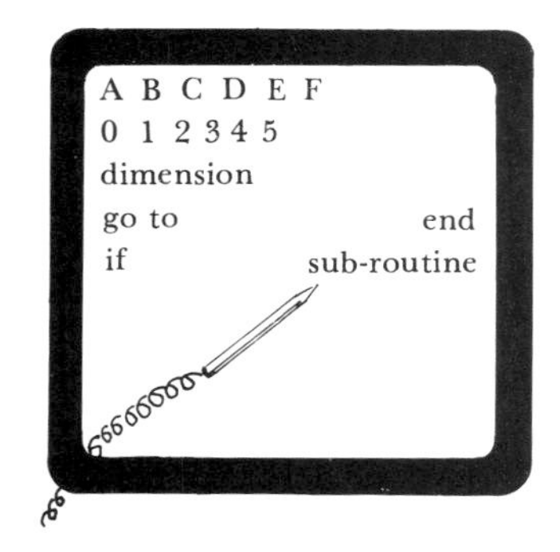


**Figure 5.25.** *Input of alphanumerical values*

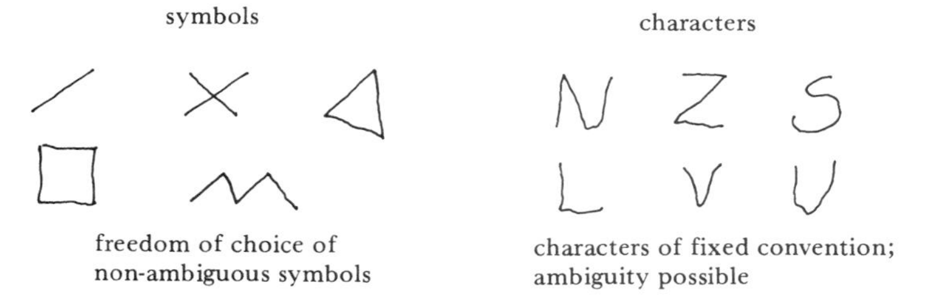


**Figure 5.26.** *Recognition of symbols and characters*

2. Use of a real-time character recognition device: even if the techniques used to construct symbol recognition are applied, character recognizers are more difficult to use, since alphabetical symbols are fixed by convention and cannot be modified. Some characters are naturally ambiguous (see Figure 5.26) and present considerable problems. This is the essential difference between characters and the symbols which are chosen specifically to avoid such confusion. In Figure 5.26, the number of lines in each symbol varies, and thus can be used for purposes of identification. Despite the fact that excellent character recognition systems are currently available, the introduction of alphanumerical values using a graphic tablet is, generally speaking, uncommon.

### *5.2.4.3 Collection of coordinates*

This is one area in which graphic tablets can be used successfully; although there are no special techniques involved, the following facts should be noted:

1. Tablets can be used in point by point mode, that is to say the coordinates are read by validation of the position of the pen, or continuously (each position of the pen is considered significant and is recorded by the system). This mode of operation is typical of real-time symbol recognition devices.
2. It is possible to place documents on a tablet and locate points on them. In this way, a convenient technique which involves manually numbering the contents of charts or introducing graphs is used. It should be noted that this provides a permanent method of introducing sets of alphanumerical values.
3. The precision afforded by tablets is quite good; working on a flat surface means that data can be introduced precisely and without the operator's arm becoming tired, as is often the case when using a light pen.

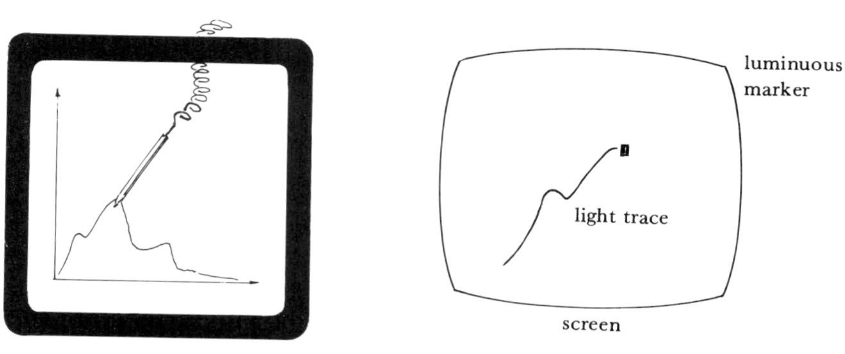


**Figure 5.27.** *Collection of coordinates*

It should be noted that when coordinates are provided using a graphic tablet, a corresponding trace is usually displayed on the screen. This trace is formed by a light marker which follows the movements of the stylus (see Figure 5.27). This can be used to verify the data received by the computer.

### *5.2.4.4 Identification*

Since the tablet only provides a coordinate pair (x, y), identification is carried out indirectly, by tracking on the screen. Once the general area containing the element to be designated is found (see Figure 5.28), an algorithm (based on the same model as that used for proximity

**Figure 5.28.** *Identification*

constraints, see section 5.2.1) is used to locate the element. The necessity of using a virtual visual display list is thus restated here, particularly for terminals with storage tubes or television scanning (raster) terminals. However, this is a relatively expensive means of calculation, since the cost is directly proportional to the number of graphic elements to be processed. The response time can be as much as several seconds, for a list made up of two or three thousand elements.

It should also be said that graphic tablets can be used in all dialogue functions, but that sometimes the cost of the software is high – and the procedures involved can be lengthy.

## 5.3 Functional aspect

### 5.3.1 ELEMENTARY FUNCTIONS

There are many different types of communication device available; these are difficult to compare since they are based on a number of criteria:

1. suitability for dialogue;
2. degree of ergonomic adaptation;
3. cost of software, both for writing and use.

There is a great temptation to design dialogue techniques simply as if they were cooking recipes, with the interactive system basically depending on the menu of available techniques. This should be avoided as it consists of making the dialogue subordinate to the communication system. In section 5.2, it was shown how each of the dialogue functions described could be used with each of the devices considered. It became evident that the devices could be used for all functions, with the exception perhaps of the function keyboard. Table 5.1 presents a summary of this. Two additional devices have been included: the *reticule* and the *joy-stick*. The similarity (apart from the use of continuous coordinate reading) in the way these two devices are used should be noted.

| | *identification* | *menu* | *values* | *coordinates* |
|---|---|---|---|---|
| *light pen* | direct designation on screen of component to be identified | direct designation on screen of command | input character by character from alphabet zone | point by point, continuous tracking |
| *alphanumerical keyboard* | giving element name, symbol guiding | typing command name | typing character chain | typing series of coordinates |
| *function keyboard* | symbol guiding with directional buttons | press button | — | — |
| *graphic tablet* | symbol guiding | symbol guiding, divided zones, symbol recognizer | divided zones, character recognizer | point by point, continuous |
| *reticule* | direct designation | direct designation | — | point by point |
| *joy-stick* | symbol guiding | symbol guiding | — | point by point, continuous |

**Table 5.1.** *Suitability of communication devices for various functions*

Table 5.2 lists the ergonomic criteria; it can be seen that, strictly speaking, the communication systems are not interchangeable. The table also shows significant differences in the collection of coordinates, which in certain circumstances, would be sufficient reason for rejecting a device.

Table 5.3, concerning the cost of software, reflects the cost of program development as well as the cost of using it. Identification of an element on a calligraphic plotting (vector) screen using a light pen takes a few milliseconds, whereas action carried out on a storage tube screen using a tablet or reticule can take several seconds.

The tables show that during the design of interactive software, the programmer is able to reason in terms of the function rather than the communication device. The advantage of this is that it allows a certain degree of flexibility in the system, in that the primitives are no longer linked to the hardware at the application level. A single function can then be carried out in different ways according to the final configuration. One effect of this is that, in some situations, the functional approach will allow work to be continued (though perhaps to a less satisfactory level) if a device breaks down, whereas an approach centred on hardware would not allow this.

| | *identification* | *menu* | *values* | *coordinates* |
|---|---|---|---|---|
| *light pen* | excellent but part of screen hidden | excellent but part of screen hidden | – | (a) good but imprecise (b) very imprecise |
| *alphanumerical keyboard* | seldom used | can be tedious | usual method excellent | tedious |
| *function keyboard* | – | excellent | – | – |
| *graphic tablet* | excellent | (a) excellent (b) good but inflexible (c) excellent | (a) very tedious (b) limited at present | (a) excellent (b) excellent |
| *reticule* | excellent | excellent | – | tedious |
| *joy-stick* | excellent | excellent | – | (a) excellent (b) imprecise |

**Table 5.2.** *Ergonomic criteria associated with various communication devices*

| | *identification* | *menu* | *values* | *coordinates* |
|---|---|---|---|---|
| *light pen* | * | * | – | (a) * (b) *** time |
| *alphanumerical keyboard* | * | * | * | * |
| *function keyboard* | – | * | – | – |
| *graphic tablet* | **** | (a) * (b) * (c) **** | (a) * (b) **** | (a) * (b) *** time |
| *reticule* | **** | * | – | * |
| *joy-stick* | **** | * | – | (a) * (b) ** time |

**Table 5.3.** *Cost of software used in various communication devices: * inexpensive; **** very expensive*

If the designer treats the dialogue as a whole, teaching the CAD/CAM system will be made easy. This approach will allow the designer to reason in terms of the actions to be undertaken, corresponding to the effect desired at a given moment, without it being necessary to worry about the ability of the hardware to carry out the action. Thus, once a dialogue function is completed, an indication of the type of action expected is displayed on the screen. The operator chooses the type of system considered to be most appropriate for the action required.

For example, during collection of coordinates, any one of the following devices could be used: light pen, graphic tablet, alphanumerical keyboard or any other means available at the level of the actual console.

In addition to this freedom of choice of hardware, it should be noted that the method suggested allows the elementary actions to be managed using identical methods. During execution of a request for dialogue function, the operator can use the following operations:

1. control of the number of elementary actions performed, in a situation in which a maximum has been determined: if this maximum is reached, the system returns to the calling program;
2. control of the number of actions by the use of a signal at the end of the dialogue, allowing the operator to interrupt the sequence of elementary actions;
3. cancellation of the last elementary action carried out;
4. cancellation of the set of elementary actions carried out from the start of the function.

The similarity of actions is appreciated most at the operator level.

### 5.3.2 COMPOSITION OF FUNCTIONS

Designers rarely work by carrying out single processes; they generally link processes together to form combinations which may sometimes be repeated. The most simple mechanism for composing elementary functions is one in which the same action can be repeated several times: selecting several elements from the menu, taking a number of coordinate pairs, inputting values, designating elements, etc. The idea is that all the functions should benefit from this mechanism, so as not to disturb the functional balance. However, this type of extension is not sufficient in itself, and sometimes new dialogue primitives must be created.

The addition of new dialogue primitives arises from the fact that methods using interactive techniques (although it can be effected by combining two elementary actions) are never carried out under ideal conditions. A typical example concerns the positioning of part of a drawing on a screen. This action can be broken down into two parts:

1. designation of part of the drawing;
2. designation of a point on the screen allowing the definitive (or temporary) location of display of the designated element.

The primitives mentioned allow this function to be simulated. There is, however, an extremely useful technique which consists of moving the designated element using a designation device (light pen, tablet or other) until an ideal position is attained. However, this technique cannot, unfortunately, be applied without the use of expensive software. The following primitive:

PLACE (nb, tabname, tabx, taby)

can be used and allows the operator to repeat nb placements, with a record of work completed being stored in the tables tabname (designated elements) and tabx, taby (definitive retained positions). Thus, the techniques mentioned over can be carried out at the level of the basic software.

The introduction of this new primitive shows that the combinations of actions implicit in the introduction of a repetition factor are not sufficient. A vertical combination has been obtained, ie one in which the same type of elementary actions are not used together. However, in certain types of interaction it is necessary to program a situation, like for example, allowing a possibility of expecting either a menu or a set of identifications, in order to designate the elements and then the action to be taken, then another series of elements and a new action, and so on. So the question of completing a series of actions of different types arises – this is called '*horizontal combination*'. To establish a horizontal combination, two types of primitive can be used:

1. declarations of actions;
2. activations of dialogue actions.

The declarations of action allow horizontal layers of actions to be specified by defining the interface in which the results will be recorded. In passing, similarity to declarations of data should be noted. These declarations can be carried out using pre-defined dialogue primitives, to which identification parameters are added. These primitives are not operative. The function is activated by using the primitive:

DIALOGUE (p, m, v, i)

in which the variables p, m, v, i allow the type of action used to be specified, with the following convention:

p, m, v, i = 0 no action of this type

p, m, v, i > 0 an action of this type, framed by the number p, m, v, or i (p for position, m for menu, v for value and i for identification).

From the operator's point of view, sequences can be created from several types of action without having to run through long and sometimes tedious lists of menus. One problem is to know whether the use of different devices for each of the functions can always be freely developed without causing ambiguity, since several functions must coexist. It is important to know the extent to which the software is able to deduce, during the first intervention, which action is envisaged

| *combination* | *light pen* | *graphic tablet* | *alphanumerical keyboard* | *function keyboard* |
|---|---|---|---|---|
| p m v i | p m i | p | p v | m s |
| p m v | p m | p | p v | m s |
| p m i | p m i | p | p | m s |
| p v i | p i | p | p v | s |
| m v i | m i | | v | m |
| p m | p m | p | m | m s |
| p v | p | p | p v | s |
| p i | p i | p | p | s |
| m v | m | | v | m |
| m i | m i | | | m |
| v i | i | | v | |
| p | p | p | p | s |
| m | m | | | m |
| v | | | v | |
| i | i | | | |

**Table 5.4.** *Horizontal composition of dialogue functions*

according to the device used. A quick survey of all possible situations reveals that ambiguities are rare, since they would arise in anomalous situations and can be solved using a supplementary signal.

Table 5.4 gives examples of possible situations which could arise in systems using light pens, tablets, alphanumerical keyboards and function keyboards. In each case, the function carried out by the communication device carried in the abscissa has been noted (the letter s indicates a system function). The following should be noted:

1. No problems arise from use of a graphic tablet;
2. The choice of a light pen for the collection of coordinates is made with the help of a function key (*key system*). Since differentiating between a menu element and a figure element during identification is simple, no ambiguity arises.
3. Problems arise only when two functions are to be carried out using either a function keyboard or an alphanumerical keyboard. It should be noted that the number of ambiguous cases amounts to eight out of a total of 45 possibilities offered by the software. Final ambiguities can be resolved using a supplementary key. The operator is warned of the ambiguity by a signal, and then notes his intention using this key. In all the other situations, the operation cannot be modified.

This section will end with an example, not of composition, but of extension of the elementary functions. This extension will be based on the possibility of manipulating a new form of expression, the *grapho-numerical expression.*

When using geometric modelling software, the operator constantly needs to give values to the parameters involved in the construction of the model. The following alternatives are available:

1. either the exact value the parameter is to be given is known (or it can be calculated easily); or,
2. this value is calculated as a function of the geometric data induced by the model on which the operator is working.

Provision of an exact value occurs in all systems. It consists of an input of real numbers. However, the numbers produced by the model are more difficult to use. The problem may, for example, involve expressing the fact that the distance of a straight line (to be created) relative to an existing line is equal to twice the radius of an existing circle to which a given value is added. One solution to this problem is to use a graphic input adapted to graphonumerical values, ie one which allows the values to be calculated according to elements existing in the model. This can be carried out using two basic functions:

1. the identification which allows objects to be designated on the screen;
2. the acquisition of an alphanumerical chain which represents an arithmetical expression in which valued, basic graphic functions can appear. A basic graphic function can be a function of the valued model, such as the distance between two identified straight lines, the radius of an identified circle or the length of an identified segment, etc.

The user can also define variables which can be valued, and use standard operators (*, /, —, +) and normal mathematical functions.

*Example* EG : 2 D (d1, d2) + R (c)
distance of radius from circle C, straight line d1 to straight line d2

Starting with an equation of this type, it is possible, not only to define graphonumerical expressions, but also to obtain parametrization of the values. If this expression is recorded as it is (see Figure 5.29), modification of an element of the model or of a value will automatically be taken into account during evaluation of the expression.

### 5.3.3 PERSONALIZATION OF DIALOGUE

One of the main benefits of the functional approach is that dialogue is more easily personalized, ie better adapted to the operator. The approach linked to the communication systems tends to make the programmer decide in advance (when writing software for use with a CAD/CAM system) which device should be chosen by the operator, since the dialogue primitives make specific mention of the devices to be used (see Figure 5.30a). The main drawback of this method is that the dialogue is fixed at a stage when the final user is not known, and thus cannot be personalized.

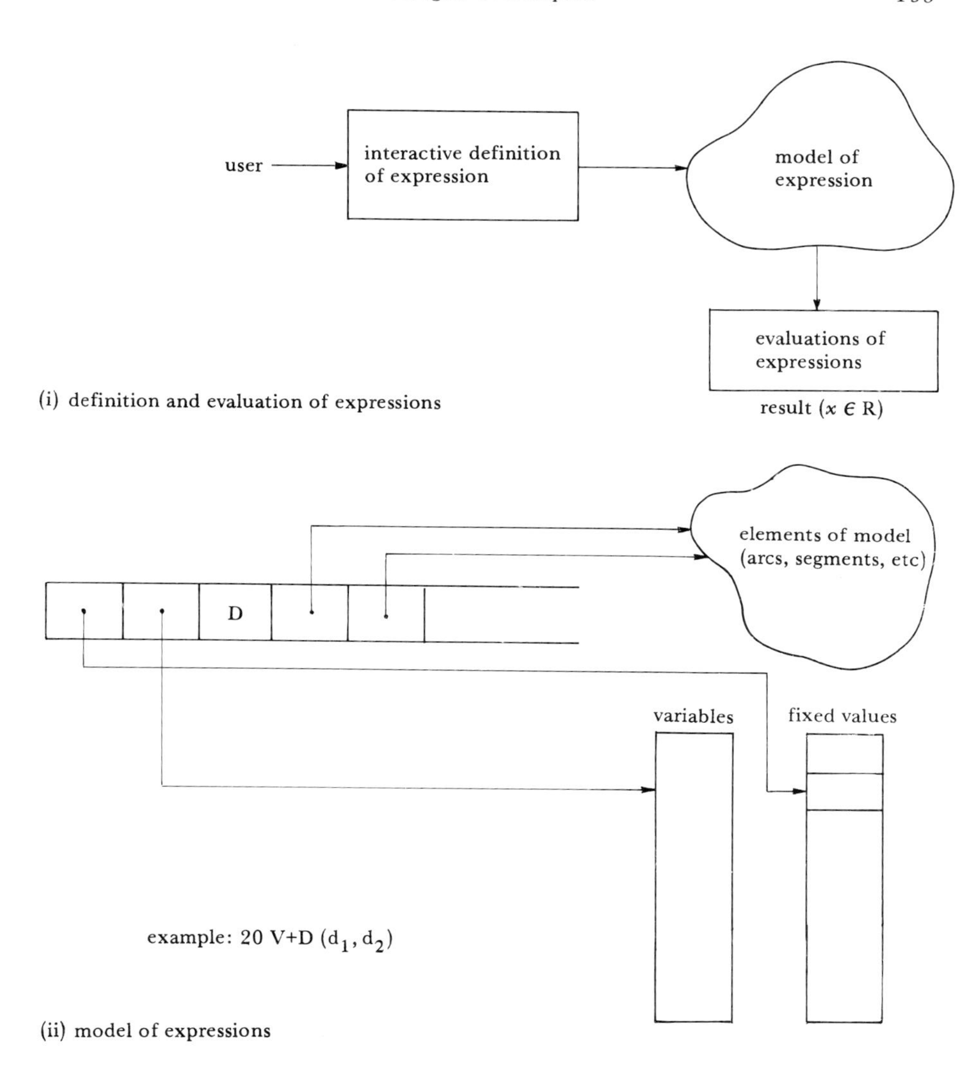


**Figure 5.29.** *Graphonumerical expressions*

The functional approach, on the other hand, leads to the programmer using only primitives which describe the dialogue in terms of function, and does not need to consider the hardware (see Figure 5.30b). During execution of a functional primitive, the software will allow a choice of device – the operator will decide the most convenient one to use. Thus, for a coordinate collection operation, the operator could:

1. use a light pen to indicate a starting point on the screen;
2. use a graphic tablet to continuously plot a curved line;
3. use an alphanumerical keyboard to introduce precise values.

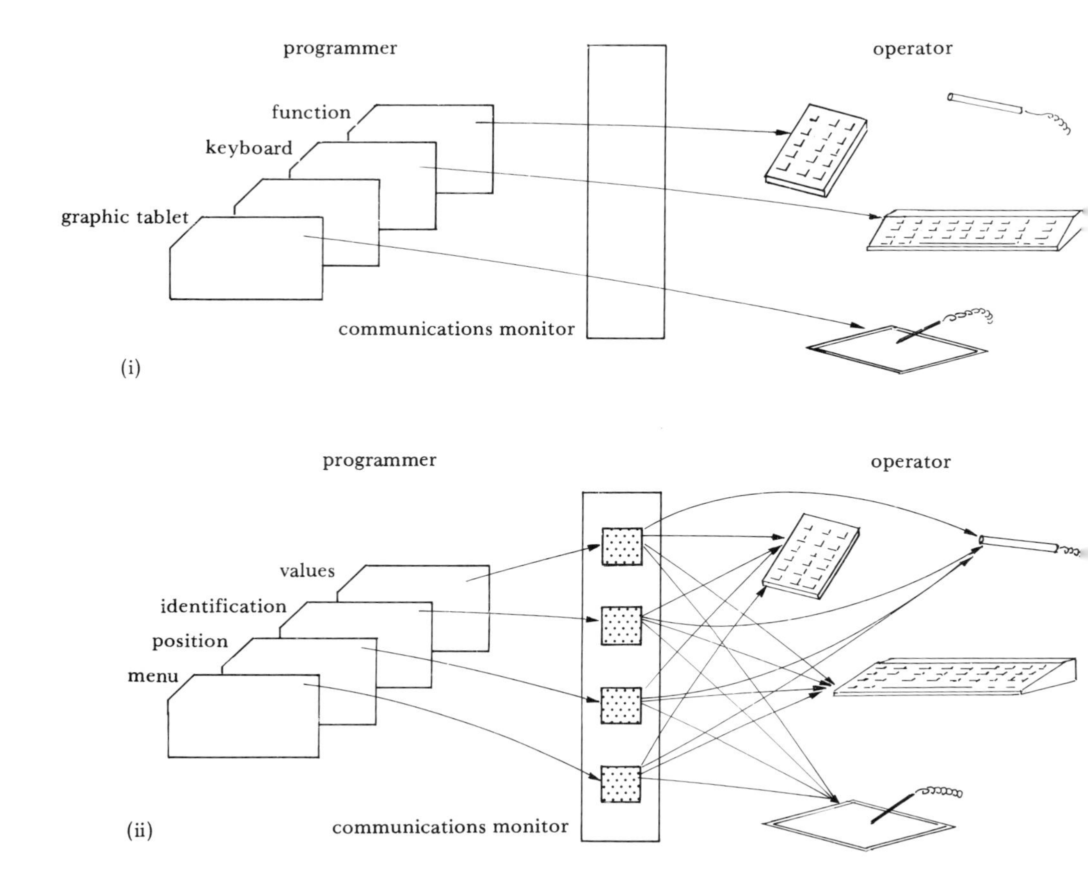


**Figure 5.30** (*i*) *Dialogue in the device-linked approach and* (*ii*) *in the functional approach*

These operations may be used interchangeably. In the same way, for selection of an action from the menu, the operator may wish to:

1. use a function keyboard;
2. use a light pen on a menu on the screen;
3. use a graphic tablet.

It is interesting to note that the behaviour of every operator varies considerably, and that the use of one system rather than another is more often affected by personal preference than for any specific reason. Being able to offer the greatest choice is an important factor in ensuring the operator achieves optimum results.

To conclude, it should be noted that other techniques can be added to this personalization:

1. the use of symbol recognition devices in real time with dynamic dictionaries;
2. training with a system of work sequences, allowing the operator to create semi-automatic operator modes.

The functional approach can make the application of these techniques easier, in that it does not take the details of the hardware into consideration but concentrates on the progress of the work.

## 5.4 Construction graphics

### 5.4.1 GENERAL POINTS

Construction graphics have two main uses:

1. graphic comprehension of logical or numerical information. The designer offers a transcription in the form of graphic elements, or values (moving a cursor by a given distance to express a desired value), or links between objects (to indicate that two points displayed are linked logically, a line is constructed between them);
2. comprehension of solely graphic information, such as coordinates.

The use of graphic processes has given rise to the development of a number of techniques, each one with advantages and drawbacks and each successful in its own way. Indeed, there are so many that it would be impossible to list them all here. The essential point is that the introduction of data, whether graphic or not, is carried out in association with a model of the CAD/CAM system, whether the model is geometric or another type. It was shown in Chapter 3 that a model is very often based on a set of primitives, and the construction of a design is assisted by the use of these primitives. This can be achieved, as already shown, by real programming. The use of graphic construction tools will allow this programming to be symbolically represented by graphic signs. It is clear that a draughtsman would be more accustomed to handling graphic symbols than programming primitives, which explains the importance of this masking.

It is intended to make computer systems based on the activation of programs, both comprehensible and accessible to someone untrained in computing, and perhaps, more accustomed to graphic expression. The extent of such masking can differ. For example, consider a sub-program for the creation of a circle tangential to a straight line and a circle (as discussed in section 3.2.2.1). The header of this sub-program is as follows:

```
subroutine CTGDCR (A, B, C, X1, Y1, R1, XC, YC, IR)
```

The parameters have the following significance:

| | | |
|---|---|---|
| A, B, C, | straight line parameters | supplied parameters |
| X1, Y1, R1 | centre and radius of circle | |
| R, XC, YC | centre and radius of reply circle | resultant parameters |
| IR | IR = 1 no solution | |
| | IR = 0 solution found | |

An example of graphic transcription could be as follows:

1. selection of CTGDCR sub-program, using the menu;

2. specification of the straight line: several methods can be used, depending on the complexity of the graphic transcription:
   (a) specification of two points on the screen;
   (b) specification of a point on the screen and of a constraint line parallel to a given direction (perpendicular to another straight line, tangent to a circle, etc). These indications can also be provided with the help of the menu (choice of constraint) and by designing the object defining the constraint;
   (c) identification of an existing line;

3. specification of the circle: here, also, a number of methods can be used:
   (a) specification of the centre by a point on the screen, with the radius indicated directly on a graduated scale displayed on the screen;
   (b) specification of three points on the screen;
   (c) specification of the centre and its tangent with another object;
   (d) identification of existing circle;

4. the reply can be ambiguous, because in certain situations several circles may be found, and for this reason validation will be requested. There are several techniques that may be used:
   (a) a point may be given before calculation of the reply indicating the area in which the object might be located;
   (b) all the possible locations of the circles can be displayed on the screen so that the operator can designate the one to be retained (or deleted).

With this example in mind, it is easy to understand why two CAD/CAM systems would allow different techniques to be used for the same project (depending on the degree to which graphic transcription is to be used relative to the direct introduction of values). In general, a mixture of graphic and alphanumerical techniques are used.

Figure 5.31 shows an example of a graphic output corresponding to the seven line program which accompanies it. In looking for parameters which could benefit from graphic transcription, the rotational object which forms the base of the scene should be noted. It is obtained from a generator made up of 11 points. This generator can be understood graphically, by collection of coordinates. The rotational object is

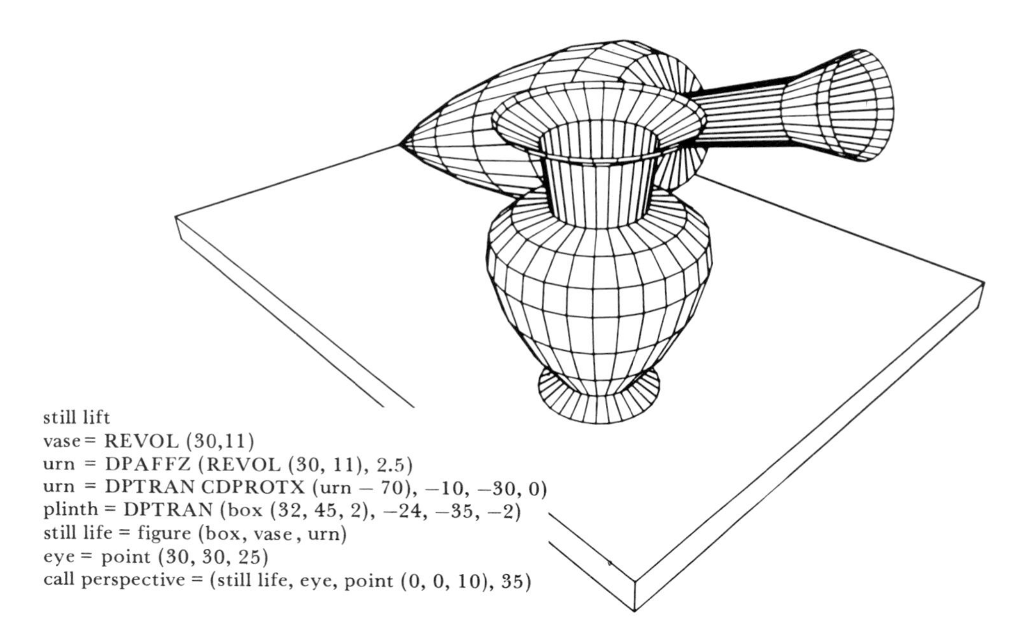


**Figure 5.31.** *An example of model programming with graphic output*

formed by copying this generator 30 times, with each copy being made after a rotation through 12°. The number of copies can be given graphically, but is more likely to be given at the keyboard. In the same way, the design of the plinth (a parallelipipedic box) could be carried out graphically by providing graduated scales for the length, breadth and height, instead of supplying values directly. The positioning of the objects can be carried out from three viewpoints, with the operator directly designating the locations.

Another important aspect of construction graphics is the degree of automation that can be associated with it. The need for automation arises from the fact that it is often necessary to acquire a large amount of documentation (maps, plans or catalogues) when establishing a new CAD/CAM application. There are two main techniques available:

1. interactive numbering systems, such as graphic tablets (this requires the operator to be in attendance and is not very quick);
2. passive (or automatic) numbering systems, such as cameras or contour tracking numbering systems: the problem with this technique is to find a method for automatic recognition of the basic elements present in a document, bearing in mind that using a sensor to sample a document can lead to potential errors that are not easily overcome.

It is interesting to note that these two aspects correspond to the drawing/picture dichotomy:

1. Interactive graphics has been the field in which information is most commonly introduced in the form of line drawings, whilst using graphic tablets and other devices for interactive comprehension oriented towards the collection of isolated points.
2. Image processing (acquisition, refinement, extraction of graphic primitives) is traditionally used for shape recognition.

Until recently, the calculation time associated with this method was prohibitive, and inhibited the use of dialogue.

However, with the development of television-type visual display consoles (which allow images to be produced) and the progress made in both software and hardware, particularly in terms of calculation power, these two branches of computer science have been brought closer together. Progress is still to be made in the area of automatic acquisition of scenes, and it is hoped that the use of images will help to reduce the bottle-neck of data to be acquired, before any work can be started on a new product.

### 5.4.2 TWO-DIMENSIONAL CONSTRUCTION

There is obviously a direct relationship between the points (coordinates) acquired on a plane and the image produced from them in a plane. Two-dimensional construction tools are particularly well adapted to the comprehension of information to be displayed on a flat surface. The variety of techniques available arises from the diversity of geometric shapes that can be created, as well as the graphic transcription that can be used to introduce the value of each parameter. Some representative examples of the ways in which a CAD/CAM system can assist a designer will now be discussed.

Consider the construction of a circle tangential to a straight line and a circle, discussed earlier in terms of its graphic variants. Figure 5.32 shows the various solutions possible once the circle and the straight line references have been specified. To help the system, the designer simply indicates the area of interest (collection of coordinates) which then immediately removes any ambiguity. This is a good example of the work routine involved between machine, which performs a number of calculations, and operator, who supplies the information necessary for the satisfactory completion of the calculations. It is clear that no fully automatic solution is possible.

Another example is provided by the tools which enable a drawing to be modified. This technique is one in which the elements of the drawing used as supports during construction are eliminated. Figure 5.33 shows two examples of this:

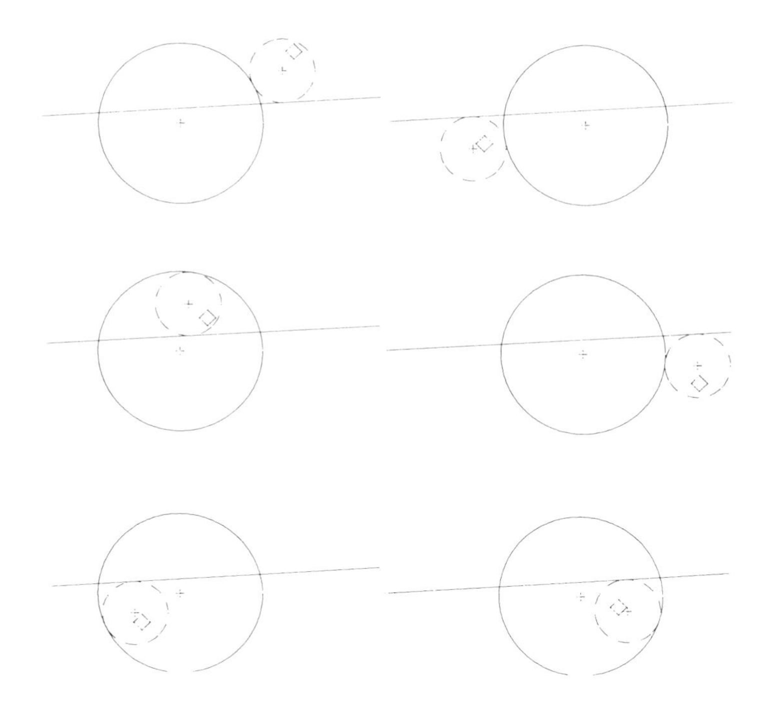

**Figure 5.32.** *Construction of a circle tangent to a straight line and a circle*

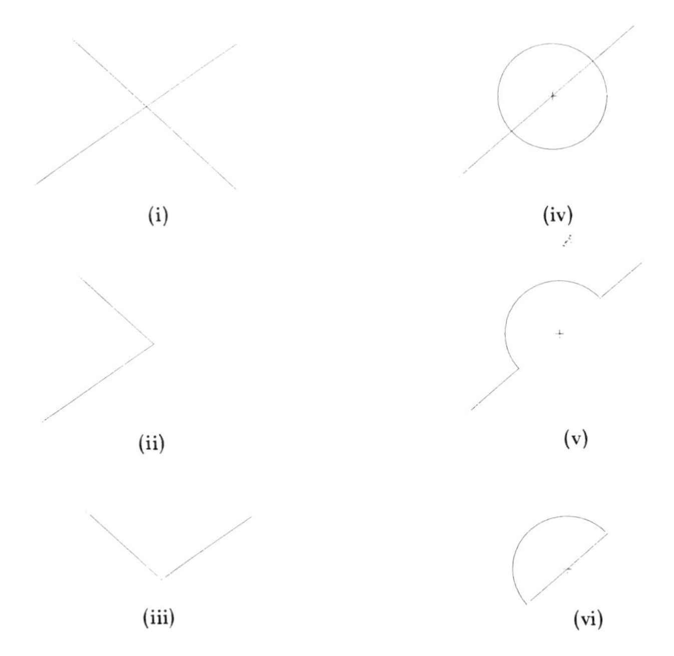


**Figure 5.33.** *Examples of refinement operations*

1. The processing of straight line segments, such that starting an initial situation with four potential segments (i), the operator can obtain the final drawing by designating redundant segments. In this example, the required drawing consists of an angle formed by two straight line segments (ii and iii).
2. The processing of a straight line segment and a circle (iv), such that by designation of the redundant parts of the segments, the operator can either obtain an arc or circle prolonged at each end by a line segment (v) or a half circle (vi).

Designation of an element can lead either to it being deleted or retained, as required. The CAD/CAM system locates elements concerned in the operation, calculates the new primitives (eg to replace two intersecting segments with four segments having a common vertex) and then deletes, after designation, the redundant elements. These simple operations can be obtained to give more complex results, combining different lines. It may be necessary to transform these lines into contours – see Figure 5.34 where the forms obtained define an interior and an exterior. A contour will be defined as a list of ordered objects (lines).

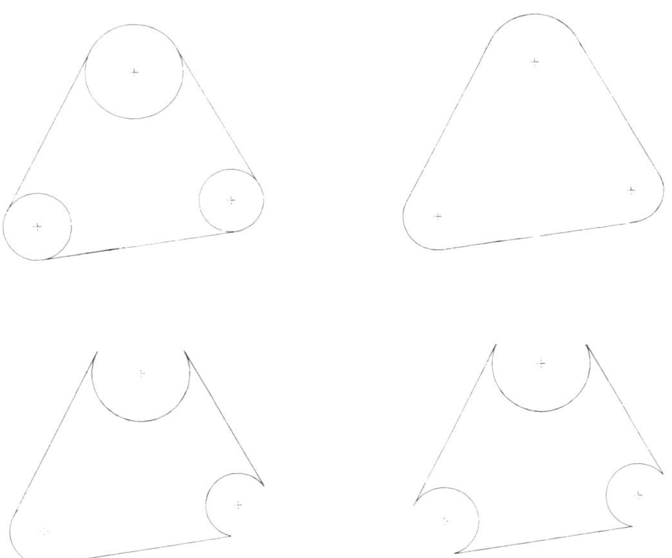

**Figure 5.34.** *Examples of contours after refinement operations have been carried out*

The operator constructs this contour interactively, by designating the different elements of which it is composed and altering the direction of any element required, so that, on completion, the whole contour can be followed in one direction. As the contour is defined, indications can

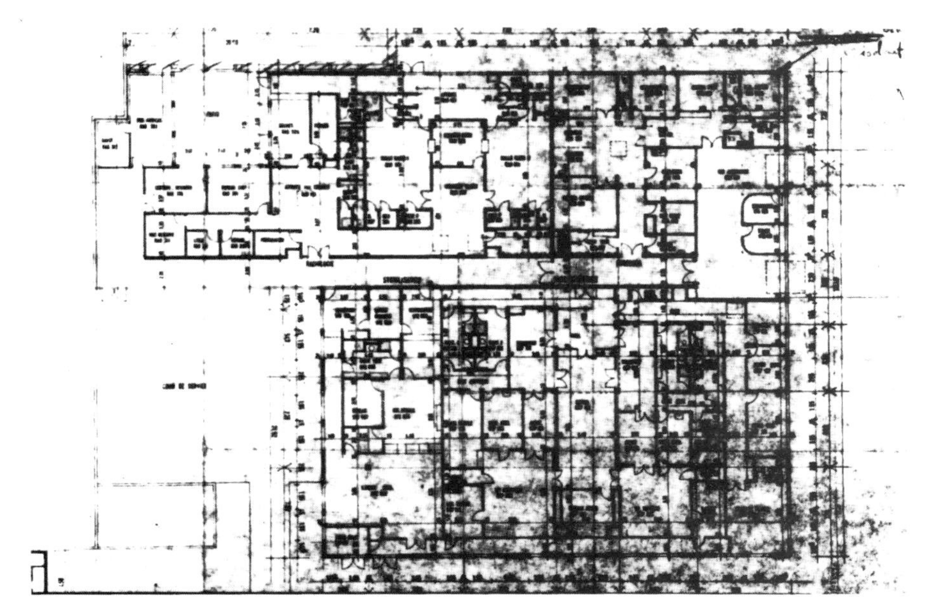

**Figure 5.35.** *A pilot study plan*

be made, such as those indicating the direction of the designated object, which allow the designer to view what must be altered.

These examples give an idea of the range of graphic comprehension tools available. These tools all require operator intervention and can therefore only be used for relatively short periods. It is clear that comprehension of large amounts of data would become tedious, and a more highly automated method should be used. The next example concerns the numbering of plans, and could also apply to any two-dimensional object (printed circuits, for example). The techniques discussed here, were first described by Gangnet *et al.*, 1980 and are taken from an architectural CAD application. This requires that, at a given moment, the geometry of a project should be available for study. A plan such as that shown in Figure 5.35 would require about 2 hours' work if an operator were to tackle it using a graphic tablet, and this would be for the geometry only. To automate the comprehension of this type of plan sufficiently to produce a first version which could be modified interactively, a camera is connected to the computer. The software is used solely to record the essentials of shape, and the interactive software used allows the details completing the plan to be introduced. In terms of shape recognition, the problem is to find the straight line segments present in a numerical image. A numerical image takes the form of a matrix of values, the value at any point depending on the level of greyness detected by a camera scanning the image. Figure 5.36

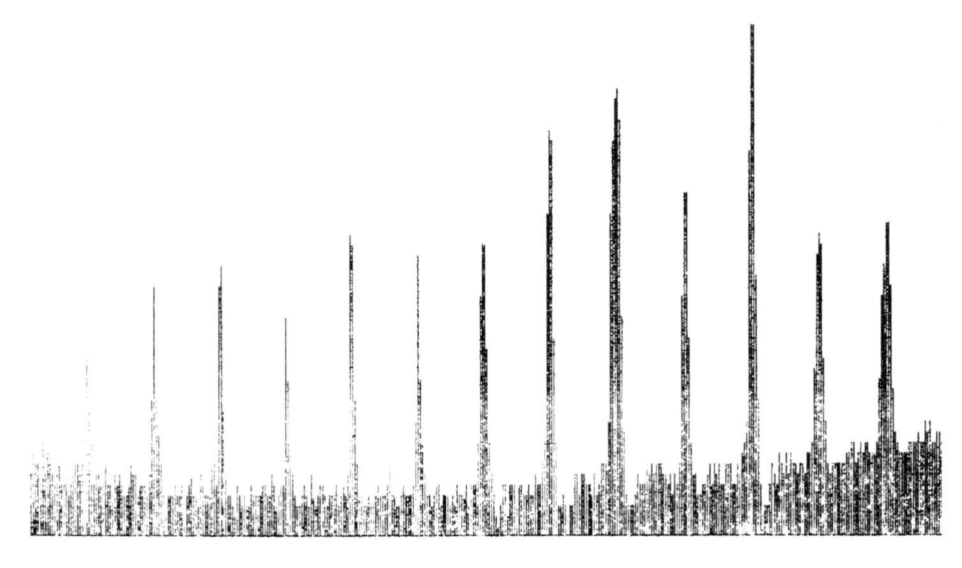

**Figure 5.36.** *Image recorded by a camera after scanning one line*

shows an example of what a camera perceives whilst scanning one line. This image shows that:

1. the passage from the background to a line is shown by a marked difference in values, represented here by peaks: to find the lines the peaks produced in the image will be detected;
2. the width of the peaks is variable, which means that the lines viewed by the camera will unfortunately not be very straight, since a line can have a variable thickness over all its length;
3. there are important variations in the background noise, caused by variations in lighting during detection.

Figure 5.37 shows the results of the comprehension phase. The image is said to be in its crude form. To avoid disturbance from background noise, a threshold value is used to eliminate all points which are insufficiently dark. A threshold image is thus produced, as shown in Figure 5.38. Using this figure, the straight line segments can be derived; this involves:

1. recognition of a straight line segment by verifying that a certain number of closely related points follow a particular direction;
2. determining the extreme ends of the segments recognized, so as to be able to replace the sets of points with a straight line.

The result of this analysis is shown in Figure 5.39.

A number of errors are immediately apparent: many of the lines are not parallel to the horizontal or vertical, lines vary in direction, and

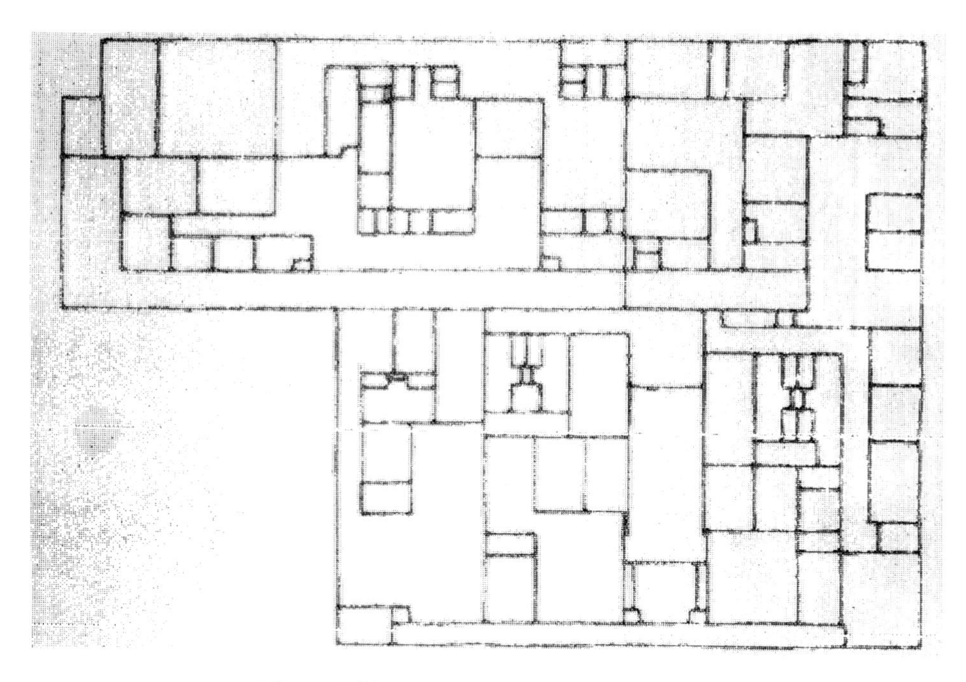

**Figure 5.37.** *Image shown in its crude form*

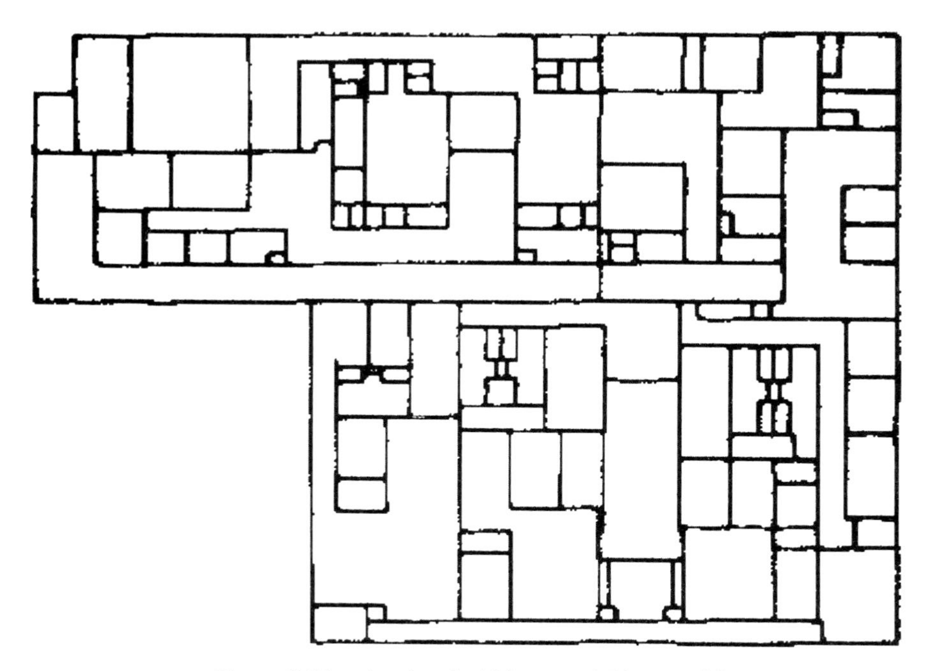

**Figure 5.38.** *The threshold image of Figure 5.37*

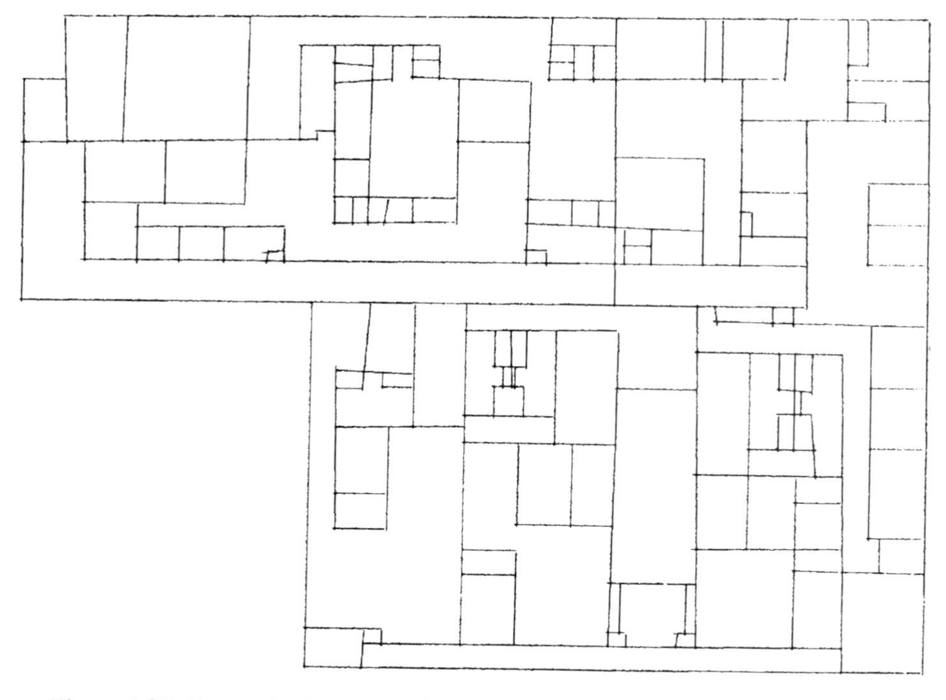

**Figure 5.39.** *Recognized segments (no indication is made of the thicknesses of the lines)*

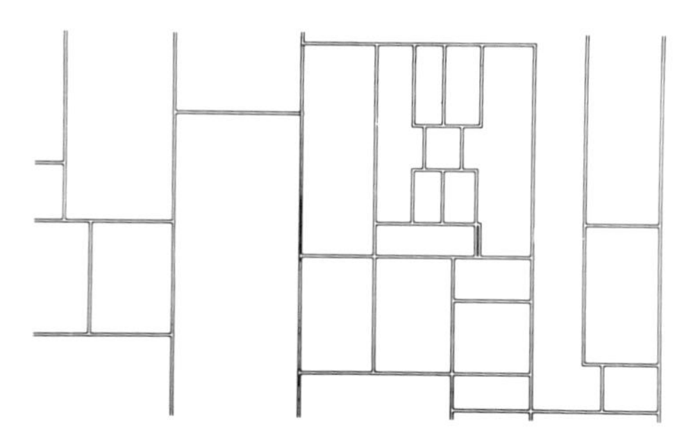

**Figure 5.40.** *Recognized segments after realignment*

some errors occur at the extremities. At this stage the imposition software is used, which allows the segments to be realigned automatically, as shown in Figure 5.40. The numbering of this type of plan takes up to 10 minutes, which is clearly a considerable improvement.

The type of sensor used has a considerable influence on the numbering technique. For example, automatic numbering devices are available which can follow lines or contours. The process resembles that using a curve follower of the tracing table type, but with the pen replaced by a camera. To start, the operator places the camera on a line and the computer then pilots the camera by moving it along the lines, ie along the sequences of black dots. The problem is to develop an algorithm capable of following lines, recognizing if it has already passed through a certain area, and able to display all the lines to be numbered without forgetting any and without repetition.

To conclude, it can be said that this technique allows the geometry of an object to be easily established. Any semantics must, however, be introduced at a later stage of interactive processing, in which the structure of the objects represented is associated with their significance (distinction is made automatically between specification lines and definition lines, etc).

### 5.4.3 THREE-DIMENSIONAL CONSTRUCTION

An additional difficulty arises in the definition of graphic tools for the construction of three-dimensional objects: How can the third dimension be restored when the output medium is two-dimensional? This problem can be overcome in a variety of ways, and the techniques used depend to a large extent on the geometric model, and thus on the type of object being described.

The technique consists of describing the object from a number of viewpoints, the same point being shown from at least two views. The problem for the designer is to use a work method which will allow him to define a point on any of the necessary views. This will enable definition of views necessary for the precise definition of the whole object. Some graphic tablets are equipped with several pens, with which direct differentiation can be made for a given point, and indicates to which view the coordinates being acquired must be related. Some objects are better suited than others to two-dimensional techniques. The definition of rotational objects has already been mentioned in connection with Figure 5.31 – here it was sufficient to draw a generator, and subject it to a rotation about an axis defined by the operator. This type of facility can also be used on objects defined by a contour and a depth, as shown in Figure 5.41. In this type of processing:

1. The drawing of the contour itself is made using two-dimensional primitives provided by the CAD/CAM system. This means that the contour can be recorded in a form corresponding to a two-dimensional model, eg by storing the construction operations and the necessary elementary primitives (straight line segments, arcs of circle, etc).
2. The two-dimensional model must be converted to a three-dimensional type. In the example, the contour must be divided into a series of segments of equal length which will form the bases for the facets automatically created by the CAD/CAM

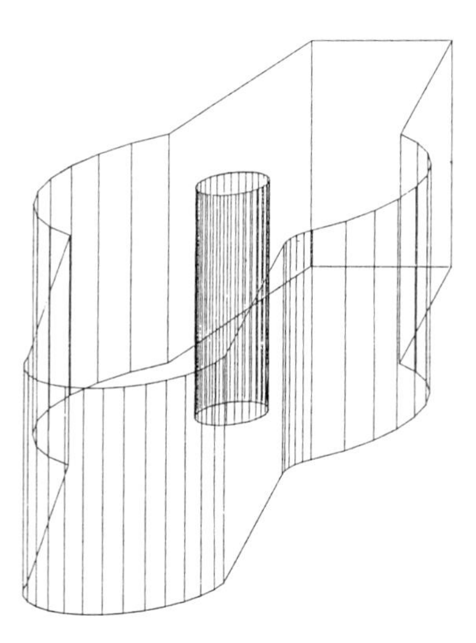

**Figure 5.41.** *Definition of an object by contour and depth*

system. These facets happen to be rectangles, the second dimension of which will constitute the height (or depth) of the object. While these facets are being created, the software calculates the coordinates of the introduced vertices, as well as listing the facets created so as to integrate them into the geometric model.

The advantages of using these graphic techniques are clear. The designer is relieved of having to perform a large number of tedious tasks, which are often sources of error. For example, the numbering of vertices and faces is typical of the sort of activity which can be performed automatically by a CAD/CAM system.

There are also techniques available for processing more complex objects. Huffman has concentrated on a particular category of objects, trihedral solids, which are characterized by the fact that they consist of three planes meeting at each vertex of a polyhedron. By studying the images produced by these objects, Huffman was able to establish that the number of possible configurations of lines was very small (layout of visible contours) – but only if those solids which are physically possible were considered. The Huffman technique consists of recognizing these configurations and associating labels with each vertex (see Figure 5.42), which makes it possible to determine, for example, whether the trihedrons are re-entrant or salient (marked with minus or plus signs, respectively). If any of the vertices cannot be labelled, the object is not physically viable. This technique has been applied to the analysis of photographs of objects. The first phase of analysis consists of extracting the straight line segments which represent the contours (and thus the visible vertices), as in the example of numbering mentioned above. Once the lists of segments have been completed, the

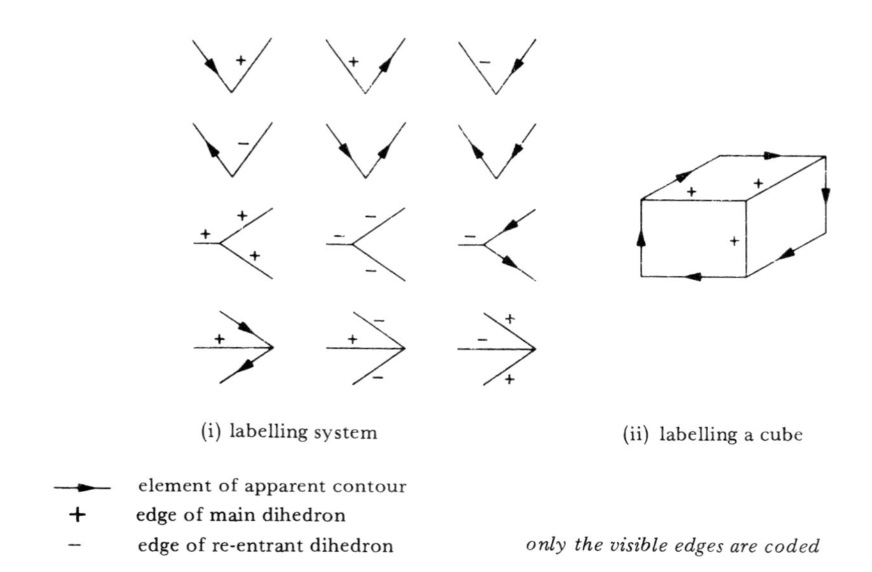


**Figure 5.42.** *The Huffman technique*

labelling phase commences. The phases of aquisition of the image and numbering of the segments may be replaced by drawing on a graphic tablet. The problem for the operator is that only the straight line segments which would be visible should be drawn, and in some cases it may be difficult to distinguish these. It should be noted that several views may be necessary to define an object correctly. The Huffman technique has been extended by Sugihara, who studied the possible configurations while considering those vertices which could be hidden. Sugihara showed that the number of possible configurations for solid trihedrons was not excessive (see Figure 5.43), which meant that it would be possible to introduce trihedral objects using a graphic tablet, with the operator drawing all the vertices of the object and specifying their characteristics (signs, graphics). From this point, the labelling operation follows the methods described by Huffman. Moreover, the grammar devised by Sugihara allows differentiation of groups of lines, leading to unambiguous identification of different objects represented by similar drawings (see Figure 5.44).

One area in which considerable research is currently being conducted is that of recognition of objects based on a number of photographs (or images). This is based on a number of points:

1. a priori knowledge of the objects or groups of objects to be identified; a library of object models is used, and once they have been displayed the resemblance of the images presented to any of these models is verified;
2. use of shadows and the play of light on the surfaces analysed to

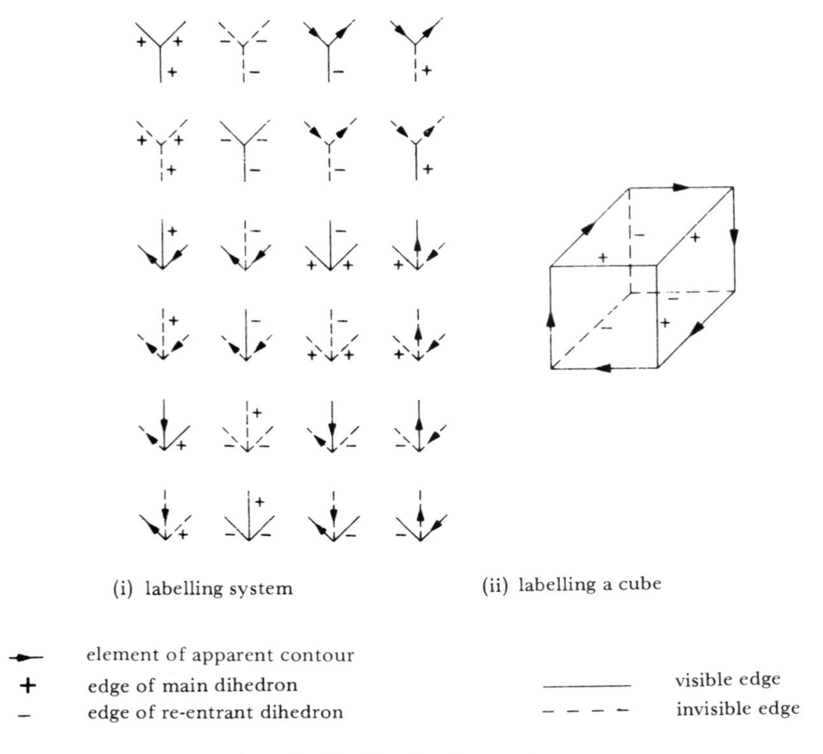


**Figure 5.43.** *The Sugihara scheme*

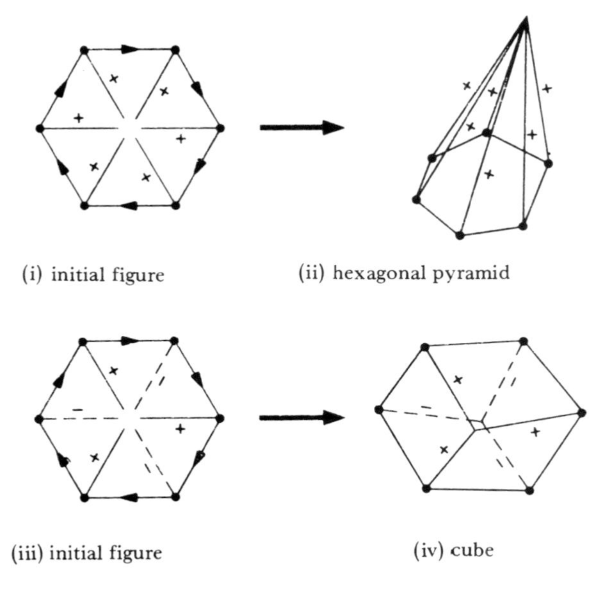


**Figure 5.44.** *Differentiation between similar drawings*

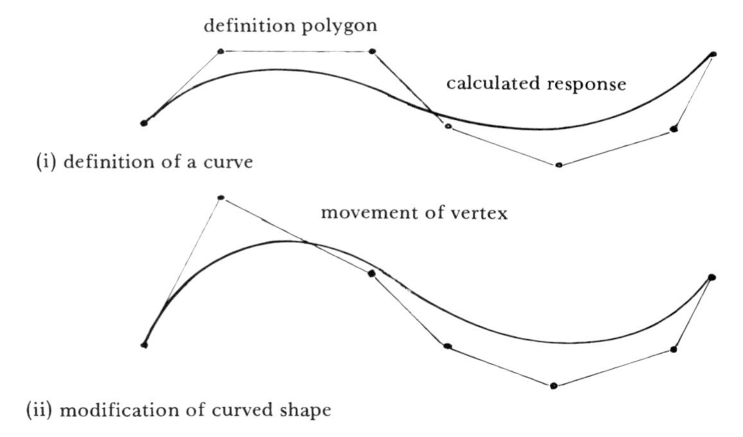


**Figure 5.45.** *Interactive creation of a skew curve*

provide a better understanding of the orientation of different parts of the object; this technique can be applied effectively to both objects surrounded by flat facets as to those formed of squared, skew surfaces.

However, there are considerable difficulties:

1. The viewing angle is generally not known, and this can complicate the search for parameters of deformation, such as the deformation caused by perspective.
2. It is difficult to link several views automatically, but this condition is essential to the efficient comprehension of an object.

To conclude this discussion, mention should be made of a field in which three-dimensional construction and modification tools are highly effective, that is the field concerned with *skew surfaces.* Although visual display tools are not as highly developed for use in cases involving faceted objects or solids, the properties of curves used to define the squares on skew surfaces can provide the designer with interactive tools which are well suited to his work method. With Bezier curves or B-Spline curves in particular, the designer can work on an approximate curve which gives the general shape of the exact curve desired (see Figure 5.45). If the exact curve is to be modified, the designer can carry out the operation on the approximate curve, moving the vertices in the required directions. The resulting curve thus follows the movement of the vertices and, with a little experience, a designer can rapidly make a calculated curve coincide with an ideal curve. It is paradoxical that using current technology such complex objects can be easier to produce than solids or groups of flat facets (setting aside the use of shape libraries and operations for combination of shapes, etc; in fact, construction tools of the truly graphic type are relatively seldom used in this method of definition).

*Chapter 6*

# Applications

The following examples illustrate the concepts put forward in previous chapters.

## 6.1 Client plan of a ball-race

*Illustrated concepts: parametrized model, communication graphics*

A plan of a ball-race consists of a drawing showing the various specifications and is usually in page format (see Figure 6.1). The ball-race containing a row of ball bearings can be defined by two types of parameters:

1. geometric parameters, such as the outer diameter of the ball-race, the diameter of the ball bearings, etc – twenty or so parameters are sufficient to describe the geometry of a ball-race;
2. logical parameters, eg whether or not there are joints or deflectors, the number of ball bearings in the race, the type of casing used, etc.

From these parameters a plan of a ball-race can be defined automatically. The problems that occur in the implementation of this type of software are not geometric (once the correct parameters are defined, the geometric calculations are very simple) but rather are a matter of page layout (since the aim is to create communication graphics). In effect, the page layout should be as perfect as possible without the need of intervention by the user. However, this can cause problems, eg with the choice of the specifications. Likewise, the choice of scale should be made automatically.

The software should allow the automatic output of plans of a ball-race consisting of a row of ball bearings (extension to other types of bearing is also possible) with the following functions:

1. the creation of a plan (that shows the various parameters);
2. the modification of one or more of the parameters;
3. the management of a library of data on the ball-race.

This application calls specifically for the use of communication graphics. Suitable software allows the realization of a plan in about

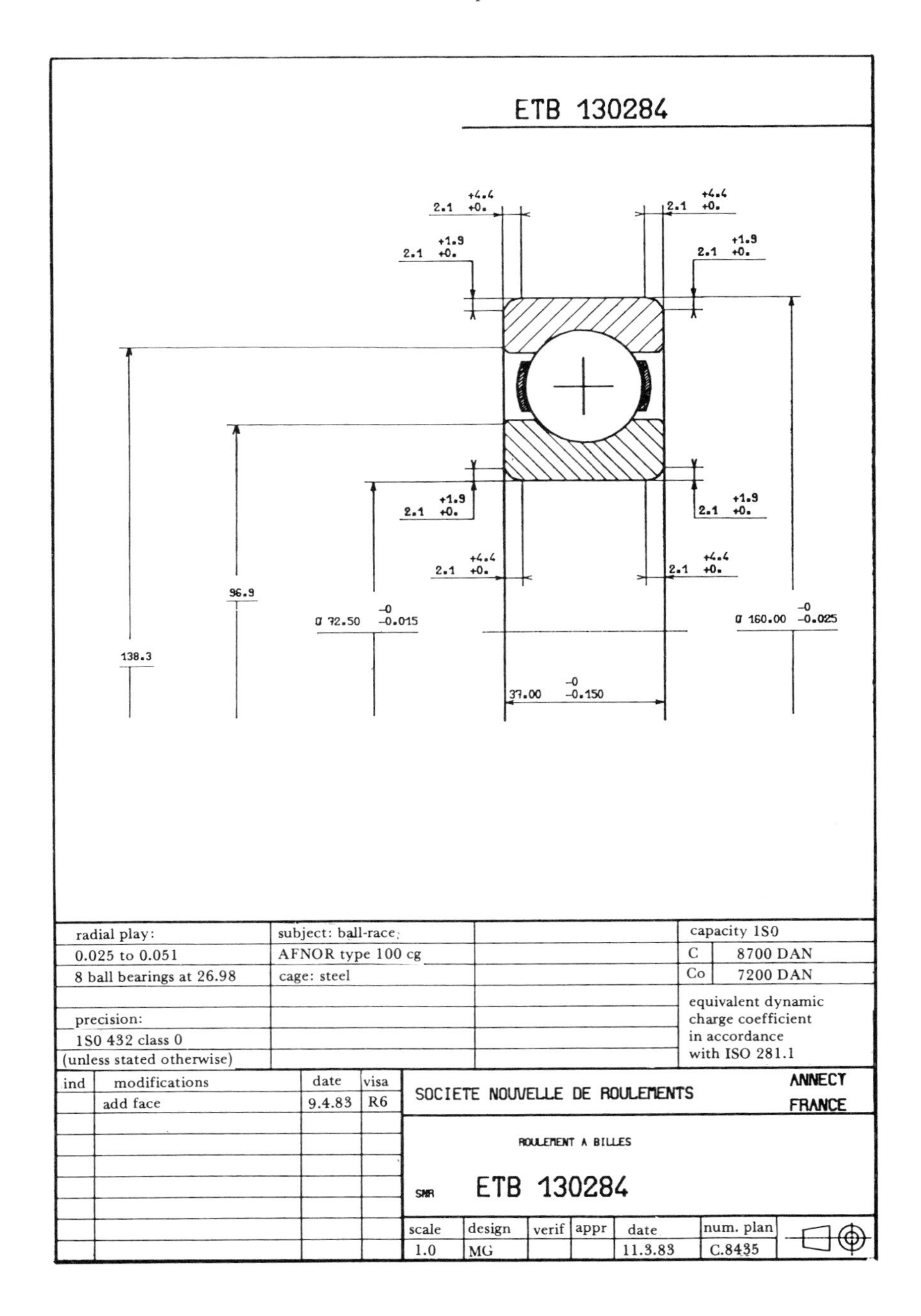


**Figure 6.1.** *Example of a plan of a ball-race*

15 minutes compared with the 4 hours which would be required to achieve this manually. Given that the development of software for such an application may take from a few days to several weeks (the time being dependent on the degree of completeness of the definition of the problem, the difficulties of page layout, etc), it is relatively easy to calculate the potential profitability. At present the SNR Company is developing more wide-reaching methods to disseminate the use of CAD.

## 6.2 Design and manufacture of wooden shutterings

*Illustrated concepts: parametrized model, construction documents*

This example concerns a company which specializes in producing wooden shutterings. Shuttering is used as a mould and requires that (Ricard, 1982):

1. a chosen shape is produced in concrete;
2. the desired texture of concrete is obtained;
3. the stability of the concrete is ensured.

There are two major methods of manufacture:

1. 'rapid shutterings' – a range of building products which are obtained from a simple dimensional adaptation using calculations carried out during study;
2. 'special shutterings' – products requiring specialized studies.

The 'rapid shutterings' method of manufacture illustrates parametrization. The Ricard Company is gradually adopting a method of design/manufacture involving a CAD/CAM system specially developed for that purpose. In order to limit cost, Ricard have established a link, via a computer network, with a computer bureau (CISI) which deals with data processing developments.

As with the previous example, the first task which has proved to be most important is to define the families. Previous work has allowed the automation of calculations, and the shape of the shuttering should result in the definition of standard families. The solution consists of a definition of the type of mould (the structure that will hold the concrete) and of the type of structure used as a support (to keep the mould rigid). The choice of solution for the mould and the supporting structure is made taking into account one or more characteristic dimensions.

The processing development has been created specially for this application. It has been implemented using APL language which allows rapid development (in this example, given the small number of interactions and the simplicity of the operating calculations, the performance aspect does not have priority).

standard type: double beam
job number (nnnn), delay (JJ/MM/AA), number (nn)?:1234A 15/4/83 1
universal (1) or rapid (2) ? : 1
length ? : 7000
height left side, right (only one if same) ? : 450
width left base ? 500
width right base (press return if same as left) ? :
core joint (press return if no joint) ? :
length of side panels (press return if only one) ? :
CP length on panel one (if no CP joint press return) ? :
accessory (press return if no accessory) ? : tie-beams
accessory (press return if no accessory) ? :

**Figure 6.2.** *Data entry*

*1 universal double beam (7000 x 450 x 500 + 500)

| | | | | | | | |
|---|---|---|---|---|---|---|---|
| A | 15 | 1844 | 100 x 50 | planed | 95 x 47 | 138.300 | pine |
| B | 30 | 477 | 100 x 50 | planed | 95 x 47 | 71.350 | pine |
| C | 15 | 166 | 100 x 50 | planed | 95 x 47 | 12.450 | pine |
| D | 2 | 7000 | 100 x 50 | planed | 95 x 47 | 70.000 | pine |
| E | 2 | 7000 | 100 x 50 | planed | 95 x 47 | 70.000 | pine |
| F | 21 | 395 | 100 x 50 | planed | 95 x 47 | 41.475 | pine |
| G | 21 | 395 | 100 x 50 | planed | 95 x 47 | 41.475 | pine |
| H | 30 | 350 | 90 x 12 | | | 0.945 | bark |
| I | 60 | 250 | 90 x 12 | | | 1.350 | bark |
| J | 2 | 7000 | 477 x 27 | planed | 477 x 24 | 180.306 | pine |
| K | 1 | 7000 | 100 x 27 | planed | 95 x 24 | 18.900 | pine |
| K | 1 | 7000 | 360 x 27 | planed | 360 x 24 | 68.040 | pine |
| L | 1 | 7000 | 100 x 27 | planed | 95 x 24 | 18.900 | pine |
| L | 1 | 7000 | 360 x 27 | planed | 360 x 24 | 68.040 | pine |
| M | 2 | 7000 | 465 x 10 | | | 6.510 | plastic |
| N | 1 | 7000 | 500 x 15 | | | 3.500 | plastic |
| O | 1 | 7000 | 500 x 15 | | | 3.500 | plastic |
| P | 1 | 7000 | 489 x 15 | | | 3.423 | plastic |
| Q | 1 | 7000 | 489 x 15 | | | 3.423 | plastic |
| R | 1 | 7000 | 404 x 12 | | | 2.828 | bark |
| S | 12 | 694 | 150 x 75 | planed | 145 x 72 | 93.690 | pine |

*cubage:*
pine 893.126
bark 5.123
plastic 20.356

*ratio:*
pine 45.568
bark 0.261
plastic 1.039

*equipment to integrate:*
2 stirrups 12

*equipment for delivery:*
12 tie beams 1930 25
= ⟩ 24 plywood
= ⟩ 36 crown
= ⟩ 30 ½ screw
= ⟩ 6 centring braces

**Figure 6.3.** *Updated cataloguing*

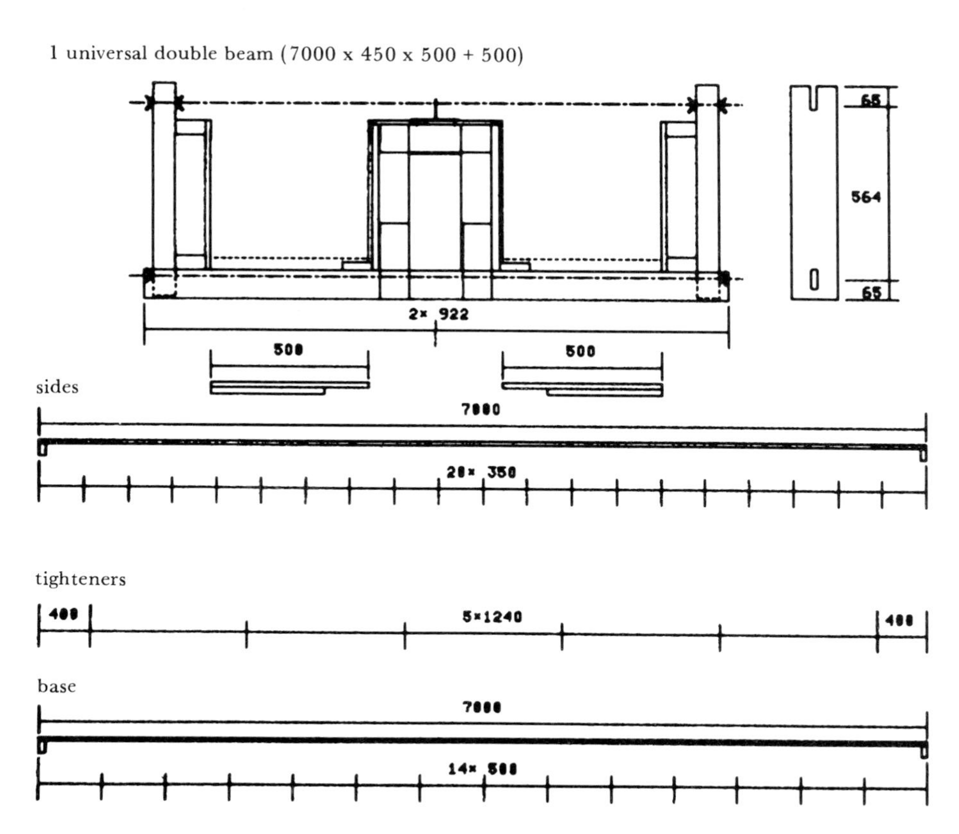


**Figure 6.4.** *Automatic plan*

A module is written for each type of shuttering and outlines the assembly of the component parts of the structure. An evaluated plan is automatically traced and the catalogue of the shuttering is updated (compare Figures 6.2 and 6.3 with 6.4). For these modules the data is provided by a user dialogue and from tables containing details of the nature and approximate dimensions of the raw materials. The results are catalogued in tables which will then be used as scales. The organization of the modules is by fixed tree type (one for each type of shuttering). Each node corresponds to a decision function in the pathway which allows elaboration of the shuttering being designed. These functions operate on decision tables to which access is governed by scales.

This application is fixed and for each addition a new program must be written by CISI. Use of computer-aided systems helps to speed up production processes and manufacturing errors can be reduced to a large extent. The development of such a system towards a state where all the company's products are designed in this way would necessitate the installation of a graphic editor with facilities for parametrization.

## 6.3 Installation of a drainage system

*Illustrated concepts: development of a work document, different aspects of documentation*

This example concerns the study of a drainage system (software developed by Ecole Nationale Supérieure de Mécanique de Nantes for SAFER of Toulouse and CANA of Anencis). Initially, a general layout of points selected at random is established. The first work document is a simple two-dimensional output of this point survey (see Figure 6.5). From this data a second document is produced which includes the contour lines (calculated automatically by the machine) and a relatively complex layout (showing rivers, roads, etc). This document (see Figure 6.6), called a topographic base plan, acts as a basis for the pedologists' work.

The installation of drainage hatches and of the drains themselves takes place interactively on-screen with the help of a numerical tablet. Figure 6.7 shows an example of a completed network: note the development of the main collector pipe indicated by the bold line (which can be found at the middle of the plot).

Also shown here is the communication document for use by the company contracted to construct the drainage network. This shows the different parameters that must be considered for each section of the drain, such as the height of the land, the depth, the angle of inclination, the length, etc. Figure 6.8 shows the document which illustrates the profile associated with the main sewer. There are documents of this type for each section or group of sections.

**Figure 6.5.** *Point collection*

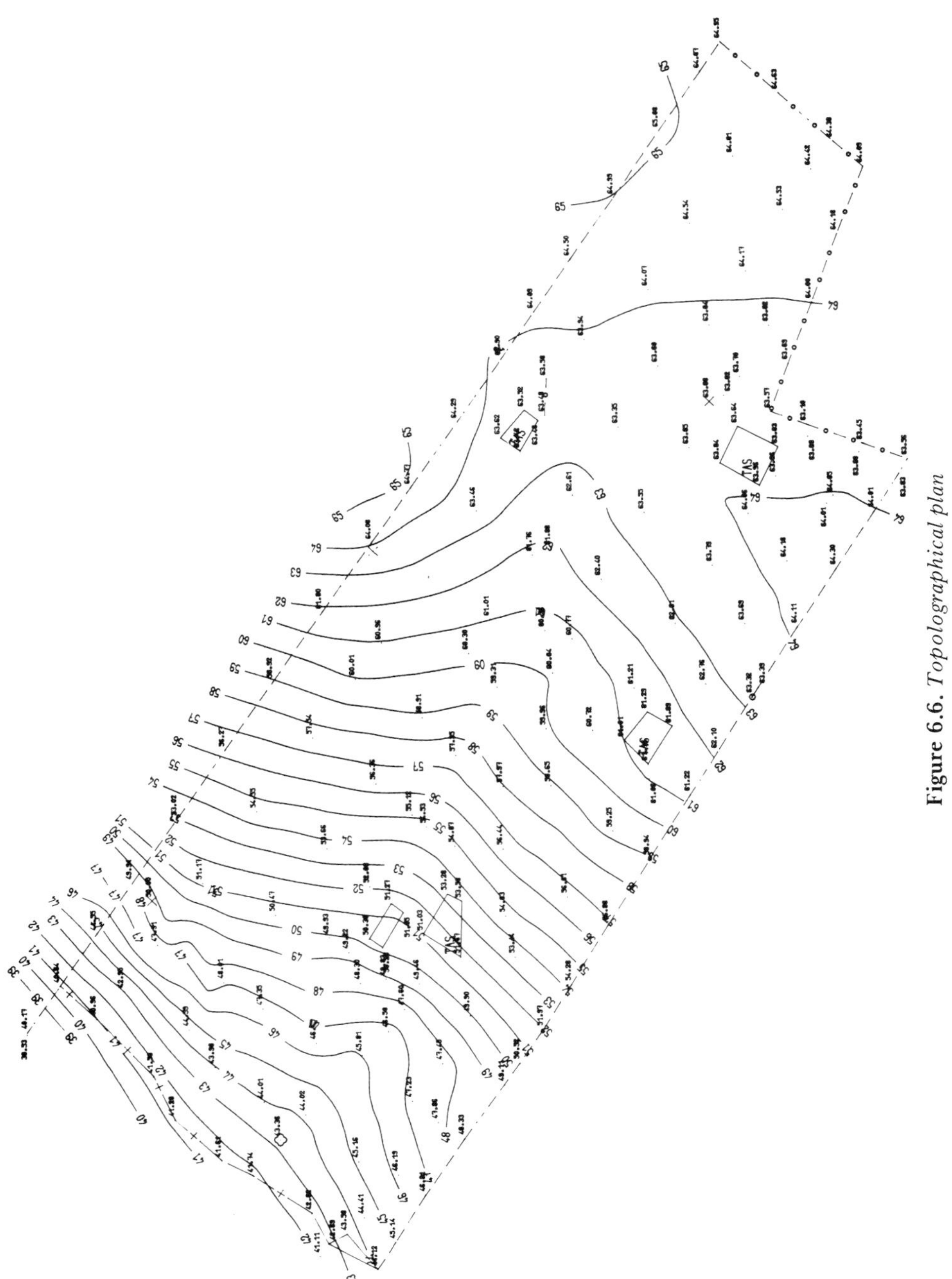

**Figure 6.6.** *Topolographical plan*

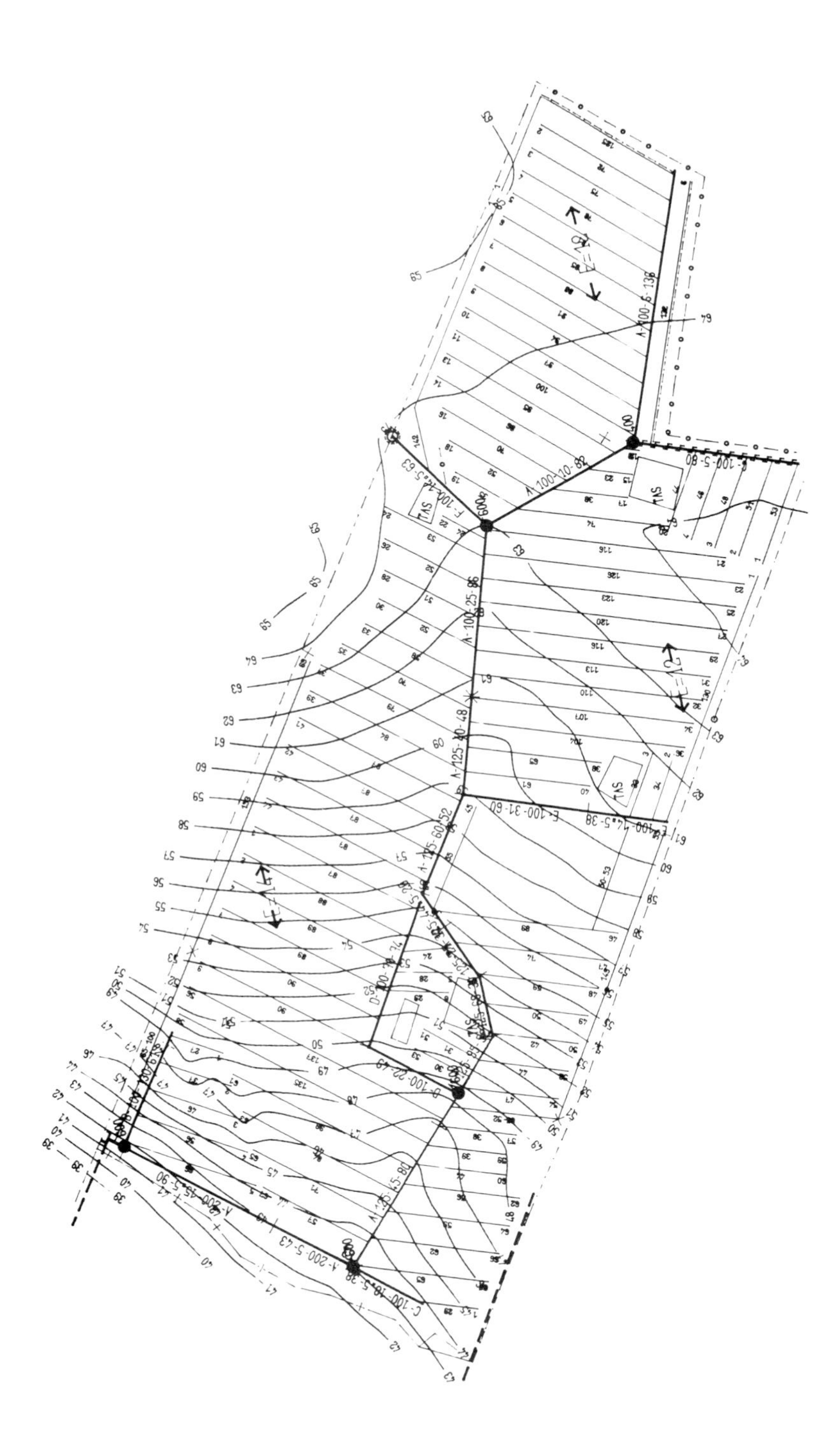

**Figure 6.7.** *Plan for the installation of drains*

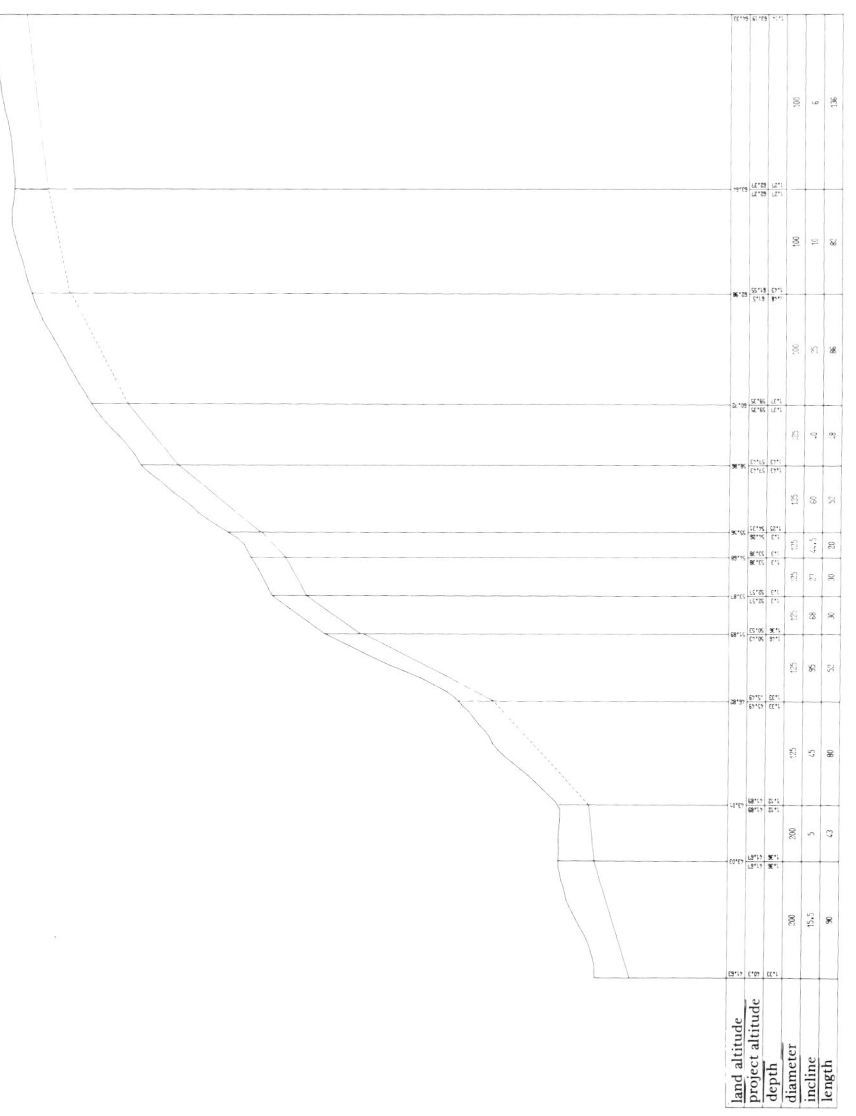


**Figure 6.8.** *Longitudinal profile of the main drain*

## 6.4 Electronics design

*Illustrated concepts: two-dimensional graphics, comprehension graphics, automation*

Certain graphic aids may be used in the field of electronics for the production of integrated circuits and the development of printed circuits. The use of colour may help to make a design easier to understand (see plates between pages 144 and 145). The example shown in Figures 6.9 – 6.12 was developed by the Crouzet Company on the SCI-CARDS system. Rather than choosing a completely automatic or completely interactive solution, it is often useful to apply an algorithm for solving a large part of the problem, leaving the operator to resolve any ambiguities. It can be seen from the figures that, after initial manual positioning, the CAD system offers a better solution. From this point, the use of CAD improves the result interactively. Furthermore, this method of operation can be applied in different areas, eg in the clothing industry. In this case the problem is to position pieces of cloth in the best possible way (and thus economize on materials). The method of positioning may, depending on the stock, allow improvements to be made interactively by the operator.

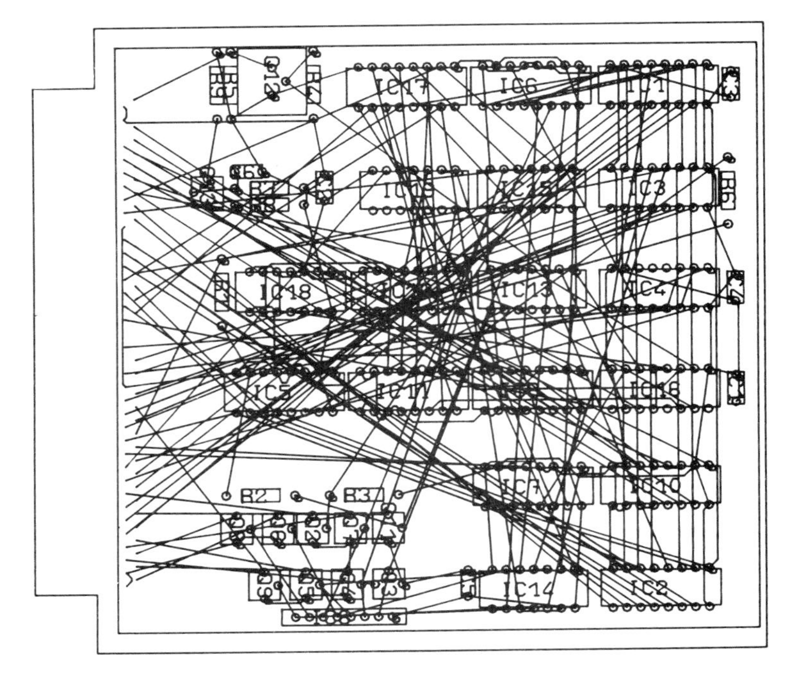


**Figure 6.9.** *Initial positioning*

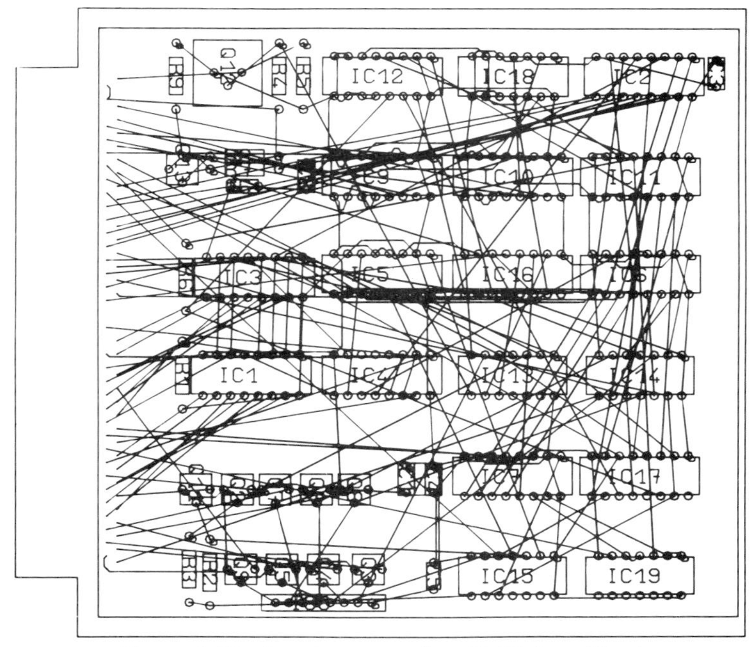


**Figure 6.10.** *Another example of initial positioning*

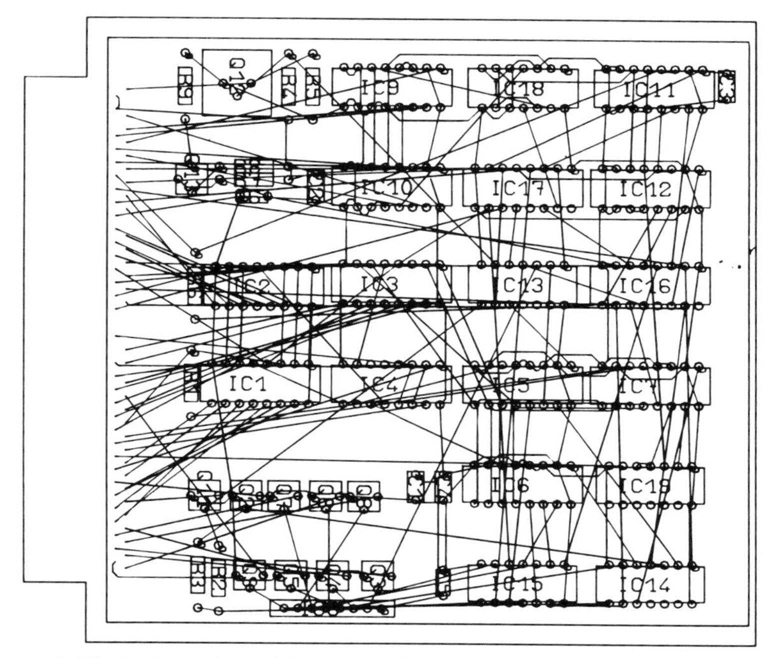


**Figure 6.11.** *Automatic positioning of the components shown in Figure 6.10*

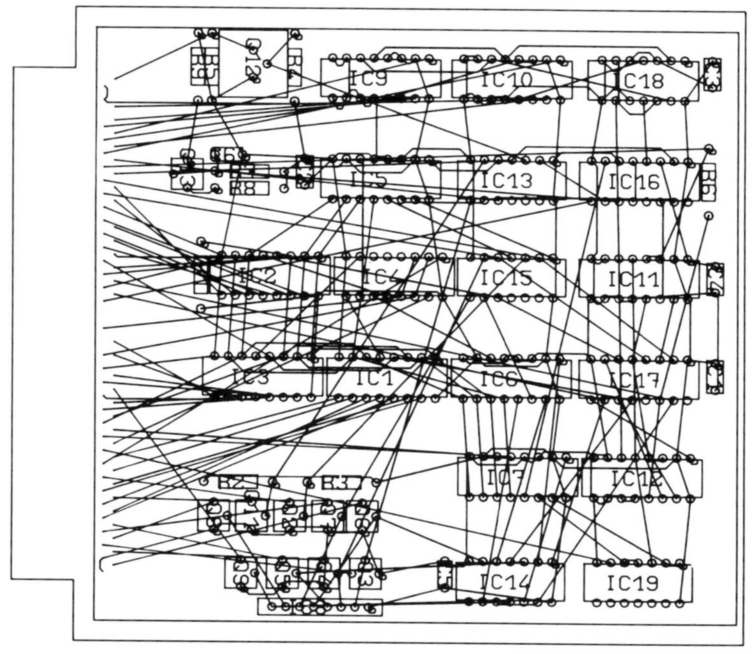


**Figure 6.12.** *After manual modification of the automatically positioned components shown in Figure 6.10*

## 6.5 Design of circuit-breaker mechanisms

*Illustrated concepts: technical drawing, the model for the implementation of a kinematic application, independence relative to hardware*

This concerns an application of CAD in the field of low voltage circuit-breaker mechanisms (it should be noted that there are important differences between 'high', 'medium' and 'low' voltage circuit-breaker mechanisms) (Figure 6.13). The functions that a low voltage circuit-breaker should perform are:

1. to control and switch off nominal and faulty currents;
2. to comply with standards regarding the dielectric medium and thermal dissipation.

A complex kinematic system could be installed to perform two functions:

1. to simulate the mechanism which allows the positive opening–closing and the break in continuity of the appliance; this is linked to the locking and disengaging devices adopted;
2. to check the interference between parts, one of the biggest difficulties in the design of a low voltage mechanism being the very large overlap in the design plan between the different functions that the appliance has to carry out (it is not unusual to have 50 basic parts in an object the size of a cigarette packet).

Thus, the design develops in three basic stages:

1. the functional design of the mechanism;
2. the assembly of this mechanism: the parts can be represented in draft form because the working of the mechanism takes place fundamentally in one plane (its constituent parts are in parallel plans);
3. test models.

The CAD system takes into account the first two phases. Using a functional and then spatial simulation, it is possible to check the 'correct' working of the mechanism (the spatial verifications dealing with parts that overlap, etc are made visually). In order to allow the designer to describe, to assemble and to test a low voltage circuit-breaker mechanism from a kinematic point of view, the MECAN (MICADO, ENSIMAG, MERLIN-GERIN) software was developed. Its basic characteristics are as follows:

1. the setting up, the modifications and the kinematic tests are done with the help of a graphic screen and using associated dialogue techniques (calligraphic, designation, graphic tablet, etc);
2. a good degree of independence is ensured regarding the computer and the graphic methods (screens, dialogue methods, etc), partly

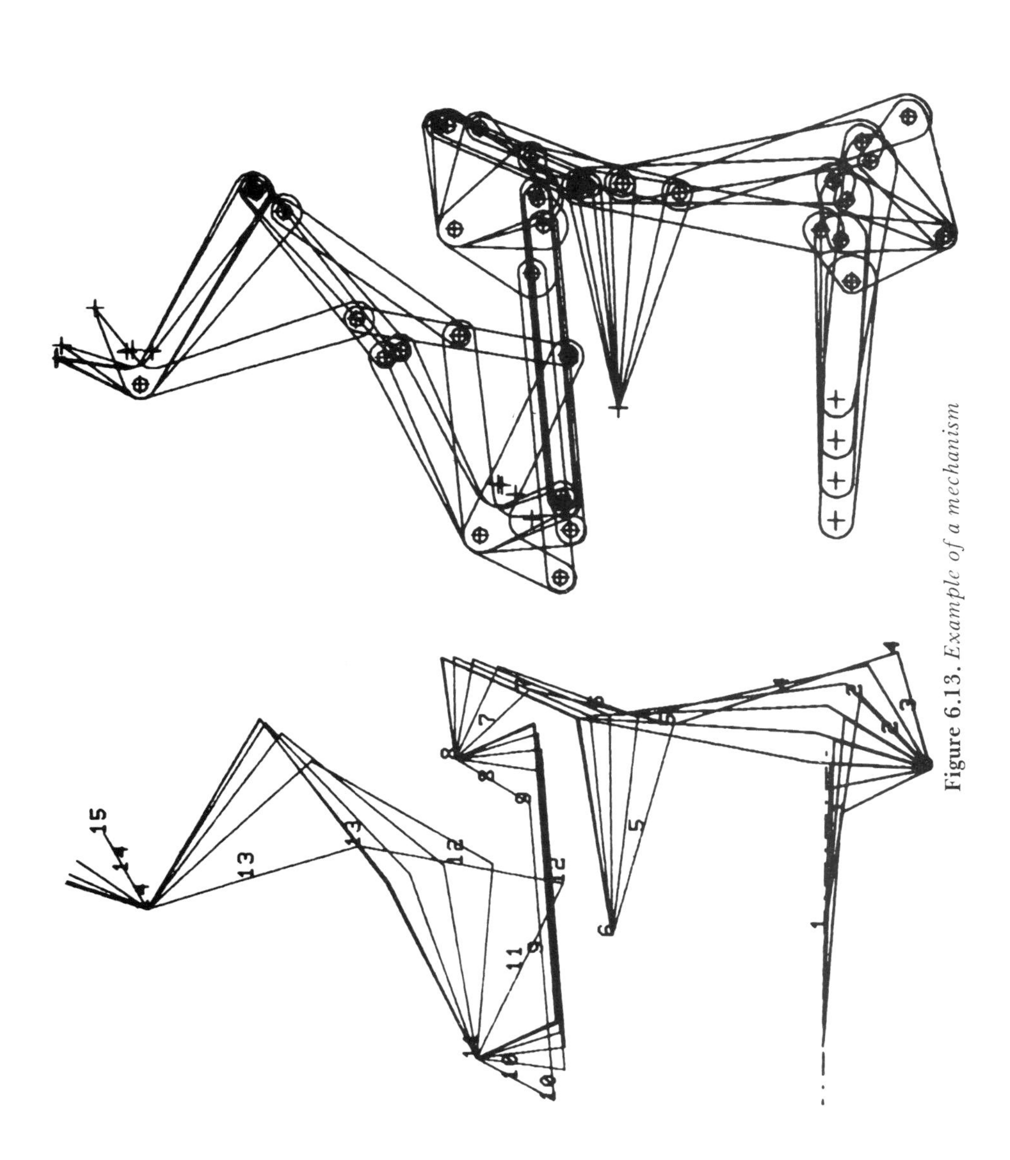

**Figure 6.13.** *Example of a mechanism*

through the use of the GRIGRI software (or the use of TEKTRONIX 4014 and IMLAC 3205);
3. extension tools which can be developed by the manufacturer are provided.

## 6.6 Architectural design

*Illustrated concepts: two and three-dimensional models, use of models for comprehension and communication graphics*

In architecture, interactive graphic techniques are used for the following reasons (Figure 6.14):

1. a three-dimensional model allows better management of the project and allows for integration on-site, testing of different methods of procedure, etc;

2. a two-dimensional model:
   (a) implementation of plans (sections) with the help of libraries of parametrized elements; these will constitute the final dossier (communication graphics) intended for the client;
   (b) use of the geometric model (the two-dimensional model is sufficient for most operations) to obtain specification documents (both quantitative and estimated), measurements, etc.

It is evident that using such models, the comprehension tools can assume a considerable importance. This is the case with the visual display of a project from different 'angles of view', eg (Figure 6.15):

1. general visual display of a group of buildings to determine their overall appearance;
2. visualizing details of a building, or group of buildings;
3. visual display of a specific aspect, eg electric circuits or water-pipes.

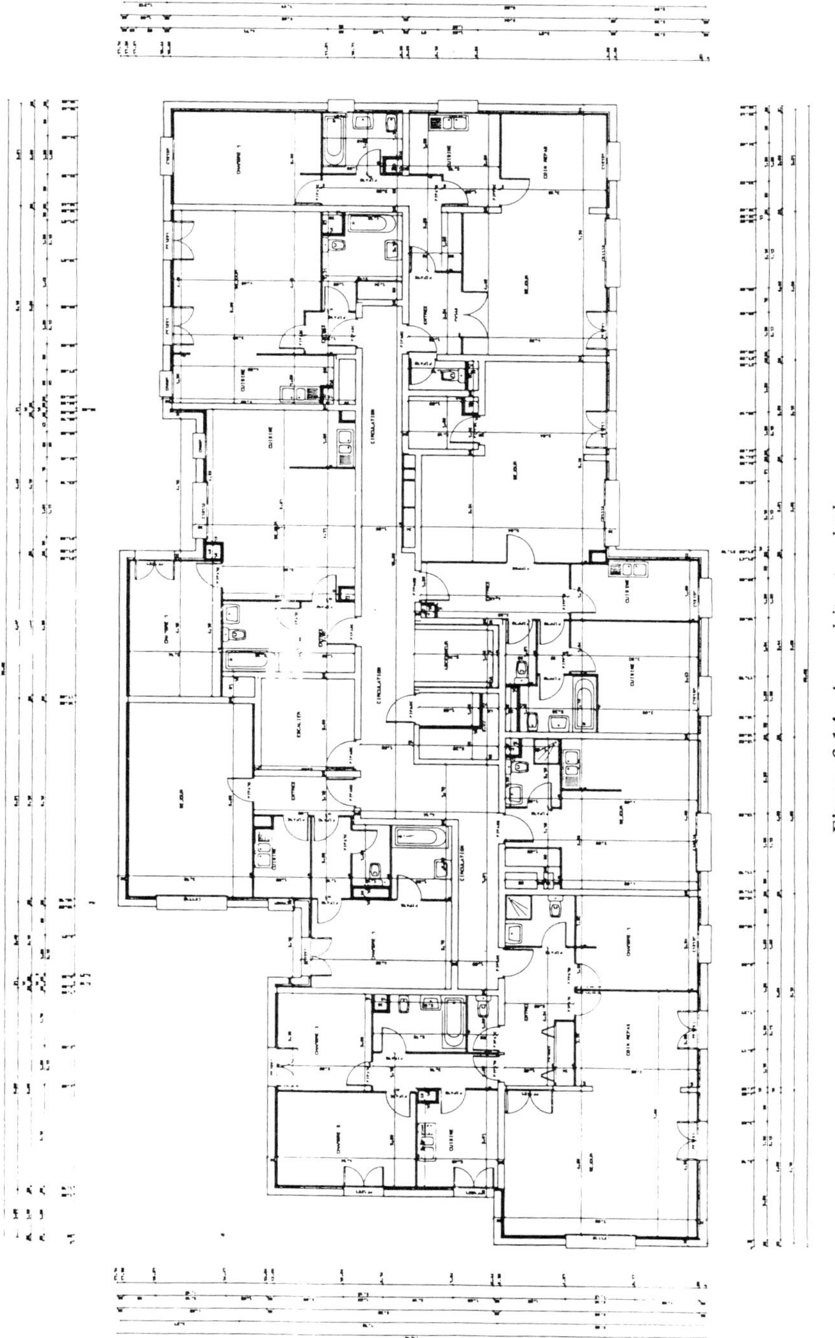

**Figure 6.14.** *An architectural plan*

**Figure 6.15.** *Plans of the elevation of a building*

## 6.7 Structural installation

*Illustrated concepts: calculation, line model and visual display*

To study the installation of a 'rig' type structure from a barge, two modules may be used:

1. a FLOAT program to calculate the balance point of a structure that is floating freely in water and determines the stability of the balance point;
2. a LAUNCH program to calculate the required trajectories of the rig and the barge to allow launch of the rig from the barge – the rig will then float at a position according to its balance point.

The principal stages in the calculation are (Figure 6.16):

1. calculation of the initial balance of the rig and barge together, taking into account the ballast of the barge;
2. application of the towing force on the rig which then starts to slip on the launching rails of the barge;
3. rotation and slip of the rig around the crane of the barge;
4. separation of the rig from the barge;
5. rig in its floating position (predetermined by FLOAT).

This is then followed by the anchoring of the rig and the raising of the crane.

The following procedures need to be represented graphically in three dimensions:

1. the trajectories of the rig and barge;
2. the variation of parameters plotted against time (position of the centre of gravity, effects of the movement of the crane, speed, acceleration, etc).

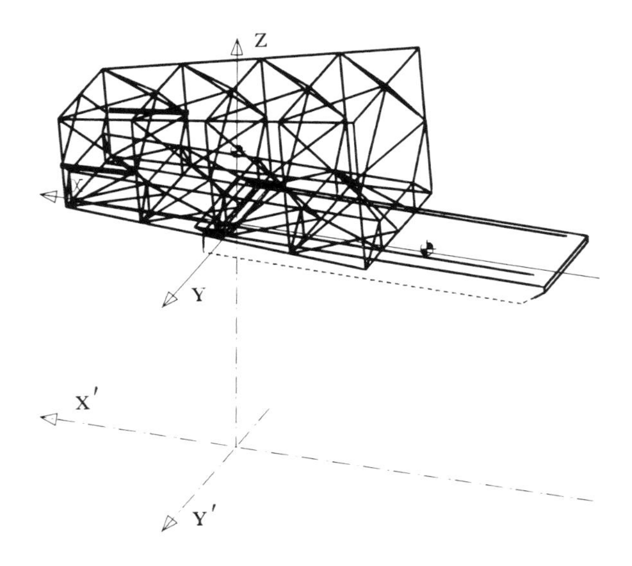


T = 0 seconds

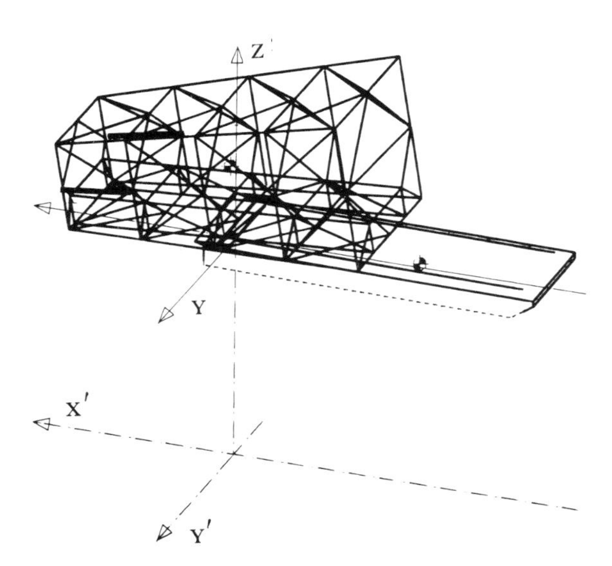


T = 10 seconds

**Figure 6.16.** *The launching of a rig from a barge*

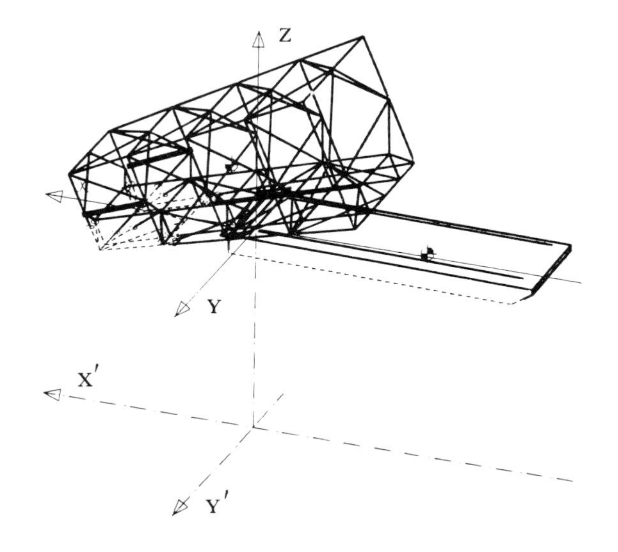


T = 15 seconds

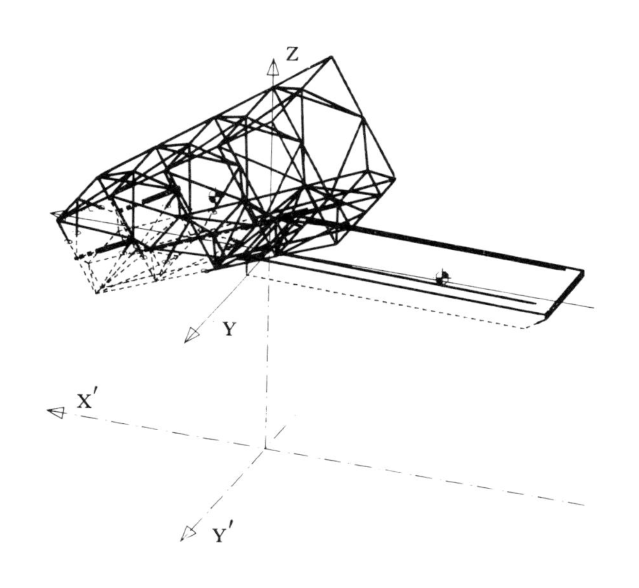


T = 17.5 seconds

**Figure 6.16.** *(contd)*

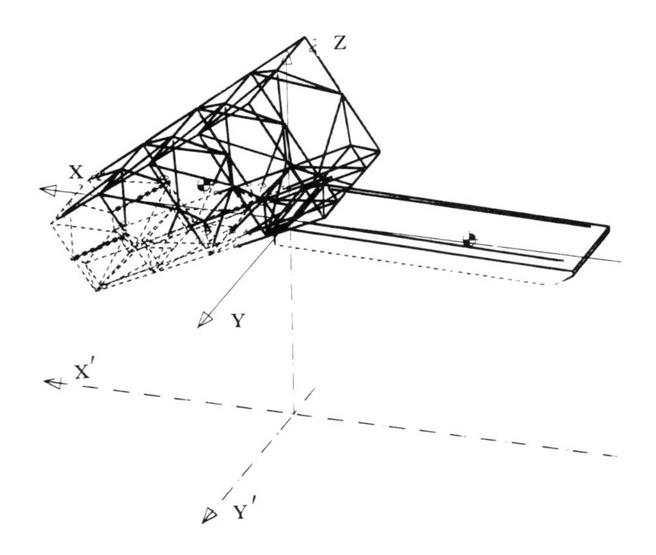


T = 20 seconds

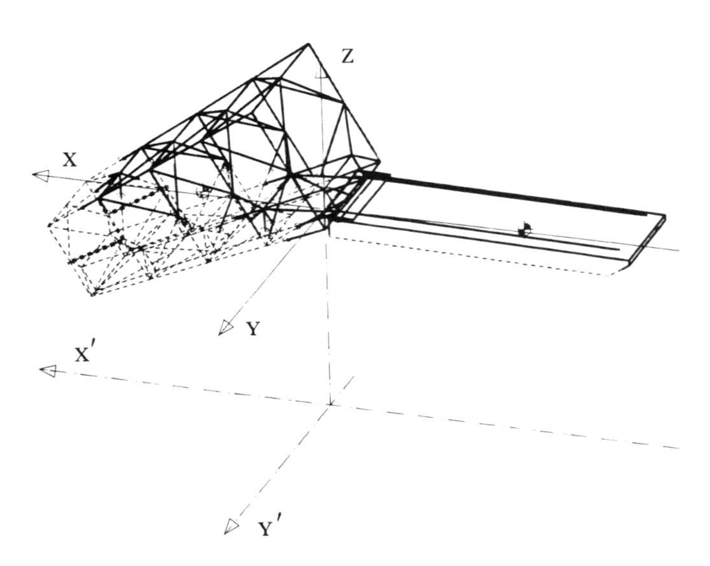


T = 25 seconds

**Figure 6.16.** (*contd*)

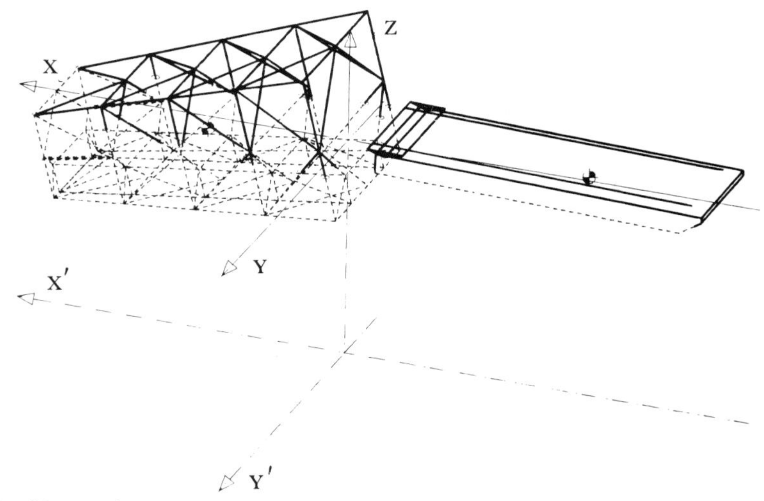


T = 30 seconds

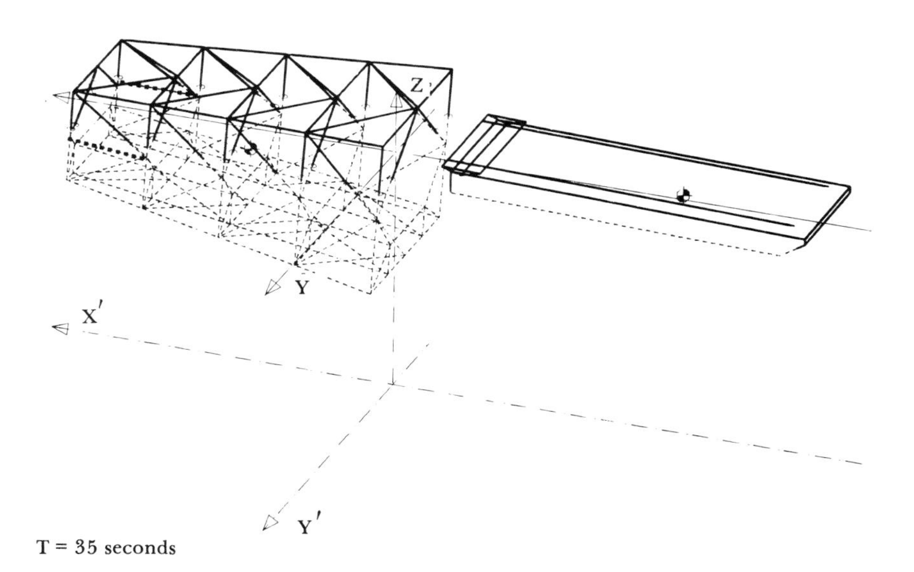


T = 35 seconds

**Figure 6.16.** (*contd*)

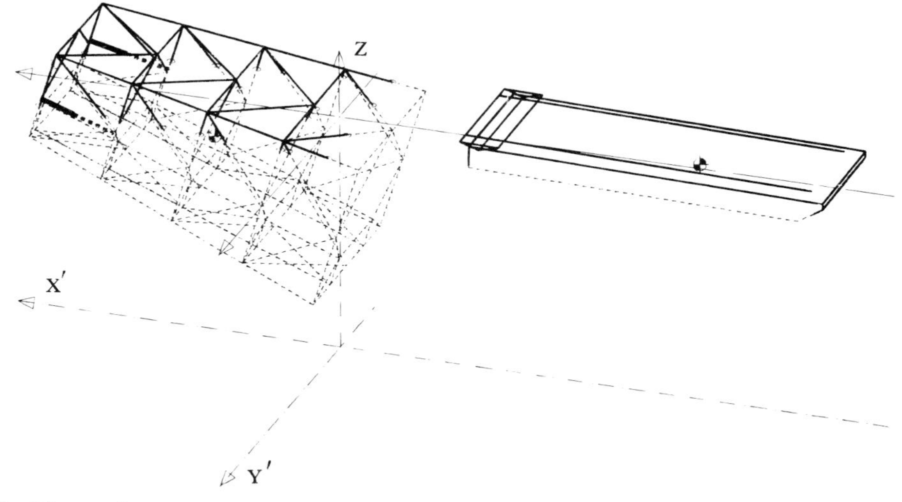


T = 50 seconds

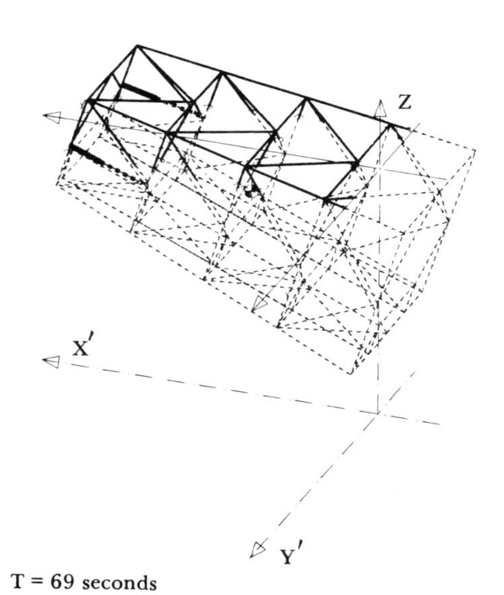


T = 69 seconds

**Figure 6.16.** (*contd*)

## 6.8 Studies relating to the construction of power stations

*Illustrated concepts: elimination of hidden parts, extension, detection of collisions*

Part of the research into the construction of power stations concerns the installation of different circuits which necessitate the use of a large number of pipes. Since 1982, the management team of Electricité de France have been using the PDMS (Plant Design and Management System) program, developed at CADCentre Limited in Cambridge, UK. This program allows the management of comprehensive data bases dealing with installation projects. It is possible to study the arrangement of pipes to ensure that they do not intersect; the production of additional plans are also possible. Figures 6.17 and 6.18 show the design of a building for use in a nuclear power plant (the building is shown without a roof so that the arrangement of pipes can be seen more clearly).

First, the installation of the large pipes is carried out (see Figure 6.17). Once these are in place the small diameter pipes are set out (see Figure 6.18). Figure 6.19 shows the layout of pipes as seen from the inside of the building. Once the unit is complete (see Figure 6.20; only the pipes are shown), it becomes difficult to see which, if any, of the pipes intersect.

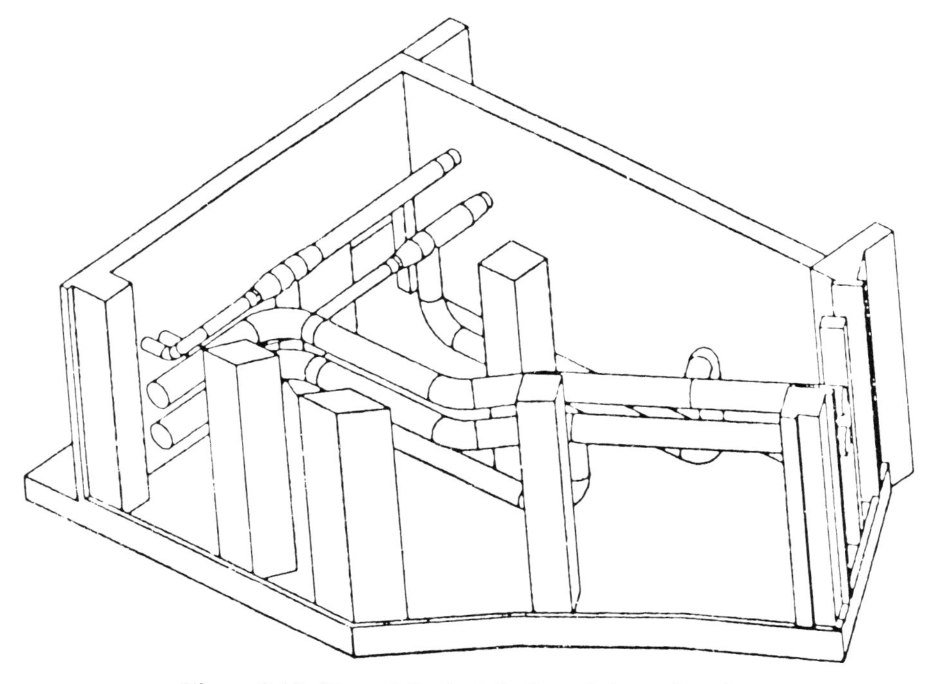

**Figure 6.17.** *Plan of the installation of the major pipes*

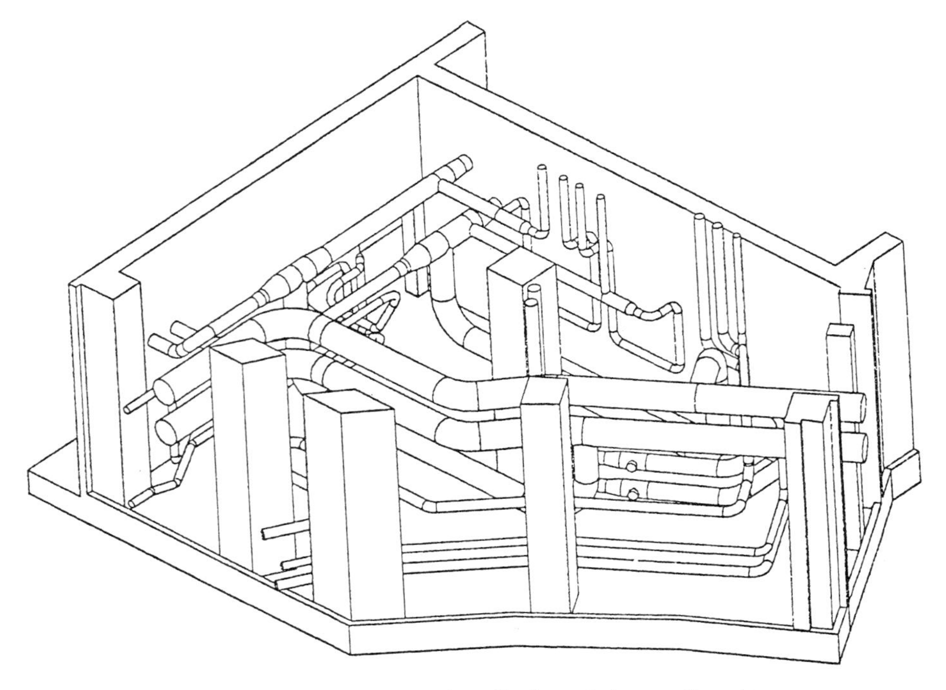

**Figure 6.18.** *Plan of the installation of the smaller pipes*

The PDMS program uses an automatic verification module to detect intersections (CLASHER) which, using the restrictions outlined and stored as each pipe is constructed, provides a list of pipes which intersect but are not intended to do so. Enlargement of a particular area allows collisions between pipes to be located. Figure 6.21 is an enlargement of the right-hand side part of Figure 6.20.

Another type of document can be produced which is useful during the actual construction of the pipes. This document, shown in Figure 6.22, is a verification isometry of a pipe line. This is an example of a two-dimensional graphic output from a three-dimensional model.

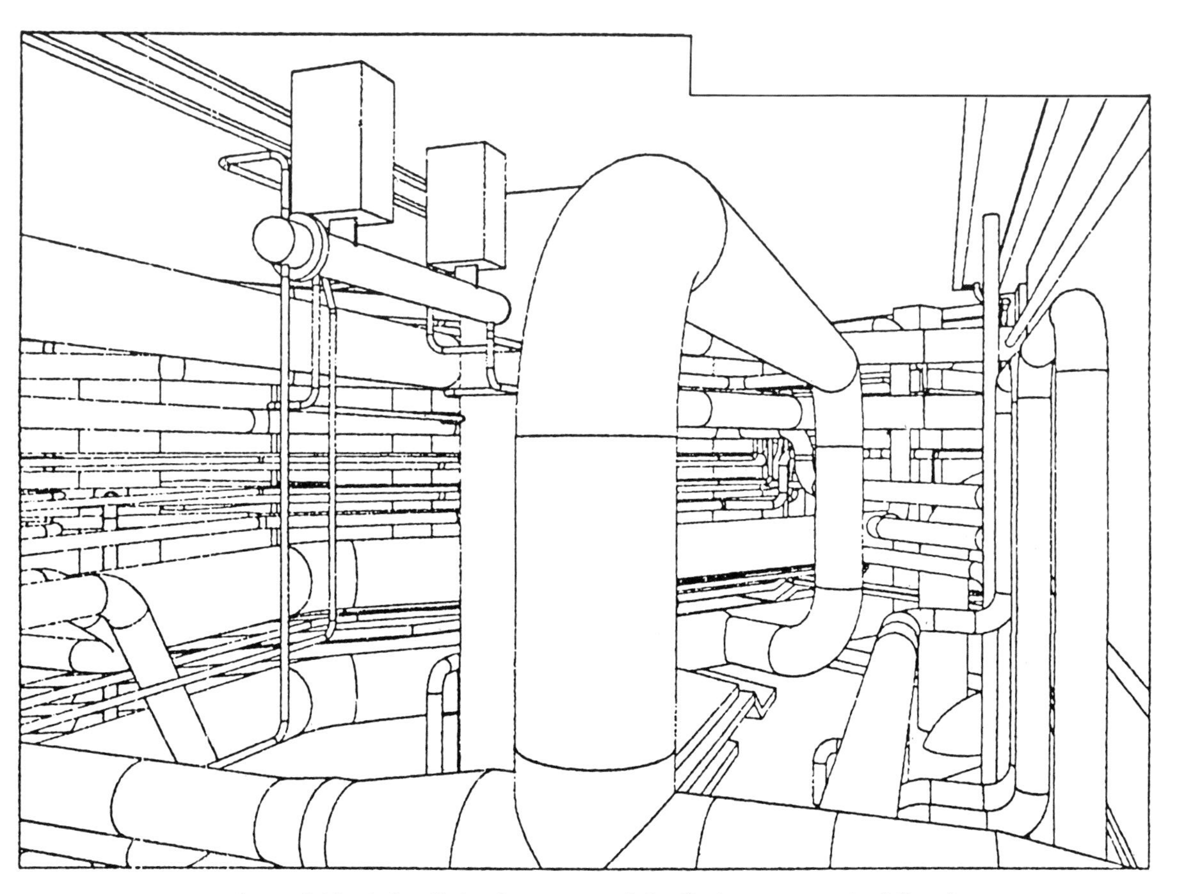

**Figure 6.19.** *A detailed enlargement of the final arrangement of the pipes*

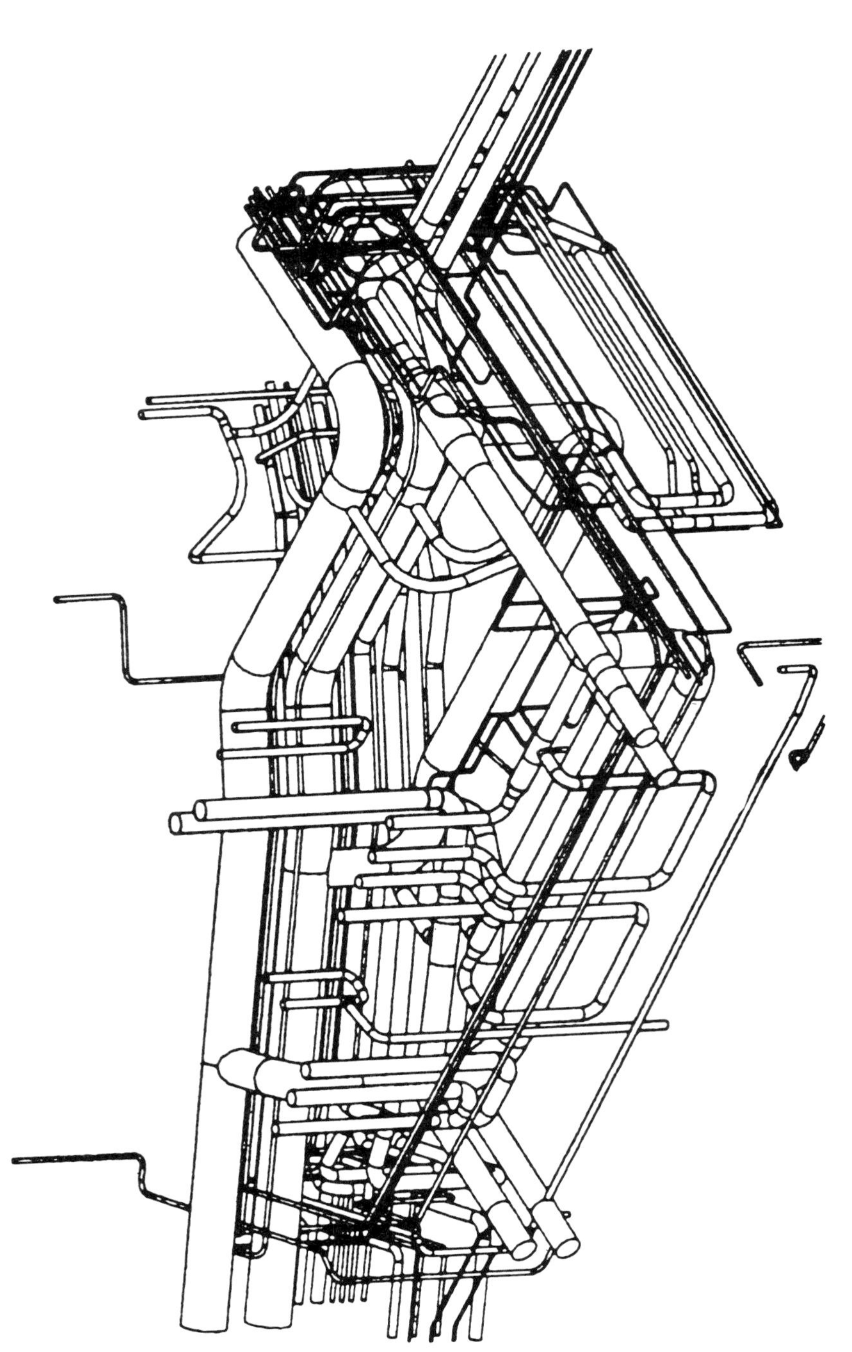

**Figure 6.20.** *A plan of the final unit*

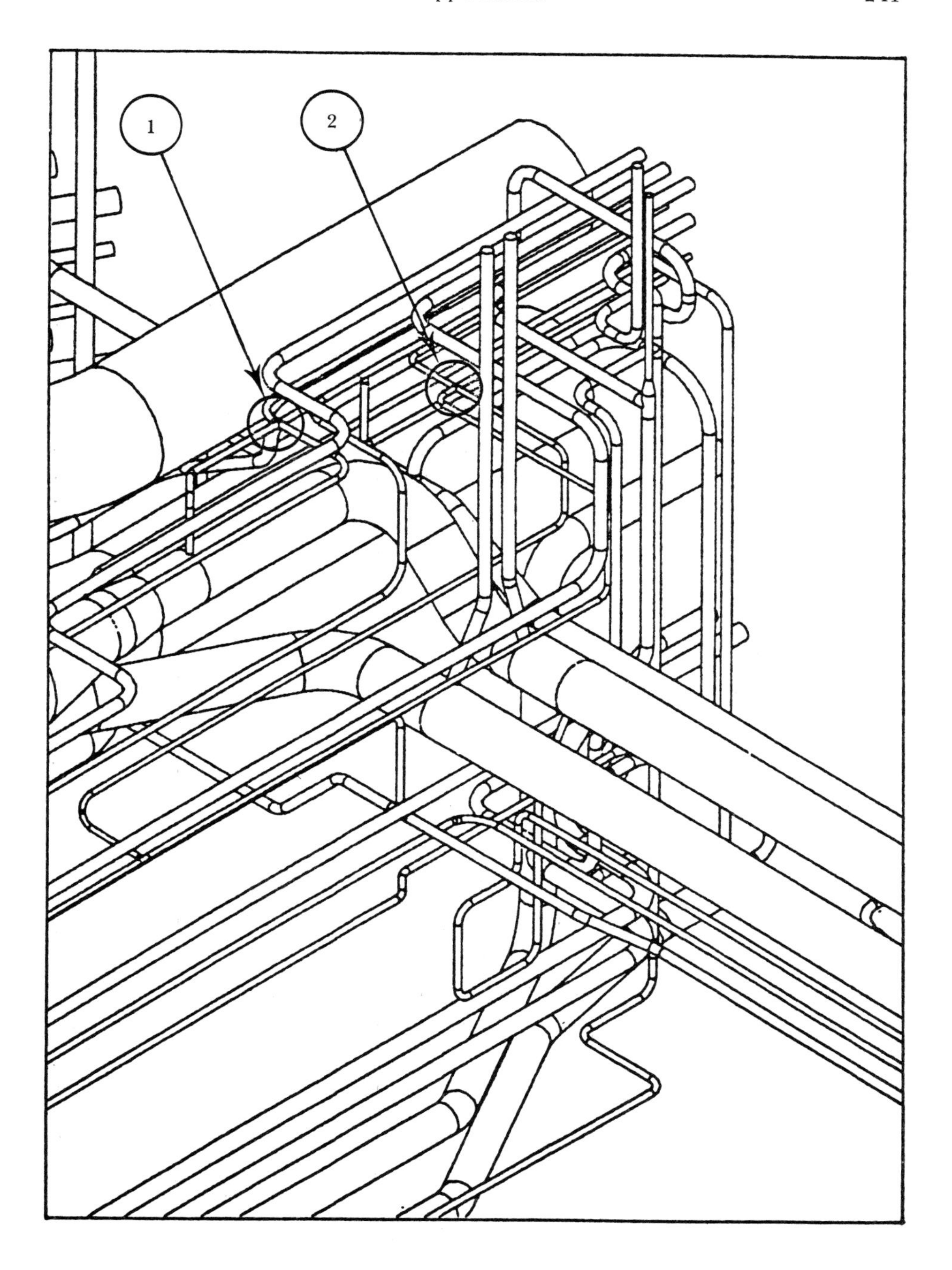


**Figure 6.21.** *A detailed enlargement showing the location of two collisions*

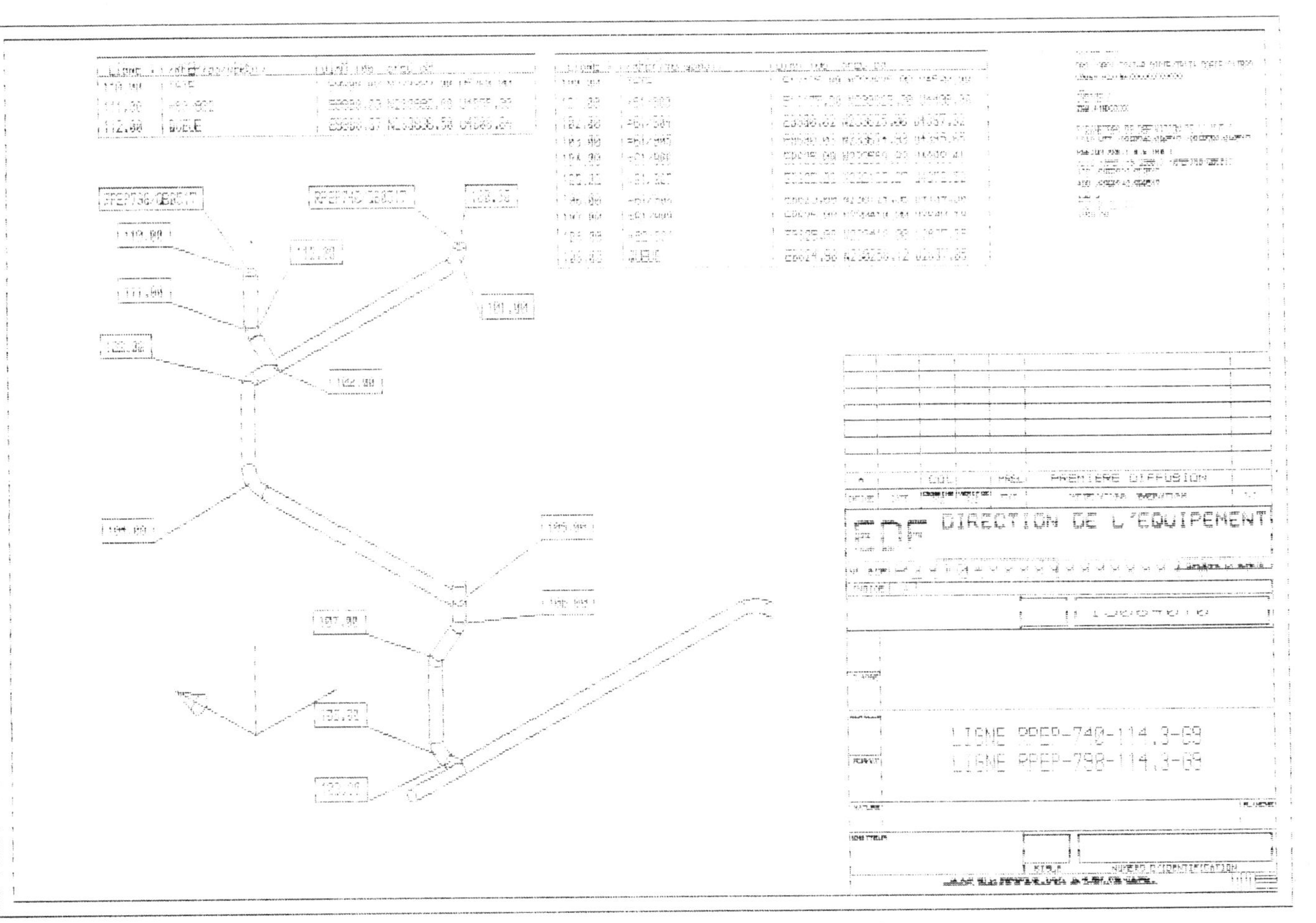


**Figure 6.22.** *Isometry for the testing of a pipe line*

## 6.9 Design and production of automobile body-work

*Illustrated concepts: variety of models, integration of the design–manufacture process*

The Renault Company has used CAD/CAM methods for the design of body-work for the past 10 years. The design of body-work is usually done manually, resulting in the production of a scale model. The UNISURF three-dimensional software in interactive mode is used for modifications of the model (see Figure 6.23). The model is then numbered by a photogrammetic method. Division into squares and definition of the parts of the body-work to be pressed is also carried out using the UNISURF software.

In the preparatory stage before manufacture UNISURF is used to determine the best form (balance and assembly) and RA3D is used for the preparation of technical drawings based on sections produced using UNISURF (see Figure 6.24).

The manufacturing stage can be divided into:

1. Standard manufacturing techniques (drilling, milling, etc), which at present are programmed manually (ELAN), but which, in the future, might be managed by a RA3D post-processor.
2. Machining control and adjustment of shape: the machining process is based on the shapes defined using UNISURF and the definition of manufacturing parameters (movement of tools, etc) using SURFAPT. Control is established using mini-UNISURF. The adjustment phase is always manual, but it is interesting to note that it is much less important now due to the use of CAD/CAM (significant improvement has been achieved at this level).

CAD/CAM techniques are not used to any extent at the assembly stage; however, several robot simulations (eg soldering robots) have been initiated using RA3D (robot movements are always established through a teaching mode).

There are over 50 UNISURF and 50 RA3D systems in use at present, mainly in the fields of car manufacture and aeronautics – the geometric model is used for numerous calculations, eg aerodynamics, distortions, etc (see plates between pages 144 and 145 for examples of these).

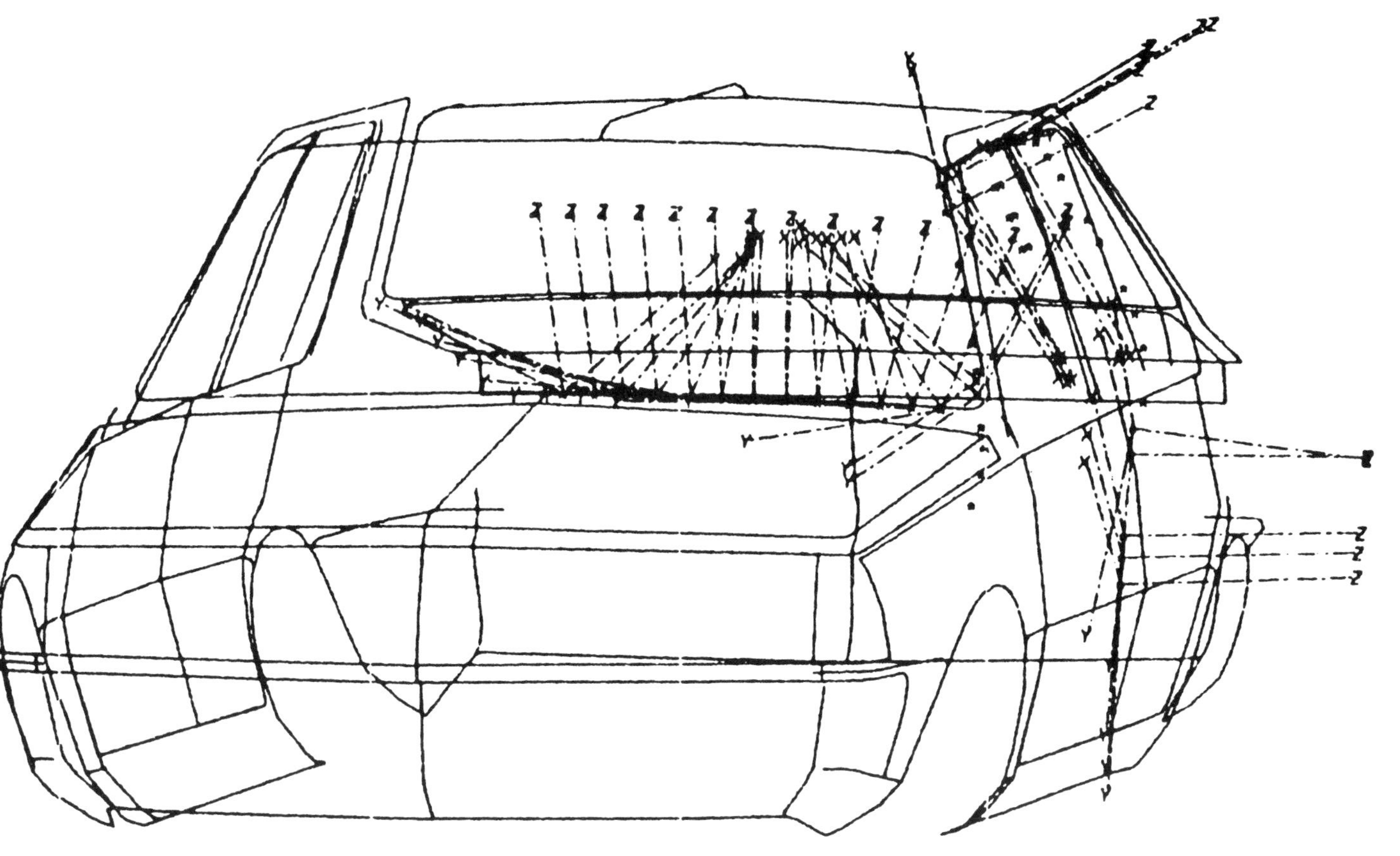

**Figure 6.23.** *Bodywork designed using UNISURF showing the definition of the tracking of a robot gripper*

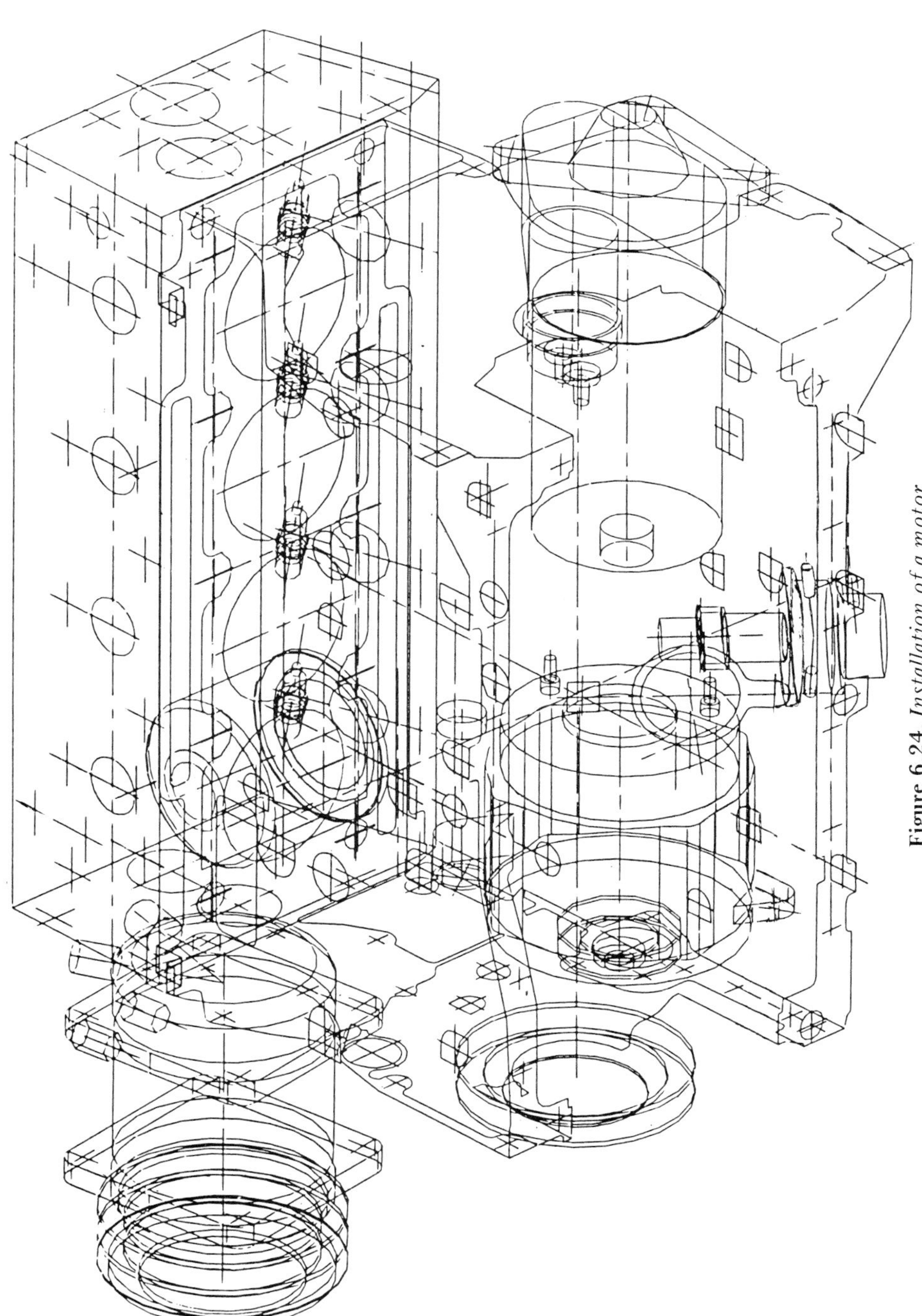

**Figure 6.24.** *Installation of a motor*

## 6.10 Design of turbines

*Illustrated concepts: complex surface, calculations*

The design of a turbine necessitates the definition of a wheel, a set of blades, a shaft and a group of components for carrying, controlling, distributing and then collecting the water (piping, valves, sluices, tanks). The shape of the blades is determined and calculated by section in several planes. This gives an approximation from which the engineer can, using SYSTRID software, produce a three-dimensional visual display. It is possible to modify the shape of the blades interactively, SYSTRID being used to achieve smoothing of the concave and convex surfaces. Once the shape of the blades has been completely specified, the other components of the turbine are defined (see Figures 6.25 – 6.27). The CAD/CAM techniques used in such studies involve the use of a 'surface' type software (SYSTRID) and those types (for instance, the MAO program designed by Neyrpic Co) which allow improved integration of the modifications arising during the project and modelling stages. Design of the large industrial turbines manufactured by Bergeron Co requires the use of surface software (UNISURF) and calculation functions based on a solid model (EUCLID).

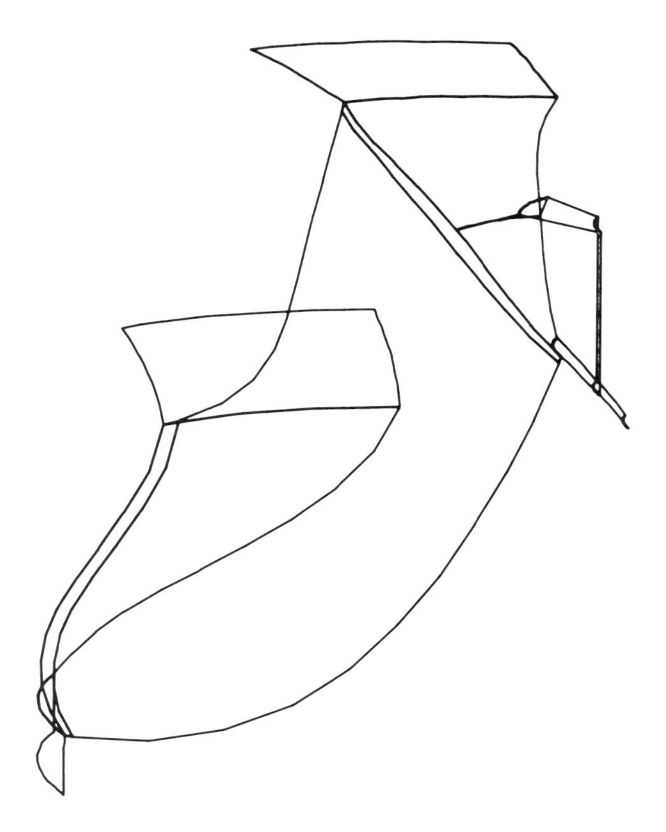

**Figure 6.25.** *A surface produced using SYSTRID software*

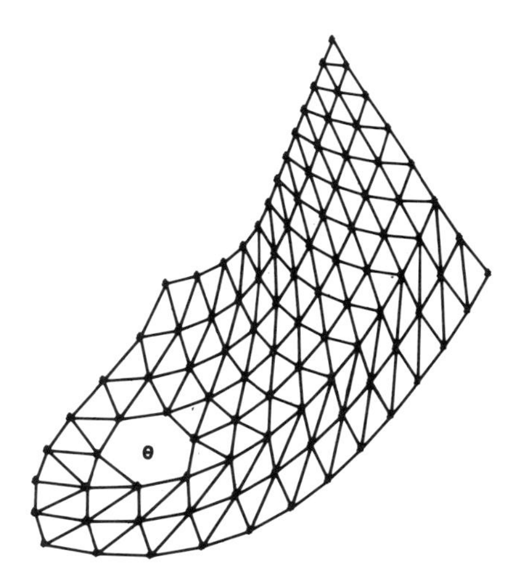

**Figure 6.26.** *A design for a blade showing the grid structure*

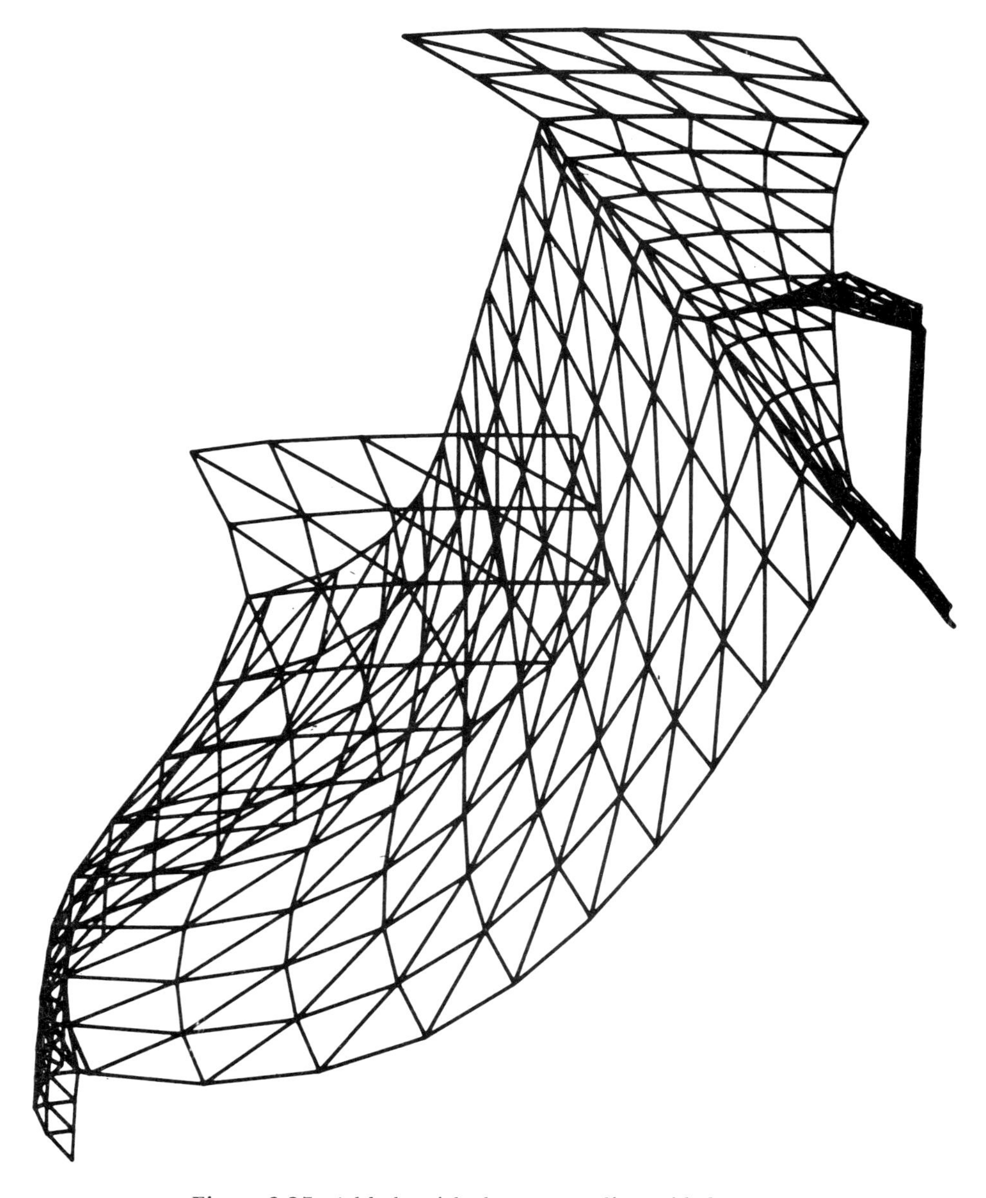

**Figure 6.27.** *A blade with the surrounding grid shown*

*Chapter 7*

# The finite element method

*by Richard G Budynas*

It was stated earlier, in Chapter 1, that computer graphics is often incorrectly interpreted as computer aided design (CAD). That is, the impressive utilization of the computer and its peripheral hardware to produce electronic images tends to be symbolic of the 'ultimate' usage of the computer in design. On the other hand, in many circles of engineering design, the finite element method is considered interchangeable with the term CAD. The method was used in industry long before the advent of computer graphics. In truth, the finite element method is only one of the many CAD tools available today. However, this widely used method is a highly versatile and powerful design tool and became such as one of the earliest emerging design techniques of the digital computer age. From the matrix methods developed in structural engineering, the basis of the finite element method began in the 1950s (Turner et al., 1956) and development continued slowly into the 1960s. Since then, the rapid growth of computer technology spurred an almost overwhelming development of the capabilities and user utilization of the finite element method. Today, it is interactive computer graphics which is enhancing and extending the use of CAD tools such as finite elements and consequently is becoming an integral *part* of CAD.

In design, the finite element method is utilized to predict the behaviour of some state property (force, stress, displacement, velocity, acceleration, temperature, voltage, acoustical pressure, etc.) within a given region or continuum of space. In general, the state variable will vary in a continuous (analog) manner within three-dimensional space and will be dependent on the conditions of the geometry and material of the continuum, the initial constraints imposed on the continuum, and the location within the continuum for which the value of the state variable is desired. A complete analysis of the given continuum should somehow provide the value of the state variable for all locations within the region. This problem type falls into the category referred to as 'field problems', for which the exact solution must be expressed in terms of continuous equations, since the overall problem geometry is continuous in nature. 'Closed-form' solutions of these types of problems can only be obtained for simple geometries.

Real design problems, on the other hand, tend not to be of simple geometric form, and alternative means of obtaining solutions must be employed. Highly idealized mathematical models can crudely approximate 'ball-park' continuous solutions, for which some engineering judgements can be made, or, for more accurate solutions, prototype models can be fabricated and tested experimentally. The latter method, however, can prove to be rather costly, especially if many design iterations become necessary. If the problem can be discretized (digitized) in some fashion, the digital computer and its myriad of capabilities can be harnessed to provide the engineer with a powerful design machine with seemingly limitless power. The finite element method supplies this capability of approaching the solution of field problems by digital methods. The solutions will also be approximate, but relatively easy to improve in accuracy and to implement into design modifications. A complete description of this method, however, would be quite involved mathematically and would need to include the many complex subtleties which exist in its applications. Many books, periodicals, and newsletters are devoted to this vast topic. This chapter, therefore, can provide only a superficial treatment of the nature of the technique. The intention here is to give an overview of the method and its relationship with interactive graphics. In order to provide some physical examples, the finite element method will be demonstrated by using some simple structural models.

## 7.1 General points

### 7.1.1 METHODOLOGY

To begin to illustrate the method, consider a simple extension spring as shown in Figure 7.1. If a force F is applied to the lower end of the

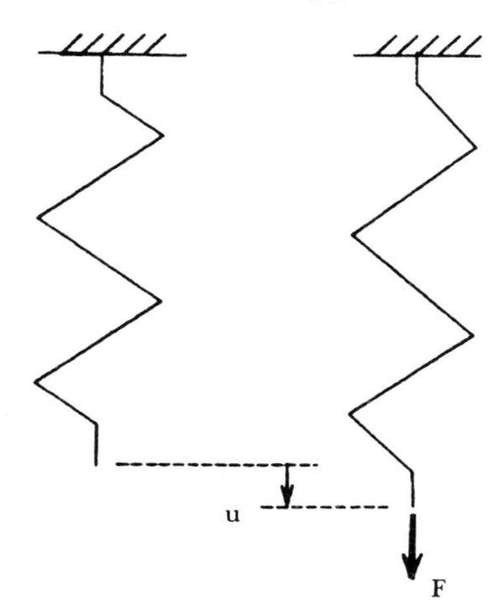


**Figure 7.1.** *The deflections of a simple spring*

spring, the end will move downward to a new position. The amount of displacement of any given point within the spring is dependent on the geometry and material of the spring, the constraints of fixing the top of the spring and applying the given force F, and the location within the spring. To be specific in this case, consider the deflection of the lower end. Assume that the deflection u is directly proportional to the force. That is,

$$u = cF$$

where c is a constant depending on the geometry and material of the spring and provides a measure of how flexible the spring is. In many instances it is more convenient to express this equation as

$$F = ku$$

where k is simply 1/c, and is a measure of the stiffness of the spring.

Next, consider the two springs a and b in series shown in Figure 7.2. Forces are applied to points 2 and 3 (called nodes). The force transmit-

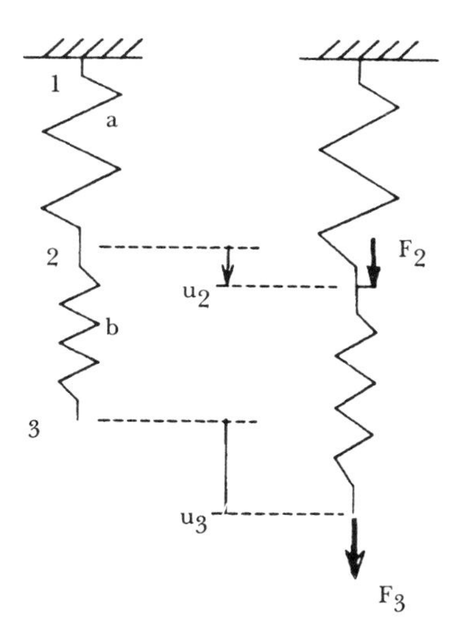


**Figure 7.2.** *Two springs in series*

ted through spring a is $F_2 + F_3$, whereas the force transmitted through spring b is only $F_3$. It should be obvious that the deflection of node 2 is

$$u_2 = c_a(F_2 + F_3)$$

and the deflection of node 3 is

$$u_3 = u_2 + c_b(F_3)$$

where $c_a$ and $c_b$ are the flexibilities of springs a and b, respectively.

Notice how the deflection of node 3 depends on the deflection of node 2 and the conditions of spring b (force and spring property). Node 2 connects to node 3 through spring b. This is an important concept about how the continuous behaviour of a continuum is put into discrete form. This behaviour is also true for node 2 and its relationship to node 1. Note that the deflection of node 1 is zero, and the flexibility and force of spring a are $c_a$ and $(F_2 + F_3)$, respectively. Now, to complicate things, consider the introduction of a third spring c and node 4 as shown in Figure 7.3, where node 4 is also fixed. It is no longer obvious how to approach the determination of the forces transmitted through each

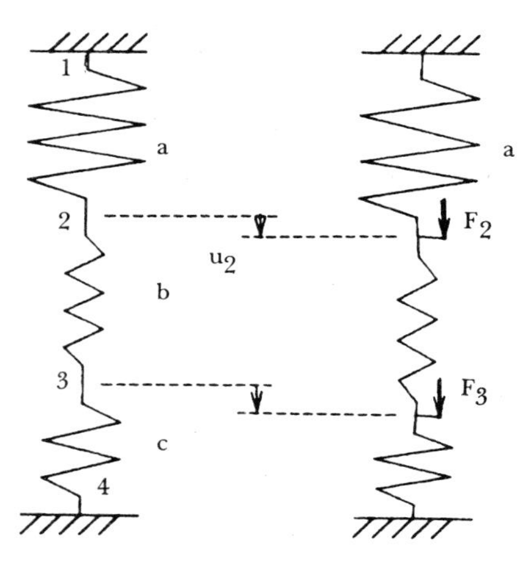


**Figure 7.3.** *Three springs in series with both ends fixed*

spring and the deflections of nodes 2 and 3. A different procedure must be followed. Instead of initially specifying the deflection of each node as a function of the applied forces, the force at each node is related to the nodal deflections. This is done using the stiffness property of each spring. For the system shown in Figure 7.3, it can be shown that*

$$
\begin{aligned}
F_1 &= k_a u_1 - k_a u_2 \\
F_2 &= -k_a u_1 + (k_a+k_b)u_2 - k_b u_3 \\
F_3 &= -k_b u_2 + (k_b+k_c)u_3 - k_c u_4 \\
F_4 &= -k_c u_3 + k_c u_4
\end{aligned}
$$

where, for purposes of generality, forces are also included at nodes 1 and 2.

* For more information on the mathematical development of the following, consult any textbook on structural mechanics (for example, Budynas, 1977).

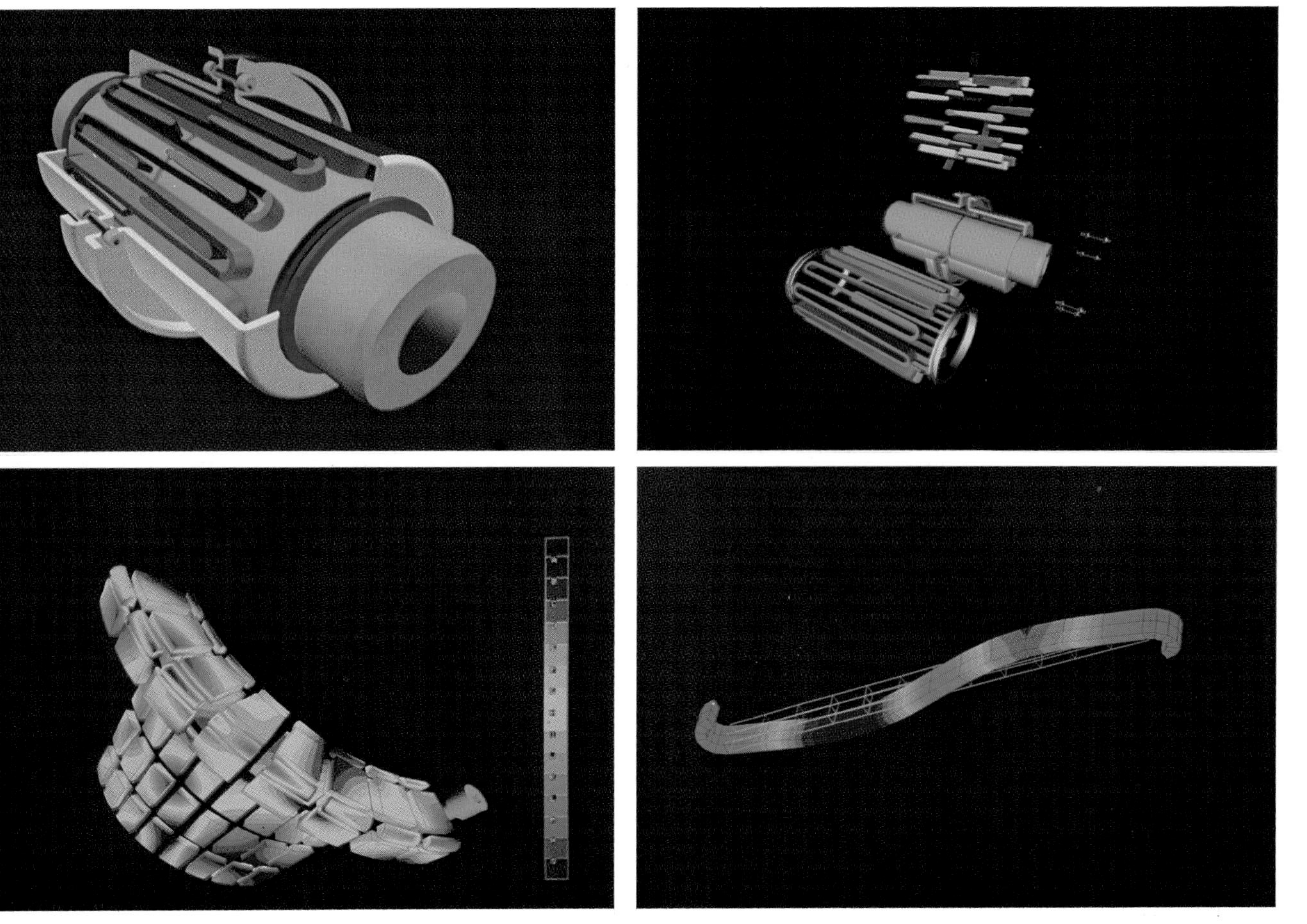

*Finite element analysis of a coupling (PATRAN-G, PDA Engineering)*

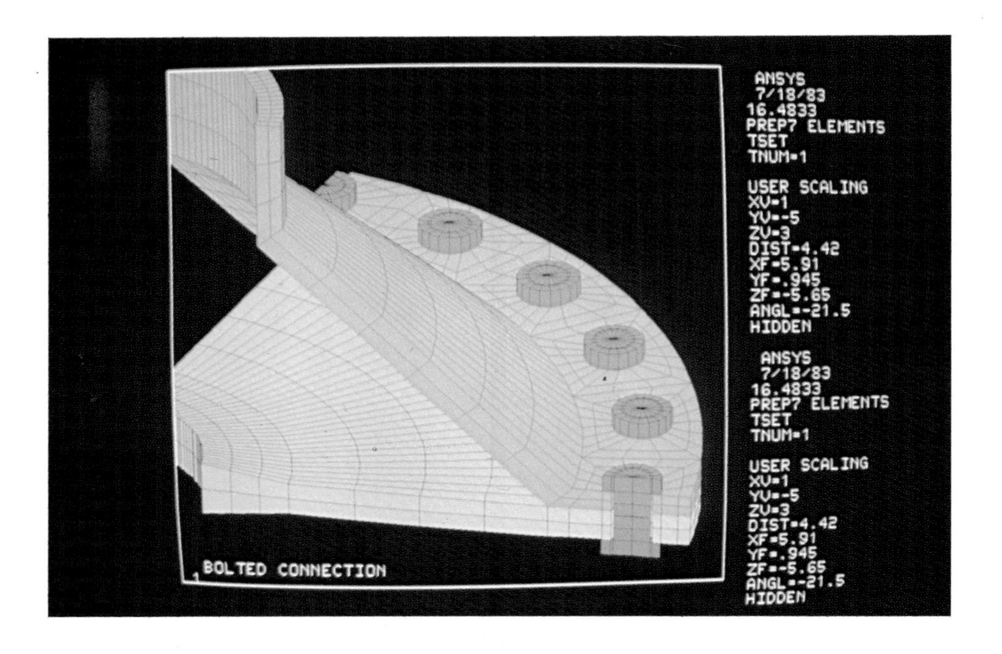


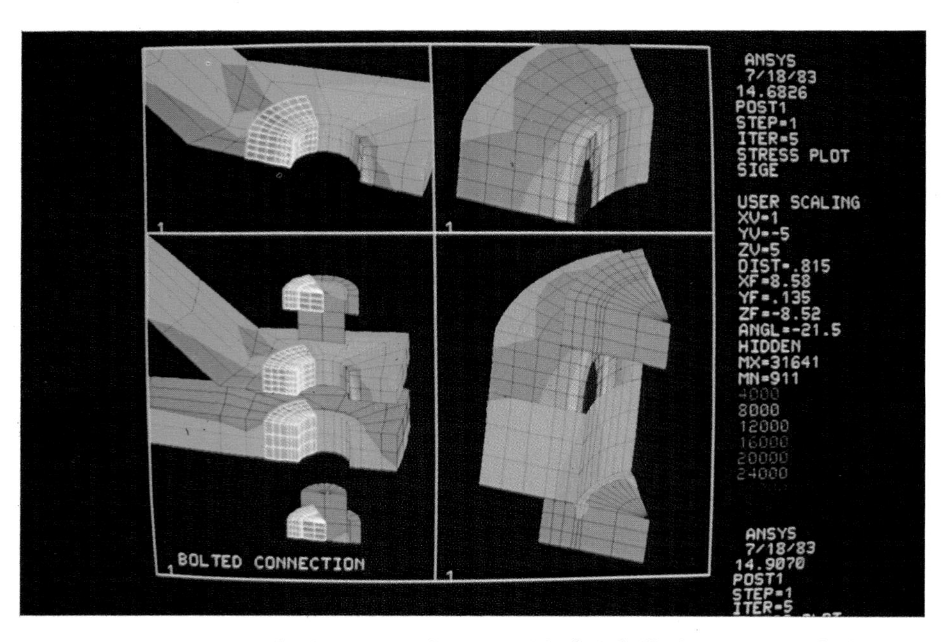


*Finite element analysis of a rotating assembly (ANSYS, Swanson Analysis Systems, Inc.)*

The system of equations can be best expressed in matrix form as

$$\begin{bmatrix} F_1 \\ F_2 \\ F_3 \\ F_4 \end{bmatrix} = \begin{bmatrix} k_a & -k_a & 0 & 0 \\ -k_a & (k_a+k_b) & -k_b & 0 \\ 0 & -k_b & (k_b+k_c) & -k_c \\ 0 & 0 & -k_c & k_c \end{bmatrix} \begin{bmatrix} u_1 \\ u_2 \\ u_3 \\ u_4 \end{bmatrix}$$

force matrix — stiffness matrix — deflection matrix

Each specific force equation can be reproduced as follows. To obtain, say, the equation for $F_3$ (the *third* equation), simply take the *third* row of the stiffness matrix and multiply each term from left to right individually with each term in the column of the deflection matrix from top to bottom. Then, add the pairs of multiplied terms to yield the equation for $F_3$. Notice the characteristics of the nodal force equations. A given nodal force is dependent on the deflections of the particular node and the immediately adjacent nodes, and the stiffness of each adjoining spring. If a node does not exist (say, that above node 1 or below node 4), it will not exist in the equation. The matrix equations can be expressed in shorthand notation as

$$[F] = [k][u]$$

where the brackets [ ] indicate a matrix of terms. The finite element method then seeks to invert the equation to solve for each deflection in the [u] matrix. Symbolically this can be expressed as

$$[u] = [k]^{-1}[F]$$

where $[k]^{-1}$ is called the *inverse* matrix of [k]. Obtaining the inverse is beyond the scope of this book. Therefore, the remaining discussion will be descriptive only. In general, prior to inversion, the [k] matrix must be modified to account for the fact that some of the displacements are already known. This is normally done by *partitioning* the matrix equations. Basically, the equation most dependent on the given displacement (boundary) condition is eliminated and the remaining equations are modified to account for the given boundary condition. In the current example, it is known that $u_1$ and $u_4$ are zero. The direct equations involve $F_1$ and $F_4$. Thus, these equations are eliminated and the equations for $F_2$ and $F_3$ are retained with the values of $u_1$ and $u_4$ substituted in and placed together with the known values of $F_2$ and $F_3$. This results in

$$\begin{bmatrix} F_2 + k_a u_1 \\ F_3 + k_c u_4 \end{bmatrix} = \begin{bmatrix} (k_a+k_b) & -k_b \\ -k_b & (k_b+k_c) \end{bmatrix} \begin{bmatrix} u_2 \\ u_3 \end{bmatrix}$$

or simply

$$[F_m] = [k_m][u]$$

where $[F_m]$ and $[k_m]$ are the *modified* force and stiffness matrices, respectively. Next, the inverse $[k_m]^{-1}$ is obtained, where

$$[u] = [k_m]^{-1}[F_m]$$

This results in

$$\begin{bmatrix} u_2 \\ u_3 \end{bmatrix} = C \begin{bmatrix} (k_b+k_c) & k_b \\ k_b & (k_a+k_b) \end{bmatrix} \begin{bmatrix} F_2 + k_a u_1 \\ F_3 + k_c u_4 \end{bmatrix}$$

where

$$C = 1/(k_a k_b + k_b k_c + k_c k_a)$$

Once the inverse is obtained, the remaining operations are trivial. All of the deflections are now known, and therefore all of the spring forces can be easily solved for, as well as the end forces $F_1$ and $F_4$. For example, the force in spring b is

$$F_b = k_b(u_3 - u_2)$$

The end (constraint) forces are found by substitution of the known deflections into the original force equations. For example, to determine the reaction at node 4, recall that the original equation for $F_4$ is

$$F_4 = -k_c u_3 + k_c u_4$$

### 7.1.2 RANGE OF DESIGN APPLICATIONS

The finite element method is quite versatile in solving field problems. If a given commercial application program such as MSC/NASTRAN or ANSYS does not have a solution sequence for a particular type of problem (such as acoustics), it is possible to modify the input data file so that the problem can be solved by analogy. That is, the field equations for a number of types of problems are very similar (for example, structural stresses, heat transfer, fluid flow, vibrations, and electromagnetic radiation). The differences occur in the physical nature of the state variables. For example, in structural stress problems some key state variables are force, deflection, stress, and stiffness modulus, whereas in the case of conduction heat transfer, the similar state variables are heat flow, temperature, heat flux, and conduction heat transfer coefficient. Table 7.1 provides a list of direct solution capabilities of MSC/NASTRAN. Table 7.2 provides a list of additional problem types which can also be solved by analogy.

3. Specific calculations for modelling purposes, for example, mass properties.
4. The final deflections of each node for each of six degrees of freedom for each subcase.
5. The values of various types of stresses and/or forces in each element for each subcase. Stresses could include normal stresses in three directions, up to six shearing stresses, three principal stresses, the maximum shearing stress, and the Von Mises stress. All of the output stresses might be for the element, the nodes, or perhaps uniquely oriented points associated with the solution process.
6. Item 5 might be repeated for strains. Strain is a state variable related to stress and deflection.
7. Item 5 might be repeated for strain energy.
8. The constraint forces, which are initially unknown.

This sample of input and output data for a structural analysis problem is by no means complete. The intent here is to make a point of the large number of types of data and values which must be in the form of either input or output to be scrutinized by the analyst. There is certainly much room for error or omission if the analyst performs these tasks manually, as was once the case when it was necessary to keypunch input data. Furthermore, sifting through the many pages of output data in an attempt to make sense of the results can be even more tedious and carries the certain risk that something subtle, yet critical, might be overlooked. *Interactive graphics* for handling both input and output can relieve the analyst of this overly laborious and error-prone task. The discussion of how interactive graphics plays its role in finite element data handling will be continued at the end of this chapter. Before that point, further discussion of the procedures necessary to carry out a finite element solution from start to finish will serve to demonstrate clearly the power that interactive graphics brings to finite elements. In continuing the discussion of the finite element method, it will be necessary to demonstrate several physical concepts. To do this effectively, the discussion will focus on a specific area of analysis served by the finite element method. Because of the origins of the method, probably the most widely active area of design employing finite elements is that of structural analysis.

## 7.2. Applications in structural analysis

### 7.2.1. BASIC CONSIDERATIONS

Structural analysis is only one subgroup of problems which can be addressed by the finite element method. However, it constitutes by far the largest class of problems solved in CAD applications today. Structural analysis can be broken down further into several specialized topic areas. A partial list follows:

Static analysis
  Linear
  Nonlinear
Dynamic analysis (vibration analysis)
  Normal modes
  Frequency response
  Transient response
  Complex eigenvalues
Buckling

A very basic structural analysis of a design would involve a linear static analysis and might also include a normal modes analysis. The static analysis would be performed to determine the levels of stress throughout the part(s), or to determine the nature of the deflections of the part(s), or to do both. A normal modes analysis might be undertaken to determine what excitation frequencies the design is most sensitive to and what shape the structure deforms to when vibrating at each of the resulting frequencies.

Information on stress from the statics analysis will enable the analyst to determine how close the design is to yielding or fracture. Knowing where the stresses are high and how they vary will assist the designer in modifying the design by perhaps combining changes in materials, geometry, loading, or mounting. In many instances, a knowledge of how the design deforms is of more interest to the designer. It is not uncommon for a designer to create a very rigid structure in an attempt to minimize deflections, and consequently not be very interested in the magnitude of stresses in the structure. The designer still might be interested in how the stresses vary because this might indicate which areas are contributing more to the deflections at a given location.

As indicated earlier, the normal modes analysis provides the excitation frequencies to which the structure is sensitive. These frequencies are called *resonant* frequencies or *eigenvalues*. For each eigenvalue, the normal modes analysis provides a relative deflection field for the structure. This is called the *mode shape* or *eigenvector*. Each set of eigenvalues and eigenvectors is referred to as a *mode* (of vibration). If the design is somehow coupled to any device which is operating with a component of frequency at or near any eigenvalue of the design, the mode associated with that eigenvalue will be excited and the designed structure will begin to vibrate according to the mode shape for that frequency. The mode shape obtained from the normal modes analysis is a set of *relative* nodal deflections. If one can imagine a set of relative nodal deflections with values which are negative to those of the first set, the mode of vibration is one where the structure 'moves' from one set to the other making a 'round trip' each period of vibration. (A period of vibration is the reciprocal of the frequency.) The deflection file is relative and only provides a *shape* which the structure keeps through each vibration cycle. The absolute magnitude of the deflections the structure undergoes is dependent on how much energy is required for a given deflection magnitude and how much energy is available from the excitation source at that frequency. The normal modes analysis does not provide for this evaluation. The analysis only serves to alert the designer to the resonant frequencies, and the mode shapes assist the designer in making structural modifications, much in the manner of the deflection results of the statics solution.

### 7.2.2. EXAMINING SOME SIMPLE MODELS

*Statics solution*

Some simple one-dimensional spring problems were examined in an earlier section. Consider the structure in Figure 7.4. The platform shown

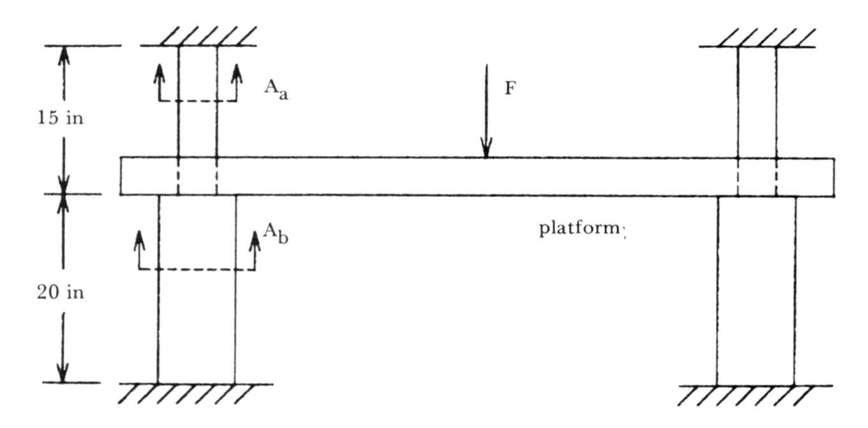


**Figure 7.4.** *Statics example problem*

is being supported equally by four steel step shafts. (Two are in line with the two shown and hence not visible.) The step shafts are connected at each end to a relatively rigid structure. The combined weight of the platform and the applied force F is 10,000 lb. The shaft dimensions are those prior to loading conditions. For simplicity, it is assumed that little or no bending of each shaft occurs, that no buckling of the lower halves of the shaft occurs, and that each shaft supports 2500 lb, as shown in Figure 7.5. Both ends of the shaft act as two springs in series, similar to the case discussed earlier. Here, some additional equations will be given without proof (again, consult a structural mechanics reference book for details). Consider the single rod element together with a

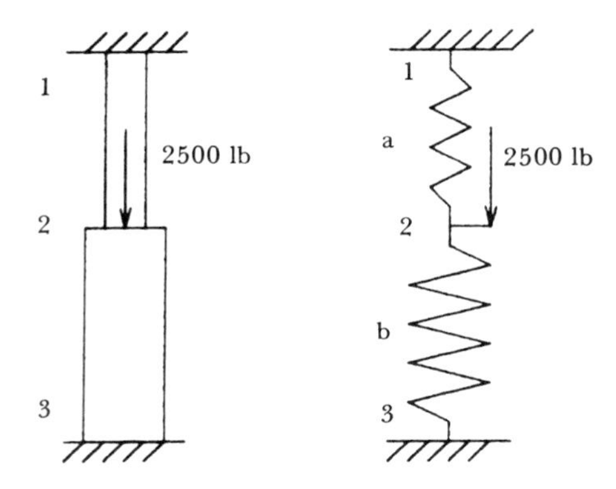


**Figure 7.5.** *Supports modelled as springs*

local xy coordinate system as shown in Figure 7.6(i). After loading, the rod may move as a whole and change length as shown in Figure 7.6(ii).

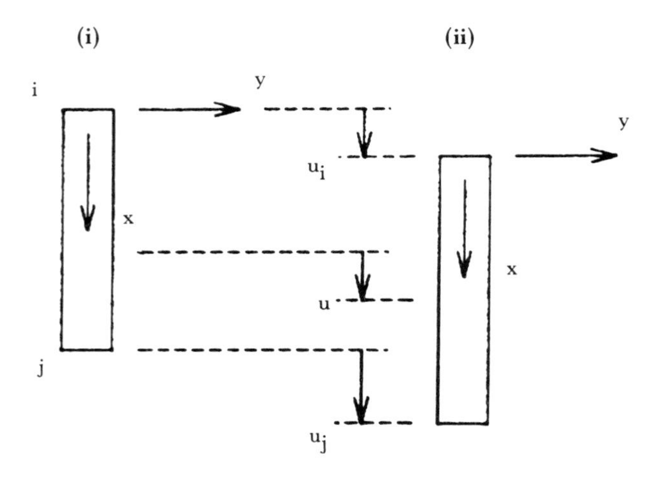


**Figure 7.6.** *Deflections of a rod element*

The deflection of any point within the rod will be *assumed* to be linear in x. If the deflections of nodes i and j are $u_i$ and $u_j$, respectively, then it can be shown that the deflection of any point on the rod located at some *original* value of x (according to Figure 7.6(i)) is given by

$$u = u_i + (u_j - u_i)(x/L)$$

Furthermore, it can be shown that the stress (force per unit area) is constant within the rod and is

$$s = (u_j - u_i)(E/L)$$

where E is a material property, called the *modulus of elasticity*. E is a measure of stiffness and for steel is approximately $30 \times 10^6$ lb/in$^2$. Stress is related to force and the cross-sectional area of the rod. The rod behaves the same as a spring, where the spring stiffness k of the rod is given by

$$k = EA/L$$

Returning to Figure 7.5, the matrix equation is

$$\begin{bmatrix} F_1 \\ F_2 \\ F_3 \end{bmatrix} = \begin{bmatrix} k_a & -k_a & 0 \\ -k_a & (k_a+k_b) & -k_b \\ 0 & -k_b & k_b \end{bmatrix} \begin{bmatrix} u_1 \\ u_2 \\ u_3 \end{bmatrix}$$

where

$$\begin{aligned} k_a &= E_aA_a/L_a = (30 \times 10^6)(0.1)/15.0 = 2 \times 10^5 \quad \text{lb/in} \\ k_b &= E_bA_b/L_b = (30 \times 10^6)(0.2)/20.0 = 3 \times 10^5 \quad \text{lb/in} \\ F_2 &= 2500 \text{ lb} \\ u_1 &= u_3 = 0.0 \end{aligned}$$

From the displacement boundary conditions, the $F_1$ and $F_3$ force equations can be eliminated, and $u_1$ and $u_3$ substituted into the $F_2$ equation. This results in

$$F_2 = (k_a+k_b)u_2$$

Solving for the unknown displacements in this case is trivial, since only $u_2$ is unknown. Solving for $u_2$ yields

$$u_2 = F_2/(k_a+k_b) = 2500/[(2 \times 10^5) + (3 \times 10^5)] = 0.005 \quad \text{in}$$

The stress in the top half of the shaft is

$$\begin{aligned} s_a &= (u_2 - u_1)(E/L_a) = (0.005-0.0)[(30 \times 10^6)/15.0] \\ &= 10000 \quad \text{lb/in}^2 \end{aligned}$$

whereas the stress in the lower half is

$$\begin{aligned} s_b &= (u_3 - u_2)(E/L_b) = (0.0-0.005)[(30 \times 10^6)/20.0] \\ &= -7500 \quad \text{lb/in}^2 \end{aligned}$$

where positive values indicate tension and negative values indicate compression.

Once an element is mathematically defined in terms of its stiffness matrix, it need not be redefined each time it is used. All that is necessary is an accounting system which relates the element stiffness in terms of the element nodes and then all of the element stiffness matrices are merged into one large system stiffness matrix. Each term in the system stiffness matrix corresponds to a specific degree of freedom of a specific node. That term is the summation of all like terms from the individual element stiffness matrices (same degree of freedom, same node). For example, for the step-shaft problem, the individual stiffness matrices were

$$[k]_a = \begin{bmatrix} k_a & -k_a \\ -k_a & k_a \end{bmatrix} \quad [k]_a = \begin{bmatrix} k_b & -k_b \\ -k_b & k_b \end{bmatrix}$$

The only node and degree of freedom common to both is node 2 displacement in the x direction, namely $u_2$. Then the system stiffness matrix becomes

spring a

$$[k] = \begin{bmatrix} k_a & -k_a & 0 \\ -k_a & (k_a + k_b) & -k_b \\ 0 & -k_b & k_b \end{bmatrix}$$

spring b

Here it is easy to see where the two individual stiffness matrices are.

Since an element need not be redefined mathematically whenever it is formulated, the element definition can be placed in the application program's element library, so that the element may be called for any time the analyst needs it. The spring which was previously defined could now be placed into an element library. However, since it is only one-dimensional, its use would be quite limited. The spring could be made three-dimensional very easily using a *coordinate transformation*, since the spring can be considered a vector of variable length. This would give the spring six degrees of freedom, three degrees of freedom at each node (end), corresponding to translation in three directions. The stiffness matrix for this element would be six by six, containing 21 uniquely different terms. The matrix equation for the element is

$$[F] = [k][u]$$

where the [F] and [u] matrices contain six force and six displacement terms, respectively, corresponding to three directions at each of two nodes. The stiffness matrix [k] can be written as

$$[k] = k[n]$$

where k is the stiffness constant and [n] is associated with the coordinate transformation. If, instead of a spring, an elastic rod element is desired, k can be replaced by EA/L of the rod. Then, for a rod element,

$$[k] = (EA/L)[n]$$

MSC/NATRAN has a three-dimensional rod element in its library called the CROD element. NASTRAN uses the letter C in front of many of its element names to indicate a connectivity of nodes. NASTRAN's CROD element also has the capability of transmitting torsion.

To understand how each element is inserted into the system stiffness matrix, consider using the rod element in a two-dimensional truss problem as shown in Figure 7.7. Here, each node has two translational

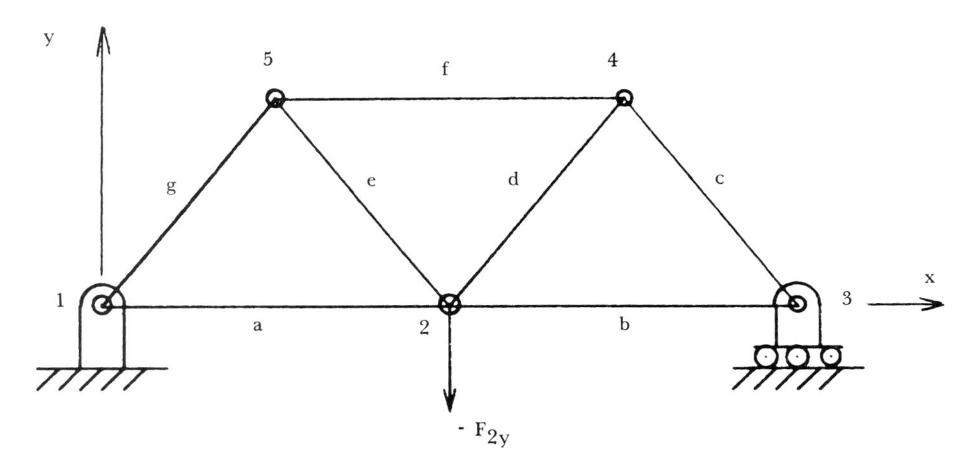


**Figure 7.7.** *Two-dimensional truss structure*

degrees of freedom. Thus each element stiffness matrix will be four by four. The stiffness matrix for element d, for example, is of the form

$$\begin{bmatrix} F_{2x} \\ F_{2y} \\ F_{4x} \\ F_{4y} \end{bmatrix} = \begin{bmatrix} d_1 & d_2 & d_3 & d_4 \\ d_2 & d_5 & d_6 & d_7 \\ d_3 & d_6 & d_8 & d_9 \\ d_4 & d_7 & d_9 & d_{10} \end{bmatrix} \begin{bmatrix} u_{2x} \\ u_{2y} \\ u_{4x} \\ u_{4y} \end{bmatrix}$$

where the terms $d_i$ represent the stiffness coefficients for the d element, dependent on stiffness and orientation of the element. Symmetry of the matrix is shown by indicating the uniquely different terms. For simplicity, it is common practice not to show the terms below and to the left of the diagonal, since those terms are understood to be mirrored across the diagonal, that is,

$$\begin{bmatrix} F_{2x} \\ F_{2y} \\ F_{4x} \\ F_{4y} \end{bmatrix} = \begin{bmatrix} d_1 & d_2 & d_3 & d_4 \\ & d_5 & d_6 & d_7 \\ & & d_8 & d_9 \\ & & & d_{10} \end{bmatrix} \begin{bmatrix} u_{2x} \\ u_{2y} \\ u_{4x} \\ u_{4y} \end{bmatrix}$$

The stiffness matrix for the d element can be expressed in the system stiffness matrix as

$$\begin{bmatrix} F_{1x} \\ F_{1y} \\ F_{2x} \\ F_{2y} \\ F_{3x} \\ F_{3y} \\ F_{4x} \\ F_{4y} \\ F_{5x} \\ F_{5y} \end{bmatrix} = \begin{bmatrix} - & - & - & - & - & - & - & - & - & - \\ & - & - & - & - & - & - & - & - & - \\ & & d_1 & d_2 & - & - & d_3 & d_4 & - & - \\ & & & d_5 & - & - & d_6 & d_7 & - & - \\ & & & & - & - & - & - & - & - \\ & & & & & - & - & - & - & - \\ & & & & & & d_8 & d_9 & - & - \\ & & & & & & & d_{10} & - & - \\ & & & & & & & & - & - \\ & & & & & & & & & - \end{bmatrix} \begin{bmatrix} u_{1x} \\ u_{1y} \\ u_{2x} \\ u_{2y} \\ u_{3x} \\ u_{3y} \\ u_{4x} \\ u_{4y} \\ u_{5x} \\ u_{5y} \end{bmatrix}$$

where the dashes indicate terms to be added from the remaining elements. Consider for all elements that the first node is the lower of the two node numbers, and the subscript scheme for stiffness terms is the same as that used for the d element just described. Merging all elements into the system stiffness matrix yields the matrix on page 265. Completing the problem is similar to the step-shaft problem where the stiffness matrix is partitioned according to the displacement boundary conditions (in this case, $u_{1x} = u_{1y} = u_{3y} = 0$), and the displacements are solved for by matrix inversion.

There are many techniques for solving the inverse problem, and since real design models may result in very large stiffness matrices, much effort has been expended in increasing computational efficiency. One method, which is related to the reduction of storage requirements, requires bandwidth optimization. In general, a large stiffness matrix will contain many off-diagonal zero terms. If these terms can be isolated, they need not be stored, resulting in a savings in storage requirements for problem solution. These terms were not isolated in the previous truss problem. If the nodes of the truss are re-ordered as shown in Figure 7.8, the resulting stiffness matrix will be that shown on page 265. Note that all zero terms have been isolated in the system stiffness matrix. That is, beyond the dashed line in the matrix, all terms are zero. The width SB is called the *semi-bandwidth*, and, when determined, provides the program a means of terminating storage of unnecessary data. As the model is being developed, it may become difficult or impossible for the analyst to keep track of how to number the nodes most efficiently to reduce the semi-bandwidth to a minimum. Fortunately, there are several algorithms available to assist the analyst. These optimization algorithms can be used to renumber the nodes for the analyst prior to submitting the input data file to the application

$$[k] = \begin{bmatrix}
(a_1+g_1) & (a_2+g_2) & a_3 & a_4 & 0 & 0 & 0 & 0 & g_3 & g_4 \\
 & (a_5+g_5) & a_6 & a_7 & 0 & 0 & 0 & 0 & g_6 & g_7 \\
 & & (a_8+b_1+d_1+e_1) & (a_9+b_2+d_2+e_2) & b_3 & b_4 & d_3 & d_4 & e_3 & e_4 \\
 & & & (a_{10}+b_5+d_5+e_5) & b_6 & b_7 & d_6 & d_7 & e_6 & e_7 \\
 & & & & (b_8+c_1) & (b_9+c_2) & c_3 & c_4 & 0 & 0 \\
 & & & & & (b_{10}+c_5) & c_6 & c_7 & 0 & 0 \\
 & & & & & & (c_8+d_8+f_1) & (c_9+d_9+f_2) & f_3 & f_4 \\
 & & & & & & & (c_{10}+d_{10}+f_5) & f_6 & f_7 \\
 & & & & & & & & (e_8+f_8+g_8) & (e_9+f_9+g_9) \\
 & & & & & & & & & (e_{10}+f_{10}+g_{10})
\end{bmatrix}$$

SB

$$[k] = \begin{bmatrix}
(a_1+g_1) & (a_2+g_2) & g_3 & g_4 & a_3 & a_4 & 0 & 0 & 0 & 0 \\
 & (a_5+g_5) & g_6 & g_7 & a_6 & a_7 & 0 & 0 & 0 & 0 \\
 & & (e_1+f_1+g_8) & (e_2+f_2+g_9) & e_3 & e_4 & f_3 & f_4 & 0 & 0 \\
 & & & (e_5+f_5+g_{10}) & e_6 & e_7 & f_6 & f_7 & 0 & 0 \\
 & & & & (a_8+b_1+d_1+e_8) & (a_9+b_2+d_2+e_9) & d_3 & d_4 & b_3 & b_4 \\
 & & & & & (a_{10}+b_5+d_5+e_{10}) & d_6 & d_7 & b_6 & b_7 \\
 & & & & & & (c_1+d_8) & (c_2+d_9+f_9) & c_3 & c_4 \\
 & & & & & & & (c_5+d_{10}+f_{10}) & c_6 & c_7 \\
 & & & & & & & & (b_8+c_8) & (b_9+c_9) \\
 & & & & & & & & & (b_{10}+c_{10})
\end{bmatrix}$$

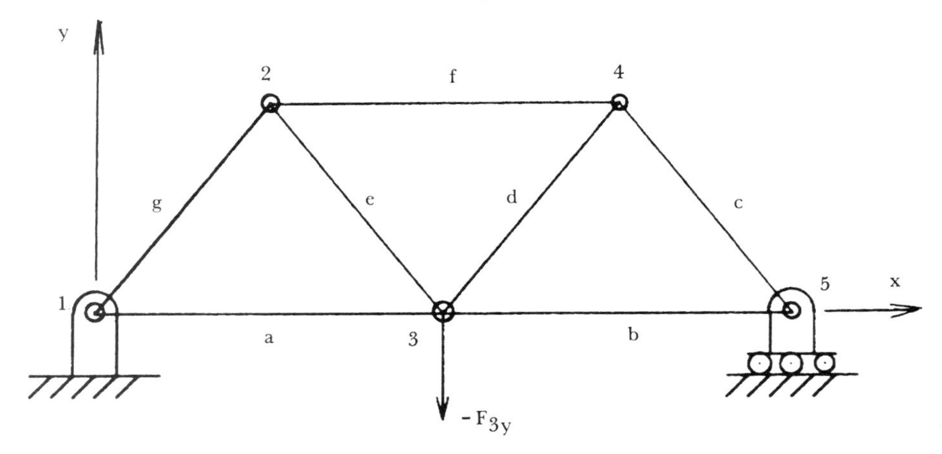


**Figure 7.8.** *Two-dimensional truss problem with nodes renumbered*

program; or, internal to the application program, the nodes can be renumbered in a manner which is transparent to the analyst. That is, the original node numbers are used for input and output information, and the program renumbers the nodes only for solution and converts all results back into the original node numbers.

In some finite element programs, other forms of optimization are necessary. For example, wavefront solutions are independent of node numbering but depend on element numbering.

*Normal modes solution*

The normal modes analysis is a dynamic solution. The static analysis is based on the matrix equation $[k][u] = [F]$ as indicated earlier. A dynamic solution must take into account the acceleration of mass within the model. That is,

$$[M][\ddot{u}] + [k][u] = [F]$$

where $[M]$ is the mass matrix associated with the element masses which are distributed in some manner to each node and $[u]$ are the nodal accelerations. The normal modes solution analyzes the 'free' vibration of the structure. That is, the applied forces $[F]$ are ignored. Thus the equation analyzed is

$$[M][\ddot{u}] + [k][u] = [0]$$

where $[0]$ is a column matrix containing only zero terms. Free vibration is harmonic (sinusoidal) in nature. That is,

$$[u] = [U] \sin \omega t$$

where w is the free vibration frequency and $[U]$ are the nodal vibration amplitudes. The second time derivative yields

$$[\ddot{u}] = -\omega^2 [U] \sin \omega t = -\omega^2 [u]$$

Thus, the free vibration equation becomes

$$\left\{-\omega^2 [M] + [k]\right\} [u] = [0]$$

The solution of this equation is beyond the scope of this discussion. However, this type of problem is classified as an eigenvalue problem. If there are N degrees of freedom in the model, there will exist N values of $\omega$ which satisfy the equation. These frequencies are the eigenvalues referred to in the previous section. For each specific eigenvalue, there is a particular displacement matrix [u] which will complete the solution of the above equations. However, since there are more unknowns than equations available, it is impossible to obtain a complete solution to [u]. A solution can be found where only one constant term is unobtainable. That is, if

$$[u] = C[q]$$

the matrix [q] can be determined, whereas the constant C cannot. The matrix [q] is directly proportional to [u]. Thus, [q] is similar to a displacement matrix. However, since the value of C is unknown, [q] can only be considered to be a displacement *shape*. The matrix [q] is the mode shape or eigenvector referred to in the previous section.

If the model contains many degrees of freedom N, the eigenvalue solution is quite extensive and, consequently, the solution process can be very slow. Fortunately, there are methods available which can reduce the degrees of freedom to speed up the solution process.

The results of a normal modes analysis will be provided in Section 7.3.

### 7.2.3 ELEMENT FORMULATIONS

Various element formulations have been developed in an attempt to improve the modelling and solution processes. Once formulated, the element definition and solution formulation reside in the application program library, where they may be recalled at any point in the modelling. In some instances, the element library may not contain an element suitable to the given problem. The analyst may then be required to develop a new element tailored to the particular situation. Some application programs conveniently allow for this possibility.

The basic element formulations fall into three categories: line, surface, and solid elements. Table 7.3 provides a sampling of some of the elements which exist in the MSC/NASTRAN applications program library. Many other elements exist, such as the gap element (for nonlinear analyses) and the viscous damper element (for dynamic analyses). In the input data file, recall that NASTRAN prefaces the element name with a C, which denotes node connectivity.

## 7.3 The solution procedure

In order to describe completely the procedures followed in performing a finite element analysis, a simple model will be analyzed in this section by applying the statics and normal modes solutions of the applications program MSC/NASTRAN. The fundamental steps in a finite element solution include

1. problem definition,
2. modelling,
3. input data file creation, and
4. review of the output results.

The description will be given as if the analysis were being performed completely manually, without the aid of graphics or computer automation save that of the solution sequences of the application program itself. Although MSC/NASTRAN does provide some graphics results capabilities (postprocessing), as well as automated mesh generation, these capabilities are generally not interactive.*

### 7.3.1 DEFINING THE PROBLEM

The problem selected is one at an intermediate level, in order to demonstrate some complexity without becoming overly involved. Figure 7.9 shows a steel platform which is to be used as an optics bench. Thus the

* MacNeal-Schwendler Corporation (MSC) does market an interactive graphics package called GRASP. Although GRASP can be used in conjunction with MSC/NASTRAN, it is considered a separate package, and any discussion of GRASP would be more appropriate to Section 7.4.

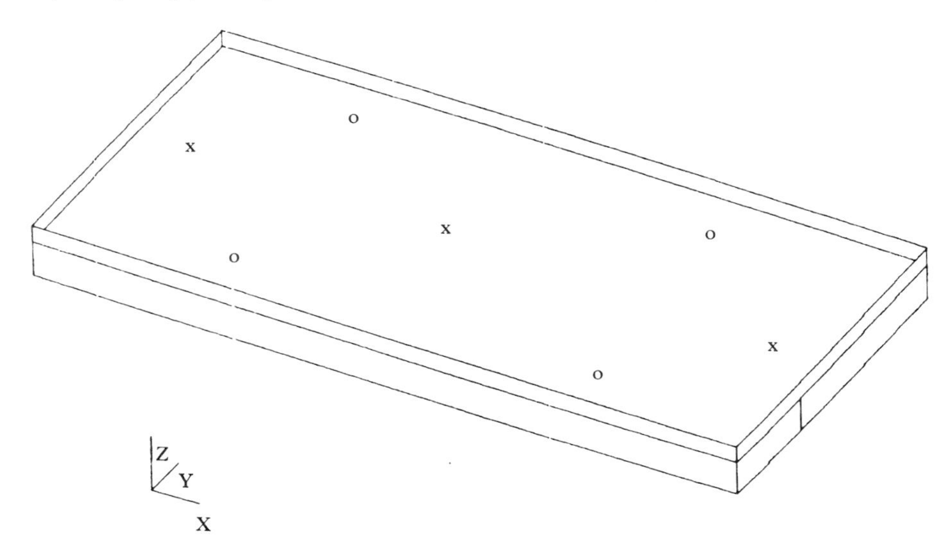


**Figure 7.9.** *Optics bench problem: top view*

| | Name | Shape | Number of grid points | Connected components[1] | Applications |
|---|---|---|---|---|---|
| LINE ELEMENT | ROD | 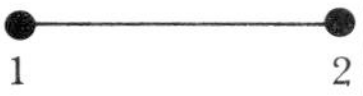 1 ●———● 2 | 2 | T,R | Pin-ended rod, reinforcement; torsional spring. |
| | CONROD | 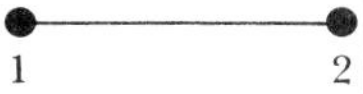 1 ●———● 2 | 2 | T,R | Alternate form of ROD element. |
| | TUBE | 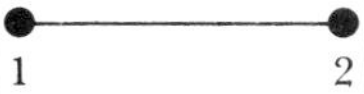 1 ●———● 2 | 2 | T,R | Alternate form of ROD element. |
| | BAR |  1 ●———● 2 | 2 | T,R | Straight untapered beam; a simplified subcase of the BEAM element. |
| | BEAM |  1 ●———● 2 | 2 | T,R | Straight beam; includes taper, warping,[2] shear relief, and separation of shear center from neutral axis as options. |
| | BEND | 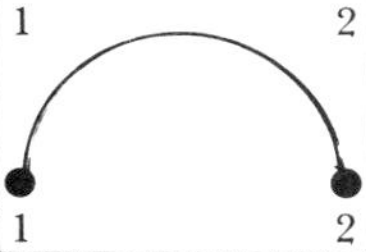 1, 2 | 2 | T,R | Curved beam; pipe elbow. |
| SURFACE ELEMENTS | QUAD4 | 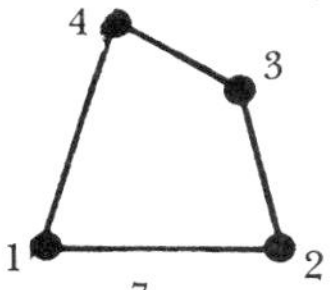 1, 2, 3, 4 | 4 | T,R | Membrane; plate; shell. |
| | QUAD8[3] | 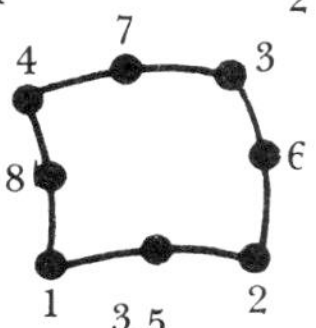 1, 2, 3, 4, 5, 6, 7, 8 | 8 | T,R | Membrane; plate; shell. |
| | TRIA3 | 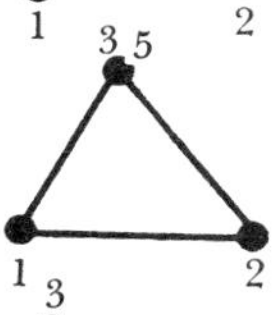 1, 2, 3 | 3 | T,R | Membrane; plate; shell; prefer QUAD4 when practical. |
| | TRIA6[3] | 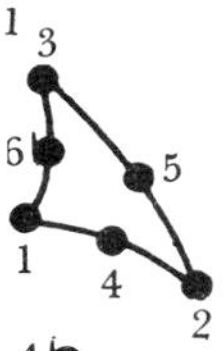 1, 2, 3, 4, 5, 6 | 6 | T,R | Membrane; plate; shell; prefer QUAD8 when practical. |
| | SHEAR | 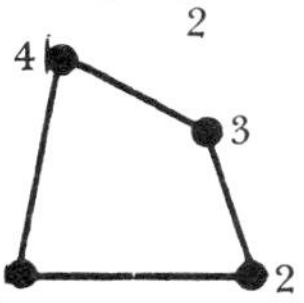 1, 2, 3, 4 | 4 | T | Shear panel; thin reinforced shell. |

(1) T = translational components of motion; R = rotational components of motion.
(2) The BEAM element requires an additional scalar point at each end if the warping option is selected.
(3) Any or all edge points may be deleted.

**Table 7.3.** *Some basic elements of MSC/NASTRAN*

| | *Name* | *Shape* | *Number of grid points* | *Connected components*[1] | *Applications* |
|---|---|---|---|---|---|
| SOLID ELEMENTS | HEXA[3] | 1, 2, 3, 5, 6, 7, 8, 9, 10, 13, 14, 15, 17, 18, 19, 20 | 20 | T | Solid; thick shell. |
| | PENTA[3] | 1, 2, 4, 5, 6, 7, 10, 11, 13, 14, 15 | 15 | T | Solid; thick shell; prefer HEXA when practical. |
| | TETRA | 1, 2, 3, 4 | 4 | T | Solid; prefer HEXA or PENTA when practical. |
| | HEX20[3] | 1, 2, 3, 5, 8, 9, 10, 13, 14, 15, 17, 18, 19, 20 | 20 | T | Solid; crack tip element; prefer for nearly incompressible materials; isotropic material only; prefer HEXA for thick shells. |
| | TRIAX6 | 1, 2, 3, 4, 5, 6 | 6 | T | Solid of revolution with axisymmetric loading; including orthotropic material. |
| OTHER ELEMENTS | ELAS1<br>ELAS2<br>ELAS3<br>ELAS4 | 1, 2, 1 | 1 or 2 grid points or scalar points | One component | Concentrated spring; prefer ROD when practical. |
| | GENEL | 3, 5, 2, 1, 4, Any shape | Any number of grid points and scalar points | T,R | To model a structural part whose stiffness or flexibility matrix is known at the connection points. |
| | CONM2 | M | 1 | T,R | Concentrated inertia at a grid point; includes mass, c.g. offset and moments of inertia. |

(1) T = translational components of motion; R = rotational components of motion.
(3) Any or all edge points may be deleted.

**Table 7.3** *(continued)*

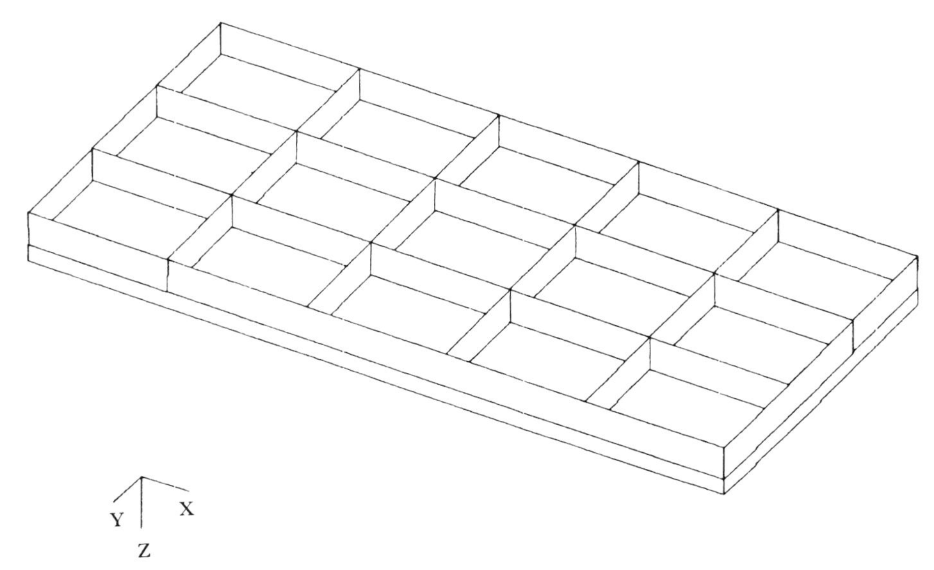


**Figure 7.9.** *Optics bench problem: bottom view*

main concern will be one of deflections (the first observation in the analysis). The top surface of the platform is a thin, flat plate for the mounting of optics, and the plate is stiffened along its perimeter with ribbing. The bottom view reveals an inner network of ribs which serve to stiffen the interior surfaces of the mounting plate. The optics bench will be bolted to a massive granite block by means of the four holes in the plate. For the sake of clarity, the optics mounting holes are not shown. For the problem at hand, three optical devices, each weighing 5 lb, are to be mounted at the locations indicated by the x's.

Specifying the intent of the analysis completes the definition of the problem. A static analysis of the plate is to be performed, in which the weight of each optical element will be considered to be an applied force, and the weight of the optics bench itself will be treated by gravity loading. The deflections of the bench will be requested as well as the stresses throughout and the forces transmitted to the granite block. Second, a normal modes analysis will be performed, in which the mass of each optical element will be treated as a concentrated mass element. Only the first five eigenvalues (frequencies) and eigenvectors (mode shapes) will be requested.

### 7.3.2 MODELLING THE PROBLEM

There are many ways to model a given problem. The intent here is not necessarily to attempt to demonstrate good modelling practice, but to show what steps are taken in the modelling effort. In approaching this task the analyst considers which, if any, elements in the program library would do a satisfactory job of closely conforming to the given problem. What is satisfactory may be subject to question, but this point will not be debated now. The analyst in the optics bench problem decided to use the plate element referred to as the QUAD4 element. This decision was based primarily on the relatively small wall thickness of the members. The ribs might be better modelled using BAR elements; however, for this example this approach was not taken. Once the types of element are more or less decided upon, the analyst has to determine the size of the mesh, that is, how large or small the elements should be. There are many rules which govern this decision. Here, the main plate was divided into 60 equal-sized elements requiring 77 nodes. If BAR elements were used to model the ribs, another 76 elements would need to be defined with no additional nodes being necessary. (However, prescribing the BAR elements is not a trivial matter.) Using QUAD4 elements for the ribs required 184 more elements with 156 additional nodes. (One can see the disadvantage of this approach.)

In the past, the analyst would sketch the element mesh manually several times before being satisfied with the gridwork. Then the analyst would determine the exact placement of each node and keypunch the node identity and location onto a single card. Then each element would be identified with the corresponding node numbers, and details regarding material properties, loading, boundary conditions, etc, would be keypunched in. This was quite a task, even for a simple geometry like the optics bench currently under discussion. To illustrate this, the element mesh for the optics bench is shown in Figure 7.10, where hidden lines are included. In the following sections, the resulting I/O data files for this model are described.

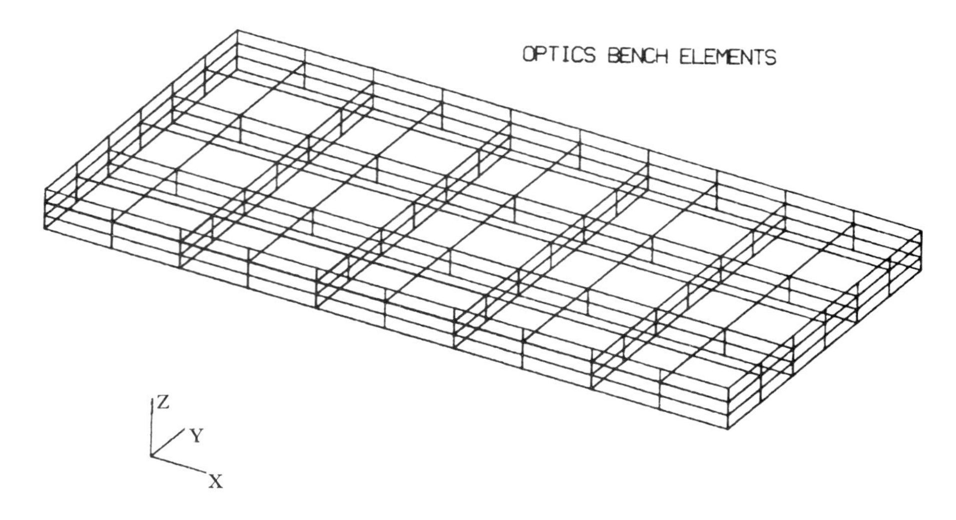


**Figure 7.10.** *Modelling the optics bench with quad elements*

### 7.3.3 THE INPUT DATA

A sample of some of the input data for running the statics solution of MSC/NASTRAN for the optics bench model is shown in Table 7.4.

```
BK. DAT; 5                         16-AUG-1984 13: 12                          Page 1
ID         BUDYNAS, RG
TIME       20
SOL        24
CEND
TITLE = OPTICS BENCH
SUBTITLE = STATICS SOLUTION
LOAD = 100
SPC = 200
OLOAD = ALL
DISPLACEMENT = ALL
SPCFORCES = ALL
STRESS = ALL
BEGIN BULK
PARAM, AUTOSPC, YES
GRAV  101, , 386. 4, 0. 0, 0. 0, -1. 0
FORCE      102          37          0       1. 0 0.       0.      -5. 00000
FORCE      102         115          0       1. 0 0.       0.      -5. 00000
FORCE      102         216          0       1. 0 0.       0.      -5. 00000
LOAD, 100, 1. 0, 1. 0, 101, 1. 0, 102
SPC1       200     123456          73
SPC1       200     123456          79
SPC1       200     123456         161
SPC1       200     123456         167
GRID         1              25. 0000    2. 00000-1. 00000
GRID         2              25. 0000    2. 00000-0. 50000
GRID         3              25. 0000    6. 00000-1. 00000
GRID         4              25. 0000    6. 00000-0. 50000
GRID         5              25. 0000    10. 0000-1. 00000
GRID         6              25. 0000    10. 0000-0. 50000
GRID         7              25. 0000    2. 00000-0. 50000
GRID         8
                                                                   0. 000
                        10                   107        104    102 0. 000
COUAD4     233          10          52        46         47     53 0. 000
COUAD4     234          10          46        55         56     47 0. 000
COUAD4     235          10          55        48         49     56 0. 000
COUAD4     236          10          48        62         63     49 0. 000
COUAD4     237          10          62        50         51     63 0. 000
COUAD4     238          10          50        66         67     51 0. 000
COUAD4     239          10          53        47         59     54 0. 000
COUAD4     240          10          47        56         57     59 0. 000
COUAD4     241          10          56        49         60     57 0. 000
COUAD4     242          10          49        63         61     60 0. 000
COUAD4     243          10          63        51         64     61 0. 000
COUAD4     244          10          51        67         65     64 0. 000
PSHELL      10          50    0. 25000        50
MATI        50     3. 000+7   1. 154+7  0. 30000   7. 320-4 0. 0. 0.  M    1
+M   1  0.         0.         0.
ENDDATA
```

**Table 7.4.** *MSC/NASTRAN input data file for a statics analysis*

The input data file is divided into three parts: the executive control, case control, and bulk data.* The executive control is the information from the first line to CEND, and provides user control over MSC/NASTRAN executive functions. For this example, only the program ID, maximum run time, and the statics solution are specified (Solution 24 is the basic statics solution). Many other control functions can be executed here to modify the overall solution format. Some of these functions are rigid format 'ALTERS', direct matrix abstraction

* The input data file is still referred to by many as the input data deck, and line entries in the input file as input data cards. Thus it is not uncommon to see reference to the executive control deck, the case control deck, and the bulk data deck.

programming 'DMAP', checkpoint specification, restart, and diagnostic print requests 'DIAG'.

The case control provides user control over the I/O requests. For the optics bench, the input information relates a load identification (LOAD = 100) and displacement boundary condition identification called the single-point constraint identification SPC (SPC = 200). The identification numbers reappear in the bulk data where the values of the appropriate input variable are entered. The output requests are to print out the following: title and subtitle for each page as indicated, all applied loads (OLOAD = ALL), all six degree of freedom displacements for all nodes (DISPLACEMENT = ALL), all forces where constraints are imposed (SPCFORCES = ALL), and all stresses for each element (STRESS = ALL). The additional I/O requests which are available are too numerous to elaborate on at this point. Here, output plotting can be specified for graphics results. The case control is also used to instruct the program with regard to the many subcases (variations in initial conditions) which can be executed within a single run.

The bulk data defines the physical problem which is being solved by the finite element program, and is appropriately introduced by BEGIN BULK. The first ten lines beyond this point convey information on displacement boundary conditions (SPC) and applied loading (FORCE and GRAV). If a degree of freedom exists with no stiffness, a zero will be entered in the system stiffness matrix and the inverse will contain terms divided by zero. If this occurs, a solution cannot be obtained, and an error message will be received. PARAM, AUTOSPC, YES will automatically eliminate a degree of freedom which has no associated stiffness. Shown next are the specifications of some of the 233 GRID points (nodes), some of the 244 CQUAD4 elements, and the material property values of each element (PSHELL, MAT1). In all, there are 505 lines of input data with 3214 separate data entries. Note that mesh generation algorithms do exist which can reduce the amount of actual input entered, but what is being demonstrated in this example are the actual entities which must be dealt with in terms of the overall problem definition and solution. MSGMESH is the mesh generator for MSC/NASTRAN and in itself is quite involved and, more important, non-interactive.

Table 7.5 gives an idea of the form of the input for the normal modes solution (SOL 3). For the example problem, the number of degrees of freedom is slightly less than 1400 (233 nodes times 6 degrees of freedom per node minus the degrees of freedom eliminated by AUTOSPC). To perform a complete normal modes solution would require a large amount of computer time, to determine approximately 1400 eigenvalues and the corresponding mode shapes. This would involve 1400 times 1400 displacement quantities. Normally a dynamic reduction method is employed, where only a limited number of the lowest frequency modes are solved for. In the optics bench example, only the first five modes

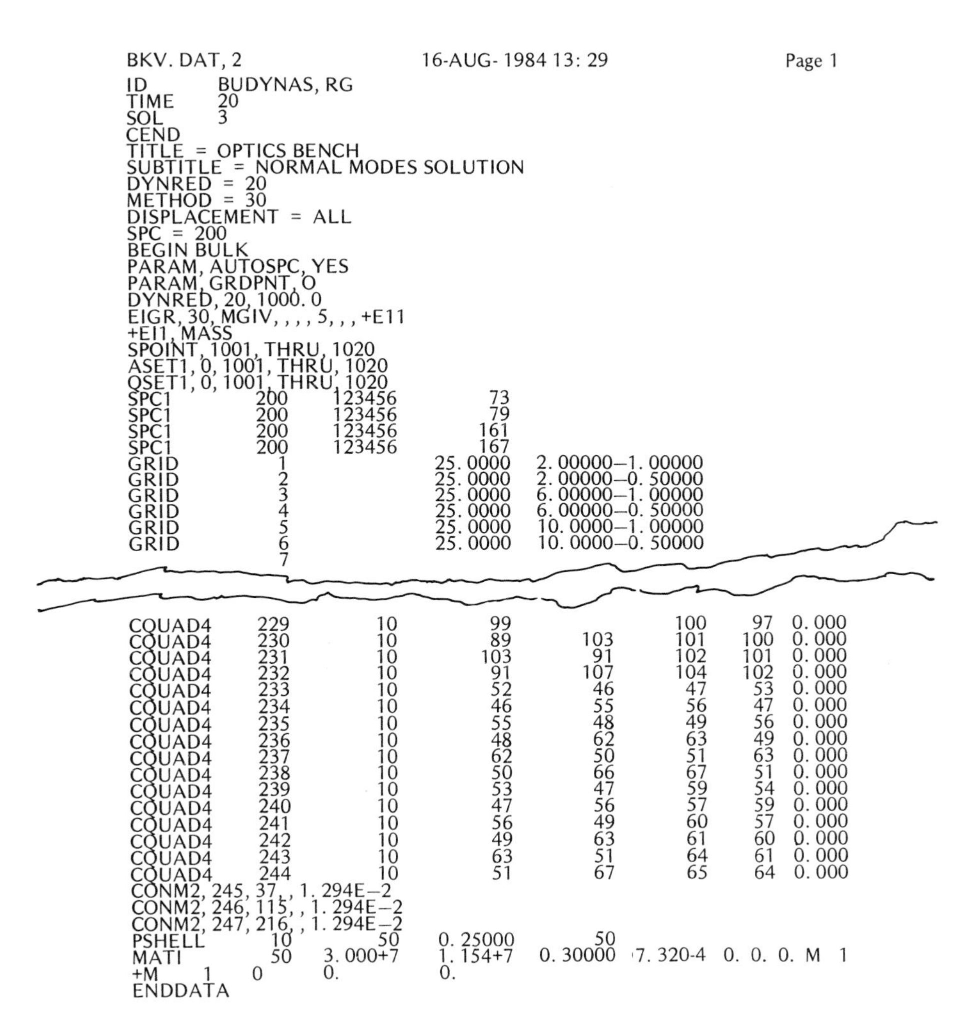

```
BKV. DAT, 2                    16-AUG- 1984 13: 29                    Page 1
ID       BUDYNAS, RG
TIME     20
SOL      3
CEND
TITLE = OPTICS BENCH
SUBTITLE = NORMAL MODES SOLUTION
DYNRED = 20
METHOD = 30
DISPLACEMENT = ALL
SPC = 200
BEGIN BULK
PARAM, AUTOSPC, YES
PARAM, GRDPNT, O
DYNRED, 20, 1000. 0
EIGR, 30, MGIV, , , , 5, , , +E11
+E11, MASS
SPOINT, 1001, THRU, 1020
ASET1, 0, 1001, THRU, 1020
QSET1, 0, 1001, THRU, 1020
SPC1         200     123456          73
SPC1         200     123456          79
SPC1         200     123456         161
SPC1         200     123456         167
GRID           1                25. 0000  2. 00000-1. 00000
GRID           2                25. 0000  2. 00000-0. 50000
GRID           3                25. 0000  6. 00000-1. 00000
GRID           4                25. 0000  6. 00000-0. 50000
GRID           5                25. 0000  10. 0000-1. 00000
GRID           6                25. 0000  10. 0000-0. 50000
               7

CQUAD4       229         10          99                100     97  0. 000
CQUAD4       230         10          89        103     101    100  0. 000
CQUAD4       231         10         103         91     102    101  0. 000
CQUAD4       232         10          91        107     104    102  0. 000
CQUAD4       233         10          52         46      47     53  0. 000
CQUAD4       234         10          46         55      56     47  0. 000
CQUAD4       235         10          55         48      49     56  0. 000
CQUAD4       236         10          48         62      63     49  0. 000
CQUAD4       237         10          62         50      51     63  0. 000
CQUAD4       238         10          50         66      67     51  0. 000
CQUAD4       239         10          53         47      59     54  0. 000
CQUAD4       240         10          47         56      57     59  0. 000
CQUAD4       241         10          56         49      60     57  0. 000
CQUAD4       242         10          49         63      61     60  0. 000
CQUAD4       243         10          63         51      64     61  0. 000
CQUAD4       244         10          51         67      65     64  0. 000
CONM2, 245, 37, , 1. 294E-2
CONM2, 246, 115, , 1. 294E-2
CONM2, 247, 216, , 1. 294E-2
PSHELL        10         50   0. 25000          50
MAT1          50    3. 000+7  1. 154+7   0. 30000  7. 320-4  0. 0. 0. M  1
+M     1       0    0.        0.
ENDDATA
```

**Table 7.5.** *MSC/NASTRAN input data file for a normal modes analysis*

are requested. The reduced degrees of freedom were accommodated for in the SPOINT, ASET1, and QSET1 lines. Performance of the dynamic reduction and corresponding reduction method are identified in the case control as DYNRED = 20, and METHOD = 30, respectively. In the bulk data, DYNRED calls for an upper bound of 1000 Hz on the eigenvalues. EIGR specifies the modified Givens method of dynamic reduction and requests the first five eigenvalues. Note that the forces due to the optical elements are omitted, but their masses are accounted for by using the three CONM2 elements. This could also have been used in the statics input in place of the FORCE entry, since gravity loading (GRAV) is specified.

#### 7.3.4 THE OUTPUT RESULTS

Table 7.6 provides a sample of some of the output generated for the statics solution. In all there were 48 pages of output which included the echo of the input data (sorted), grid point singularity table (and the results of AUTOSPC), an information message related to model conditioning, the displacements of each degree of freedom of each node,* the load vector at each loaded node (in this case this means all nodes, since gravity loading is specified), forces of single-point constraint (reaction forces at mount locations), and 16 pages of stress data where, at each element centroid, six stresses are evaluated for both top and bottom fibers of the plate element.

Table 7.7 provides a sample of some of the output generated for the normal modes solution. In all there were 47 pages of output which included the echo of the input file, sequence processor output (in this solution, an internal nodal optimization is required for computing efficiency), output from the grid point weight generator (information regarding the mass properties of the model), grid point singularity table, the eigenvalues, and five separate relative displacement files for each degree of freedom for each node for each eigenvalue.

## 7.4 The role of interactive graphics

The preceding sections attempted to describe briefly what the finite element method is, how it works, what its role is in engineering design, and how to apply it. As stated earlier, there is much to the method, and to become proficient in any one specific area of finite elements, an individual has a long road of learning ahead. The intent in this chapter is simply to make the reader aware of the vast amount of information which must be processed by the analyst and the computer. The previous section described what is necessary in using a specific commercial application program in applying the finite element method to a specific problem. Although the example was quite simple by normal application standards, an extremely large amount of I/O was generated. Keeping track of the validity of the problem definition via the input and the values and trends of the output results for design decisions is quite an accounting function for the analyst. Since most of this involved I/O is intimately related to the physical nature of the problem task, what better justification exists for the application of modern *interactive graphics* methods? A concise description of interactive graphics and commercial finite element codes is presented by Fong (1984). In finite

* T and R refer to translation and rotation, respectively. The numbers 1, 2, and 3 refer to the system x, y, and z directions, respectively. Thus, for example, T2 refers to translation in the y direction and R3 refers to rotation about the z axis.

OPTICS BENCH
STATICS SOLUTION

AUGUST 16, 1984 MSC/NASTRAN 7/20/83 PAGE 16

DISPLACEMENT VECTOR

| POINT 1D | TYPE | T1 | T2 | T3 | R1 | R2 | R3 |
|---|---|---|---|---|---|---|---|
| 1 | G | −3. 699990E−05 | −4. 824681E−06 | −2. 555422E−04 | 0. 0 | 3. 875174E−05 | −4. 894423E−07 |
| 2 | G | −1. 751211E−05 | −2. 052251E−06 | −2. 556184E−04 | 0. 0 | 3. 934117E−05 | −1. 360155E−07 |
| 3 | G | −3. 124452E−05 | 8. 754340E−17 | −2. 688855E−04 | 0. 0 | 3. 462093E−05 | 1. 821235E−16 |
| 4 | G | −1. 396481E−05 | 1. 853003E−16 | −2. 690889E−04 | 0. 0 | 3. 445712E−05 | 1. 267315E−16 |
| 5 | G | −3. 699990E−05 | 4. 824681E−06 | −2. 555422E−04 | 0. 0 | 3. 875174E−05 | 4. 894422E−07 |
| 6 | G | −1. 751211E−05 | | | | | |
| | G | | | | | | |

OPTICS BENCH
STATICS SOLUTION

AUGUST 16, 1984 MSC/NASTRAN 7/20/83 PAGE 21

LOAD VECTOR

| POINT 1D | TYPE | T1 | T2 | T3 | R1 | R2 | R3 |
|---|---|---|---|---|---|---|---|
| 1 | G | 0. 0 | 0. 0 | −3. 535560E−02 | 0. 0 | 0. 0 | 0. 0 |
| 2 | G | 0. 0 | 0. 0 | −7. 071120E−02 | 0. 0 | 0. 0 | 0. 0 |
| 3 | G | 0. 0 | 0. 0 | −3. 535560E−02 | 0. 0 | 0. 0 | 0. 0 |
| 4 | G | 0. 0 | 0. 0 | −7. 071120E−02 | 0. 0 | 0. 0 | |
| 5 | G | 0. 0 | 0. 0 | −3. 535560E−02 | | 0. 0 | |
| 6 | G | | | | | | |

OPTICS BENCH
STATICS SOLUTION

AUGUST 16, 1984 MSC/NASTRAN 7/20/83 PAGE 26

FORCES OF SINGLE−POINT CONSTRAINT

| POINT 1D | TYPE | T1 | T2 | T3 | R1 | R2 | R3 |
|---|---|---|---|---|---|---|---|
| 73 | G | −1. 338900E+01 | −4. 436881E+00 | 1. 274800E+01 | 2. 502397E+00 | −8. 083197E+00 | 0. 0 |
| 79 | G | −1. 338900E+01 | 4. 436881E+00 | 1. 274800E+01 | −2. 502397E+00 | −8. 083197E+00 | 0. 0 |
| 161 | G | 1. 338900E+01 | −4. 436881E+00 | 1. 274800E+01 | 2. 502397E+00 | 8. 083197E+00 | 0. 0 |
| 167 | G | 1. 338900E+01 | 4. 436881E+00 | 1. 274800E+01 | −2. 502397E+00 | 8. 083197E+00 | 0. 0 |

OPTICS BENCH
STATICS SOLUTION

AUGUST 16, 1984 MSC/NASTRAN 7/20/83 PAGE 28

STRESSES IN QUADRILATERAL ELEMENTS (QUAD4)

| ELEMENT | FIBRE | STRESSES IN ELEMENT COORD SYSTEM | | | PRINCIPAL STRESSES (ZERO SHEAR) | | | MAX |
|---|---|---|---|---|---|---|---|---|
| ID. | DISTANCE | NORMAL−X | NORMAL−Y | SHEAR−XY | ANGLE | MAJOR | MINOR | SHEAR |
| 1 | −1. 250000E−01 | −1. 905639E+00 | 1. 055621E+00 | 4. 539000E−01 | 81. 4783 | 1. 123633E+00 | −1. 973650E+00 | 1. 548641E+00 |
| | 1. 250000E−01 | 7. 501152E+00 | −5. 873105E+00 | 1. 626166E+00 | 6. 8339 | 7. 696037E+00 | −6. 067990E+00 | 6. 882013E+00 |
| 2 | −1. 250000E−01 | 9. 451104E+00 | 6. 931558E+00 | 8. 503397E+00 | 40. 7865 | 1. 678754E+01 | −4. 048763E−01 | 8. 596208E+00 |
| | 1. 250000E−01 | 8. 324300E+00 | −1. 939285E+00 | −2. 823328E+00 | −14. 4090 | 9. 049681E+00 | −2. 664665E+00 | 5. |

**Table 7.6.** *Some MSC/NASTRAN output for a statics analysis*

OPTICS BENCH
NORMAL MODES SOLUTION

AUGUST 16, 1984 MSC/NASTRAN 7/20/83 PAGE 14

O U T P U T F R O M G R I D P O I N T W E I G H T G E N E R A T O R

REFERENCE POINT = O

M O

| | | | | | | | |
|---|---|---|---|---|---|---|---|
| * | 1. 319670E–01 | 0. 000000E+00 | 0. 000000E+00 | 0. 000000E+00 | –1. 404525E–02 | –7. 918020E–01 | * |
| * | 0. 000000E+00 | 1. 319670E–01 | 0. 000000E+00 | 1. 404525E–02 | 0. 000000E+00 | 1. 649588E+00 | * |
| * | 0. 000000E+00 | 0. 000000E+00 | 1. 319670E–01 | 7. 918020E–01 | –1. 649588E+00 | 0. 000000E+00 | * |
| * | 0. 000000E+00 | 1. 404525E–02 | 7. 918020E–01 | 6. 184274E+00 | –9. 897525E+00 | 1. 755656E–01 | * |
| * | –1. 404525E–02 | 0. 000000E+00 | –1. 649588E+00 | –9. 897525E+00 | 2. 865616E+01 | 8. 427150E–02 | * |
| * | –7. 918020E–01 | 1. 649588E+00 | 0. 000000E+00 | 1. 755656E–01 | | 3. 481514E+01 | * |

OPTICS BENCH
NORMAL MODES SOLUTION

AUGUST 16, 1984 MSC/NASTRAN 7/20/83 PAGE 20

R E A L E I G E N V A L U E S

| MODE NO. | EXTRACTION ORDER | EIGENVALUE | RADIANS | CYCLES | CENERALIZED MASS | GENERALIZED STIFFNESS |
|---|---|---|---|---|---|---|
| 1 | 1 | 1. 762378E+06 | 1. 327546E+03 | 2. 112855E+02 | 1. 000000E+00 | 1. 762378E+06 |
| 2 | 2 | 2. 263036E+06 | 1. 540339E+03 | 2. 394230E+02 | 1. 000000E+00 | 2. 263036E+06 |
| 3 | 3 | 4. 643459E+06 | 2. 154869E+03 | 3. 429580E+02 | 1. 000000E+00 | 4. 643459E+06 |
| 4 | 4 | 5. 228276E+06 | 2. 286542E+03 | 3. 639145E+02 | 1. 000000E+00 | 5. 228276E+06 |
| 5 | 5 | 1. 289138E+07 | 3. 590456E+03 | 5. 714388E+02 | 1. 000000E+00 | 1. 289138E+07 |
| 6 | 6 | 2. 395913E+07 | 4. 894807E+03 | 7. 790327E+02 | 0. 0 | 0. 0 |
| 7 | 7 | 2. 500814E+07 | 5. 000813E+03 | 7. 959042E+02 | 0. 0 | 0. 0 |
| 8 | 9 | 3. 609059E+07 | 6. 007544E+03 | 9. 561304E+02 | 0. 0 | 0. 0 |
| 9 | 8 | 4. 177675E+07 | 6. 463494E+03 | 1. 028697E+03 | 0. 0 | 0. 0 |
| 10 | 12 | 7. 244605E+07 | 8. 511524E+03 | 1. 354651E+03 | 0. 0 | 0. 0 |
| 11 | 11 | 7. 692794E+07 | 8. 770857E+03 | 1. 395925E+03 | 0. 0 | 0. 0 |
| 12 | 10 | 9. 660275E+07 | 9. 828670E+03 | 1. 564281E+03 | 0. 0 | 0. 0 |

OPTICS BENCH
NORMAL MODES SOLUTION

AUGUST 16, 1984 MSC/NASTRAN 7/20/83 PAGE 32

R E A L E I G E N V E C T O R N O 3

EIGENVALUE = 4. 643459E+06
CYCLES = 3. 429580E+02

| POINT ID. | TYPE | T1 | T2 | T3 | R1 | R2 | R3 |
|---|---|---|---|---|---|---|---|
| 1 | G | –1. 006628E+00 | 1. 805613E+00 | –6. 828443E+00 | 0. 0 | 1. 062482E+00 | –3. 794110E–01 |
| 2 | G | –4. 731573E–01 | 9. 720932E–01 | –6. 830572E+00 | 0. 0 | 1. 074361E+00 | –1. 625491E–01 |
| 3 | G | 6. 725147E–09 | 1. 857245E+00 | 2. 650675E–08 | 0. 0 | –5. 786543E–09 | –3. 599119E–01 |
| 4 | G | 3. 761372E–09 | 9. 903628E–01 | 2. 660407E–08 | 0. 0 | –6. 118864E–09 | –1. 504803E–01 |
| 5 | G | 1. 006628E+00 | 1. 805613E+00 | 6. 828443E+00 | 0. 0 | –1. 062482E+00 | –3. 794110E–01 |
| 6 | G | | 9. 720932E–01 | | | | –1. 625491E–01 |
| 7 | G | | | | | | |

**Table 7.7.** *Some MSC/NASTRAN output for a normal modes analysis*

elements the use of interactive graphics to manipulate input data is termed *preprocessing*, whereas the manipulation of output results is called *postprocessing*.

### 7.4.1 PREPROCESSING – CREATING THE MODEL INTERACTIVELY

The object of a preprocessor is to assist the analyst in creating an input data file compatible with the finite element application program. Some preprocessors were originally designed to work with specific application programs such as SUPERTAB for SUPERB, GRASP for MSC/NASTRAN, and PREP7 for ANSYS. A graphics processor is quite an investment. Consequently, vendors generally do not want to limit their processors to only their application programs. Once a processor is developed for one application program, it is not overly difficult to expand it to dovetail with others. In fact, processors have been developed by organizations which have not initially written any finite element application code, but translate their processor code to many commercial application programs. PDA/PATRAN-G is a classic example of this. Its success in graphic processing has enabled the developers to offer their own finite element capability.

Preprocessing must begin by developing the problem geometry. In some cases where the design evolved from an interactive graphics drafting workstation and the design resides in an accessible data base, the latter could provide the essential problem geometry. This is where standardization such as IGES becomes important (see Section 3.4). If not, the preprocessor might be required to enable the analyst to reproduce the problem geometry in a data base. PATRAN-G has both capabilities. If total processing is to be performed using PATRAN's data base, there are three phases. The first two are primarily for preprocessing, whereas phase three is for postprocessing. Figure 7.11 shows an overview of the structure of PATRAN-G. Phase one establishes the geometry of the model. Geometric construction entities include grids,* lines, patches (surfaces), and hyperpatches (solids). Entities which vary through space are n-order parametric cubic functions, where n corresponds to the order of the entity (lines = 1, patches = 2, hyperpatches = 3). PATRAN offers a myriad of geometric construction directives, and, although menus assist the user somewhat, PATRAN is more command driven. Consequently, the user requires some training and experience to become proficient. Table 7.8 shows only one of the many directives offered by PATRAN in its geometric model phase, namely, the translate directive.

The geometric entities create a skeleton with which many phase two entities can be associated. Phase two forms the analysis model. That is,

* It is unfortunate that NASTRAN uses the term grid to mean node. PATRAN uses grid for geometry, and node for finite element node.

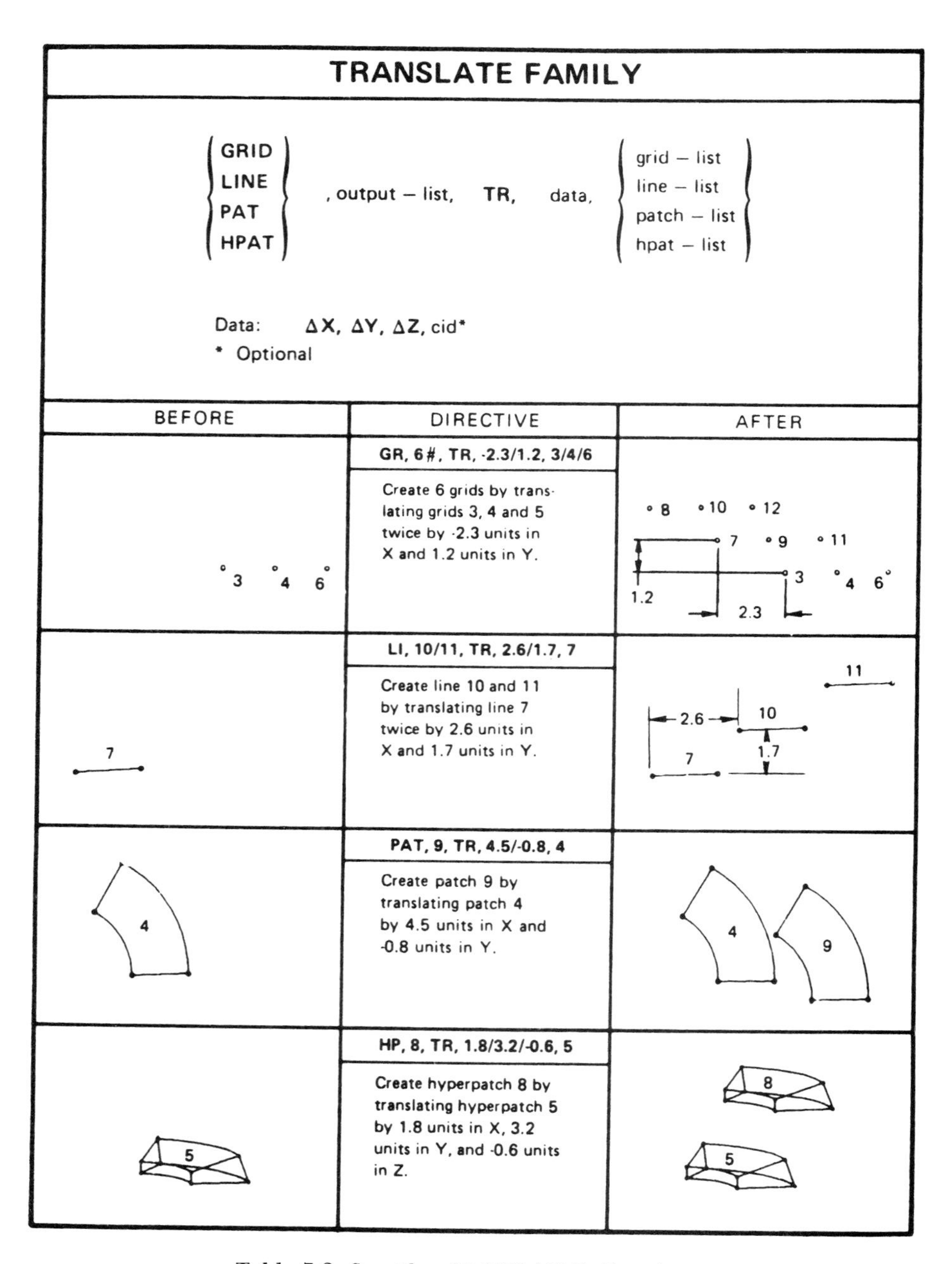

## TRANSLATE FAMILY

{GRID / LINE / PAT / HPAT}, output – list, **TR**, data, {grid – list / line – list / patch – list / hpat – list}

Data: ΔX, ΔY, ΔZ, cid*

* Optional

| BEFORE | DIRECTIVE | AFTER |
|---|---|---|
| | **GR, 6#, TR, -2.3/1.2, 3/4/6**<br>Create 6 grids by translating grids 3, 4 and 5 twice by -2.3 units in X and 1.2 units in Y. | |
| | **LI, 10/11, TR, 2.6/1.7, 7**<br>Create line 10 and 11 by translating line 7 twice by 2.6 units in X and 1.7 units in Y. | |
| | **PAT, 9, TR, 4.5/-0.8, 4**<br>Create patch 9 by translating patch 4 by 4.5 units in X and -0.8 units in Y. | |
| | **HP, 8, TR, 1.8/3.2/-0.6, 5**<br>Create hyperpatch 8 by translating hyperpatch 5 by 1.8 units in X, 3.2 units in Y, and -0.6 units in Z. | |



Table 7.8. *Sample of PATRAN-G directives*

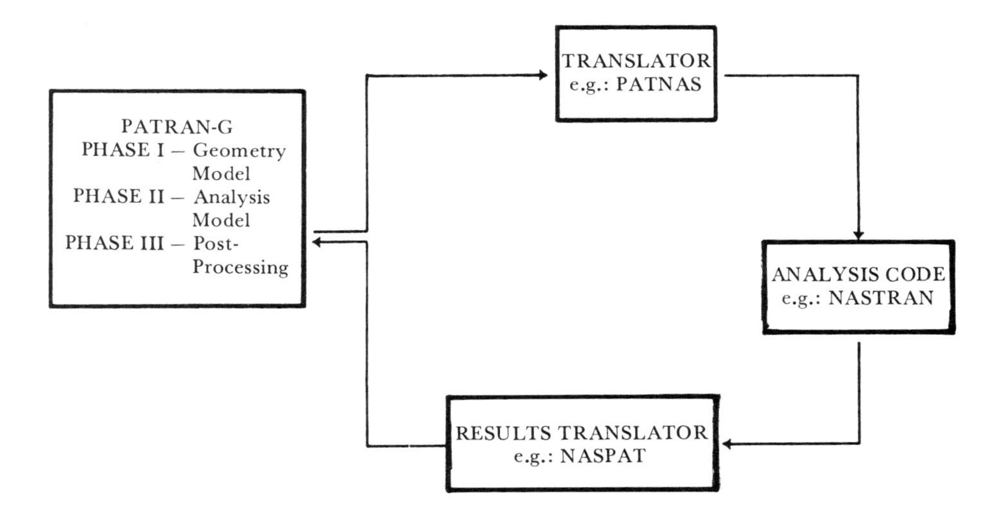


**Figure 7.11.** *PATRAN-G overview*

the entities of phase two will be used to create the input data file for the finite element application program. Nodes, elements, material property identification, loads, and boundary conditions can be linked with the geometric entities to generate the final analysis model. The almost instant graphical response of the computer to phase one or phase two commands allows the kind of results verification which makes computer graphics valuable to the analyst. If the processor software is designed to be very versatile and 'user friendly' (interactive), then the full power of interactive computer graphics can be realized. PATRAN effectively allows the user to backtrack, make modifications, and check for and correct errors easily. For example, the optics bench discussed in the previous section was actually generated by PATRAN-G. Since surface elements were to be used in the analysis (CQUAD4 elements), patches corresponding to the main plate and ribs were created in phase one. In all, 11 patches were created fairly easily. In phase two, the node mesh was automatically generated for each patch. Since there were only five distinctly different patch geometries, this required only five simple commands. Since several of the patches intersected, redundant nodes were formed in each patch. Automatic nodal equivalencing, once requested, eliminates these overlapping nodes. The creation of the 244 elements required only one simple command, which specified that all patches were to contain quad elements. The patch skeleton served to attach the remaining properties associated with the quad material identification, loading, and displacement boundary conditions. Once the user considers the modelling finished, there are many visual verification checks which can be made to ensure that the actual modelling truly conforms to what the user intended.

Some of the modelling capabilities and verification checks that PATRAN provides are the following:

1. Window and view; interactive manipulation of windowing (zoom, move, etc) and viewing angles.
2. Contour and fringe plotting.
3. Automated nodal equivalencing and visual verification.
4. Built-in bandwidth/wavefront optimization algorithms.
5. Hidden-line plots. Figure 7.12 shows the top and bottom views of the elements of the optics bench using hidden lines. This offers the advantage of reducing the confusion that results when all lines are viewed.

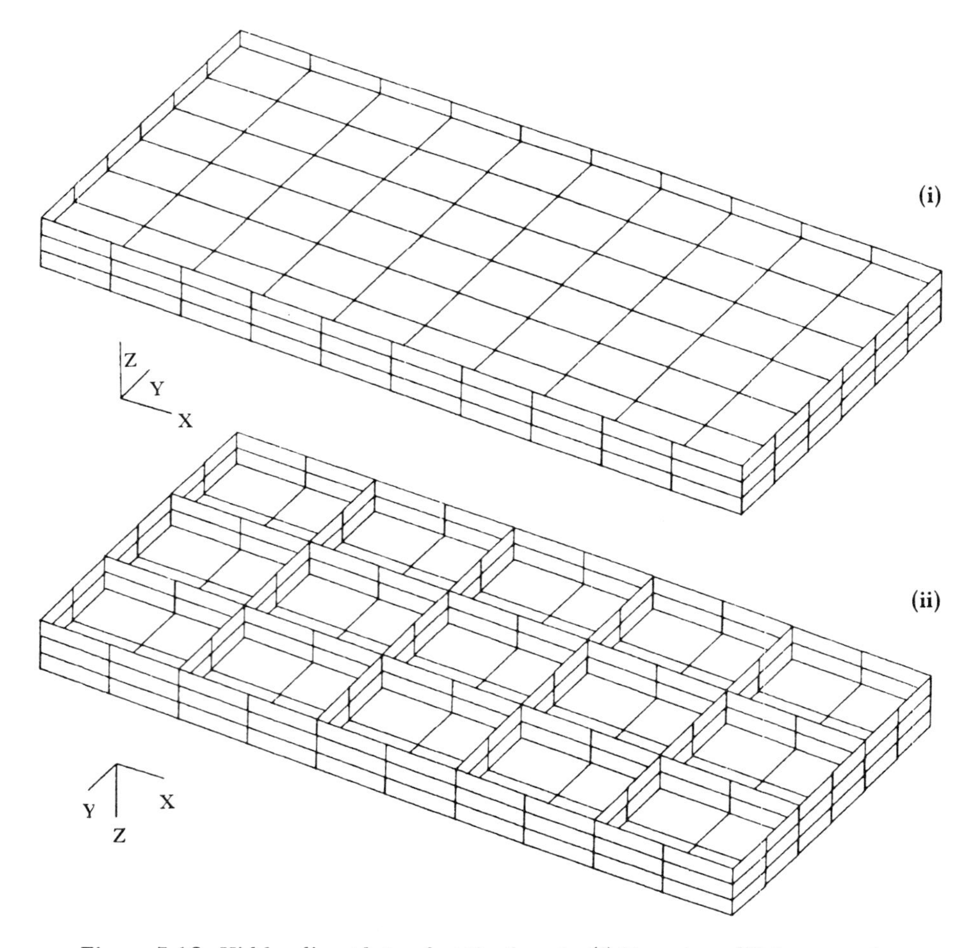


**Figure 7.12.** *Hidden-line plots of optics bench: (i) Top view; (ii) bottom view*

6. Shrink plots. Figure 7.13 shows the top and bottom views of the elements of the optics bench using both shrink and hidden line plots. The shrink plot enables verification that an element is actually present. Without shrink, one is not completely sure that the boundary lines of the element one sees are not just the boundary lines of *adjacent* elements.

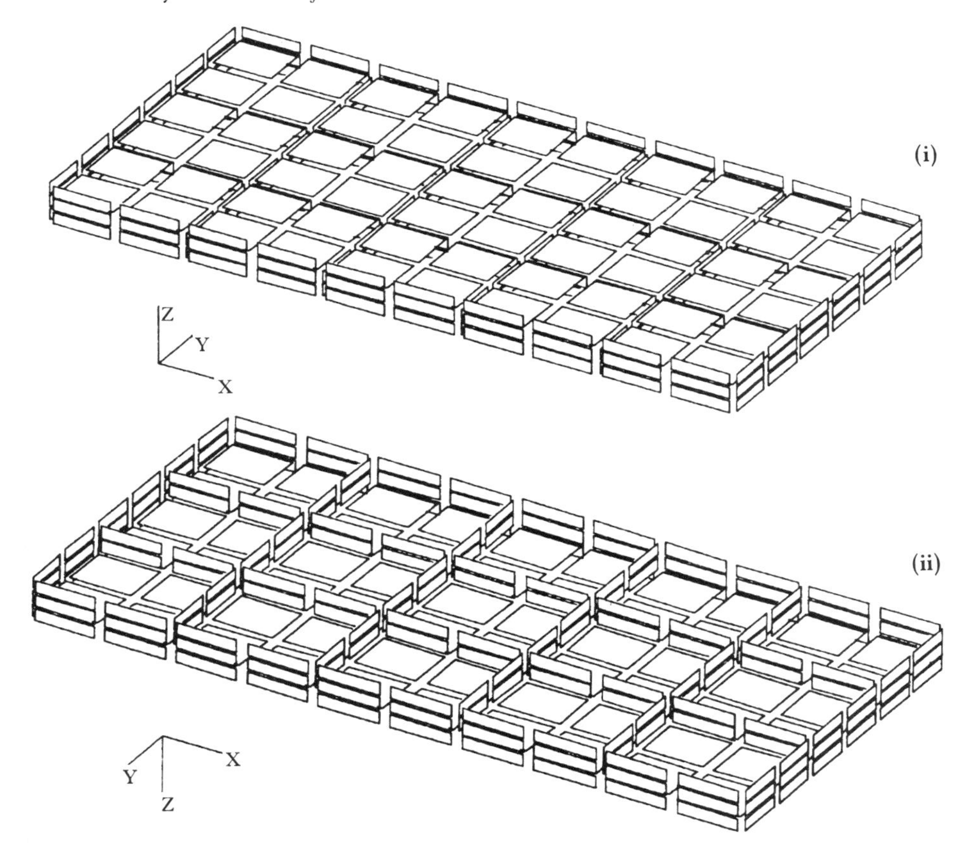


**Figure 7.13.** *Hidden-line plots with the shrink option on: (i) Top view; (ii) bottom view*

7. Fill-hide plots. Any parameter connected with the elements can be specified (such as material property identification or surface normals) and associated with a colour code. Upon command, the three-dimensional model is graphically re-created beginning at the back plane. As the re-creation proceeds towards the front plane, anything that is truly hidden is overdrawn by whatever is hiding it. Each element is drawn in a solid colour corresponding to whatever parameter has been previously specified. Thus, the user

can 'walk' through the model, see every element and its associated property, and 'freeze' the plotting at any point.
8. Interference detection and close proximity checks.
9. Visual checks of free edges and cracks, prescribed constraints, and applied loads.
10. Multiple screens. Various views can be presented on the same screen.

When the analyst is satisfied with the analytical model, he or she then directs PATRAN to create a neutral output file containing the phase two data. This file is then read into a translator program, which will create an output file which is in the form required by the application program. For example, the translator PATANS will create a file for ANSYS, or the translator PATNAS will create the bulk data file for MSC/NASTRAN. A small amount of editing may be required in order to create the final input data file for the finite element application program.

The file is then processed by the finite element program, where specific output files are created. These output files are then submitted to another translator to be put into a form of neutral file that can be returned to PATRAN for phase three, postprocessing.

### 7.4.2 POSTPROCESSING – REVIEWING THE FINITE ELEMENT RESULTS INTERACTIVELY

Typically, the result of the finite element analysis is the most difficult part of the process to review without the aid of graphics. As long as computer graphics has been available, it has been utilized at this stage of the finite element analysis. However, the power of computer graphics increases most dramatically with the addition of colour, and more importantly, *interactive* capability. Combined with the analysis model capabilities discussed in the previous section, PATRAN-G has these added features for postprocessing:

1. Contour and fringe results plots. Stress or displacement files can be reviewed in a fashion like that discussed for the analysis model.
2. Animation of vibration modes or deformation history.

Figure 7.14 shows some results of the static solution of the optics bench. Shown are superimposed views of the deformed and undeformed structure, and a contour plot of how the maximum shearing stress varies throughout the structure. Figure 7.15 shows part of the results of the normal modes solution, where the first four mode shapes are presented. The first two mode shapes are bending and can be seen fairly easily in the views provided ((i) and (ii)). The next two mode shapes are difficult to see and other views may be necessary to obtain a better understanding of the motion.

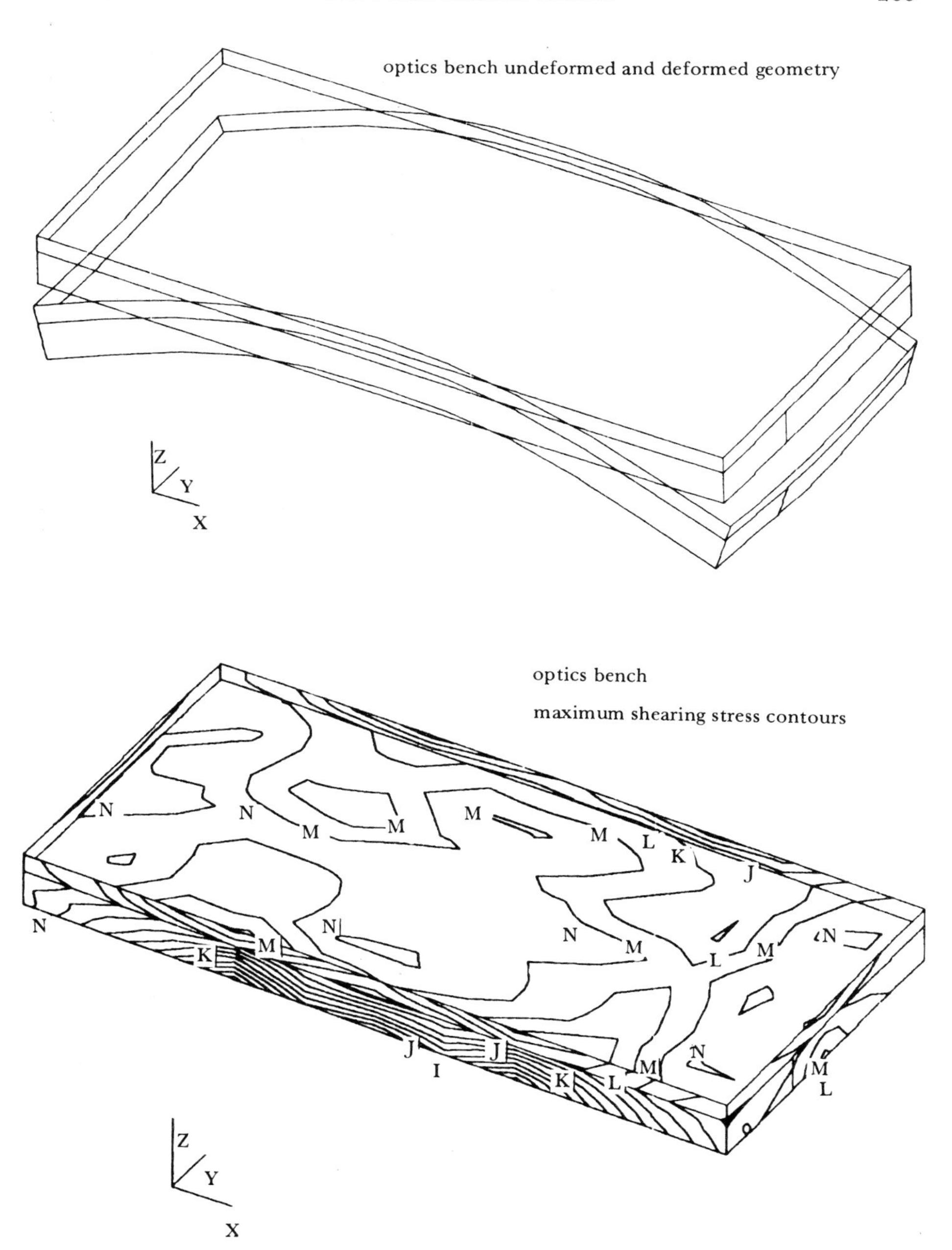


**Figure 7.14.** *Statics analysis results: (i) Deformed and undeformed geometry of optics bench; (ii) maximum shearing stress contours: 50.0 = A; 46.8 = B; 43.6 = C; 40.3 = D; 37.1 = E; 33.9 = F; 30.7 = G; 27.4 = H; 24.2 = I; 21.0 = J; 17.8 = K; 14.6 = L; 11.3 = M; 8.11 = N; 4.88 = O*

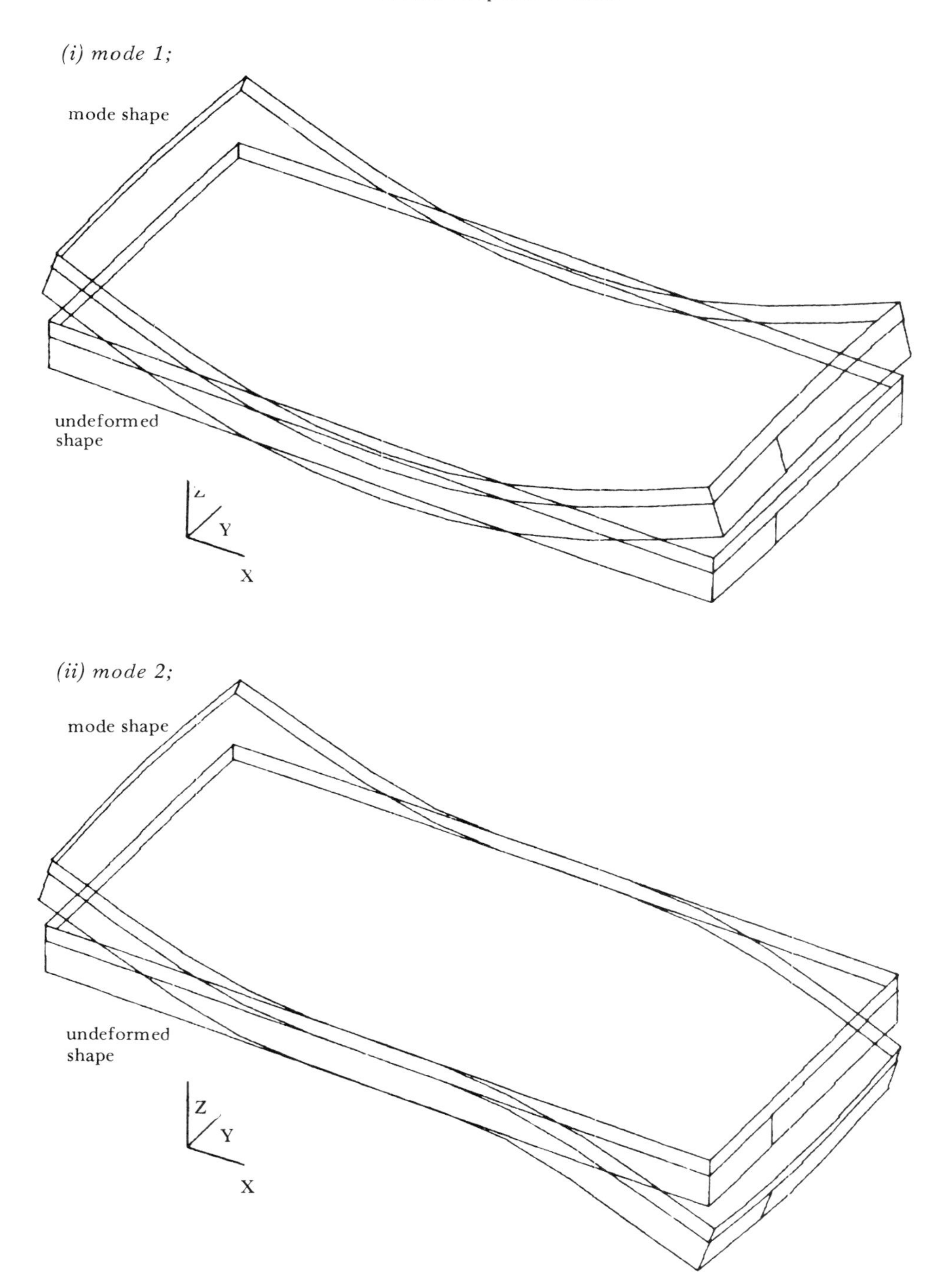


**Figure 7.15.** *Normal modes analysis results: modes 1 and 2*

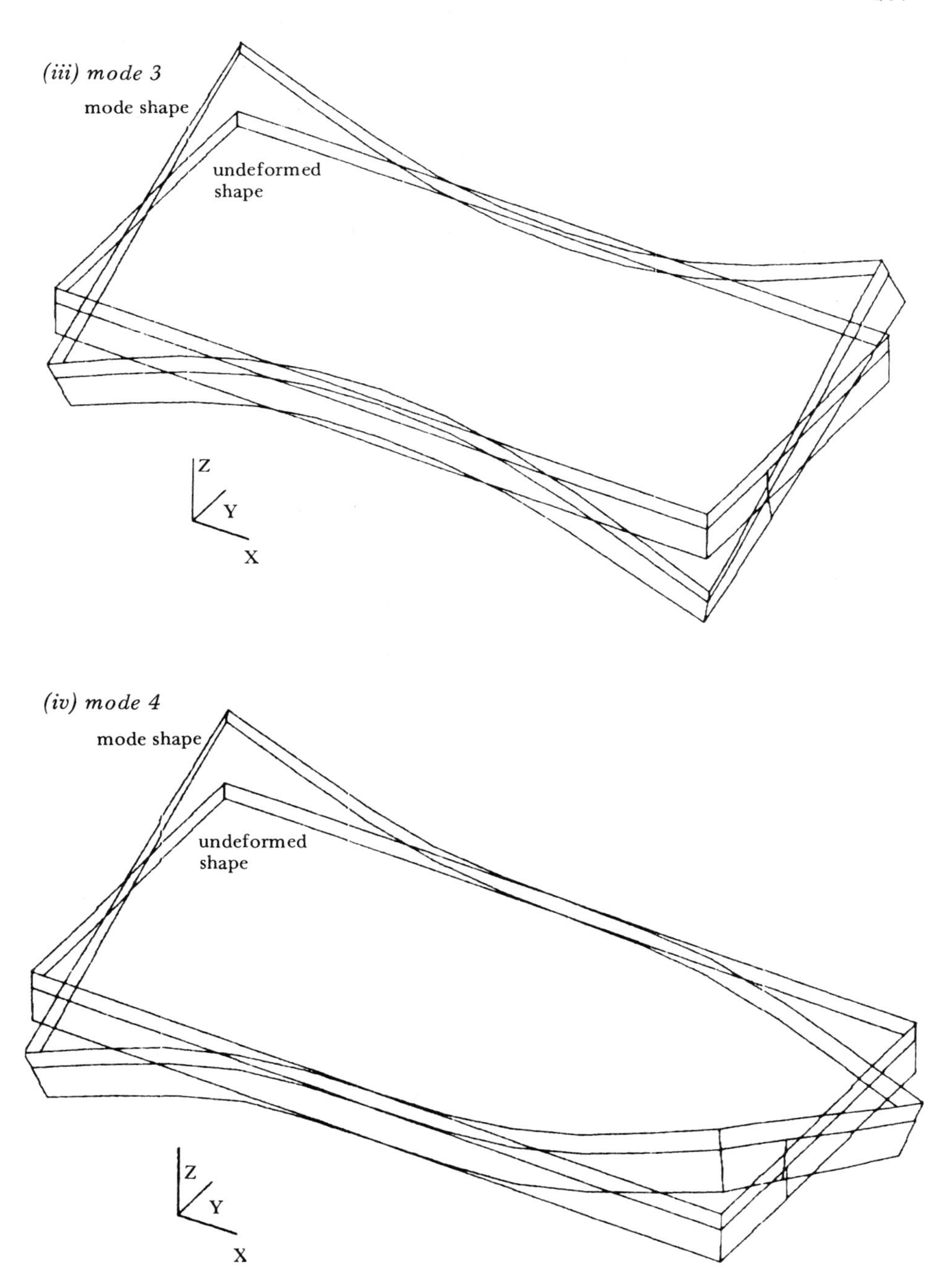


**Figure 7.15.** *Normal modes analysis results: modes 3 and 4*

To understand the added dimension of colour, refer to the last page of the colour insert section in the middle of this book. The last page, front and back, contains colour reproductions of pre- and postprocessing. The front page contains four views of a shaft coupling which was modelled using PDA/PATRAN-G. The top views show the model assembly and exploded view, whereas the lower views show the results of the finite element analysis. Part of the coupling flange is shown where the stress fringe pattern is observed with the element shrink option on. Because of symmetry, only portions of a complete structure need be analyzed. For example, the remaining view shows the analysis results of one complete length of the coupling spring member. The undeformed wire-frame view of the elements is shown together with the stress fringes superimposed on the deformed spring.

The back of the last colour page insert contains two views of a model and results as performed by ANSYS's PREP7 pre- and postprocessor. The problem was that of a rotating flange, and the results in the lower view depict the stresses induced by the rotation and assembly stresses. Note the multiple screen view.

## Bibliography

Budynas, R.G. *Advanced Strength and Applied Stress Analysis* McGraw-Hill, New York, 1977.

Fong, H.H. Interactive graphics and commercial finite element codes. *Mechanical Engineering* **106** (6) June 1984.

Turner, M.J.; Clough, R.W.; Martin, H.C.; Topp, L.J. Stiffness and deflection analysis of complex structures. *J. Aero. Sci.* 23, 1956.

# Bibliography

Azema, J. *Grammaires de Graphes – Algorithmes d'Analyse: Application* Thesis, Grenoble, 1975.

Barnhill, R.E.; Riesenfeld, R.F. *Computer Aided Geometric Design* Academic Press, London, 1974.

Bernard, A. CATIA: système tri-dimensionnel de CFAO. In *MICAD 82* Paris, September 1982.

Borgerson, B.R.; Johnson, R.H. Beyond CAD to computer aided engineering. In *IFIP 80* Tokyo, October 1980.

Boyse, J.W.; Gilchrist, J.E. GM solid: interactive modelling for design and analysis of solids. In *Proceedings of IEEE – CG and A* March 1982.

Braid, I.C. *Designing with Volumes* Cantab Press, Cambridge, 1974.

Brooks, R.A. Symbolic reasoning among 3-D models and 2-D images. *Artificial Intelligence* 1981, 17.

Brown, C.M. PADL: a technical summary. In *Proceedings of IEEE – CG and A* March 1982.

Brun, J.M. La gestion des données dans EUCLID. *Private Communication* 1983.

CISI *Notice de Présentation du Logiciel CONDOR* 1982.

Dassault Systemes *Présentation du Logiciel CATIA* 1981.

Freeman, H. Computer processing of line drawing images. *ACM Computing Surveys* 1974, **6**(2).

Galimberti, R.; Montanari, U. An algorithm for hidden line elimination. *CACM* 1969, **12**(4).

Gangnet, M.; Coquillard, S.; Haiat, J.C. Numérisation par caméra de plans de bâtiment. In *MICAD 82* Paris, September 1982.

Gardan, Y. A system for the interactive description of parametrized elements (PARAM 2D). In *Prolamat 82* Leningrad, 1982.

Gardan, Y. *Eléments Méthodologiques pour la Réalisation de Systèmes et CFAO et leur Introduction dans les Entreprises* Thesis, Grenoble, December 1982.

Gardan, Y. *Systèmes de CFAO* Hermes Publishing (France), April 1983.

Gardan, Y. *La Realisation des Logicels Graphiques Interactifs* Livre Editions Eyrolles, 1982.

Giambasi, N.; Rault, J.C.; Sabonnadiere, J.C. *Introduction à la Conception Assistée par Ordinateur* Hermes Publishing (France), 1983.

Gips, J. Shape grammars and their uses: artificial perception, shape generation and computer aesthetics. *Interdisciplinary Systems Research* Birkhaüser Verlag, Basel, 1975.

Hillyard, R. The build group of solid modellers. In *Proceedings of IEEE – GC and A* March 1982.

Huffman, D.A. Realizable configurations of lines in pictures of polyhedra. In *Machine Intelligence* edited by Elcock and Michie, Ellis Horwood, London, 1977.

Jared, G.; Stroud, I. Local operators in the build system. In *Prolomat 82* Leningrad, 1982.

Lucas, M. *Contribution à l'Étude des Techniques de Communication Graphique avec un Ordinateur, Éléments de Base pour les Logiciels Graphiques Interactifs* Thesis, Grenoble, December 1977.

Massabo, A.C.; Moal, Y.; Stark, J. SYSTRID 1. In *Proceedings of Eurographics 79* Bologne, October 1979.

Matra Datavision *Notice de Presentation EUCLID* 1982.

Micado *Notions d'Utilisation Interactive et Programmee (Primitives) de GRI 2D* 1983.

Morvan, P.; Lucas, M. *Images et Ordinateur: Introduction à l'Infographie Interactive* Larousse, France, September 1976.

Narashiman, R. Syntax directed interpretation of classes of pictures. *Communication of ACM* March 1966(3).

National Bureau of Standards A technical briefing on the Initial Graphics Exchange Specification (IGES). *NBSIR 81-2297* July 1981.

Newman, S.; Sproull, R.F. *Principles of Interactive Computer Graphics* McGraw Hill, New York, 1979.

Renault *Présentation de RA3D* 1981.

Requicha, A.G. Representation for rigid solids — theory, methods and systems. *Computing Survey* 1980, 12(4).

Requicha, A.G.; Voelcker, H.B. Solid modelling: a historical summary and contemporary assessment. In *Proceedings of IEEE — GC and A* March 1982.

Ricard, A. Une Experience d'utilisation d'outils de CAO pour la conception et la fabrication de coffrages bois. In *MICAD 82* Paris, September 1982.

Rodgers, D.F.; Adams, J.A. *Mathematical Elements for Computing Graphics* McGraw Hill, New York, 1976.

Shaw, A.C. A proposal language for the formal description of pictures. *Technical Report GSG28 of the Stanford Linear Accelerator Laboratory* 1967.

Sutherland, I.E.; Sproull, R.F.; Shumacker, R.A. A characterization of ten hidden surface algorithms. *ACM Computing Survey* March|1974, 6(1).

Voelcker, H.B.; Requicha, A.G. Geometric modelling of mechanical parts and processes. *Computer* December 1977.

# Index

# Acknowledgements

The publishers would like to thank the following institutions for allowing reproduction of certain illustrations contained in this book.

Matra-Datavision (Figures 1.9, 3.31, 4.6, 4.16, 4.20, 4.31); Dassault Systèmes (Figures 1.10, 3.2, 4.27); Computervision (Figure 1.11); SNR (Figures 3.5, 6.1); University of Grenoble-Sigma Archi (Figure 4.1); University of Nantes (Figures 4.2-4.4, 4.9-4.12, 4.15, 4.18, 4.24, 4.26); CISI (Figures 4.14, 4.32, 4.35); Control Data (Figure 4.30); LIMSI (Figure 5.31); Micado (Figures 3.3, 5.41); Crouzet (Figures 6.9-6.12); Merlin-Gerin (Figure 6.13); SIFRA (Figures 6.14, 6.15); EDF (Figures 6.17-6.22); Neyrpic (Figures 6.25-6.27).